TRAVEL
IN THE
ANCIENT
WORLD

TRAVEL
IN THE
ANCIENT
WORLD

Lionel Casson

HAKKERT
TORONTO
1974

First published in 1974

© George Allen & Unwin Ltd 1974

ISBN 0-88866-542-3

Library of Congress Catalog Card No 73 91249

Hakkert
554 Spadina Crescent
Toronto, Canada M5S 2J9

Printed in Great Britain
in 12 point Fournier
by Unwin Brothers Limited
The Gresham Press
Old Woking Surrey

To Mimi Rae

AUTHOR'S PREFACE

This book is the first full-scale treatment, in any language, of travel in the ancient world.

Chronologically it goes from the voyages recorded in Egyptian inscriptions of Old Kingdom times to the Christian pilgrimages of the fourth to the sixth centuries A.D. Topically it covers all the major aspects: the motives for travel, particularly those other than trade and government business; the mechanics of travel on land and sea; inns, bars, restaurants, and other facilities available to the traveller; above all, the nature of ancient tourism—the standard itineraries, the favoured sites and sights, museums, guides, guidebooks, tourist behaviour.

The Roman Imperial period, for which our information is fullest, was dealt with comprehensively by Ludwig Friedländer in the sections on '*Verkehrwesen*' and '*Die Reisen der Touristen*' in his magisterial *Darstellungen aus der Sittengeschichte Roms*. However, the last edition dates back to 1922, and the intervening years have not only increased our knowledge in all respects but altered significant data on which Friedländer had to rely. For periods other than the Roman Imperial, there is no comprehensive work available, not even an out-of-date one. More or less useful studies of certain aspects may be found scattered in miscellaneous books and periodicals, but by no means of all. The mechanics of travel by sea, souvenirs, tourists' mail—these and a number of other topics have hitherto received nothing beyond casual mention.

I have written with both the student of the ancient world and the general reader in mind. On behalf of the latter I have included brief historical introductions to the various periods dealt with and have avoided spangling the pages with footnote

A*

numbers. However, since our knowledge of antiquity is so imperfect that the authority for the statements we make is as important as the statements themselves, following the text I have provided complete documentation, citing wherever possible standard works that give the relevant literary, archeological, epigraphic, papyrological, and numismatic sources, and, where not, the sources themselves.

Place-names always present a problem. I have sometimes used ancient forms, sometimes modern. My guiding principle has been ease of recognition. Consequently I speak of Milan and Lyons rather than Mediolanum and Lugdunum, of Nicaea and Sidon rather than Iznik and Saida. When there was little to choose between the two, I favoured the ancient (e.g. Tibur over Tivoli, Puteoli over Pozzuoli).

My greatest debt is, as ever, to my wife, who gave her invariable multi-faceted assistance, from pointing an unerringly critical finger at parts that needed rewriting to patiently typing draft upon draft of the manuscript. I owe particular thanks to Bluma Trell, whose expert knowledge of the Roman East put me on many a fruitful trail. Others, too, have given me welcome help—Blanche Brown with questions of art history, Annalina and Mario Levi with the Roman imperial post, Naphtali Lewis with papyrological points, Arthur Schiller with matters involving ancient law, Richard Scheuer and Joy Ungerleider with Holy Land travel. Ernest Nash, Director of the Fototeca Unione at the American Academy in Rome, gave me his customary knowledgeable assistance in choosing and obtaining illustrations, and Moshe Dothan, Assistant Director of Israel's Department of Antiquities and Museums, kindly supplied the photograph for Figure 20a.

CONTENTS

ILLUSTRATIONS

MAPS

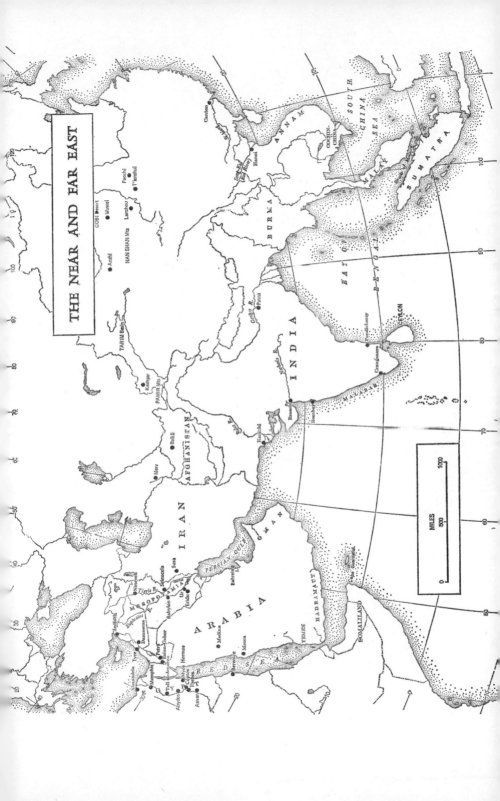

THE NEAR AND FAR EAST

MILES
0   500   1000

Canton

Annam
Hanoi

Peachi
T'ienshui
Lanchou

GOBI Desert

SOUTH
CHINA
SEA

Anshi
Wuwei
NAN SHAN Mts

SUMATRA

MALAY

BURMA

BAY
OF
BENGAL

COCHIN-
CHINA

TARIM Basin

PAMIR Mts

Kashgar

Ganges R.
Patna

INDIA

Narbada R.

CEYLON

Pondicherry

Cranganore

MALABAR

AFGHANISTAN

Merv

Balkh

Karachi

Broach
Bombay

IRAN

Susa
Seleucia
Nineveh

OMAN

PERSIAN GULF

Tigris R.

MESOPOTAMIA

Ur
Eridu

Bahrein

HADRAMAUT

ARABIA

Babylon

Cape Guardafui

Antioch

Damascus

Tyre
Euphrates R.

Petra

Ezion-Geber

Medina

YEMEN

SOMALILAND

Alexandria

Hormoz

Memphis

Mecca

Tell el-Amarna

RED
SEA

Coptos
Thebes

Berenice

Abydos

Aswan

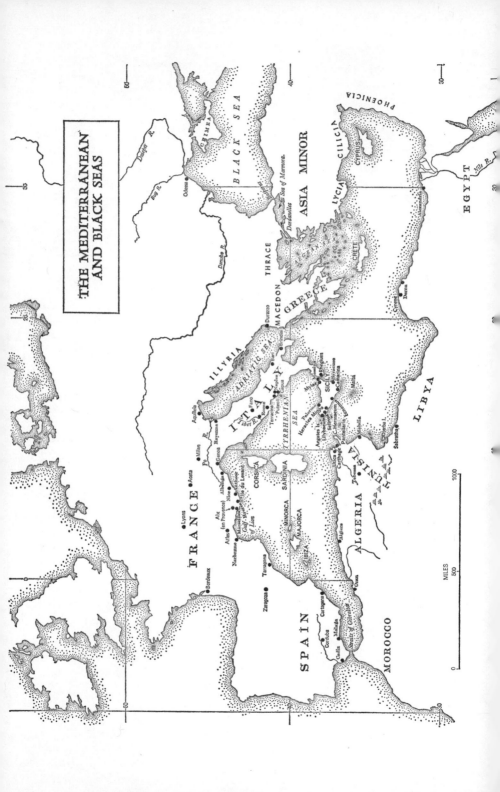

THE MEDITERRANEAN
AND BLACK SEAS

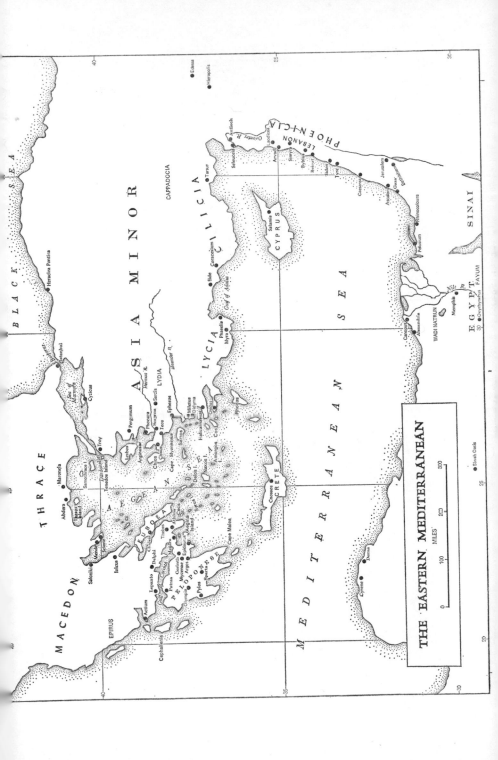

THE EASTERN MEDITERRANEAN

MILES

0   100   200   300

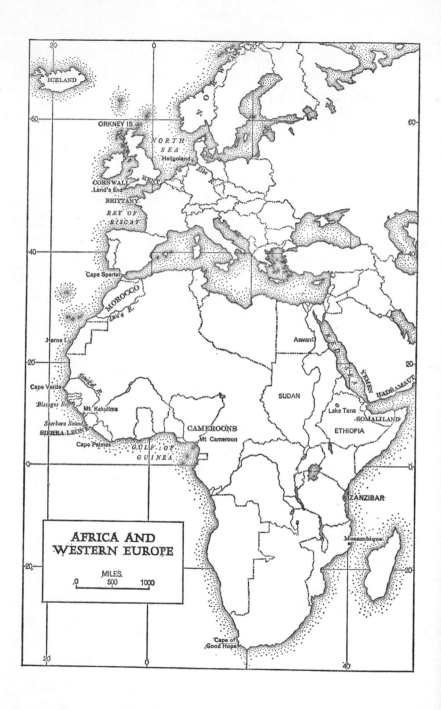

ICELAND

ORKNEY IS.

NORTH SEA

Heligoland

CORNWALL
.Land's End
BRITTANY

*BAY OF
BISCAY*

Cape Spartel

MOROCCO
Dra'a R.

.Herne I.

Cape Verde
Bissagos Bay
Mt. Kakulima
Sherboro Sound
SIERRA LEONE
Cape Palmas

*GULF OF
GUINEA*

CAMEROONS

Mt. Cameroon

Aswan

SUDAN

RED SEA

YEMEN

HADRAMAUT

Lake Tana
.SOMALILAND
ETHIOPIA

ZANZIBAR

Mozambique

AFRICA AND WESTERN EUROPE

MILES
0   500   1000

'Cape of
Good Hope

PART ONE

THE NEAR EAST AND GREECE

I

In the Beginning: 3000–1200 B.C.

Men built the first clusters of cities in the lands between the Tigris and the Euphrates and put together the first unified nation along the banks of the Nile. Inevitably the new pattern of life brought in its wake new patterns of movement. Now couriers began to shuttle from centre to centre, officials to move about their spheres of responsibility, traders to make the circuit of the markets, throngs to drain out of the countryside and flood into holy spots on festival days.

At the outset, such travel must have been fairly limited— down or along the three great rivers, in and about the hills and valleys and plains of Syria and Palestine, along their coasts. The horizon expanded dramatically not long after 3000 B.C., when shipwrights learned to design vessels able to go relatively safely and comfortably over open water. These hauled cargoes across the eastern Mediterranean between Egypt and the Levant, up and down the Red Sea between Egypt and Arabia, over the Persian Gulf and Indian Ocean between Mesopotamia and the northwest shores of India.

We do not know exactly who pioneered the building of seagoing craft. It could well have been the Egyptians since, gathered along an eminently navigable river, they turned to the water very early in their civilized existence. 'When the Nile overflows the countryside . . . ,' writes Herodotus, 'the whole of Egypt becomes a sea, and only the towns stick out above the surface of the water. When this happens, people use boats right in the middle of the land and not just along the course of the river. Anyone going from Naucratis to Memphis sails right by the pyramids.' He is reporting what he saw during a visit about 450 B.C., but he could have written the same words had he been there two and a half millennia earlier. The Nile and its tributaries and canals always offered the Egyptians the easiest and quickest way to go anywhere, and in certain areas, such as the marshes of the delta, just about the only way. Egyptians were even able to sail upstream, since the prevailing wind luckily blows from the north. By the first half of the fourth millennium B.C., they were travelling about in canoes and rafts made of bundles of reeds of the papyrus plant that grew in profusion along the banks, the famous bulrushes in which the baby Moses was left. By 2700 B.C., they were using sturdy rivercraft of wood. Half a century later we hear of a flotilla of forty ships that crossed from the Lebanese coast to the mouth of the Nile.

Mesopotamia has two great rivers, but neither was as useful as the Nile; though both are navigable, there is no convenient prevailing wind to waft craft upriver. By the third millennium B.C. small wooden riverboats were in common use; when it was time to return from a downstream voyage, they inched their way against the current at the end of a towline pulled by a file of hauliers. Armenian rivermen, who started out in the far north and hence had a long way back, facilitated matters by using light rafts buoyed by numerous inflated skins; as Herodotus tells it, each raft had 'aboard a live donkey, the larger ones several. After arriving at Babylon and disposing of the cargo, the frames of the boat . . . they auction off, load the hides on the donkeys, and walk back to Armenia'. The buoyed raft, as it happens, was well suited for negotiating the rapids that occur where the Tigris cuts through the mountains of Kurdistan; if it struck a rock, the most it suffered was a few punctures, which could be repaired in a few moments. In the calm lower reaches the Mesopotamians favoured large round coracles, particularly for ferrying from bank to bank. These, made of patches of leather sewn about a framework of branches, were big enough to carry chariots, even heavy loads of building stone.

Where water transport was not possible, as in Palestine and Syria, which have few navigable streams, travellers at first either walked, or rode donkeys. From about 3000 B.C. on, vehicles were available. The earliest examples are attested among the Sumerians, the gifted people of northern Mesopotamia who share with the Egyptians the honour of so many pioneering contributions to civilization. They are heavy wagons with a box-like body borne on four solid wheels and drawn by teams either of oxen or onagers, a type of wild ass. Some remains dating about 2500 B.C. have been excavated, and these all belong to wagons that were quite small, the bodies only twenty inches or so broad and the wheels twenty to forty inches in diameter. This may have been the size that onagers pulled, since any larger wagon of so massive a style would be too much for them; indeed, pictures of the age more often than not show the beasts hitched in teams of four rather than just two. The two-wheeled cart seems to have made its debut slightly later than the wagon; it also was a massive affair fitted with solid wheels Around 2300 B.C. the horse was introduced into the Near East as a draught-animal, and within a few centuries a lighter type of cart, drawn by horses or mules, came into being, a fast and handy conveyance for kings, princes, high dignitaries, and the like.

And then, about 1600 B.C., kings and princes and dignitaries had a new instrument put at their disposal—the chariot. The chariot was in effect a horse-drawn cart designed for use in warfare. Its size and weight consequently had to be kept to an absolute minimum, and since it was solely a nobleman's weapon, expense was no object in achieving this end. By the first half of the second millennium, carpenters had learned the technique of using heat to bend wood. This enabled them to replace the ponderous disc wheels of an earlier day with wheels made of spokes—usually there are four, sometimes six—running to a rim of curved, carefully joined felloes, and to replace the cart's heavy all-wood body with one made of a curved wooden frame overlaid with a covering of hides or wicker. A chariot found in the tomb of Tutankhamen (1352–1344 B.C.) even has a featherweight floor of interlaced leather thongs. So light were chariots that Homer's hero, Diomed, as he is about to steal one from the enemy, ponders whether to haul it or just pick it up and carry it. The new invention enjoyed worldwide popularity. Within two or three centuries after its appearance in the Near East, it had penetrated westward to Greece, Crete, and northern Europe, and eastward to India and China.

The Near East knew only one type of harness and used it indiscriminately on massive wagons and cockleshell chariots, the yoke. Every vehicle had, extending from the centre of its front side, a draught-pole with a horizontal crossbar near the outer end. The arrangement was obviously designed for hitching a team of oxen, with one animal on either side of the pole, and the crossbar, the yoke, sitting on their shoulders. When onagers and horses entered the ranks of draught animals, no accommodation was made for them: they were unimaginatively used in pairs in the same harness. However, since they lack the prominent shoulders of an ox, they had to be bound to the yoke by a band passed over the breast (cf. Fig. 1). As they threw themselves into the pull, this pressed against the windpipe and impeded any effort to use their full strength. Wherever the chariot wandered, it took this inefficient harness with it, northward into Europe, eastward as far as China. The Greeks and Romans, as we shall see (181 below), did very little to remedy the situation. The Far East, it so happens, did develop a harness suitable for horses, but adopted it only fitfully and sparingly. One proper way to hitch a horse to a vehicle is between shafts (cf. Fig. 11), and several bronze models of light gig-like carts with what appear

to be shafts have turned up in archeological sites in India that
date around the beginning of the second millennium B.C. Even
if these are, indeed, examples of shafts, none other are attested
until over 1,500 years later, in China of the fourth century B.C.
At this late date the Chinese became the first people to appre-
ciate fully the value of shafts; they adopted them as the
standard system, giving up the yoke that they had borrowed
from the West and had been using up to then.

Covered wagons date from at least 2500 B.C., to judge from
some clay models that have been found. Fitted with an arched
canopy, they resemble the famous Conestoga wagon of the
nineteenth century and no doubt, like it, served to transport
families with their worldly possessions. The pharaoh who
employed Joseph could very well have had such vehicles in
mind when he instructed him to tell his brothers to take
'wagons out of the land of Egypt for your little ones, and for
your wives, and . . . your father', in order to bring them all
from Canaan to Egypt.

Able-bodied travellers generally eschewed conveyances and
went by foot or, if they could afford it, by donkeyback. They
never went by horseback, for the art of riding a horse lay
many centuries in the future (51 below). Litters for some
reason are not mentioned until quite late, but they surely were
known in earlier times.

A walker or animal needs only a track. A vehicle needs a road,
and this could well have been one of the major reasons why
traders did not regularly go about in carts or wagons: in this
early age there were not many routes that could take wheeled
traffic. In a Sumerian hymn attributed to Shulgi, king of Ur
from about 2100 to 2050 B.C., he boasts that he went from
Nippur to Ur—a distance of some 100 miles—and back in a
single day despite a fierce hailstorm on the return lap. If there
is a kernel of truth behind his words it is that he made a fast
trip between the two cities, and this implies the existence of a
carriage road. There surely was one, and a good one at that,

between Babylon and Larsa in the days of Hammurabi, ruler of the Babylonian empire from 1792 to 1750 B.C. In a letter to an official at Larsa he orders certain personnel to be sent to him as fast as possible, specifying that they are to 'travel day and night and so get to Babylon within two days'. The two cities are about 120 miles apart; if we allow from thirty-six to forty-eight hours, it means he was counting on an average speed of $2\frac{1}{2}$ to $3\frac{1}{2}$ miles per hour, and this is almost as good as travellers in mule-drawn carts did on the highly touted Roman roads two millennia later (188–9 below). The 'way of the land of the Philistines' which the Israelites so carefully avoided during the Exodus, the route that, running along the coast from the mouth of the Nile up to Tyre and Sidon and Beirut and beyond (cf. 190–1 below), served as the main link between Egypt and the Levant, was also able to take wheeled traffic, at least for most of the way. Joseph's wagons no doubt followed it when they brought his family to Egypt.

Yet even the finest of these highways offered but a bare minimum. Paving was almost non-existent. The Hittites, the powerful people who dominated Asia Minor from c. 1800 to 1200 B.C. thanks in good part to their finely developed chariot corps, paved the mile and a third that lay between their capital and a nearby sanctuary to sustain the weight of the heavily loaded wagons they used in processions on festal days, but their war chariots rolled over the countryside on dirt roads. Bridges too were a rarity; there were practically none in Egypt and Mesopotamia, where flooding posed a well-nigh insoluble problem for contemporary engineers. Vehicles either forded or were carried across on ferries, an operation that at times could involve dismantling them in order to squeeze them aboard some modest-sized reed boat or coracle. Then there was the question of maintenance. 'I enlarged the foot-paths, straightened the highways of the land,' claims Shulgi in the hymn that tells of his lightning-like ride. But not every Mesopotamian monarch was a Shulgi, and there must have been long periods when nobody bothered to 'straighten' the roads.

Things seem to have been somewhat better on the island of Crete, where the impressive civilization of the Minoans flourished from 2000 to 1500 B.C., and in the Greek peninsula, where the equally impressive Mycenaean civilization flourished from 1600 to 1200. Both peoples went in for extensive road-building. On Crete archeologists have traced the remains of a highway that ran from a port on the south coast north to the capital at Cnossus; it was two lanes wide all the way, averaging 13 feet in breadth, it was strengthened where needed by terracing walls of hewn stone, and a monumental viaduct also of hewn stone carried it for the final stretch to the palace at Cnossus. In Greece roads dating from Mycenaean times have been identified not only around Mycenae itself but at Pylos, in Boeotia, even southern Thessaly. Usually they were one-lane, but some, with an average width of 11½ feet, were for two-way traffic. Bridges and culverts kept them passable during the rainy season, and at the approaches to towns they might even have a bit of paving; there is a stretch, for example, leading up to the Lion Gate at Mycenae. All in all, Greece in the thirteenth century B.C. probably had a better system of roads than it did in the third.

The concern for roads among the Mycenaeans very likely stems from their fondness for chariot riding. In the Near East the chariot served only for war or hunting. The Mycenaean gentry seem to have added a third use—travel. A wall-painting found at Tiryns, one of their great centres, depicts an elegant chariot with crimson body, white trim, yellow wheels, white draught-pole wrapped with black thongs and red reins. In it is shown not a driver accompanied by a warrior or hunter but a pair of ladies going for a ride; the stylized background reveals it is a ride in the country. The obvious conclusion is that the nobility used their chariots for getting about—and they could hardly have done much getting about in these light vehicles without fairly decent roads.

So much for the ways and means of travel in its infancy. Let us turn to the people who did the travelling.

In Egypt it was above all men of the government. By 3200 B.C. the valley of the Nile from the First Cataract northward to the coast was under the sway of a single ruler. From the capital at Memphis, just below the apex of the delta, the pharaoh sent his administrators and agents and messengers up and down the river. In the sacred precinct of Osiris at Abydos, for example, where every Egyptian yearned to leave a memorial, excavators have found any number belonging to officials who had set them up when they happened to pass through on some government assignment. 'I reached Elephantine [at the First Cataract]', reads one left by a chamberlain of Amenemhet II (1929–1895 B.C.), 'as I had been ordered . . . I returned by the route I took out [i.e. sailed back down the river]. I moored at Abydos. I left my name in the place of the god Osiris.' The pharaoh's men not only shuttled up and down the river but plodded across the eastern desert to Sinai where, from at least 3000 B.C., the Egyptians were mining copper and extracting turquoise; there must have been a stream of work gangs, pack donkeys, porters, officials, and the like going back and forth over the wastes. At times Egypt's representatives ventured beyond the nation's frontiers, northward into the Levant or southward into the Sudan. A prince Harkhuf, for example, who lived sometime between 2300 and 2200 B.C., made three trips to the Sudan, as we learn from a short autobiography he had carved upon his tomb. The first was:

to open up the way to this country. I did it in seven months and brought back from it all kinds of good and rare presents . . . His Majesty sent me a second time . . . I set forth [from the First Cataract] . . . and returned . . . in the space of eight months. I returned and brought presents from this country in very great quantity . . . His Majesty sent me a third time . . . I returned with 300 asses loaded with incense, ebony, oil, leopard skins, elephant tusks, boomerangs, and all good products.

He had been, it would appear, in charge of a series of trade missions.

Harkhuf did not himself penetrate darkest Africa; he went no further than between the Second and Third Cataract. Here there must have been a trading post, the end of a caravan trail that ran to the highlands and jungle to the south. A few centuries later, by 2000 B.C., the Egyptians learned to bypass the land routes, and the middlemen these inevitably involved, by turning to the water and sending ships down the Red Sea directly to the shores of Ethiopia and perhaps even Somalia.

In Mesopotamia too there was much moving about of government personnel. It started somewhat later than in Egypt. The Sumerians, who were the earliest civilized people there, went in for individual city-sized states rather than a unified nation, and it was not until after 2700 B.C. or so that the powerful among these began to taste the joys of subjugating neighbours. Various aggressive rulers put together sizeable empires, and by the twenty-first century B.C. the official traffic between a capital and its subject cities was heavy enough to justify the creation of a government-run communications service (35–6 below).

In early Egypt commerce was in the hands of the pharaoh; business trips, like Harkhuf's, were just another form of official travel. Traders from other lands did on occasion make their way into the valley of the Nile, such as the group of Levantines leading loaded donkeys that we see on a painting in a tomb of the twentieth century B.C. The Egyptians, not the most modest of peoples, refer to them as official foreign representatives and to their goods as tribute, but it is more than likely that they were private merchants on the road for their own profit.

In Mesopotamia private enterprise flourished mightily.

Caravans were a common sight on the roads, loaded rivercraft on the streams. 'Thirty years ago', runs a letter written about 2000 B.C. by two business partners in Assur to a trio of customers whose account was in arrears, 'you left the city of Assur. You have never made a deposit since, and we have not recovered one shekel of silver from you, but we have never made you feel bad about this. Our tablets have been going to you with caravan after caravan, but no report from you has ever come here.' Assur was in northern Iraq and the addressees lived in a town in the heart of eastern Anatolia; caravans went to and fro frequently enough to provide an informal postal service.

Letters such as this and other records of business life, written on clay tablets, which if undisturbed can last for centuries, have been recovered by the thousands from the soil of Mesopotamia. They reveal not only the extent of the commercial traffic of the time but its sophistication. Caravan traders worked on credit, using money or goods entrusted to them by a merchant-banker, usually on some sort of profit-sharing basis. The keeping of careful records was mandatory, and a body of law grew up to take care of the various contingencies that might arise. From the famous law code of Hammurabi we learn that any traders who lost their goods through enemy attack—presumably either the king's enemies or just highway robbers—did not have to repay, but if they returned without making a profit they had to give the banker double what had been advanced; apparently not to come back with a profit was either a flagrant breach of contract or *prima facie* evidence of fraud. Those who dealt in ship cargoes also worked on credit but without any profit-sharing. The banker extended an ordinary interest-bearing loan, the borrower kept all the profits, and the banker was spared all the risks; even if the vessel went down, he was still entitled to his principal plus interest. The network of overseas trade was impressively widespread: from the second half of the third millennium, ships made their way down the Arabian Gulf to Saudi Arabia and along the coasts of Iran and Afghanistan as far as the northwest coast of India.

Government couriers, officials with their entourages, traders with their jars and bales of goods—these are the people one saw on the roads and rivers day in and day out. But at certain times of year all this was dwarfed to insignificance by the mass influx of worshippers to a sacred spot on the occasion of its deity's festival. In Egypt, where religion outstripped all other interests and where a convenient river made travelling any-where in the country relatively easy, such events set vast throngs in motion. Herodotus, describing what surely had been going on for thousands of years before his day, reports that:

the Egyptians meet to celebrate festivals not once a year but a number of times. The biggest and most popular is at Bubastis . . . , the next at Busiris . . . , the third at Sais . . . , the fourth at Heliopolis . . . , the fifth at Buto . . . , the sixth at Papremis . . . When they gather at Bubastis this is what happens. They go there on the river, men and women together, a big crowd of each in each boat. As they sail, some of the women keep clicking castanets and some of the men playing on the pipes, and the rest, both men and women, sing and beat time with their hands. Whenever they pass a town they bring their craft close inshore and do as follows: some of the women keep on as I have just described, but others scream and make fun of the women in the town, still others dance, and still others stand up and expose themselves. They carry on this way at every town along the river. And when they arrive at Bubastis, they celebrate the occasion with great sacrifices, and more wine is consumed at this one festival than during the whole rest of the year. According to the locals, up to seven hundred thousand people gather there, including men and women but not children.

The attendance figure Herodotus was given is no doubt exaggerated but, however much we discount it, we are still left with an enormous number of people on the move at one time.

And lastly, from about 1500 B.C. on, we can discern in Egypt sure signs of tourism, of travel for simple curiosity or pleasure. It appears there and not in Mesopotamia because the Nile valley is blessed with an abundance of good building stone which the pharaohs began to employ for their grandiose tombs and temples as early as 2700 B.C. As a result, Egyptians of later ages found themselves living in a veritable museum, surrounded by structures of hoary antiquity. In the great days of the New Kingdom, from 1600 to 1200 B.C., when Thutmose and Akhenaton and Ramses and other such renowned figures held the throne, the step pyramid of Djoser at Sakkarah, the Sphinx at Gizeh, the three great pyramids at Gizeh, the pyramid complex at Abusir, and the like, were already over a thousand years old. On their walls we find messages left by people who had made a special trip to see these impressive witnesses to the might of their past. Each monument was a hallowed spot, so the visitors always spent some moments in prayer, yet their prime motivation was curiosity or disinterested enjoyment, not religion. 'Hadnakhte, scribe of the treasury', reads one such message, dated 1244 B.C., on the wall of a chapel connected with Djoser's pyramid, '. . . came to make an excursion and amuse himself on the west of Memphis, together with his brother, Panakhti, scribe of the Vizier'. From a wall of the chapel to the goddess Sekhmet in the pyramid complex at Abusir we learn that in 1261 B.C. a scribe named Ptah-Emwe and his father, also a scribe, and perhaps a third scribe 'came to contemplate the shadow of the pyramids after having been to present offerings to Sekhmet'. They were tourists no less than the sightseer of today who, at some famous cathedral, takes time to make an offering of a candle.

Scribes were such regular visitors to these monuments that they even worked out a formula to record their presence, and, since they were an unimaginative and conservative lot, kept using it with little variation for hundreds of years. 'Scribe

1 Greek cart drawn by a pair of mules. Sixth century B.C. Note the wheels, a primitive type of spoked wheel.

2 Greek coins used internationally in the fifth century B.C.: Athenian silver decadrachm with olive branch, owl, and the first three letters of the name Athena; electrum stater of Cyzicus with two golden eagles; gold Persian daric with darius holding a bow and spear.

3 Greek horseman in travelling garb with broad-brimmed hat (*petasos*) and short cloak (*chlamys*). C. 500 B.C.

So-and-So,' it goes, 'of the clever fingers came to see the temple of the blessed King So-and-So.' One example, written sometime in the thirteenth century B.C. in Djoser's pyramid complex, adds that it was done 'in the view of the whole body of the School of . . . The Nine'—in other words, a school for scribes conducted a visit *en masse*, like the groups of school-children we see today making the rounds of sights.

These repetitive simple-minded inscriptions attest not only the existence of the tourist but also that some of the charac-teristic features of his behaviour were established very early in his career. The chief reason for the messages seems to have been the age-old urge to leave one's name in a place one has been to, to leave one's calling card as it were. They are not formally chiselled on the stone but either hastily written with paint and a brush or scratched in with a sharp point of some kind; the latter method was so common that the technical term we give to such scribblings is graffiti, Italian for 'scratch-ings'. Some visitors could not be bothered with the whole formula; they got right to the heart of the matter and put down just their names: 'The scribe Pennewet', 'The scribe Wia', and so on. If most of the signers are scribes, this is only to be expected; they were the ones who knew how to write. Despite the smug reference to their 'clever fingers', i.e. their skill, their performance was often far from perfect—so much so that one member of the profession was moved to indite an irate blast on a wall of the chapel in Djoser's complex:

The scribe of clever fingers came, a clever scribe without his equal among any men of Memphis, the scribe Amenemhet. I say: Explain to me these words [presumably some illiterate graffiti he saw]. My heart is sick when I see the work of their hands . . . It is like the work of a woman who has no mind; would that we had someone who could have denounced them before ever they entered in to see the Temple. I have seen a scandal; they are no scribes such as Thoth [patron god of scribes] has enlightened.

B

Another characteristic of tourist behaviour that appears in these early days is the drive to bring home mementoes, typical or exotic, from places one has visited. Harkhuf, the envoy who was sent by the pharaoh to carry out trading missions in the Sudan (28 above), on the return from his fourth and last mission acquired as a present for his ruler the African souvenir *par excellence*, a pygmy trained in native dances. It was an inspired choice because, when he sent a message ahead to announce what he had with him, the pharaoh went into a dither of excitement at the news. 'Hurry,' he wrote back, 'and bring with you this dwarf . . . Get stalwart men who will be around him on the deck, beware that he does not fall into the water. Also get stalwart men to pass the night around him in his tent. Make inspection ten times in the night.'

Not only do souvenirs go back to these earliest days of travel but so does the buying of bargains or specialties abroad to satisfy requests from friends or relatives. Here is a letter that a certain Uzalum received sometime around 1800 B.C. from Adad-abum, either a young friend or, if the word 'father' is meant literally, a grown son; Adad-abum was probably in Eshnunna, just north of Baghdad, and Uzalum away in one of its subject cities:

I have never before written to you for something precious I wanted. But if you want to be like a father to me, get me a fine string full of beads, to be worn around the head. Seal it with your seal and give it to the carrier of this tablet so that he can bring it to me. If you have none at hand, dig it out of the ground wherever (such objects) are (found) and send it to me. I want it very much; do not withhold it from me. In this I will see whether you love me as a real father does. Of course, establish its price for me, write it down, and send me the tablet. The young man who is coming to you must not see the string of beads. Seal it (in a package) and give it to him. He must not see the string, the one to be worn around the head, which you are sending. It should be full (of beads) and should be beautiful. If I see it and dislike (?) it, I shall send it back!

Also send the cloak, of which I spoke to you.

When a holiday throng of Egyptians descended on Busiris or any of the other sites that Herodotus lists, they found no formal facilities for their food and lodging. Like the hundreds of thousands who congregate today for festivals of rock music, they slept in the open and fed themselves as best they could, leaving the locals to clean up after them.

At the other end of the scale were those on government assignment, who had everything provided for them. In the pharaoh's answer to Harkhuf's message about the pygmy, he reminds his envoy that 'commands have been sent to the Chief of the New Towns . . . to command that sustenance be taken from him in every store-city and every temple, without stint'. In other words, Harkhuf and his entourage were to be cared for at temples and government depots along the way. Presumably this was the standard procedure in Egypt for all who were travelling on official business. In Mesopotamia, some cities even had a fully organized government post. Shulgi in his hymn asserts:

> I enlarged the footpaths, straightened the highways of
>   the land,
> I made secure travel, built there 'big houses',
> Planted gardens alongside of them, established
>   resting-places,
> Settled there friendly folk,
> (So that) who comes from below, who come from above,
> Might refresh themselves in its cool,
> The wayfarer who travels the highway at night,
> Might find refuge there like in a well-built city.

In plain language, he established along the highways fortified settlements whose *raison d'être* was the maintenance of sizeable government hostels—rather attractive ones, if we can take him at his word. They were to serve all passersby, the high, who would certainly be largely official travellers, and the low, for the most part probably traders. He may have instituted the same kind of service we find in operation at Lagash about this time, one that ensured efficient movement of her administrators, couriers, and army personnel between the capital and the subject cities, most of which were 100 to 250 miles away and one even more than 400. Each man's travel orders included an issue of food rations, which were enough to carry the recipient just one day's march; at the end of this he presumably found himself at a government hostel where he put up for the night and received food for the next day on the road. The amount and quality of the rations went according to rank: administrators, for example, ate distinctly better and more than ordinary dispatch riders. The men travelled on foot except for the very highest officials, whose allowance included fodder for animals; it is very likely that they got fresh mounts as well at each stage.

None of these Mesopotamian hostels have survived. The earliest hostel of which we have remains is in Crete, where it was erected some time around 1500 B.C. It was a small elegant structure placed alongside the highway from the south coast just at its approach to the palace at Cnossus; travellers, after the long ride across the island, would have refreshed themselves here before entering the palace. On the lowest level are rooms with the remains of storage jars and bins for grain; these must have been connected with the kitchen. On a higher level was a handsome loggia, about eighteen by twelve feet overall, decorated just under the ceiling with a gaily painted frieze depicting flowers and birds. This could have been a dining-room. Alongside it was an equally handsome little pavilion enclosing a pool for washing the feet. The pool was roughly six feet by four feet six inches in size, deep enough for Minoans (who were quite small, perhaps averaging five foot four in height) to take a hip-bath in, and surrounded by a fine paving of smooth stone slabs. Just beyond was a room in which bath-tubs were found; this must have been where the guests took a complete scrub.

To judge from Shulgi's words, at least some of the roadside government hostels in Mesopotamia welcomed casual non-official travellers. In town they put up at the local inn, for private hospitality seems to have played no great role in these parts. Mesopotamian public houses go back to at least the first half of the third millennium B.C., but supplying beds for strangers was more or less incidental, since their chief business was supplying drinks and women. The tavern-keepers themselves were mostly women; barmaid and madame must be the second and third oldest female professions. Drinks were date-palm wine and barley beer, and there were strict regulations against watering them; in Hammurabi's code the punishment for watering beer, neatly fitting the crime, was death by drowning. Decent people did not patronize taverns. A lady who had retired from the priesthood, for example, if caught entering one, was burned alive; the assumption was that she was going there to fornicate. A requirement that tavern-keepers on pain of death should report all customers who were felons indicates the general level of the clientele; it was not particularly savoury. Neither were the surroundings. A document of the first half of the second millennium B.C. states: 'If a man urinates in the tavern in the presence of his wife, he will not prosper . . . He should sprinkle his urine to the right and the left of the door jambs of the tavern and he will prosper.'

The government hostels were in a sense part of a primitive postal system: they helped expedite authorized couriers on their way. Such couriers, however, carried only official mail—or whatever else they might be persuaded or bribed into slipping into the government pouch. Non-official mail went the way it was to go throughout ancient times: in the hands of whatever traveller came along who was headed in the right direction. The businessmen in Assyria who corresponded with associates in Asia Minor (cf. 30 above) entrusted their letters to the caravans that shuttled between the two localities. The letter quoted earlier requesting a traveller to send back a string of beads (34 above) refers to 'the young man who is coming to you'; the 'young man' may have been a fellow townsman who by good luck was starting on a round trip to where the addressee was staying and so was able to carry the letter down and the purchase back. A man of Larsa who, c. 2000 B.C., wrote to his sister, closed by saying, 'I am now sending you a man (who travels overland) with the sacred barge of the god Adad. Send me by him one hundred locusts and food worth one-sixth of a shekel of silver.' Here again the letter-carrier seems to be someone who happened to be making a round trip to where the addressee lived.

Overland travel in this age was both hard and dangerous. It meant following roads that were often mere donkey tracks. It meant fording streams or, if the traveller was fortunate enough to find a ferry in operation, waiting for the ferryman. Above all, it meant plodding along in sun or wind or rain, any of which can be punishing in the Near East. Here is an Egyptian official, the pharaoh's seal-bearer, on the subject; he was sent on a mission across the desert to Sinai (cf. 28 above) in the year 1830 B.C. or so and left an inscription there that is eloquent:

This land was reached in the third month of the second season, although it was not at all the season for coming to this mining area [indeed it was not; the time was close to the beginning of June]. This seal-bearer . . . says to the officials who may come to this mining area at this season: Let not your faces flag because of it . . . I came from Egypt with my face flagging. It was difficult, in my experience, to find the skin for it, when the land was burning hot, the highland was in summer, and the mountains branded a blistered skin.

Even worse than the hardships were the dangers, above all brigandage. It was so widespread that Hammurabi's code, as mentioned above, excused a trader from repaying a loan if his goods had been stolen. One of Hammurabi's ways of meeting the problem was to throw the burden on the local authorities: he ruled that they were to compensate any victim of highway robbery in their territories. When law and order broke down the situation was well-nigh hopeless. 'Men sit in the bushes', moaned an Egyptian writing between 2200 and 2100 B.C., a period of crisis in the valley of the Nile, 'until the benighted traveller comes, in order to plunder his load. The robber is a possessor of riches.' Shulgi's words glorifying his road-building (35 above) emphasize the protection he supplied, and one of the impressive features of Crete's road between Cnossus and the south coast is a series of fortified posts for highway police.

Sometime around 1130 B.C. or so, an Egyptian priest named Wenamon compiled a report of a business trip he had taken. By an almost miraculous stroke of fortune a copy has survived, a tattered roll of papyrus that a group of Egyptian peasants came upon one day when looking for fuel. It is the earliest detailed account of a voyage in existence, and its bald, intensely personal narrative suddenly turns a light on in the darkness, enables us to get some feeling of what it was like to travel twelve centuries before the birth of Christ.

Wenamon was attached to the temple of Amon at Thebes in upper Egypt. The high priest there selected him to under-take the journey to Lebanon to purchase a load of its famous cedar, needed for building the ceremonial barge used in the annual festival. Wenamon's first move was to make his way down to the delta, pay his respects to the local ruler there, and enlist his aid. He presented a letter of introduction from the high priest, his credentials or passport as it were, and was received graciously. Passage was arranged for him on a vessel bound for Syria, and, on 20 April, fifteen days after leaving Thebes, the ship raised anchor, sailed down to the river's mouth, and, as Wenamon puts it, 'embarked on the great Syrian sea'.

So far things had gone very well, and at the first port of call it seemed that Wenamon's luck would hold out. His vessel put in at the town of Dor, a little to the south of Carmel, where a tribe of sea raiders called the Tjeker had established a colony less than a century earlier. The local ruler, Beder, hastened to dispatch to the newly arrived envoy 'fifty loaves of bread, a jar of wine, and a joint of beef'. Wenamon, who, as the narrative makes clear, held a glowing opinion of his own importance, took the gifts in gracious stride as being no more nor less than his due. This was the last time luck was to smile on him; his very next words reveal a horrendous misfortune. As he tells it in his businessman's language, 'A man of my ship made off, having stolen one vessel of gold amounting to five *deben* [about 1·2 lbs], four vessels of silver amounting to twenty *deben*, a sack of silver—eleven *deben*. Total of what he stole: five *deben* of gold, thirty-one *deben* [about 7·5 lbs] of silver.' Every cent the poor fellow had been carrying was gone, his travel allowance as well as the cash he had been given to pay for the lumber.

Wenamon did about the only thing he could, under the circumstances. 'In the morning I got up,' he reports, 'and went to the place where the prince was and said, "I have been robbed in your harbour and since you are prince of this land you should start an investigation to look for my silver."' Beder was not one to be taken in by such bluff. At the same time he was decent enough to offer to help. 'I don't care how important a person you are,' he replied, 'I refuse to recognize the complaint that you have just lodged. If it had been a thief who belonged to my land who went on your boat and stole your silver, I would have paid it to you from my treasury until they had found this thief of yours—whoever he may be. Now about the thief who robbed you—he belongs to you! He belongs to your ship! Spend a few days here visiting me, so that I may look for him.'

After nine days of visiting Wenamon got impatient. At this point the papyrus is tattered, and we can only try to guess from scraps of sentences just what happened. Wenamon left Dor, continued on his way, and somewhere between Tyre and Byblus, perhaps in the port of Sidon, he solved his desperate problem by a desperate remedy: he carried out a bit of robbery on his own. He held up some Tjeker and took thirty *deben* of silver from them. The papyrus is still mutilated at this point, but the sequel shows that something of this sort happened. He had no qualms: his money had been stolen in a Tjeker harbour, and this was Tjeker money. 'I am taking your silver,' he told his victims, 'and it will stay with me until you find mine or the thief who stole it. Even though you did not steal, I am taking it.'

If Wenamon thought that his troubles were now over, he could not have been more wrong. The moment he dropped anchor in the harbour of Byblus, where he intended to buy the lumber, the harbour-master met him with a short but unambiguous message from Zakar-Baal, the ruling prince: 'Get out of my harbour!' The most reasonable explanation for the unexpected order is that the Tjekers had sent a wanted-for-theft message ahead to Byblus and, since they were his neighbours on the south and had a reputation as formidable sea raiders, the prince was not anxious to start any trouble with them. A man of Wenamon's stamp, however, who had just pulled himself out of a hole by a successful piece of hold-up work, was not going to let a little thing like this stop him. For twenty-nine days he hung around the harbour, even though each morning the harbour-master duly reported with the same message. Zakar-Baal, curiously enough, went no further than this. He had to stay on the right side of touchy neighbours, but at the same time he did not want to lose a profitable sale if he could help it. So he chose this interesting expedient of issuing an order and doing nothing to back it up.

Finally the prince granted the poor envoy an interview— and Wenamon found himself up against a tough negotiator.

B*

Since the stolen money fell far short of covering the cost of the timber, Zakar-Baal made him send back to Egypt for a cargo of goods to make up the difference. It took eight months for the shipment to arrive and the timber to be cut and hauled and loaded. At long last Wenamon received clearance to leave with his precious purchase—and that very morning, as if sent by the gods of retribution, eleven Tjeker warships sailed into the harbour to demand justice for the thirty *deben* of silver that had been stolen from them a year ago. At this point, Wenamon tells us, he sat down on the beach and cried.

Zakar-Baal was on the spot. He had an obligation to Wenamon—but at the same time he had no intention of getting on the wrong side of the Tjekers. His solution was a highly original compromise. 'I cannot arrest a messenger of Amon in my territory,' he told the Tjekers, 'but let me send him off and then you go after him to arrest him.' In other words, Wenamon was to shove off somewhat ahead of his enemies, was to have, as it were, a sporting chance. He no doubt had his own ideas of how sporting a chance a vessel chartered for hauling timber had against a crack squadron of sea raiders.

The next portion of the narrative is tantalizingly bald. 'He loaded me on board,' Wenamon writes, 'he sent me away. The wind drove me to the land of Alashiya' (Cyprus or the coast of Asia Minor to its north). This wind, which took him in a direction almost opposite to what he wanted, must have been one of the southeasterly gales that are common along the Syrian coast. Wenamon probably considered it just another to add to his list of tribulations, but actually it very likely proved his salvation: the Tjekers, either because their ships were too light or because they thought the gale would save them the job, apparently did not bother to give chase.

When the vessel landed, unquestionably a good deal the worse for wear, a group of natives promptly descended upon it and hustled Wenamon off to kill him. Their villages had very likely suffered their share of pirate raids, and this would be looked upon as a welcome opportunity to square accounts. At this point, however, Wenamon's luck finally changed. He pushed his way to the palace of the Queen and 'found her just as she was going from one of her houses and entering into another. I greeted her. I asked the people who stood around her, "Isn't there one of you who understands Egyptian?" Someone answered, "I understand it." I said to him, "Say to your mistress—" ' but the speech is unimportant and probably represents what, years later at his desk in Thebes, he reckoned he ought to have said rather than what a soaked and exhausted and frightened wayfarer actually did say. The important point is that the queen listened. 'She had the people called and, as they stood before her,' writes Wenamon, 'she said to me, "Spend the night—" ' and here the papyrus abruptly breaks off. These are the last words we have from this extraordinary writer. We do not know—and probably never will, unless by another miracle the rest of the document is discovered—how he got back home or whether the timber arrived safely. We only know that he did get back, or else the report would never have been written.

2

In the Beginning:
1200–500 B.C.

Sometime around 1200 B.C. the world of the eastern Mediterranean underwent a profound change. Hordes of invaders
of obscure origin, the 'Sea Peoples' as historians call them,
slowly but inexorably swept over it, leaving ruin in their wake.
When the dust of their devastations died down, the Bronze
Age was at an end, the Iron Age had begun, and a new cast
had taken up the key roles in the drama of ancient history.

The Egyptians managed to beat off the attackers at their
very doorstep, the mouth of the Nile, but the effort, along
with other factors, exhausted what little energy they had left.
They soon lapsed into a long twilight of living in the past that
was to fossilize their country and make it the prime tourist
attraction of ancient times. In Asia Minor the newcomers
smashed the power of the Hittites. Syria and Palestine, which
hitherto had been more or less divided between Egyptian and
Hittite spheres of interest, were now left leaderless, and this
enabled a number of relatively minor peoples, Canaanites and
Israelites and Phoenicians, to make their presence felt. In
Mesopotamia the end of the turmoil brought to the fore a
nation that was soon to put together the greatest empire the
Near East had ever seen, the Assyrians. The change, however,
that in the long run most effected the course of history took
place in the peninsula of Greece.

Since the attackers came from the north, it stood directly in their path. As they overran it, they came upon the still-flourishing Mycenaeans, those Bronze Age Greeks who from about 1500 B.C. dominated the trade of the eastern Mediterranean (cf. 27 above), whose kings dwelt in great palaces, ran extensive bureaucracies, and had themselves buried in grand style. The invasion stamped out this civilization so thoroughly that Greece went into eclipse, to live through a dark age lasting three or four centuries. When the curtain of obscurity finally parts it is to reveal the ancestors of the superbly gifted people we know from history.

In the beginning this new race of Greeks led a poor and primitive life, a far cry from that of their predecessors, the wealthy and highly organized Mycenaeans. The great kings of those times were now reduced to the status of local chieftains little more powerful than the aristocracy surrounding them, the impressive towns with their royal palaces to mere villages where nobles and peasants alike lived on farms. Cheaper and more durable iron weapons and tools substitute for bronze. This is the age that appears in Homer's poems, particularly the *Odyssey*. Though he purports to sing of Agamemnon and Nestor and other rich and great lords of the pre-invasion days, though he includes in his story many of the features of their civilization—war-chariots, costly armour, precious gifts of gold and silver—the basic setting is by and large a time not too far removed from his own century, the end of the eighth or beginning of the seventh B.C.

In this world travel by sea is still the most expeditious way of getting from place to place. But the great maritime powers of the previous millennium—Minoans, Mycenaeans, Egyptians —have now all been replaced by a new nation of traders, the Phoenicians. From about 1100 B.C. they monopolized the Mediterranean for some four hundred years until the Greeks learned the ways of the sea well enough to challenge them successfully. Solomon (c. 965–922 B.C.) used Phoenician sailors to carry on trade with India, reopening lines of commerce that had existed a thousand years before (30–1 above). A little over a century later Phoenician seamen, working ever further westward, founded a colony at Carthage, and eventually passed through the Straits of Gibraltar into the Atlantic to plant one at Cadiz. By 600 B.C. they had circumnavigated Africa (61 below). 'Phoenicians, famed for their ships, came into port,' says Odysseus' swineherd as he embarks on the tale of how he became a slave, 'greedy rascals with thousands of trinkets in their black ship.' He was a child at the time, son of the local king; the new arrivals, ready for illegitimate as well as legitimate business, lured him aboard, carried him away, and sold him off to Laertes, Odysseus' father.

In Homer's verses there is much talk of travel, both on sea and land, but only the de luxe travel of kings and princes. The Phaeacians, inhabitants of a kind of maritime Shangri-La, take Odysseus home to Ithaca in a crack fifty-oared galley and let him stretch out to sleep on the afterdeck, sharing the space with the ship's officers. When Odysseus' son Telemachus sets forth to find out what happened to his long absent father, he has a twenty-oared galley at his command; on the way out he shares the afterdeck with Athena, on the way back with a refugee prince he had befriended.

On land Homer's heroes do their travelling in chariots. Telemachus goes by chariot from Pylos to Sparta, Helen's daughter from Sparta all the way to Phthia, the birthplace of Achilles in Thessaly. In the dark age the chariot had become almost obsolete among the Greeks, surviving only for racing. These journeys, then, are anachronisms, reminiscences of Mycenaean times when nobles and their ladies went about the countryside in such conveyances (27 above). They are legendary as well: the first trip would have involved two days of steady riding over mountainous country, and the second still more; even the Mycenaeans did not have carriage roads between the places involved, and there certainly were none in the dark age, or for that matter, throughout most of Greek history.

Transport was chiefly by pack-animal, particularly mules. Where the terrain permitted, wheeled vehicles were used; thus Priam hauled the ransom for Hector's corpse across the plain between Troy and the Greek camp in a 'handsome new-made well-wheeled mule-drawn wagon', and in the Phaeacians' idyllic island, Scheria, Nausicaa carried the family wash to the riverside in a 'well-wheeled mule-drawn wagon'. Homer happens to mention only four-wheeled wagons, but the two-wheeled cart surely was known.

The accommodations enjoyed by the heroes were no less luxurious than their modes of travel. For they put up at each other's houses, where they were handsomely wined and dined and sent off loaded down with gifts. Telemachus, after a stay with Menelaus and Helen at Sparta, left with a silver bowl and a robe woven by Helen's own fair hands. His hosts had once been guests themselves of the King and Queen of Thebes in Egypt; on their departure the King presented Menelaus with two silver tubs, two tripods, and ten pieces of gold, and the Queen gave Helen a gold distaff and a silver basket with gold-plated edges for holding wool. There was a price to be paid for all this: when an erstwhile host returned a visit, he expected the same level of hospitality and gifts of equal value. The gold and silver things that Homer talks about so freely are again anachronisms, luxuries that the long departed Mycenaeans had enjoyed. We get a glimpse of the true state of affairs at this time when he describes where people went to sleep. A chieftain of the dark age occupied a simple farmhouse that had room only for his family; at nightfall he and his wife would go off to their bedchamber, but his guests, no matter how distinguished, would bed down under an open porch that runs along the front of the building.

Entrée to the house of some important local involved more than just food and shelter—it meant that the visitor had the strong arm of his host to shield him from a small community's instinctive distrust and fear of strangers. Otherwise, in this age which knew no central authority, his sole protection was people's respect for religion, their willingness to abide by heaven's law, which clearly and unambiguously enjoined hospitality. 'Stranger,' says Odysseus' swineherd to the beggar that he does not know is his master in disguise, 'it is not right for me to scorn a stranger, even if someone worse than you should come along. For both strangers and beggars all come from Zeus.' Homer was well aware that not everybody was so gratifyingly obedient to god's will. He gives the other side of the picture in Odysseus' contretemps with the Cyclopes, who 'pay no heed to aegis-bearing Zeus and the blessed gods' and view unexpected guests as just so much food for supper.

Homer rarely sings of everyday folk. Only in his report of Odysseus' vicissitudes when masquerading as a beggar is there a hint of what might befall the anonymous traveller. Odysseus' first encounter in this guise was with his swine-herd, who, as a godfearing man, honoured the laws of hospitality. In his own home he did not do as well. 'You're out of your mind, stranger,' sneers one of Penelope's maids when he insisted on staying in the main hall and tending the lights, 'why don't you go to the smith's or the town loggia to sleep?' If nobody took a stranger in, the most he could hope for was room to bed down under a public loggia or, even better, in the local smithy, where the warmth from the forge would keep off the night chill.

Similar conditions existed at this time in parts of the Near East as well, as we learn from the early books of the Old Testament, which, roughly speaking, are more or less contemporary with Homer. The two angels sent to Sodom incognito to test the populace would have spent the night in the town square, had not Lot insisted that they come to his house. Lot, being no native of the place, had decent manners; the townspeople, 'wicked and sinners before the Lord exceedingly', when they got wind of the presence of strangers, besieged the house in a body, and only divine intervention prevented violence. A chapter in the Book of Judges relates a similar incident. A Levite, who was bringing a concubine from her city back to his home, found himself at nightfall in Gibeah, inhabited by members of the tribe of Benjamin. Since no one offered hospitality, he camped in the town square until eventually an old man—as in Lot's case no native of the town—came along and took him in. During dinner a lawless gang descended upon the house and began to threaten; he was able to buy them off only by giving them the concubine to abuse. As the chapter points out at the outset, this happened 'when there was no king in Israel', i.e. when the land, like Homer's Greece, lacked a strong central authority. At such times there was too little traffic to justify the existence of inns, and travellers had to depend on haphazard private hospitality and trust to luck they would escape being molested.

Men went on foot and alone, as Jacob did when he paid his visit to Laban. The well-to-do, particularly when travelling with women, might take along servants and donkeys: the man and concubine in the incident reported in Judges were wealthy enough to travel this way, as was the Shunammite woman befriended by Elisha. Kings and princes rode mules. Chariots were strictly for war; they are never spoken of in connection with travel, even though in places there were roads they might have used. The Philistines, for example, when returning the ark which they had captured, transported it from Ekron by a wagon or cart drawn by cows which, heading under divine guidance straight for Bethshemesh, 'went along the highway'.

While David and Solomon were building a small and ephemeral kingdom in Palestine, off to the northeast in the middle reaches of the Tigris the Assyrians were laying the foundations of a vast empire. It lasted almost three centuries, from about 900 to 612 B.C., when Cyaxares' Medes joined a reinvigorated Babylon to destroy the capital at Nineveh so thoroughly that some two hundred years later Xenophon's Greeks passed the ruins with no idea of what they were seeing.

What made the Assyrians great was their instinct for

discipline and organization; they were the Romans of their age. It enabled them to create a military force that conquered and held most of the Near East and a bureaucracy that administered what had been conquered with ruthless efficiency. To permit the troops to move swiftly in any direction and to facilitate rapid communication between the capital and the surrounding territories, Assyria's rulers laid down a network of roads. 'I took my chariots', says Tiglath-Pileser I, describing a campaign he made in 1115 B.C. deep into the rocky terrain of Kurdistan, 'and my warriors, and over the steep mountains and through . . . wearisome paths I hewed a way with pickaxes of bronze, and I made passable a road for the passage of my chariot and my troops.' Assyrian military roads were no mere tracks. They had to accommodate not only the Assyrian chariots, specially heavy affairs borne on eight-spoked wheels and carrying up to four men, but also the Assyrian battering rams, which look like primitive tanks and were so ponderous they sometimes were fitted with three pairs of wheels.

The main routes were carefully kept up, were marked with road signs at given distances, and every six miles or so there was a guard post which offered not only protection but the opportunity to communicate with the next down the line by means of fire signals. Along roads through desert, there were wells and small forts at appropriate intervals. As in the previous age (26 above), road surfaces were never more than packed dirt, paving being reserved for the approaches to temples or sanctuaries that had to take processional vehicles on festival days. In these stretches, the roadbuilders reveal a technique almost the match of the Romans. A processional way at Babylon dating about 600 B.C. has a foundation layer of bricks set in asphalt, and upon this a surface of heavy limestone slabs, each a little over forty-one inches square, with the joints between them sealed with asphalt. Work of this quality was expensive; even the treasuries of Assyria and Babylon could afford little of it.

The same was true of permanent bridges in stone. They were

put up only where absolutely essential, as across the Euphrates at Babylon, the span, erected most probably in the time of Nebuchadnezzar (605–562 B.C.), that Herodotus so admired. Seven piers still stand, or at least their brick cores, since originally they were sheathed in stone. Each is about sixty-nine feet long and twenty-nine and a half feet wide. Herodotus describes how the engineers diverted the course of the river to put them up; since cements that would set in water were not known until Roman times, this was the only way it could have been done. Removable planks spanned the distance between piers, making the structure into a drawbridge— although Herodotus has a more picturesque explanation, that the planks were taken up every night to prevent people on either side from crossing over to rob each other.

Assyria's roads were used regularly by the king's messengers as well as the army, for the palace maintained an efficient government post. It included a network of 'officials for the forwarding of the royal correspondence', stationed in key centres—in other words, postmasters to supervise the movement of couriers and mail. The written documents dug up in Assyria include a number of hand-lists giving the names of places along a given route and the distances between them. These probably were in the first instance for military use, but could well have been issued to couriers also. They are the forerunners of the *itineraria* of the Romans (186 below), the travel guide in its most primitive form.

During the years when the Assyrian star was rising men finally learned to ride horses.

The horse, as we have seen (23 above), started its career as a draught animal, first substituting for donkeys or mules to pull ordinary carts and wagons and then coming into its own as the draught animal for that most prized form of cart, the chariot. This promotion took place about 1600 B.C. However, the further promotion to riding animal was delayed for over half a millennium longer. Refugees might *faute de mieux* leap on an available team, servants ride strays back to the stable, or horse thieves make a getaway on their loot (when Odysseus and Diomed took Rhesus' famed steeds from under the noses of the Trojans, Odysseus 'mounted the horses, then whipped them, and eagerly the pair flew toward the hollow ships'), but these were all exceptional cases. An Egyptian relief shows Amenhotep III (1398–1361 B.C.) in his chariot—and it is his captives who ignominiously sit astride the horses.

Then, shortly before the beginning of the first millennium B.C., pictures of mounted warriors start making an appearance. The art of riding most likely arose among the nomads of the steppe lands, in South Russia and Asia Minor and Iran, and from there moved on into the surrounding areas. Its reception was cordial but reserved: the chariot continued to be the preferred military weapon for many years, as we can tell from the Bible's account of the fighting between Philistines and Israelites or from the reliefs illustrating the Assyrian army in action. By 875 B.C. or so, the Assyrians had unbent sufficiently to add cavalry, although they still remained as devoted as ever to their chariots. Subsequent armies turned increasingly to cavalry until, by the fifth century B.C., the chariot had become obsolete for all military intents and purposes in the West (it lasted a good deal longer in the Far East).

From the outset through most of ancient times, riders made do with a minimum of equipment. They guided their horses with a simple snaffle bit and rode either bareback or on a horsecloth or simple pad (Fig. 3). Spurs do not appear until the fifth century B.C., the stirrup and nailed horseshoe not until more than a thousand years after that (181 below).

As draught-animals horses had served almost exclusively for warfare. They were somewhat more widely used as riding animals, but not much. Expensive to buy and maintain, they were for cavalrymen, government dispatch carriers, or wealthy sportsmen. Ancient travellers preferred to go on donkeyback or to be pulled by mules.

The Medes had made a spectacular entrance onto the stage of Near Eastern history with the destruction of Assyria's capital in 612 B.C. Half a century later Cyrus the Great of Persia (559–530 B.C.) knit them together with his own people to form an empire even more impressive than the Assyrians'. His successor but one, Darius the Great (521–486 B.C.), consolidated Cyrus's conquests and perfected the loose but effective machinery of government that enabled the Persians to rule successfully a conglomerate of subject lands stretching from Iran to Egypt.

One secret of their success was swift and sure communication between the capital and the most distant centres. To effect this, the Persians took over the network of roads and the government post that the Assyrians had built up and expanded and refined both. Their so-called 'royal road', maintained primarily for government couriers but open to all, ran from Sardis, near the east coast of the Mediterranean, some 1600 miles to Susa, the Persian capital, not far from the head of the Persian Gulf. There were rest houses and inns for royalty or other notables at fixed intervals of about ten to fifteen miles depending upon the terrain, forts at strategic points, ferries for crossing water. Ordinary wayfarers could average some eighteen miles a day on it, and traverse the whole in three months. The Persian dispatch service, efficiently organized into stages, probably did it in one-fifth the time. The mounts were supplied by the king, the riders formed an elite unit, and the administrative head of the service was one of the government's high dignitaries. Herodotus, though he never saw the men in action and had to depend on hearsay, was tremendously impressed. He reports:

There is nothing on earth faster than these couriers. The service is a Persian invention, and it goes like this, according to what I was told. Men and horses are stationed a day's travel apart, a man and a horse for each of the days needed to cover the journey. These men neither snow nor rain nor heat nor gloom of night stay from the swiftest possible completion of their appointed stage. The first man, having covered his, hands the dispatches to the second, the second to the third, and so on, the dispatches going from one to the other through the whole line.

The roads the couriers raced over were built to take wheeled traffic no less than horses and pack-animals. As a matter of fact, they were able to accommodate a particularly demanding vehicle much favoured by the Persians, a *de luxe* four-wheeled closed carriage. The Greeks called it a *harmamaxa*, 'chariot-wagon', since it combined the grace and speed of a chariot with the capacity of a wagon. The Persian elite used it for, among other things, shuttling their harems about; it had a roof and sides that could be closed in by curtains, thereby discreetly screening the occupants from view. Aristophanes, satirizing the Athenian diplomats who tried to justify their high salaries by big talk of hardships, introduces an envoy to Persia who complains: 'Well, first we had to cross the plains. It was exhausting. There we were, travelling in *harmamaxai*, lying at our ease, shaded by awnings. We had a terrible time.' The *harmamaxa* that outdid all *harmamaxai* was the one that was specially built, taking two years in the making, to bring Alexander's body from Babylon, where he had died, to his tomb at Alexandria. It was in the form of a colonnaded Greek temple, was roofed with scales of gold, was gorgeously decorated, and—unique among ancient conveyances—had some form of shock absorber (cf. 350 below). No less than sixty-four mules were needed to haul it. The road from Mesopotamia to Egypt at the time, no question about it, must have been first class.

Perhaps the most notable contribution to travel made by this road-conscious nation was in an area where there were no roads at all. For the Persians, if they did not inaugurate the cross-desert camel caravan, are at the least responsible for its key role in the trade of the Near East.

One must be careful, in tracing the use of the camel, to distinguish between the two-humped or Bactrian camel and the one-humped, the dromedary. The first is woolly and hence fitted for colder temperatures, climbs mountains with ease, and serves exclusively as a pack-animal. The second thrives in hot weather, is useless in the mountains, and serves as often for riding and fighting as for transport. They arose in different regions and followed different paths in history.

The two-humped camel originated in Central Asia, was domesticated by at least 2000 B.C., and was in use by that time as far west as Persia. From there it made its way still further into Asia Minor and Mesopotamia. The Assyrians, always in the forefront when it came to transport, seem to have been responsible for bringing it to Mesopotamia, perhaps about the beginning of the first millennium B.C.

The history of the dromedary is more complicated and presents something of a puzzle. It probably was first tamed and bred in Arabia. Figurines of dromedaries dating from 3000 B.C. or even before have been found in Egypt, so the animal was known there in very early times—yet Egyptian records reveal no evidence whatsoever of camels as beasts of burden until thousands of years later. The Israelites must have known the dromedary back in the days of the Patriarchs, 1800 B.C. or so, for it is mentioned in Genesis; yet, since they viewed it as 'unclean', they obviously held it in scant regard. The Babylonians knew it at least as early as the fourteenth century B.C., but their regular pack-animal remained the donkey practically all through their history. One solution to the puzzle is to assume that the dromedary found favour as early as 3000 B.C. among desert peoples living on the periphery of the civilized world, who presumably used it not only for transport, riding, and fighting, but for its milk, wool, hide, and dung, even as today. This would explain how Egyptians, Israelites, Babylonians, and all others who were in contact with such peoples were familiar with the animal; not living amid desert conditions, however, they had no compelling reason to adopt it. Eventually the dromedary was introduced into Mesopotamia by Assyria in the ninth century B.C. or perhaps even earlier. After a number of campaigns waged against camel-riding peoples, the Assyrian army recognized its value and began to include it in their baggage trains.

The dromedary had thus been promoted to an adjunct to the military. But it still did not rank as a standard beast of burden. This came about when the Persians created their great empire. It brought into being an unprecedented political arrangement: for the first time in history, all of the Near East was in the hands of a single well-organized and powerful state. Hitherto transport from Mesopotamia to the Mediterranean had taken a wide arc to avoid crossing the no-man's-land of the Syrian desert. Now, without toll barriers and with a government strong enough to keep desert maurauders in hand and rich enough to plant and maintain a series of watering points, a short-cut across the desert was suddenly feasible. The Persians had learned from the Assyrians the use of the dromedary for transport, its peculiar value in the desert had been common knowledge for thousands of years, so it was a natural choice as pack-animal for the new route. The camel caravan was launched on its long career.

The year 500 B.C., to use a convenient round number, marks the moment when the Near East, so long the focus of ancient history, yielded precedence to the west, to the Greeks and Romans.

By this time, the general lineaments of ancient travel had been fixed. On the sea, sailings of merchant craft offered communication between the major ports of the eastern Mediterranean. On land, key centres were linked by carriage roads, the best of which might boast bridges and ferries, road-signs, way-stations, guard-posts. The technique of paving had been developed although still sparingly used. Travellers had their choice of wagons, carts, donkeys, horses, or camels. Along major routes there were inns, and in towns, inns and taverns. And, among the regular users of the sea-lanes and roads, the official and commercial travellers, we begin to catch a glimpse of the traveller for travel's sake, the tourist.

3

Expanding Horizons

In 500 B.C., Darius the Great's Persia bestrode the ancient world like a Colossus. He had welded the once great nations of the Near East, Lydia, Assyria, Babylonia, Egypt, into one far-flung empire. The long arm of his power reached out to control the Greek cities on the west coast of Asia Minor. Only some pocket-sized states in Greece itself lay outside his grasp. When one of them, Athens, dared to challenge him, he decided to include these too in the Persian embrace. The result was the celebrated pair of wars fought in 490 and 480–79 B.C. in which the Greeks, to their own and Persia's astonishment, defeated their gigantic enemy and thereby moved into the forefront of ancient history.

Persia had built and run a vast sprawling empire. To the Greeks bigness was anathema. They preferred to live as they had for centuries, in cities which were at the same time independent states, each, no matter how small, with its own constitution, courts, military establishment, coinage, and other appurtenances of autonomy. There never was a unified nation that called itself 'Greece'. There was Athens, Sparta, Corinth, Thebes, and so on. These were the largest; the others varied in size down to mere villages. When Athens reached its heyday in the second half of the fifth century B.C., it put together what we refer to as an empire, but this was not at all an organized whole like the Persian; it was a federation of city-states which remained city-states as before but paid tribute to Athens and submitted to her foreign policy.

The world that the Greeks moved about in stretched from the eastern shores of the Black Sea to as far west as Marseilles. It would have stretched still further, had it not been for the Phoenicians, or rather Carthage, the colony planted by them on the coast of Tunisia which eventually grew more powerful than the motherland. The close-fisted traders of Carthage had early taken over both shores of the western Mediterranean, and wanted no competitors. In 535 B.C. and during the following decades the Greeks who had founded Marseilles fought several desperate naval battles with Carthage, but all they gained was the right to stay where they were; the Carthaginians were able to cordon off the waters between the coasts of Spain and Morocco and bolt the gates of Gibraltar.

From Marseilles eastward, however, the seas were open, and they were ploughed by a multitude of freighters, Carthaginian, Phoenician, Egyptian, above all, Greek. Ships plied regularly between Marseilles and ports in Sicily and southern Italy, and from there one could get any number of sailings to Greece or Asia Minor. From Athens or Corinth in Greece trade routes reached out southward to the Levant and Egypt, eastward to Asia Minor, northward to the Hellespont, the Bosporus, and even beyond into the Black Sea, along its southern shore right up to the eastern end, along the northern as far as the Crimea. Travellers who wanted to push still further east could follow the fine roads maintained by Persia (53 above) to Mesopotamia or even into Persia itself. Travellers who sailed from Greece to Egypt could continue up the Nile to the First Cataract.

Homer had known only part of the Mediterranean, to the west no further than Sicily, to the east no further than the Hellespont; for the regions beyond he is reduced to tales of lotuseaters and Cyclopes and other marvels. By the fifth century B.C. educated or well-travelled Greeks knew the whole of the Mediterranean and the Black Sea, and had a fair idea of the size and outlines. Thanks to the information gained before

Carthage barred strangers, they knew that the western gate was the Strait of Gibraltar and that there was a vast ocean beyond; they had even heard of the British Isles. But their knowledge did not penetrate very deeply inland; the hinterland was, for them as for Homer, largely *terra incognita*. They were vague about just where the people they called Celts lived, and they thought the Danube rose in the Pyrenees. Towards the northeast, they had some solid facts about the Scythian tribes of south Russia and the region they inhabited, and they were aware that the Caspian was an inland sea, but at this point their information petered out. For Russia north of the Black Sea coast, Herodotus repeats rumours—though with his good sense he refuses to believe them—of men with goat feet, men who sleep six months of the year, griffins, and the like. Still further north he reports the existence of cannibals and of people who believe in werewolves and, beyond them, of snowy desert.

Travel through Persia had acquainted the Greeks with Asia as far east as the Indus valley (West Pakistan). Darius, upon annexing the valley in 515 B.C., sent an expedition down the Indus river to the Indian Ocean; from there his men coasted westward past the mouth of the Persian Gulf and the south shore of Arabia to enter the Red Sea and end their voyage somewhere near Suez. Reports of the accomplishment brought this part of the world within the bounds of Greek geographical knowledge, but just barely. Herodotus, for example, knows about the groves of incense trees in Arabia, but he thinks that cassia—cinnamon bark—comes from there, not realizing that, like the tender cinnamon sticks or shoots, it originated in India and further east and that Arabia was just serving as middleman for the traffic in both. And he adds lurid details of flying snakes that guard the incense trees, of bat-like creatures in the marshes where cassia was thought to grow, of how cinnamon is obtained from birds who carry off the sticks to build nests with. He knows about India's vast polyglot populations, about bamboo, about the primitive Dravidians, but he tells stories of Indian cannibal tribes who kill and eat the sick and aged and of Indian ants that are bigger than foxes and mine gold. Of what lay east of India he had no notion; he thought there was nothing but endless inhospitable desert. China, in other words, was totally beyond his ken.

By the fifth century B.C., then, the Greeks' knowledge of Asia included Arabia and the lands eastward as far as the Indus valley. For Africa, on the other hand, they had not improved much upon Homer. Herodotus has some details about the desert of the Sudan, but he speculates vainly on where the Nile rose, and to him, as to all before him, the 'Ethiopians' were still a race of supermen (110 below). The Greeks knew that Africa is surrounded by water. Indeed, if we can believe a tale that Herodotus picked up in Egypt, the Phoenicians succeeded in circumnavigating the continent some time around 600 B.C. Here is what he says (with modern equivalents substituted for his geographical names):

Africa, except where it borders Asia, is clearly surrounded by water. Necho, Pharaoh of Egypt, was the first we know of to demonstrate this. When he finished digging out the canal between the Nile and the Red Sea, he sent out a naval expedition manned by Phoenicians, instructing them to come home by way of the Straits of Gibraltar into the Mediterranean and in that fashion get back to Egypt. So, setting out from the Red Sea, the Phoenicians sailed into the Indian Ocean. Each autumn they put in at whatever point of Africa they happened to be sailing by, sowed the soil, stayed there until harvest time, reaped the grain, and went on; so that two years passed, and it was not until the third that they rounded the Pillars of Hercules and made it back to Egypt. And they reported things which others can believe if they want but I cannot, namely, that in sailing around Africa they had the sun on the right side.

Hundreds of pages have been written about this bald paragraph, debating the truth of the story, questioning whether such a tremendous feat had actually been accomplished. On one point most agree: a voyage such as Herodotus describes was feasible. There is no reason why a crew of Phoenicians could not have carried it out in the span of time and in the way he said they did. Even if the sceptics are right and Necho's ships did not make it all round Africa, some sort of expedition must have been launched and, to judge from Herodotus' details about crops sown en route, a carefully planned one at that. What is more, it must have pushed beyond the tropic to a point where the crew was able to note they had the sun on the right side, that is to their north as they worked southwest and west. The very item Herodotus singles out for disbelief is the most convincing element in his account.

About a century and a half later, there was a second attempt to sail around Africa, this time the other way, from west to east, and there is no doubt whatsoever that it was a failure. The leader reported that he got far enough to see 'a race of dwarfs who wore clothes of palm leaves' and then came to a spot where 'the ship stopped and just could not go any further'. It sounds as if he had managed to sail below the Sahara as far as Senegal or even Guinea, where he perhaps saw Bushmen living further north at that time than they do today, and then ran into the calms and hostile current of the Gulf of Guinea or the combination of adverse winds and current beyond. As a matter of fact, wind and current make the circumnavigation of Africa from east to west, as Necho's expedition did it, far easier; although a number of ancient mariners later tried it the other way, they all failed. Vasco da Gama at the very end of the fifteenth century was the first to perform the feat.

These two ventures were small-scale voyages of exploration launched probably to blaze the way for new trade routes. Around 500 B.C. or a few decades later, a grandiose expedition passed through the Straits of Gibraltar, bent on setting up colonies on Africa's west coast. It is the one voyage of discovery made by the ancients that we know of first hand, for we have the exact words of a report submitted by the commander, Hanno of Carthage. He had it inscribed in bronze and set up in his home town, and years later an inquisitive Greek made a copy which has come down to us.

'The Carthaginians commissioned Hanno to sail past the Pillars of Hercules and to found cities of the Libyphoenicians [Phoenicians residing in Africa]. He set sail with sixty vessels of fifty oars and a multitude of men and women to the number of thirty thousand, and provisions and other equipment.' So begins Hanno's report, a document of less than 650 words which, over the centuries, has provoked several hundred thousand of explanation, comment, and argument.

Hanno had clear sailing at the beginning, and so do we: his first leg was through the Straits of Gibraltar and southwest along the Moroccan shore, where he kept anchoring to set down prospective colonists. At the mouth of the Draa river he made friends with a local tribe of nomads, probably Bedouins, and, since they were familiar with the coast further south, took some along as guides and interpreters. Soon after, the expedition reached a large river with two mouths that was 'deep and wide and infested with crocodiles and hippopotami'. The first river along the coast that would satisfy such a description is the Senegal, just north of Cape Verde. Next they came to a great gulf and then, after passing a tall mountain, a second gulf with an island in it where they saw men and women 'with hairy bodies' and managed to capture three females. The guides called them gorillas, but Hanno's men could hardly have taken alive what we call by that name, even females; chimpanzees or baboons are more likely. At this point they ran out of provisions and turned back.

How far did Hanno get? The conservatives, who are probably right, hold that he never went past Sierra Leone, that he stopped short of the calms and scorching heat of the Gulf of Guinea. The first gulf, then, would be Bissagos Bay in Portuguese Guinea, the mountain Mt Kakulima (admittedly rather low to qualify for the distinction of 'tall'), the second gulf Sherbro Sound in Sierra Leone. The radicals carry him all the way to Cameroon or even Gaboon, identifying the river as the Niger and the mountain as Mt Cameroon, the highest peak in West Africa. So far as the history of travel is concerned, the argument is academic. The voyage, though one of the ancient world's great achievements in exploration, had precious little effect: it did not bring West Africa into the orbit of ancient civilization, it did not even bring lasting geographical knowledge. Claudius Ptolemy, who in the second century A.D. composed the definitive geography of the ancient world, shows the very coast that the Carthaginians colonized trending in the wrong direction, trending southeast from the Straits of Gibraltar instead of southwest. The truth was not to be known again until the days of Henry the Navigator.

4   Etruscan covered wagon drawn by a team of horses. Fourth century B.C.

5 Wall-paintings from Stabiae and Pompeii illustrating seaside villas built about the Bay of Naples. First century A.D.

4

Trade and Travel in Classical Greek Times (500–300 B.C.)

When the centre of gravity of the ancient world moved westward from Persia and the Near East to Greece, the Mediterranean assumed the role it was to play thereafter as the means *par excellence* for the travel and trade of Greece and Rome. The majority of the Greek city-states are found along its coasts, they cluster about its shores 'like frogs on a pond', as Plato put it. Though there were some important Greek settlements inland, those that achieved wealth, such as Athens, Corinth, Syracuse, Miletus, and so on, were all seaports. It was inevitable: a Greek oil dealer who, every summer, transported two or three thousand five-gallon jars weighing some 100 pounds each to a market hundreds of miles away, was able to load them all into a single ship of only moderate size—but he would have needed an endless file of donkeys or oxcarts to carry them overland. Until the coming of the railroad, the water was the only feasible medium for heavy transport and the most convenient for long distance travel.

And so Greek traders were to be found shuttling back and forth the length and breadth of the Mediterranean. You saw them in south Russian ports dickering for grain to feed Athens, on the docks of the Piraeus picking up olive oil to ship to

C

Greek colonists along the Black Sea, putting into Beirut for ship timber cut from the cedars of Lebanon, negotiating at Miletus on the Asia Minor coast for fine woollen fabrics that brought two to three times the purchase price in shops at Athens or Syracuse. The vessels they used averaged some 100 feet in length with a carrying capacity of around 100 tons. There were, of course, others much bigger, up to at least 500 tons, and others much smaller, for short coastal runs. The hulls were given comfortable, well-rounded lines, and the rig was no towering spread of canvas but a single low and broad squaresail—the ships were made, in other words, for capacity and safety, not speed. Near the stern there generally rose a small deckhouse which enclosed a few cabins. These were for the captain and the owner of the craft or the merchant who had chartered it. A cabin was nothing very elaborate, just a few square feet of space that offered a place to sleep, but it served to keep the occupants out of the rain or cold or heat. The servants who accompanied them, as well as any others who had booked passage, slept on deck. On coastal craft too small to boast a deckhouse, a merchant probably shared the deck with all the others. Aboard a big ship or small, he brought his own food with him, had his servants wait their turn to cook it in the ship's galley, and ate it on the open deck without any ceremony. He might fare better when it came to drink, if he had seen to it that several amphoras—big clay jars—of his favourite vintage were carefully stowed away in the cool damp sand carried as ballast deep in the hold. When his craft made port, his first act was to rush to the temple of Poseidon, conveniently located right at the dockside, and offer thanksgiving for a safe crossing (cf. Fig. 6).

Provided one had luck with the weather, travel by sea could be no unpleasant experience. Once a voyager had bought food and drink and stored it and his gear aboard, no further effort was required: the ship was his inn, and wind or oars did the work.

Travel by land in this age, on the other hand, was strenuous. It usually meant going by foot. People travelling light took along only a slave or two to serve as valet and carry the baggage, sacks stuffed with clothes, bedding, and provisions. More elaborate entourages included a goodly number of servants and pack animals for the gear. With rare exceptions, these were donkeys or mules; horses, as we observed before (52 above), were for racing, hunting, or the army. The animals would have a sheepskin or goatskin thrown over their backs to prevent chafe and, upon this, a wood-frame packsaddle often fitted with panniers. Those who could afford it sometimes took donkeys or mules for riding as well. The Greeks looked down on the litter or sedan-chair; it smacked of ostentation, they felt, and condoned its use only in the case of invalids or women. Demosthenes, for example, caused eyebrows to raise when he was seen in one going from Athens to the Peiraeus.

Where the roads permitted, people might take conveyances, especially when there were women in the party. The standard passenger vehicle was a small open cart, holding no more than four persons, with a light body made of boards or plaited withes; a pair of mules or donkeys drew it (Fig. 1). For long journeys there were carts covered with the traditional arched canopy (cf. Fig. 4). Before the fifth century B.C. the spoked wheel was not nearly as common as one made in a distinctive fashion with a single massive crossbar running the diameter and two lighter bars, set like chords in each semicircle, intersecting the crossbar at right angles (Fig. 1). This kind of wheel is pretty clearly a lightweight descendant of the massive solid wheel of primitive times (23 above); though still not as light as a spoked wheel, it had the advantage of being easier to make, probably not requiring the skill of a professional wheelwright. As might be expected, it is found in a good many places besides Greece, in Macedonia, Cyprus, Italy, and Etruria. In the fifth century B.C. the spoked wheel, which was stronger as well as lighter, eventually drove it out of use.

When a stouter conveyance was needed, heavy carts were pressed into service or even four-wheel wagons drawn by teams of oxen, though the Greeks always maintained a preference for two-wheel vehicles. Strictly speaking, the Greek word *apene* refers to the light passenger cart and *hamaxa* to the heavy cart or wagon, but, like ourselves, the Greeks did not always take care to speak strictly and the terms are frequently used interchangeably.

A traveller in Greece of the fifth and fourth century B.C. thought twice before taking along any vehicle, light or heavy, since roads that could handle wheeled traffic were by no means to be found everywhere. A unified network of highways could hardly be expected in a land diced up into tiny, fiercely independent states. What is more, few of them had the resources to go in for proper road-building even within their own confines; at Athens, for example, what construction and repair there was seems to have been paid for by occasional special levies on the rich. Besides, Greece is so rocky and mountainous that the cost of laying good roads would have been prohibitive, no matter how wealthy a state was. The guidebook writer Pausanias, who travelled all over the country in the second century A.D., reports that the main road to Delphi as it neared its destination was difficult even for a man on foot. A route he followed into the hills beyond Sicyon was 'impossible for vehicles because of its narrowness'; plenty of other mountain roads must have been the same. There was a pass in the Peloponnese, he tells us, that was named 'The Ladder' because travellers used to get over one part of it by means of steps chopped into the rock. A road from Corinth past Mycenae to Argos was called the 'Staff-Road', presumably because it was so difficult that those who took it needed the support of a staff. The main route from Corinth to Megara and Athens ran along the top of precipitous mountains that skirt the shore of the Saronic Gulf; here was where Sciron in the legend of Theseus had his station, where he stopped all travellers coming through, robbed them, made them wash his feet, and, while they were doing so, with one good kick sent them hurtling over the edge.

For six miles it ran along a narrow, crumbling ledge half-way up the face of an almost sheer cliff . . . So narrow was the path that only a single sure-footed beast could make its way with tolerable security along it. In stormy or gusty weather it was dangerous; a single slip or stumble would have been fatal.

This was how the road looked to travellers in the last century, and it could have been little different twenty-five hundred years earlier. At one point the emperor Hadrian gave it his attention and, thanks to the skill of Roman engineering, the track was made over into a fine carriage road able to take two chariots abreast. But this state of affairs lasted only as long as money from Rome's treasury was available to maintain it.

The Greeks did pay attention to the roads that led to their sacred places, particularly the sites of the great festivals. Wherever possible, they made them broad enough to take wheeled traffic. Travellers from the Peloponnese, for example, were able to go most of the way to Delphi in carts or wagons big enough for a family to sleep in. In some cases roadbuilders saved money and time by constructing 'rut roads', a sort of remote ancestor of the railway track (cf. Fig. 8). Instead of taking the trouble to level the entire width needed, they limited themselves to cutting out a pair of ruts, each about three to four inches deep, eight to a little less than nine wide, and some fifty-four to fifty-seven inches apart. The ruts were polished and squared carefully, and the carts, which must have had more or less a standard gauge, ran along them like a train on rails. The ruts were all that counted; the surfaces between them or alongside were left unfinished. When carved in rock, as was often the case in Greece, such a road was practically wear-proof and weather-proof. There was a rut road from Athens four hours by foot to the sanctuary of Demeter at Eleusis, from Sparta to the sacred town of Amyclae some three miles away, over stretches of the sacred way from Elis to Olympia and from Athens to Delphi. Heavily trafficked work roads were also given ruts. The road between Athens and her marble quarries at Mount Pentelicus, which carried a steady stream of lumbering ox-carts or sledges bearing ponderous loads, was paved with stone slabs to a width of sixteen feet and fitted with a double set of ruts to accommodate two-way movement. On one of the rut roads hacked in the hills north of Athens, at a certain point a projection from the rock wall was not cut away but left to stick out, and the inside rut comes to a dead stop against it; this foolproof barrier may have been connected with a toll station at this point.

Even ordinary highways that were heavily used, such as the road between Athens and Delphi or Sparta and Olympia, were here and there given double tracks. And single-tracked roads had bypasses at intervals to enable traffic going in opposite directions to get by. But no doubt there was many a stretch where, when two carts met head on, one or the other had to back up a discouragingly long way. One of the most famous murders in literature was very possibly caused by such a confrontation. The legend of Oedipus tells how he killed his father when they met, each unaware of the other's identity, on the 'cleft way', a segment of the rocky road between Delphi and Thebes. His father was coming from Thebes, riding in a horse-drawn carriage as befitted a king of heroic times; Oedipus was coming from Delphi on foot. What happened next is best told in the words Sophocles puts in Oedipus' mouth:

I walked along, and as I neared this road
I came face to face with a herald and a man,
Such as you describe, who was riding in a carriage
Drawn by horses. The herald and the man were both
Intent on driving me from their path by force.
Their groom shoves me from the road. Enraged,

I strike him. When the man sees this he waits until
I come abreast and then from the carriage brings down
Upon my head his two-pronged goad. But I
Paid him back far worse, for a second later
He had taken a blow from the staff in this very hand
And rolled out from the carriage upon the ground.
I killed them, every one.

Oedipus flared up because of what he considered humiliating
and insolent treatment. But his father may very well have
insisted on the right of way not through royal arrogance but
because his carriage wheels were locked into the grooves of a
rut road.

Greek roads offered little in the way of amenities. Shade
trees were rarely planted along the sides; a traveller either
carried a parasol or rode with the blazing sun full upon him.
There were no road signs as such, but at least at crossroads or
boundary lines there was a serviceable substitute, the *hermeia*
or 'shrines of Hermes'; Hermes, messenger of the gods, for
obvious reasons doubled as patron deity of roads. In their
earliest form these wayside shrines of his were just heaps of
stones, and passersby, as a gesture in his honour, would add
one to the heap. As time went on, the *hermeia* became more
sophisticated. In some places the helter-skelter heaps gave way
to arrangements of hewn stones; Strabo, the Greek geographer
who wrote toward the end of the first century B.C., remarks
on some extraordinary examples he saw in Egypt that were
made up of boulders no less than six feet in diameter and at
times as much as twelve. Elsewhere they took the form of an
oblong shaft, often with the upper end carved into a likeness
of Hermes. The passerby's gesture now consisted of pouring
out a libation of oil. The Greek writer Theophrastus, discussing various traits of character, describes a superstitious
man as one who, 'when he goes by the carved shafts at crossroads, pours oil on them from his flask, falls on his knees,
makes an obeisance, and only then moves on'.

An ancient description of a tourist route through Boeotia starting from Athens gives some idea of what it was like to travel on Greek roads. Although it was written toward the end of the second century B.C. or the beginning of the first, things could not have been very different two hundred years earlier. The first leg was to Oropus, a distance of some thirty miles, which the author calls 'just a day's journey for a good walker'; much of it was uphill but the 'abundance of inns offering rest and plenty of life's necessities keeps the traveller from feeling fatigue.' The second day one went on to Tanagra through olive groves and woodland along a road 'absolutely free from attack by robbers'. We are also told that Tanagra itself was 'the safest city in all Boeotia for strangers to stay in'; both statements should probably be taken with a pinch of salt. Then on to Plataea by way of 'a road rather desolate and stony . . . but not too precipitous'; it followed the slopes of Cithaeron, the forbidding mountain where the infant Oedipus had been abandoned. From Plataea on it was easy going, the way to Thebes being all along the flat, while from there to Anthedon the road, running through the fields, was good enough to take wheeled traffic.

Whether a man went by land or sea, a problem he had to consider seriously was the danger involved. Travel at this time had its risks. For those who chose the water, there was the ever-present chance of capture by pirates, or by some enemy craft if, as was usually the case, a war was going on. The Athenian navy, the finest afloat during the fifth and fourth centuries B.C., offered the best protection it could, but this only alleviated matters. One of Demosthenes' lawsuits, for example, involved a businessman who had been seized by some warship; it took twenty-six *minae*, a good £5,000 or $13,000 in purchasing power, to buy his release. Another case dealt with the property of a merchant killed by an arrow during the fight that took place when the ship he was on was attacked by pirates. A favourite plot of the comic playwrights of the day has to do with a girl who had been carried off by pirates as a child and sold into slavery; she remains in this unhappy position until the last act, when a miraculous concourse of circumstances restores her to her rightful state. Theophrastus, characterizing a coward, says he 'is the sort who, when aboard ship, imagines that every headland is a pirate galley'. No doubt about it, pirates were a prime worry for anyone who booked passage on a vessel.

Our scanty sources of information do not often mention highwaymen, but these were no doubt as much a plague as pirates. Whatever police forces a city-state maintained were for keeping order within the town walls; the open country to all intents and purposes was a no-man's land. The travellers' only recourse was to move in groups or to take along plenty of slaves; they were as much bodyguards as body servants. The satirist Lucian in one of his imaginary dialogues set in the underworld has a group of spirits discuss how people got down there; one tells of a rich Athenian who:

> was murdered by highwaymen, I think while travelling over Mt Cithaeron to Eleusis. He arrived groaning and holding his wound with both hands . . . He blamed himself for being rash: he crossed Mt Cithaeron and the district around Eleutherae, which had been left deserted by the wars, taking along only two servants for the trip—a man who was carrying four cups and five bowls of solid gold!

As a consequence, those leaving on journeys tried to hold the money and valuables they took to a bare minimum. This brought another problem in its wake—what to do about whatever was left behind. There were no such things as safe deposit boxes, but there were adequate substitutes. Temples, all of which had facilities to accommodate votive gifts to the god, often served as public treasuries, taking on deposit state moneys, and, under certain circumstances, objects or funds from private individuals. Bankers too would accept custody of valuables; a speech by Demosthenes, for example, refers to

c*

the embarrassment caused when a clerk made the mistake of handing over to one client two precious bowls that had been left by another.

Money posed the most serious concern of all because, with no instruments of credit available, it had to be carried in coin. A businessman could probably limit the amount he took and count on replenishing his funds from his associates abroad, and the aristocrat no doubt made reciprocal arrangements with the friends and relations who would put him up in the various places he visited. But even they had to carry some cash with them, while the rank and file of, say, those heading for one of the great festivals had to take enough to cover all expenses while away from home. Greek bandits could be pretty ,sure that their efforts would be rewarded, that any traveller they pounced on would have a fairly well-filled purse on him.

There was yet another difficulty connected with money: what kind was it to be? Since Greek city-states insisted on having coinages of their own, the money-changer was even more essential to travel then than now. He was to be seen in every commercial town, down at the port or in the market place or in front of some strategically located temple, seated before his little table; the word for money-changer in Greek, *trapezites*, means literally 'table-man'. He would weigh in all coins offered him in a balance to make sure they were up to the mark, and feel or smell or make ring any that looked suspicious, even test them by scratching them on a touchstone, a piece of special black jasper found only in certain stream beds in Lydia. In the west and in Greece proper, coins were mostly silver; further to the east, gold was common, and also electrum, a natural alloy of silver and gold. When Athens was in her heyday, in the fifth and fourth centuries B.C., her money became an international form of exchange, and anybody planning a voyage found it useful to lay in a supply of 'owls', the distinctive silver pieces stamped with a goggle-eyed version of Athena's sacred bird. People heading east did equally well with the electrum staters of Cyzicus, a thriving city-state on the Sea of Marmora, or with gold Persian darics, struck, as the name shows, by Darius the Great. These three (Fig. 2) were internationally accepted currencies, and they meant not only a great convenience to the traveller, but a saving as well, since the ancient money-changers' charges were not the painless fraction they are today but a murderous five to six per cent.

There was one problem the Greek traveller *was* spared: harrowing decisions about what clothes to take. The vases of the period are often decorated with genre scenes, and from these we can see that the contemporary wardrobe was relatively simple. The basic garment for men was the *chiton*, a loose sleeveless linen or woollen tunic which came down to the knee or calf and was gathered in around the waist with a belt, the *zone*. When travelling, men tended to double their *chiton* over the belt to draw it up higher and, in that way, leave the legs free and keep the hem out of the reach of dust or mud. 'As for the length of the journey', Herodotus will say, 'a well-girdled (*euzonos*) man will spend five days on it'; he is referring to someone belted up in this fashion, prepared, that is, for serious walking and not dawdling. For outer covering the traveller carried a *chlamys*, an oblong of wool that could be worn as a short cape (Fig. 3). On his feet he tied sandals securely with thongs reaching to the calf; he wore no socks or stockings since these were all but unknown throughout ancient times. On his head he clapped a sort of sombrero, the *petasos*, a wide-brimmed hat fitted with a chin strap (Fig. 3); in hot weather he could uncover simply by letting the hat slide down his back and hang from the strap, while in cold he could pull the strap tight in such a way that the brim closed in and covered his ears. He had to carry his own bedding —a feature of travel that lasted until about the last century; he would pack a *himation* or *chlaina*, a good-sized oblong of wool that served as a blanket at night and doubled as a wrap-around cloak for cold or stormy days. His wife would have a tunic like his, and, as headgear, a chic version of the broad-brimmed hat; she might also carry a parasol. She had no short cloak, just the large oblong of wool which she would wear as a mantle draped about her. Whatever was not on their backs was packed up into cloth sacks and put in the care of the slaves who accompanied them. Only exiles, refugees, or the like travelled alone; ordinary voyagers invariably took along at least one servant.

The people willing to undergo the hardships and hazards that travel in these days posed fall into a number of well-defined categories.

Traders, journeying regularly year in and year out, no doubt made up the biggest number both on land and water. But along certain roads and sea lanes at certain times of year they and any other random travellers were lost amid what was without question the largest single block of people on the move at any one time in this age—the crowds hurrying to attend the great panhellenic religious festivals. We read, in Herodotus' account (31 above), of the incredible numbers at Egyptian festivals; the Greek ones called forth similar throngs.

The notion of holding joint religious ceremonies arose early in Greek history. Groups of nearby city-states fell into the practice of coming together at a given centre to worship a divinity they honoured in common. Gradually, for reasons that are not exactly clear, four of these occasions increased in importance until they became recognized as national festivals, with Greeks from all over taking part in them. These were the Olympic Games, Pythian Games, Isthmian Games and Nemean Games. Each was dedicated to a single god and included due measure of sacrifice and prayer; they were called 'games' since one of the ways Greeks honoured a deity was to offer up to him a superlative athletic or artistic per-formance. The festivals furnished in one unique package the spectrum of attractions that have drawn tourists in all times and places: the feeling of being part of a great event and of enjoying a special experience; a gay festive mood punctuated by exalted religious moments; elaborate pageantry; the excitement of contests between performers of the highest calibre—and, on top of all this, a chance to wander among famous buildings and works of art. Imagine the modern Olympics taking place at Easter in Rome, with the religious services held at St Peter's, and you can gain some idea of what made high and low, from far and near, non-Greeks as well as Greeks, bend every effort to be on hand.

The oldest and most important of the four great festivals were the Olympic Games. These were held every fourth year in honour of Zeus at Olympia, a gracious spot along the banks of the Alpheus river in the northwest corner of the Peloponnese. The place was neither central nor easily accessible. The time of year—the blazing, dry midsummer—must have been hard on both participants and spectators, though in recompense they were spared the discouragement and discomfort of rain. The city-states were almost continuously at war with each other but this did not stop the Olympics. In common with the other three festivals which drew a panhellenic audience, it enjoyed the benefits of a 'sacred truce'. On the first full moon after 22 June, the city-state of Elis—it was located near the festival site and its most important industry was the running of the great occasion—sent out heralds called 'truce-bearers' to announce the opening of the 'sacred truce'. This meant that, for the next month, war was totally outlawed. Even bitter enemies, up to that moment locked in a struggle to the death, laid down their arms. If they did not, they were subject to a stiff fine, two *minae* for each member of the violating army. When Sparta launched an attack with 1,000 men during the Olympics of 420 B.C., Elis fined her 2,000 *minae*—perhaps four hundred thousand pounds or a million dollars in purchasing power. Since the festival lasted but five days, visitors had ample time to arrive and enjoy the spectacle free of worries about how they were to get home.

We have no idea of the total number that attended but it must have been at least in the tens of thousands. At the head of the social ladder were the embassies sent at public expense by every state, rich and solid citizens who put in an official appearance at all the functions dressed in elaborate formal garb. The wealthy were well represented, making as much or even more of a show, though not officially. Then there were the contestants, each with his entourage—and the entourage of, say, an entrant in the race for four-horse chariots, with grooms and stableboys and the like, could reach a sizeable figure. Alcibiades, that master at public relations, once entered seven different chariots—and even got sponsors to foot the bill: Ephesus gave him a magnificent tent for his lodgings, Chios supplied fodder for the twenty-eight horses, and Lesbos furnished food and wine for his entertaining (and Alcibiades was no stingy host). Then there was the rank and file of spectators. Lastly we must add all whom such a crowd inevitably brings in its wake to supply services both needed and unneeded, vendors of food and drink, guides, touts, prostitutes, hawkers of souvenirs. The mere job of supplying water must have required hundreds of men circulating about carrying jars or leading donkeys loaded down with them, for it was not until half a millennium later, in the second century A.D., that Roman engineering and a millionaire's philanthropy combined to put up an aqueduct and provide the site with running water.

At the ancient Olympics as at its modern descendant, the keynote was athletics. The oldest events, going back to the festival's earliest days, were the running races: the 'stadium' course, a single length of the stadium or about 210 yards; the 'double course' or two lengths of the stadium, comparable to our 440; and the 'long race', 24 lengths of the stadium or a little over 5,000 yards, a gruelling run, in other words, of not much less than three miles. Other events were the pentathlon (a five-part contest involving long jump, discus, running, javelin, wrestling), boxing, the pancratium (a brutal sport that combined bare-knuckle boxing with wrestling), chariot racing, and horse racing. Before and after matches spectators could walk the grounds and visit the sights, including the mighty temple of Zeus which housed Phidias's gigantic statue of the god, a celebrated work destined to be included in the list of the Seven Wonders of the Ancient World (232 below). They could stop to listen as the best modern authors delivered readings of their works or the greatest names in oratory made important addresses on vital issues, or to inspect works of art displayed by ranking contemporary sculptors and painters. These incidental attractions as well as the athletic contests must have been of all-absorbing interest since they were able to distract the visitors' attention from the crowded conditions, lack of organized facilities, and, above all, the heat. Spectators passed entire days crammed into benches like sardines, bareheaded (the Greeks generally wore hats only when travelling; cf. 75 above), and with no protection if a summer shower happened to come along. 'Don't you get scorched?' questions Epictetus, 'Aren't you all jammed in together? Isn't it hard to get a bath? Don't you get drenched when it rains? Don't you get fed up with the din and the shouting and the other annoyances?' It was so bad that a story was told of a master who brought an unruly slave into line simply by threatening to take him along to the Olympics.

The Pythian Games, dedicated to Apollo and held near his oracle at Delphi, offered somewhat different fare. There were athletics to be sure, but the emphasis here was upon song and dance; the event was akin to the international music festivals that are so important in today's tourism. There were contests in choral dancing; in singing to the accompaniment of the lyre; in musically accompanied recitations of Homer; and in the 'Pythian melody', a piece of instrumental programme music describing the mythical struggle between Apollo and a dragon that had taken place in that very locale (it was in five movements: prelude, onset of the struggle, struggle, triumph, death of the dragon). Other music festivals included singing for flute accompaniment as well, but this was barred from the Pythian Games on the grounds that the dirges and threnodies usually so sung were too sombre for the occasion. The Pythian Games were the answer to a music-lover's prayer, a unique opportunity to see the world's greatest instrumentalists and vocalists straining to outdo each other. The art lover was not forgotten, since the programme included exhibitions of sculpture and painting. The festival took place the spring of every fourth year, so scheduled as not to conflict with the Olympics.

At Corinth on the isthmus between the mainland of Greece and the Peloponnese were celebrated the Isthmian Games dedicated to Poseidon. They were held every other year, alternating between spring and summer; the keynote was athletics, although music and dance were also included. The Isthmian Games were less important than the Olympics but very likely drew almost as large crowds since Corinth was the most accessible spot in Greece; with a port on each side of the isthmus, it could be reached by water from either east or west. The fourth of the international festivals was the Nemean Games in honour of Zeus. Like the Isthmian, these were scheduled for every other year, alternating between winter and summer, and included music and athletics with emphasis on athletics.

The sacred truce that the panhellenic games enjoyed practically guaranteed a large turn-out. Local festivals did not have this advantage, yet some offered such irresistible attractions that they drew a considerable number of out-of-towners despite the dangers of travel. This was certainly true of the Greater Dionysia, the annual festival in honour of Dionysus that Athens held each March. The programme was given over entirely to music and literature—there were no athletics—and the high point was a series of competitions between writers of tragedy and comedy.

To this festival we owe the very art of the theatre. Drama

came into being as part of the rites used in the worship of
Dionysus—precisely how is obscure and has been much
debated—and was made a standard element in the ceremonies
at his festival. In the Greater Dionysia of 534 B.C., an actor
named Thespis performed a primitive play of his own composition; it was drama's formal debut. The new art then
developed with amazing speed. Thirty-five years later in 499,
Aeschylus presented his maiden effort; by 458 he had written
his Oresteia trilogy, a milestone in Western dramatic literature.
During the golden age of the Greek theatre, the second half
of the fifth century B.C., three days of the festival were given
over to plays. In the mornings the writers of tragedy put
on pieces they had newly composed for the occasion, in the
afternoons the writers of comedy. In every audience there was
a goodly number of overseas visitors; exactly how many we
cannot say but enough so that Aristophanes was once prosecuted by a demagogic leader on the grounds that the playwright, to whom nothing was sacred, was criticizing the
government in the presence of strangers. They came from all
over, undismayed by the rigours of an early spring sailing or
a trek along muddy roads; the chance to see Euripides' or
Sophocles' or Aristophanes' latest masterpiece was worth any
risk or discomfort. Skilled road companies later took the plays
from Athens to other city-states.

The theatre at Athens was a huge open-air affair, set on
the slant of a hill, with a capacity of some 14,000; the slopes
above and to the sides provided unofficial space for perhaps
as many again. All Greek theatres were big, some even bigger
than Athens'; they are the equivalent of today's sports
stadiums rather than theatres. Yet, such was the enthusiasm
for drama that often there were not enough seats to go around.
The performances, whether at Athens or on the road, were
first and foremost for the local citizens; this meant that out-
of-towners simply had to take their chances. At Athens the
best seat in the house, the front row centre seat, was for the
Priest of Dionysus, and the one alongside for the herald

who made the announcements. The next
the front row and similar choice seats, wer
the city's magistrates, official foreign guest
of embassies, and a number of recognized
both citizen and non-citizen. In addition, s
over to certain groups—a block for the
perhaps a block for each of the ten trib
population was divided. Tickets—pieces of
coin—indicated only the section and the
section, not individual seats, and the ushers
upon to settle the arguments that inevi
gate-crashers tried to wedge into benche
capacity. Theophrastus gives as an example
the man who buys a bench-full of seats for
town friends, squeezes himself in with no
and, at the next day's performance, manage
all his children plus their tutor. The Atheni
too poor to afford the price of admission
by the state out of a special fund, the 'Seein
with no official position to entitle them to se
through some local, like the friends of Th
of brazen effrontery, or simply picked the
the slopes around the auditorium.

So far as numbers were concerned, no
traveller came near matching the throngs er
festivals. But they were merely occasional
road only at certain times during certain y
category which might be seen on the roa
out was made up of the sick or infirm wendi
sanctuaries of the healing gods, of Ascle
Such places were generally set in surroundin
for their pure air and water and natural b
were mineral springs on the site. Here
merely treatment but facilities for rest an
the keen Greek mind recognized as being

sport that combined bare-knuckle boxing with wrestling), chariot racing, and horse racing. Before and after matches spectators could walk the grounds and visit the sights, including the mighty temple of Zeus which housed Phidias's gigantic statue of the god, a celebrated work destined to be included in the list of the Seven Wonders of the Ancient World (232 below). They could stop to listen as the best modern authors delivered readings of their works or the greatest names in oratory made important addresses on vital issues, or to inspect works of art displayed by ranking contemporary sculptors and painters. These incidental attractions as well as the athletic contests must have been of all-absorbing interest since they were able to distract the visitors' attention from the crowded conditions, lack of organized facilities, and, above all, the heat. Spectators passed entire days crammed into benches like sardines, bareheaded (the Greeks generally wore hats only when travelling; cf. 75 above), and with no protection if a summer shower happened to come along. 'Don't you get scorched?' questions Epictetus, 'Aren't you all jammed in together? Isn't it hard to get a bath? Don't you get drenched when it rains? Don't you get fed up with the din and the shouting and the other annoyances?' It was so bad that a story was told of a master who brought an unruly slave into line simply by threatening to take him along to the Olympics.

The Pythian Games, dedicated to Apollo and held near his oracle at Delphi, offered somewhat different fare. There were athletics to be sure, but the emphasis here was upon song and dance; the event was akin to the international music festivals that are so important in today's tourism. There were contests in choral dancing; in singing to the accompaniment of the lyre; in musically accompanied recitations of Homer; and in the 'Pythian melody', a piece of instrumental programme music describing the mythical struggle between Apollo and a dragon that had taken place in that very locale (it was in five movements: prelude, onset of the struggle, struggle, triumph, death of the dragon). Other music festivals included singing for flute accompaniment as well, but this was barred from the Pythian Games on the grounds that the dirges and threnodies usually so sung were too sombre for the occasion. The Pythian Games were the answer to a music-lover's prayer, a unique opportunity to see the world's greatest instrumentalists and vocalists straining to outdo each other. The art lover was not forgotten, since the programme included exhibitions of sculpture and painting. The festival took place the spring of every fourth year, so scheduled as not to conflict with the Olympics.

At Corinth on the isthmus between the mainland of Greece and the Peloponnese were celebrated the Isthmian Games dedicated to Poseidon. They were held every other year, alternating between spring and summer; the keynote was athletics, although music and dance were also included. The Isthmian Games were less important than the Olympics but very likely drew almost as large crowds since Corinth was the most accessible spot in Greece; with a port on each side of the isthmus, it could be reached by water from either east or west. The fourth of the international festivals was the Nemean Games in honour of Zeus. Like the Isthmian, these were scheduled for every other year, alternating between winter and summer, and included music and athletics with emphasis on athletics.

The sacred truce that the panhellenic games enjoyed practically guaranteed a large turn-out. Local festivals did not have this advantage, yet some offered such irresistible attractions that they drew a considerable number of out-of-towners despite the dangers of travel. This was certainly true of the Greater Dionysia, the annual festival in honour of Dionysus that Athens held each March. The programme was given over entirely to music and literature—there were no athletics—and the high point was a series of competitions between writers of tragedy and comedy.

To this festival we owe the very art of the theatre. Drama

came into being as part of the rites used in the worship of Dionysus—precisely how is obscure and has been much debated—and was made a standard element in the ceremonies at his festival. In the Greater Dionysia of 534 B.C., an actor named Thespis performed a primitive play of his own composition; it was drama's formal debut. The new art then developed with amazing speed. Thirty-five years later in 499, Aeschylus presented his maiden effort; by 458 he had written his Oresteia trilogy, a milestone in Western dramatic literature. During the golden age of the Greek theatre, the second half of the fifth century B.C., three days of the festival were given over to plays. In the mornings the writers of tragedy put on pieces they had newly composed for the occasion, in the afternoons the writers of comedy. In every audience there was a goodly number of overseas visitors; exactly how many we cannot say but enough so that Aristophanes was once prosecuted by a demagogic leader on the grounds that the playwright, to whom nothing was sacred, was criticizing the government in the presence of strangers. They came from all over, undismayed by the rigours of an early spring sailing or a trek along muddy roads; the chance to see Euripides' or Sophocles' or Aristophanes' latest masterpiece was worth any risk or discomfort. Skilled road companies later took the plays from Athens to other city-states.

The theatre at Athens was a huge open-air affair, set on the slant of a hill, with a capacity of some 14,000; the slopes above and to the sides provided unofficial space for perhaps as many again. All Greek theatres were big, some even bigger than Athens'; they are the equivalent of today's sports stadiums rather than theatres. Yet, such was the enthusiasm for drama that often there were not enough seats to go around. The performances, whether at Athens or on the road, were first and foremost for the local citizens; this meant that out-of-towners simply had to take their chances. At Athens the best seat in the house, the front row centre seat, was for the Priest of Dionysus, and the one alongside for the herald who made the announcements. The next best, the rest of the front row and similar choice seats, were for other clergy, the city's magistrates, official foreign guests such as members of embassies, and a number of recognized public benefactors both citizen and non-citizen. In addition, sections were given over to certain groups—a block for the corps of youths, perhaps a block for each of the ten tribes into which the population was divided. Tickets—pieces of metal resembling a coin—indicated only the section and the bench within the section, not individual seats, and the ushers were often called upon to settle the arguments that inevitably arose when gate-crashers tried to wedge into benches already filled to capacity. Theophrastus gives as an example of brazen effrontery the man who buys a bench-full of seats for a group of out-of-town friends, squeezes himself in with no ticket of his own, and, at the next day's performance, manages to jam in as well all his children plus their tutor. The Athenian citizen who was too poor to afford the price of admission had it paid for him by the state out of a special fund, the 'Seeing Fund'. Strangers with no official position to entitle them to seats either got them through some local, like the friends of Theophrastus' sample of brazen effrontery, or simply picked themselves a spot on the slopes around the auditorium.

So far as numbers were concerned, no single category of traveller came near matching the throngs en route to the great festivals. But they were merely occasional, they took to the road only at certain times during certain years. A substantial category which might be seen on the roads day in and day out was made up of the sick or infirm wending their way to the sanctuaries of the healing gods, of Asclepius in particular. Such places were generally set in surroundings carefully chosen for their pure air and water and natural beauty; often there were mineral springs on the site. Here patients found not merely treatment but facilities for rest and diversion, which the keen Greek mind recognized as being an essential part of nursing the sick. The sanctuary at Epidaurus, for example, located where Asclepius was said to have been born and hence the most venerated in the Greek world, spread over an extensive tranquil grove. The buildings included the central temple of Asclepius with a famous statue of the god and other celebrated sculptures, additional temples also housing noted works of art, colonnades for shaded walks, a stadium for athletic events, and a theatre that, seating some 17,000, was the second largest in Greece; this last monument has managed to survive the centuries and is one of the most impressive sights to be seen in Greece today.

Alongside Asclepius' temple was the next most important building, the 'dormitory'; these two were where the cures took place. All visitors who wished—and certainly most did—would spend a night in either and, asleep on the floor amid the dogs and tame snakes sacred to Asclepius, would in a dream be visited by the god and either be advised what treatment to take or be magically cured; obviously the priests of the sanctuary were not adverse to eking out the purely medical resources at their disposal with divine help. On the walls of the 'dormitory' were plaques inscribed with glowing testimonials to the god's effectiveness. 'On these tablets', writes Pausanias, who visited Epidaurus in the second century A.D., 'are engraved the names of men and women who have been healed by Asclepius, together with the disease from which each suffered, and the manner of the cure.' Archaeologists, during the excavation of the site, came across a number of such plaques. Here are some rather spectacular cures they record:

1. A man who suffered much from an ulcer on the toe was brought forth by the attendants and placed on a seat. While he slept, a serpent came forth from the dormitory and healed the ulcer with his tongue. It then glided back into the dormitory. When the man awoke he was cured, and declared that he had seen a vision; he

thought a young man of goodly aspect had smeared a salve upon his toe.

2. Lyson, a blind boy of Hermione, had his eyes licked by one of the dogs about the temple and went away whole.

3. Gorgias of Heraclea had been wounded with an arrow in one of his lungs at a battle. Within eighteen months the wound generated so much pus that sixty-seven cups were filled with it. He slept in the temple, and in a dream it seemed to him that the god removed the barb of the arrow from this lung. In the morning he went forth whole, with the barb of the arrow in his hands.

Another way the patients had of showing their gratitude was by votive offerings; excavators have brought to light hundreds of clay models, usually rather crudely made, of feet, hands, legs, ears, eyes, intestines, and so on, dedicated to the god by those who had been cured of an ailment or wound in the portion of the anatomy represented.

In addition to the 'dormitory' where patients bedded down for a single night to receive treatment, there was also a big inn where visitors, sick or well, could put up for any length of time. It included four identical square complexes set alongside one another to form a total square 250 feet by 250 feet. Each complex was laid out in the fashion that, as we shall see (88 below), was usual for Greek inns, a courtyard surrounded by a two-storey building; since each court had 20 rooms opening onto it on both the lower and upper floors, there were 160 in all. The rooms were by no means cramped: most were about 15 feet square, while those in the corners were double chambers some 15 by 30 feet.

Other sanctuaries that drew visitors, although doubtless far fewer than Dionysus', were the oracles. The two greatest were Zeus' at Dodona in northwestern Greece and Apollo's at Delphi; another important oracle of Apollo, at Didyma near Miletus, served Asia Minor. They catered first and foremost to governments, statesmen, generals, and the like, who regularly consulted them when deliberating a significant action. But they also received those who had personal questions to pose; probably the best known instance is Socrates' disciple Chaerophon's inquiring of the Delphic oracle about his master's wisdom. There were plenty of other oracular seats which were of lesser rank, and very likely people with private problems tended to patronize these, going to the one that happened to be nearest. The Boeotians were particularly well off in this regard; for some reason Apollo maintained half a dozen within their borders.

Men abroad on business, visitors to festivals, the sick or puzzled en route to sanctuaries—these accounted for the bulk of the travel that took place in the fifth and fourth centuries B.C. One more category deserves mention, even though it was infinitesimally small compared with the others—the tourists pure and simple. 'A great many Greeks went to Egypt', writes Herodotus, 'some, as might be expected, for business, some to serve in the army, but also some just to see the country itself.' He himself belonged to this last category, although there is a possibility (98 below) that he travelled for business as well as sightseeing. We are distinctly told that Solon combined the two when, after completing an arduous term as Athen's leader during a crisis, he relaxed by taking a trip abroad. Athens itself developed into a tourist attraction from the second half of the fifth century on, when the Parthenon and other exciting new buildings crowned its Acropolis; as a contemporary writer of comedy put it:

If you've never seen Athens, your brain's a morass;
if you've seen it and weren't entranced, you're an ass;
if you left without regrets, your head's solid brass!

To go in for disinterested travel required leisure and money, and those who enjoyed such privileges in the fifth and fourth centuries B.C. were but a wafer-thin crust on Greek society. The numbers, as we shall see, were to increase steadily in the succeeding centuries.

Let us turn now to what awaited a traveller upon arrival at his destination.

The answer has to be general and lacking in detail since no ancient author ever specifically described travel experiences. We have to use casual remarks dropped by historians, stray lines in ancient comedies, genre pictures on vases, and the like, then piece this in with certain information available from later centuries, and, finally, add a seasoning of plain guesswork.

To begin with, ancient travellers made it a rule to arrive by daylight. In an age that did not know the lighthouse, let alone beacons or illuminated buoys, no skipper wanted to enter a harbour in the dark. Walkers or riders were just as averse to threading their way at night through unmarked, unpaved, and unlit streets, unable to see either their way or where to jump when they heard 'Stand back'! and rubbish came flying out of a window. Street lamps lay centuries in the future, and paving was not only rare but, where it did exist, just a poorly drained layer of stone chips rammed into the surface. To add to the confusion, those most useful devices, street signs and house numbers, were yet to be invented. A character in a comedy by Plautus comes on stage looking for an address and mutters, 'My master said it was the seventh building from the town gate'; a few lines later he reports that he is 'staying at the third inn outside the town gate'. These were as precise indications as one could give. Even street names were sparingly used; only main avenues had them. In one of Terence's comedies a set of directions goes like this:

> You know that house there, the one that belongs to Cratinus, the millionaire? Well, when you get past that house, go straight down the street there to the left, then when you get to the temple of Diana go right. Then just before you get to the town gate, right by a watering pond there, you'll find a little bakery and, opposite it, a carpenter's shop. That's where he is.

By arriving during the day the stranger could at least step

around potholes, avoid piles of refuse, see where to duck in at the warning call of someone throwing rubbish, find passersby to ask the way, and stand some chance of following their instructions successfully.

In the early days, as we have noted (48 above), travellers often had no alternative to using private hospitality. And private hospitality continued to play a significant role long after the increased pace of movement had planted inns all over the land. Traders counted on being lodged with business associates, the noble or wealthy with their influential friends, and the humble with whoever would take them in. Families in different cities united by ties of friendship extended hospitality to each other from generation to generation. The ties did not have to be particularly close; indeed, there were certain households with the generous tradition of putting up all citizens from a given place regardless of whether these were personally known or not. The dwellings of the well-to-do always included at least one *xenon* or guest room; usually it had its own entrance, and sometimes it was a separate little lodge. The visitor would be invited to his host's table the day after his arrival; thereafter provisions were sent to the *xenon* or he bought them himself, and his servant prepared them. On departure, guest and host exchanged gifts.

Those who had no access to private hospitality perforce went to an inn, a *pandokeion* 'place for receiving all [comers]'. By the fifth century B.C. inns were to be found along the major roads, in most towns, and in considerable numbers in ports or big centres. The trouble was that most of them were unprepossessing, to say the least. Aristophanes' *Frogs* opens with a scene in which Dionysus decides to go to the underworld. He consults Heracles—the hero was an expert on getting there since one of his Twelve Labours had been to bring back Cerberus, Hades' watchdog—and an urgent request he makes is for a list of 'landladies with the fewest bedbugs'; as in the earliest days of travel (37 above), innkeeping was still a woman's profession. The inn in Hades where he eventually puts up, it turns out, is run by a lady with a terrifying way of carrying on about guests who do not pay—the ancestor of Falstaff's Mistress Quickly and other formidable female inn-keepers of English literature. If there were any snug comfortable hostels, we never hear of them.

We know the layout only of country inns or those built where generous space was available. They were like the hostelry at Epidaurus, a large square or rectangular central courtyard surrounded on all four sides by a shallow con-tinuous structure, usually two stories high. This was parti-tioned off into a line of small rooms, each opening onto the court or a covered passage surrounding it. The principal facade was pierced by a gateway giving access to the court. Inns in town were very likely much more cramped, as in Roman times (207 below). The traveller left his carriage or pack-animals in the court and was ushered into one of the rooms, which he might have to share with any number of other guests, depending upon the volume of traffic. The only furniture would be a pallet, perhaps also a spread; for a blanket, he used his cloak. The room would certainly be dark, with few or even no windows; this had the advantage of keeping it cool during the summer, the most popular time for travelling. If the weather happened to be cold enough to require heat, he might convince the innkeeper to send in a charcoal brazier. There were no toilets—there were none in the finest mansions in town either—just commodes, which hopefully the servants emptied promptly. In town, where there were markets, he would rent just the room and buy his own food, which his servants or the kitchen staff would prepare. In a country inn he would strike a bargain with the innkeeper for each item separately—bed, drink, meals (cf. 270 below). Rates including full board were the exception, to be found only in regions where food was so plentiful it was practically thrown in.

By the fifth century B.C. temple precincts, as we shall see in a moment (90 below), had inns of their own. Somewhat later, perhaps sparked by the example of the temples, certain cities began to run inns. One imposing example has been unearthed in a rather remote spot in Epirus in western Greece. The entrance facade was decorated with columns, the court measured an ample 46 feet six inches by 38 feet 4 inches and the rooms opening on to it—there were some eighteen on the ground floor and another dozen or so on a second floor—were furnished with tables as well as beds. Cities still maintained *leschai*, the loggias (48 above) where the populace could idle away part of the day sheltered from rain and sun, and these, though they offered no more than a roof over one's head, were better than nothing for anyone who could not afford an inn or find a household generous enough to offer its *xenon*.

As a matter of fact, Greek inns, at least those in towns or cities, offered very little more than a night's shelter. Food, as just mentioned, had to be bought elsewhere. A guest who wanted to wash off the dust of the road would go down the street to the nearest public bath carrying his own towel and his own flask of oil for rubbing down with afterwards; the establishment furnished a cleanser, usually a lye of lime or wood ashes or fuller's earth (soap proper was unknown at this time). He took off his clothes in the dressing room and made sure they were in someone's care while he was bathing, since robbing garments from dressing rooms was practically a profession, and the management assumed no responsibility. The bath itself, as we can tell from pictures on contemporary vases, was a big basin over which he leaned while an attendant sloshed water over him. A form of shower very much like those of today also occasionally appears, but we have no way of telling how widely it was used. Upper-class houses sometimes included a private bath—yet another in the long list of conveniences enjoyed by those who could stay with friends.

Inns offered so little because they were primarily for transient guests. Travellers who had to spend any amount of time in a place looked for lodgings in a private house. In ports such as the Peiraeus, Corinth, Byzantium (the Greek predecessor of Constantinople), or the like, these were plentiful—enough of them at Byzantium, for example, to give rise to a story that the men there spent so much time lounging and drinking in the wineshops, they hardly had any use for their homes and would rent them out, wives included.

At temples or sanctuaries of any importance there generally were facilities for receiving guests, both lodgings and banquet halls. The temple of Hera at Plataea in Boeotia, for example, by the fifth century B.C. boasted a two-storey inn that was over 200 feet square and had perhaps as many as 150 rooms. In Hippolytus' sanctuary at Troezon in the eastern Peloponnese, archeologists have uncovered a banquet hall with couches for fifty-six diners and in Hera's at Argos a series of three small dining-rooms that could accommodate twelve in each. At the site of the Olympic games, in the fourth century B.C. a certain philanthropist paid for the erection of a handsome hostelry that measured all of 242 by 262 feet overall and was two storeys high. It followed the layout we usually associate with ancient Greek inns (88 above), a patio surrounded on four sides by lines of rooms, all opening onto it. Here the patio was a spacious affair with an arcade of Doric columns. There were slightly more than twenty rooms on each floor, even the smallest of which were of good size, about 18 feet wide and 35 deep, while the largest, in the corners, were ample chambers more than 35 feet square. An imposing line of Ionic columns, 138 in all, ran about the whole exterior. At other than festival times, the rooms and halls at the various sanctuaries were available for rental by whatever visitors could afford them, the proceeds making a welcome addition to the temple revenues. During festivals, since they could take care of but a fraction of the thousands who flocked in, they must have been reserved for ranking notables.

Housing the crowds at any of the panhellenic games posed a monumental problem. The well-to-do usually arrived equipped to take care of themselves, with tents and household gear and a staff of servants. For the rank and file, who came with little more than a change of clothes, the local authorities provided some temporary shelters. Whoever could not jam into these simply slept under whatever cover there was—porticoes, loggias, temple porches—or bedded down in the open and hoped that it would not rain.

At the festivals there were activities, formal or otherwise, going on endlessly, so people were spared the problem of what to do with themselves. In towns of any size, visitors in search of diversion had the *kapeleia* or *potisteria* 'drinking shops' to turn to, which offered not only wine but meals and gambling and dancing girls. In most cases such establishments were extremely modest, catering to no very elevated trade; the wealthy entertained themselves and their guests at home. There were, however, exceptions, as archeologists discovered when digging at Corinth, one of Greece's most important and active seaports until Rome destroyed it in 146 B.C. Sometime in the second half of the fourth century B.C. the Corinthians put up a long elegant portico with an equally long and elegant two-storey structure behind it. The ground floor housed a line of thirty-one taverns, each with its own entrance onto the portico, and the second floor a line of two-room suites entered from a corridor approached by a staircase at either end of the portico. Each tavern was a bit over 15 feet square, had a storeroom of equal size behind, and from the storeroom a back door led to a small neatly paved area with a latrine. What is more, each tavern had in the middle of its main room the nearest thing to a refrigerator that the ancient world could supply—a well whose bottom opened onto a man-made tunnel connected with fresh springs. Here, at the end of long cords, were kept wine jugs and containers of foodstuffs submerged in the cool water. When excavated the wells turned out to be full of debris from the shops: battered wine jugs, broken flutes, knuckle bones, drinking cups. Some of the last were intact, including a number of the kind that, used for libations, had the name of the god to be honoured inscribed on them. All the names are well known—e.g. 'Dionysus', 'Love', 'Joy', 'Health',—except one: *Pausikraipalos* 'Stop-the-Hangover'. The suites above the shops were no less well fitted. Each was entered from the corridor, like the rooms in a modern hotel. The door led into a small antechamber, open at the back; here a shallow staircase of two steps, flanked by a simple column on either side, brought one to the main room. The antechamber, which was easily curtained off at night, could have been for servants.

There may have been a special reason for facilities of such unexpected luxury in Corinth at this time. From 338 B.C., when Philip of Macedon became master of Greece, to the death of his son Alexander in 323, the city was the seat of the confederacy of Greek states that Philip had created. Whenever meetings were called, every member sent delegates there. Quite possibly the suites were their living quarters and the taverns where they ate and spent their leisure.

If a delegate sought greater diversion than even such handsome taverns could offer, he could spend the evening with a courtesan, a lovely lady finely trained in all the arts—music, dance, and conversation, as well as making love—that delight a man's soul. Their prices were steep; they were a luxury that only the likes of delegates or prosperous business-men could afford. Some well-to-do merchants, in ports they visited regularly, kept girls on a retainer as it were, paying through the nose for the exclusive use of their charms. Lucian has an amusing skit in which a sailor from the Athenian navy storms at a courtesan because she threw him over for a tooth-less, balding fifty-year old merchant; the girl icily retorts that, instead of gifts of onions or cheese or cheap shoes, her new client had given her 'these earrings and a rug, and the other day two minae [about £400 or $1,000 in purchasing power] . . ., and paid the rent'.

The tourist today who gets into trouble abroad—runs out of money or has an accident or is caught up in some outbreak of violence—has his consul to turn to. The ancient Greek had his *proxenos*. The two, though differing in many key respects, served a number of the same purposes.

A *proxenos* was a person living in a city-state either as citizen or resident alien, who was officially chosen to take care of the interests of another city-state—he was, in effect, the other state's accredited representative in the one where he dwelled. He was necessarily a man of wealth and position; the family of Alcibiades, for example, was for generations Sparta's *proxenos* at Athens, Demosthenes was Thebes', Nicias, the political successor of Pericles, was Syracuse's. In the above instances each, as it happens, was an Athenian citizen serving as *proxenos* for a foreign state; more often the *proxenos* was a resident foreigner who was selected by the city in which he lived to represent the city of his origin. The *proxenos'* prime duty was to aid and assist in all ways possible any of his compatriots who turned up in the place of his residence, particularly those who had come in some official capacity. For example, in 325 B.C. the Athenian government passed a resolution designating as *proxenos* a certain Heracleides of Salamis, a city-state on the island of Cyprus. Heracleides henceforth would be expected to give hospitality to any government representatives Salamis sent to Athens, secure them admission to meetings of the Assembly, get them tickets to the theatre, and so on. He could be asked for help by any Salaminian who might be involved in a lawsuit at Athens, or for a loan by any who chanced to run short of funds while there. He could be asked to negotiate the ransom of Salaminians taken as prisoners of war. If a Salaminian died at Athens, the heirs could request him to wind up relevant financial matters there. Conversely, if Athens for some reason had to send a representative to Salamis to beg a favour or negotiate a delicate issue, Heracleides would be the natural choice. A *proxenos* received no pay from the state that appointed him. He was granted certain privileges, and unquestionably his position opened up useful business contacts and opportunities, but his prime motivation seems to have been the honour of it, his highest reward to be given public recognition in the form of an official decree carved on stone and set up in a public place—sometimes in duplicate, one in the state which appointed him and where he served and the other in the state which he represented.

Thus, as late as the end of the fourth century B.C., travel in and around Greece was neither easy nor particularly pleasant. Those who went by sea depended on the sailings of merchant-men, put up with casual accommodations once aboard, and worried about pirate attacks during the whole voyage. Those who went by land found the roads generally poor, the inns worse, and had to keep a sharp eye out for highwaymen. The wealthy were better off only in having the money to take a cabin aboard ships that offered such amenities, friends to put them up in various places, and the influence to ensure the help of their city's *proxenos* if they got into difficulties.

Most who travelled did so with specific ends in view: government representatives, businessmen, itinerant merchants, actors on tour, the sick heading for a sanctuary of Asclepius, the festival crowds en route to the panhellenic or other well-known games. But there were a few who, despite all the discouragements, travelled for the love of it. One was the man who has the distinction of being the world's first travel writer.

5

The First Travel Writer

In 490 B.C. King Darius of Persia launched an amphibious attack upon Athens—the first of the Persian Wars mentioned above (58). It was Goliath against David, a David with no secret weapon but just the traditional courage and skill of Greek men-at-arms. Athens repulsed the invasion practically single-handed. Stung by such an unexpected defeat, Xerxes, Darius' son, returned ten years later at the head of a gargantuan expedition by sea and land. The Greek city-states—or at least a good many of them—were for once alarmed enough to give up fighting each other and combine against the common enemy. They smashed Xerxes' navy at Salamis, and his army at Plataea. The two stunning victories made them overnight the foremost people in the eastern Mediterranean and marked the beginning of Athens' dazzling career as political and cultural leader.

We know about this war as we do few others, thanks to a keen-eyed, keen-minded, and widely travelled Greek who wrote about it and thereby earned himself the title of 'Father of History'. Herodotus' *History of the Persian Wars* was something totally new in literature. He was not, to be sure, the first to record the past. For over two thousand years Near Eastern monarchs had been inscribing monuments with accounts of their heroic accomplishments, and the Jews had long before drawn up the story of their vicissitudes as Jehovah's chosen people. The fundamental purpose of all these writings, however, had been to attest to the triumphant fulfilment of heaven's will. Herodotus concentrated on man's doings, and he had the vision and genius to take a vast mass of material and organize it into a narrative which would show the human motives and actions that brought Greeks and Persians into conflict and gave victory to the one and defeat to the other. What is more, to introduce the protagonists properly to his audience, he begins with an extended survey of the vast polyglot Persian empire and the neighbours who figured significantly in its history, drawing upon information he had acquired through personal observation and inquiry during long and far-ranging journeys. He has thus the distinction of being the world's first travel writer as well as historian.

We know tantalizingly little about this extraordinary man who spent the better part of his life as a tourist and used the experience so creatively. Greek writers are reticent. They assume that readers want a book for information about its subject, not its author. There is hardly a word in Herodotus' pages about what he ate, where he stayed, whom he met, what adventures he had, and the rest of it. In fact, there are not many about where he actually travelled. From a random mention that he saw a certain bowl at 'a place between the Hypanis (the Bug) and the Borysthenes (the Dnieper)' we realize that he had been to south Russia. We know he traversed Egypt as far as the First Cataract since he remarks at one point that he is reporting on the country 'as an eye-witness as far as Elephantine'. We gather he had been to Babylon because, in describing a solid gold statue eighteen feet high, he adds 'I didn't see it myself, I only report what the Babylonians tell me'.

He was born in Halicarnassus, a Greek city-state on the southwest coast of Asia Minor, in the early decades of the fifth century B.C. Halicarnassus was a vassal of Persia in those days and contributed a squadron to the navy Xerxes massed for his attack on Greece. Herodotus was probably of school age when Artemisia, the queen of Halicarnassus, brought the ships limping home from Salamis; years later he was to immortalize her by telling how that naval Amazon commanded the contingent in person and drew compliments from the king for her courage and cunning in action. He left Halicarnassus as a young man; there are vague hints of a contretemps with Artemisia's successor, so it may have been exile that started him on his wanderings. He spent the rest of his life abroad, exploring widespread parts of the Greek and Persian world. He visited Athens more than once, perhaps even taking up occasional residence, and, when Athens in 443 B.C. sent out a well-publicized colonizing expedition to found Thurii in the instep of the Italian boot, he either joined the emigrants or followed shortly after. He died there sometime between 430 and 425 B.C.

Herodotus came from good family, was well educated, and had money—only a member of the leisured class could indulge a wanderlust as he did. His interests are those of the cultivated intellectual. He is particularly keen on comparative religion; in fact, a desire to check foreign gods and ritual practices against the Greek and see which can claim priority appears to have been the prime motive for many a journey. He is a serious student of physical geography. He theorizes—accurately, as we now know—that Egypt originally had been an arm of the sea; among other reasons, his sharp eye had noticed 'sea shells appearing on the mountains', in other words, marine fossils. He analyses the hypotheses offered for the Nile's annual flood, and we can forgive him for branding the theory that it was the result of melting snow as 'especially inaccurate'; some of his contemporaries knew better but the knowledge was soon lost, and not regained until nineteenth century explorers came upon the towering Ruwenzori Mountains whose melting snows set the White Nile in spate. Studious inquiries of this kind are only to be expected of Greek intellectuals of the time; they were always seeking to discover the cause of things. What is surprising is to find in Herodotus an equally lively curiosity in matters that are norm-

D

ally businessmen's concerns. He is intrigued by modes of transport and reports in detail on certain odd craft, oversize round coracles, he saw on the Euphrates around Babylon (where they are still to be seen) and on the curious way Nile boats were put together out of short lengths of plank (they still are, at least south of the Second Cataract). He notes local products—the big fish caught at the mouth of the Dnieper that are 'good for salting' (we prefer our sturgeon smoked); the linen of special weave that Egypt produces; the cloth woven from hemp in south Russia which is so much like linen that anyone who does not know hemp cannot tell the difference; the candy, tamarisk syrup thickened with wheat flour, that was a specialty of a certain town in Asia Minor. He reports strange ways of doing business, such as the technique the Carthaginians use in trading with the natives of the west coast of Africa:

> they lay out their goods in a row on the beach, return to their ships, and raise a smoke signal; the natives see the signal, go to the beach, put down an amount of gold, and move away from the goods; the Carthaginians disembark, take a look, and if the gold seems enough for the goods take it and go off, and if not, they go back to the boats and wait, and the natives come out and add to the gold till the sellers are satisfied.

Herodotus' fellow-travellers were more often than not traders and commercial agents, and he surely whiled away many a long day on deck or donkeyback talking business with them; apparently it rubbed off on him. Was he perhaps a trader himself as well as a tourist? It was unusual for a Greek of his station—but he was an unusual Greek.

Since he tells us so little about himself, we cannot map in detail the course of his travels. He did not make one grand tour but rather a number of individual voyages. It goes without saying that he had been all over Greece and the Aegean islands; and he was at least once in Cyrene in north

Africa, an easy sail from the Aegean. In the west he knew southern Italy and Sicily well—he probably explored these areas during his stay at Thurii—but never went further westward. His exotic travelling was done in the east. One voyage took him from Ephesus on the west coast of Asia Minor to Sardis, and from there over parts of the Persian Royal Road (53 above). He sailed over much of the Black Sea, including the northern coast, which gave him the chance to visit the Greek settlements in the general area of Odessa and inquire about the Scythians and other native tribes of the hinterland who lived outside the frontier of civilization.

South of Asia Minor through Syria and Palestine to Babylon and Egypt—all was part of the sprawling Persian Empire in Herodotus' day. This made things easier for a traveller; there were no boundaries to cross, and he could cover ground swiftly—by ancient standards—on the well-maintained Persian roads. Herodotus got as far eastward as Babylon. What his exact route was is anybody's guess. Most probably he sailed to Syria and landed at some port near the present site of Antioch (not to be founded till 300 B.C.), where the distance from the coast to the Euphrates is shortest, struck east until he reached the river, and then followed the caravan track along it. His reward for weeks of arduous plodding was to come upon a vast complex:

> square in shape, with each side 14 miles long, a total of 56 miles. Babylon is not only of enormous size; it has a splendour such as no other city of all we have seen . . . The city wall is 85½ feet wide and 342 high . . . Its circuit is pierced by one hundred entrances, with gates, jambs, and lintels of bronze . . . The town is full of three- and four-storey houses and is cut through with streets that are absolutely straight, not only the main ones but also the sidestreets going down to the river.

This student of religion was naturally struck by the soaring ziggurat he saw there, the distinctive Babylonian type of temple that rises in square stages, like a stack of children's building blocks: 'in the middle of the sacred precinct a solid tower has been erected, two hundred yards along each face, upon this tower a second is set, and still another on this up to eight.' The whole city must have seemed a marvel to a man accustomed to modest-sized Greek towns with their two-storey buildings, narrow and twisting alleys, low and graceful temples. We can hardly blame him for the inflated figures he gives for dimensions; he probably got them from the guides who took him around, and he was in no position to check the numbers they must have glibly reeled off.

Somehow a sizeable part of Herodotus' survey of Syria and Mesopotamia failed to survive. Luckily we have the whole of his account of Egypt, a unique and for the most part eye-witness report that forms one of the largest single sections of his book. Herodotus went there to see the sights, but his curiosity was not at all about the things that bring people to Egypt today and not primarily about what brought them there during subsequent centuries of the ancient world. He is not the least bit interested in Egyptian art: 'the walls are full of carved figures' is his offhand reference to what must have been hundreds of yards of bas-reliefs, tastefully sculpted and painted. He cared little for Egyptian architecture as such; when taken into one of the courts of the gigantic temple at Karnak, 'it was large', he remarks, and hurries on to his point, namely the number of statues there of high priests and what calculations about the antiquity of Egypt could be made from the total. The special quality of Egyptian art and architecture, to be sure, is more or less a discovery of our own times. But Herodotus was just as little interested in Egypt's chief drawing card in all ages, her grandiose witnesses to a once mighty empire. Some of them excited his wonder—he would hardly be human if they did not—but as feats of engineering more than anything else. Take his reaction to the pyramids. To him the ramp built to carry the chunks of quarried stone from the river to the Great Pyramid and up its sloping sides was 'just about as big a piece of work as the pyramid'. His description of the monument dwells on the work gangs and how they operated in shifts, the size of the hewn blocks and how they were raised and set in place, how the monument was finished off (from the top down), how much time it all took (ten years for the ramp, twenty for the pyramid itself) and, of course, how much it cost. Here he had only a straw in the wind, but he grasped at it:

There is an inscription in Egyptian on the pyramid telling how much was disbursed on radishes, onions, and garlic for the workmen. And, as I remember very well what the guide said when translating it for me, it was an expenditure of 1,600 talents [perhaps twenty million pounds or fifty million dollars]. If this is so, what figure can we put on the rest of the expenses—for the iron used, for the food [as against mere trimmings such as onions and garlic] and clothing of the workmen?

Whatever the inscription was, a guide of the fifth century B.C. could no more read Old Kingdom hieroglyphics than those who take tourists around the pyramids today. Herodotus' guide was either telling a taller tale than usual or possibly just having fun with him—Herodotus' figure for the length of the sides of the Great Pyramid is so close to the mark (800 feet as against 760) that it looks as if he paced it off himself; perhaps the guide was getting even with a sceptical client who refused to take his word.

The only other building he describes in equal detail is the so-called Labyrinth, and this piqued his curiosity because of its amusing maze-like arrangement. He reports:

We saw the upper chambers, and they surpass any of the works of man. All the various passageways in and out of chambers and the various goings this way and that way through the courtyards produce wonder after wonder as you move from courtyard to chamber or from chamber to gallery, then into different chambers from the galleries and different courtyards from the chambers.

He thought it was a memorial building put up by a group of kings of relatively late date, the seventh century B.C.; we know now that it was a tomb-temple built by Amenemhet III in the nineteenth B.C., and excavation has shown that it does indeed have an unusually intricate and complicated ground-plan. The monument lay near the ancient Lake Moeris. To Herodotus the lake was even more of a marvel than the Labyrinth, since he assumed it was all man-made and estimated its circumference to be an imposing 420 miles—a gigantic feat of engineering in any age. Actually the lake was far smaller, less than half the size he assigns it (the remnant left today, Birket-el-Karun, measures a scant thirty miles by six), and it was mostly a natural basin, though the pharaohs' engineers get credit for some impressive improvements that enabled it to be used as a reservoir for surpluses from a high flood of the Nile.

What drew Herodotus to Egypt more than anything else was what it had to offer to the student of religion. In one of those rare moments when he talks about himself, he gives us a glimpse of the extent to which this interest determined his movements. While in Egypt he inquired into the antiquity of what he refers to as the Egyptian Heracles; exactly what deity he means by this is hard to tell. He was not completely satisfied, so, he writes, 'wanting to learn the facts of the matter from what sources I could, I sailed to Tyre in Phoenicia as well, since I had heard of a temple there, a very holy one, dedicated to Heracles'. Here he must be identifying Heracles with the Phoenicians' Melkart, the Baal of the Bible. While there, he continues, 'striking up a conversation with the priests, I asked how long ago the temple had been built . . . They said it was as old as Tyre itself . . . At Tyre I noticed another temple to Heracles, the so-called Heracles of Thasos, so I went to Thasos too . . . In fine, my researches make it clear that the worship of Heracles is very ancient.' His inquiries covered everything from the antiquity of Heracles to the number of times a day priests washed themselves. Egypt at that time was the land of religion and superstition *par excellence*; Herodotus had a veritable field day there. He looked into the selecting and sacrificing of the Apis bull sacred to Ptah, the way bulls were sacrificed to Isis, the ritual attitude toward pigs (considered unclean, and as a consequence swineherds never enter temples), what foods were taboo for priests (fish and beans), what happened at Egyptian festivals (a lot of drinking; cf. 31 above), the various sacred animals, the available types of embalming (de luxe, medium priced, cheap), and dozens of other matters. He equates Egyptian deities with Greek—Amun is Zeus, Isis Demeter, Osiris Dionysus, Bast Artemis, and so on—and spends much time arguing that the Greek gods are derived from the Egyptian—rather a waste of time from our point of view, since we know, as he could not, that the two sets of divinities are totally distinct.

Religion, customs, physical geography—all these may have provided the key motives for Herodotus' wanderings in Egypt and elsewhere, but he was not always so serious. He spent a good deal of time just 'doing the sights'. In Egypt, as mentioned above, he went to the pyramids and the Labyrinth. At Delphi he saw Croesus' famous offerings to the sanctuary, including a solid gold lion that originally weighed about 575 pounds and a silver mixing bowl that could hold about 5,200 gallons. In the temple of Hera at Samos he saw the two wooden likenesses that Pharaoh Amasis had donated of himself. At Tegea he saw hung up in the local temple the fetters the Spartans had brought to use when they invaded Tegea but which were clapped on themselves when they lost the battle. Outside of Sardis he visited the monumental tomb of Croesus' father, Alyattes. He went over battlefields—not only Marathon and Thermopylae, which he was interested in as historian, but any he happened to be near, such as the site of a decisive encounter between Egyptians and Persians. He paid a visit to the descendant of a celebrity, the grandson of a Spartan who had gained immortal fame by dying a hero's death in battle.

Like most travellers in ancient times, Herodotus went by ship whenever he could. This is why we find him reporting on so many harbours and river towns. His arrival in Egypt was by sea—he remarks that, a day out of port, sounding with the lead will pick up samples of muddy bottom at eleven fathoms—and he was lucky enough to get there when the Nile was in flood (between August and November) and so was even able to go up to the pyramids by water (21 above).

From Memphis at the apex of the delta he went by boat up the Nile, managing to get off at Thebes but missing some important stops along the way, such as the holy city of Abydos which he mentions nowhere. In Asia Minor, Syria, and Mesopotamia he went overland for the most part, not by choice but because these areas had few navigable waterways. On ship or ashore he was always an ordinary tourist, travelling in no official capacity, having no special entrée. In Greek towns he no doubt could frequently count on private hospitality and the help of people he was recommended to; elsewhere he was strictly on his own. Then there was the problem of language. Greek carried him from Italy to the west coast of Asia Minor. From there it was either Persian or Aramaic, the lingua franca of the Near East, or Egyptian. Like any good tourist, Herodotus picked up a smattering of foreign words as he went along. He casually mentions some Persian words (*artab*, the Persian dry measure, and *parasang*, the Persian measure for distance), a number of Egyptian (the typical loaf of bread was called *cyllestis*, the typical tunic *calasiris*, the typical Nile boat *baris*, a crocodile was a *champsa*), and even some Scythian (*arima* means 'one', *spu* means 'eye', the national drink of one of the remote tribes was *aschy*), and he surely must have known many more, at least in Aramaic and Egyptian, including no doubt the indispensable 'Does anyone speak Greek?'. In making the rounds of sights he inevitably depended upon Greek-speaking guides. When he went through temples, he was shown about and talked with what he calls priests, but who must have been sacristans or the like (lofty Egyptian prelates did not take tourists around, say, the great temple at Karnak any more than cardinals and archbishops take them around the Vatican). The conversations must have been carried on through his guide or an interpreter. Some of the mistakes he makes may be because he had no way of verifying what these told him. Take, for example, his report that 'the Egyptians were the first to say . . . that the soul, when the body has died, enters some other creature, each at the moment of birth, and, after making the rounds of every form of animal, fish, and bird, re-enters a newborn human body'. Thanks to the findings of the Egyptologists, we now know that Herodotus is totally wrong. Metempsychosis is foreign to the Egyptians' way of thinking; in Herodotus' day they were still clinging unwaveringly to their age-old belief that all good men at death become Osiris, the god who had been killed by a wicked brother but then lived on forever in another world. Quite possibly Herodotus' interpreter, out of his depth in attempting such a subject, put the question in a garbled form. Another possibility is that Herodotus, who was convinced of Egypt's priority in so many things, had him ask, 'Isn't it true that the soul etc.?' and the sacristan or whoever was being quizzed obligingly gave the answer that was obviously called for.

Apart from guides, Herodotus probably got a certain amount of information from the sort of people tourists generally come into contact with, porters, drivers, waiters, maids, and so on, a few of whom must have had a smattering of Greek. A conversation conducted half in pidgin Greek or pidgin Egyptian or both and half in sign-language could very well have been the source of Herodotus' description of the hippopotamus; no eye-witness could possibly compare it in size to an ox, to say nothing of giving it cloven hooves, a

D*

horse's mane, and a horse's tail. Even his own sharp eyes could trick him. All Egyptians, he writes, eat out-of-doors. Probably, as he walked village lanes at meal times, he saw family upon family cooking in front of the house as they do today; had he been invited to dine in an upper-class household, he would have learned otherwise. Egyptian women, he informs us, wear only one garment—true, no doubt, of servants or those in the fields, but other Egyptian women of the time wore two, even three. Yet, if he made mistakes, he was by no means gullible. He reports what he is told about the fabulous bird called the phoenix, but carefully adds that he never saw one himself. An island was pointed out to him that was allegedly remarkable for being afloat; 'I myself didn't observe it floating or even moving', he comments. His informants at Babylon told him that the god entered the temple to sleep in a couch left at the top; 'that's what they say', he notes, 'but I don't believe it.' Certain statues he was shown had no hands, and he was given some esoteric explanation for the absence; 'it was nonsense', he remarks, 'even I could see that the hands had fallen off through age'.

Herodotus wrote not merely to inform but to entertain. His technique is that of a skilled conversationalist, who moves easily from subject to subject to provide pace and variety, leaving one as soon as he senses his audience has had enough of it to go off on another. Just so, Herodotus steps leisurely along, slipping effortlessly from history to anthropology to geography and back again. Consider his account of Babylon. He begins by describing the walls and temples. Then he details what two highly intelligent queens did for the city: Semiramis put up dykes for flood control, and Nitocris had the course of the river changed and spanned it with a bridge (Nebuchadnezzar probably deserves the credit for this; cf. 51 above). This reminds him of the grim joke Nitocris played: she inscribed on her tomb a notice to the effect that any subsequent king of Babylon who needed money had her permission to open the grave and help himself; inevitably one of her successors fell into the trap—and found only a second notice scoffing at his greed and sacrilege. Since Nitocris' son happened to be on the throne when Cyrus the Great led his Persians against Babylon, Herodotus is minded to tell of the attack, starting with a story of how Cyrus en route punished a river for drowning a prized horse—he turned it into a creek by making his army spend a summer digging run-off channels. Finally getting to his subject proper, he adduces some facts about Babylon's wealth and resources, but soon digresses to describe the 'greatest wonder of all next to the city itself', the curious round coracles used for ferrying people and goods across the Euphrates. He closes his account with a description of some of the Babylonians' more striking peculiarities. They affect long hair, wear turbans, perfume the whole body, and carry walking sticks. Until recently they had a unique way of arranging marriages which Herodotus considers eminently sensible and regrets has disappeared: each year each village used to collect all marriageable girls and auction them off; the big prices for the beauties went into a fund to supply dowries that would ensure husbands for the homely. Another practice that gains his approval is the Babylonians' way of handling illness: 'They bring the sick into the town square, since they do not use doctors. Each invalid is then approached and given advice by passersby who have either suffered from the same sort of ailment themselves or know someone else who has . . . These prescribe what they did to recover or what they know others did who recovered. You are not allowed to go by a sick person without asking what's the matter with him.' One practice he vehemently disapproves of is the religious injunction upon every woman to go at least once in her life to the temple of the goddess of love and fertility and have relations with any stranger who comes along and picks her; 'the tall and goodlooking are soon home again, but the ugly spend a long time there, . . . some of them even three or four years'.

Or consider his account of the Scythians. Because Darius had once made a foray against this complex of tribes dwelling along the northern shore of the Black Sea in and around the Crimea, Herodotus includes an account of them—the first description in western literature of peoples living beyond the pale of civilization. It is three times as long as the report on Babylon; he had visited the region himself and been so fascinated with everything he saw and was told that he could not bear to omit any of it.

He begins, fittingly, with the question of origins. Although he is convinced that the Scythians are found in Russia for the plain and simple reason that they were pushed there out of Asia by powerful tribes in their rear, he conscientiously offers two alternatives, the view of the Scythians themselves and of the Greek settlers in a nearby colony: the Scythians were convinced that they were descended from the sons of the local god, the Greeks that they were nothing more than the progeny of a child whom Heracles, happening to be passing through on the return from one of his labours, fathered on a local creature, half-woman and half-snake. He then mentions the source of certain of his information, a poem by one Aristeas—which reminds him of a curious story about Aristeas: he fell dead in a cleaner's shop, his body suddenly disappeared, and then he himself suddenly reappeared seven years later in his home town and 240 years later in a town in southern Italy. Returning to his subject, Herodotus describes the various tribes and how they live (by agriculture, grazing, or hunting), how hard the winters are, how this affects horses very little but mules and donkeys very much—and at this point he cannot resist breaking off to tell us that in Elis in Greece mules cannot be bred at all; 'I'm digressing', he admits, 'but in this book, from the opening pages, I've been on the lookout for such digressions.'

Beyond the Scythians, he goes on to say, live the Hyperboreans 'people beyond the north-wind', and no one knows anything about them—except the priests on Apollo's sacred island, Delos. This is because the Hyperboreans dutifully send offerings there, parcels carefully wrapped in straw which they deliver to their nearest neighbours, who pass them on to their neighbours, and so on to Delos (the kernel of fact behind this story seems to be the amber trade; amber came from the far north and passed from people to people until it reached the Mediterranean). The Hyperboreans bring to Herodotus' mind the various attempts to map their remote northern abode, indeed to map the whole world, and that leads him to tell of the circumnavigation of Africa (61 above) and of Darius' exploration of the Indian Ocean (60 above), to comment on the oddness of dividing up one land-mass into three continents of quite unequal size (he thought them unequal because he thought of Europe as far bigger than the other two), and to wonder where the names Libya (his name for Africa), Europe, and Asia came from, anyway. Here he pulls himself up short— 'That's enough on this subject' and doggedly returns to the Scythians.

They are ideally fitted for self-preservation, he reports, since no one can come to grips with them: they live in wagons, feed on their cattle, and fight on horseback with bow and arrow. He then sings the praises—as any inhabitant of arid Greece would—of their well-watered land, with its great navigable streams (under the guise of the ancient names we can identify the Danube, Dnieper, Bug, and Don). He turns next to religion, always a favourite topic with him. The chief god of the Scythians, he informs us, is female. Their methods of sacrifice are totally unlike the Greeks' (who roast the meat of a victim on spits, shashlik-style): they boil the meat in a huge pot, or when they have no pot, cook it in the victim's stomach, haggis-style. Prisoners are all slaughtered as sacrifices to their god of war. As a matter of fact, the Scythians are in general a bloodthirsty lot: a youngster has no status until he has killed his man and drunk his blood, while enemies killed in battle are beheaded and scalped, and the skulls of particularly hated enemies are converted into cups. The scalps are preserved, and a warrior's reputation depends on the number he can display. When their king falls ill, he calls upon a committee of the three top soothsayers to determine the cause; they usually end up charging someone with having sworn falsely by the king's hearth (their most solemn oath)—but if the accused is able to defend his innocence, the committee is summarily burned alive. When their king dies he is given a most elaborate funeral involving a country-wide display of the body, self-mutilation on the part of the mourners, rich tomb gifts of gold, and the wholesale slaughter of horses and servants to be buried with the royal corpse or planted about the grave. After any funeral the Scythians have a special ritual for cleansing themselves. First they wash their hair. Then they go through what Herodotus calls a 'hot-airing', which seems to be nothing less than a 'trip' on hashish: they build a teepee-like tent, put in a brazier full of red-hot stones, crawl in with a handful of hemp, place it on the stones, sniff the fumes, and, as Herodotus puts it, 'get such pleasure from this "hot-airing" that they howl out loud'. Scythians will have nothing to do with foreign ways. To prove this, he relates the sad story of King Scylas who, born of a Greek mother, had a fatal weakness for Greek ways. Scylas secretly set himself up a household, complete with wife, in the nearest Greek town, where he would sneak off and spend a delicious month or more incognito living à la grecque. He went so far as to get deliriously drunk with the mobs celebrating the festival of Dionysus—and this was too much; some eye-witness blabbed to his subjects, and they promptly turned him out.

On and on Herodotus goes, spinning the narrative with unflagging interest, with unfailing charm and good humour. It seems to be a mélange, yet it is all—or nearly all—woven with art into a whole that has a studied design. To heighten the flavour he shrewdly seasons it with spicy marvels from the lands that, like the Hyperboreans', lie beyond the geographers' ken. Ethiopia, where 'men are the tallest and handsomest and longest-lived' does not count; that had been

Shangri-La to the Greeks ever since the days of Homer. But he provides a fine yarn about certain Indian tribes living in the Hindu Kush who extract gold from sand heaps thrown up by burrowing ants bigger than foxes; the Indians have to work fast and make their getaway on female camels since only these are speedy enough to outrun the ants and then only with a good head start. Herodotus is somewhat doubtful of the truth of all this and keeps reminding the audience that he had not personally seen such ants, that he got the whole story from the Persians. He tells of an island off the west African coast where gold dust is fished up from the bottom of a lake; he passes it on as perhaps just a tale—but then again maybe not. He reports on donkeys with horns, dogheaded men, headless men with eyes in their chest, one-eyed men, goat-footed men, men who hibernate for six months. It is pure nonsense, he assures us—but tells it nonetheless.

The travel writer does not merely purvey information; that is for the Karl Baedekers, the sober compilers of guide books. His role is to be the tourist's perfect companion: to be articulate, well-informed, a skilled raconteur; to include in what he tells a fair share of the unusual with a dash of the exotic; to tell it all with infinite zest. It was Herodotus who set not only the pattern but a standard.

PART TWO

TRAVEL IN
ROMAN TIMES

6

One World

When Herodotus left the Greek city-states along the coast of Asia Minor to make his way further east and south, he entered a different world. It spoke a babel of strange tongues, followed a traditional way of life inherited from forefathers who lived thousands of years earlier, and knew only rule by monarchs. Whatever Greeks were there, were transients like himself. Little more than a century later, Alexander the Great smashed the Persian empire and made his spectacular march to the borders of India, and all changed almost overnight.

As Alexander penetrated eastward, he dropped off contingents of his soldiers to found settlements; each became, as it were, an injection of the Greek way of life into the body of the ancient east. Fever cut him down in 323 B.C. before he had time to carry out what seems to have been his intention, an amalgamation of Greek and Oriental. For the next few decades his generals fought like wildcats over the carcass of his empire. When the battling ended, about 270 B.C., they had torn it into three parts. The family of the Antigonids held his ancestral throne in Macedonia with a general control over the city-states of the Greek mainland. The family of the Seleucids ruled a sprawling patchwork of parts of Asia Minor, Syria, Palestine, and Mesopotamia. The plum, the rich valley of the Nile, was in the hands of the Ptolemies.

The great conqueror's dream of an intermingled world of Greeks and Orientals was abandoned; his successors, though able men, were no visionaries. But the movement of Greeks into the newly opened east went on apace. The Seleucids and Ptolemies, each an island of Greek rulers in a vast sea of non-Greek subjects, surrounded themselves with a dependable armed force of Greek soldiers, settled permanently on the land. On top of this they actively recruited Greek technicians and administrators to staff a bureaucracy—indeed, they opened the gates to any Greeks who wanted to come in, merchants, artisans, farmers. 'Go east, young man, go east', if we may paraphrase Horace Greeley, was the watchword of the third century B.C.

And so, from 300 B.C. on, the Near East was gradually transformed. Alongside the dwellings and places of worship of age-old oriental type rose Greek temples and theatres and porticoes and the rest of the architectural apparatus of a Greek city-state. Robed and turbaned locals now shared the streets with Greeks in their light tunics, and gradually got used to the sight of Greek youths working out in the nude in the newly built gymnasia, at Greek elders shouting in violent debate at town council sessions in the newly built meeting chambers, at Greeks of all ages chattering like magpies in the newly built market-places, the agoras.

This Hellenized east became an integral part of the Mediterranean Greek world west of it. In the far west, to be sure, the great city of Carthage still ruled the seas and no Greeks—or any others—were allowed to pass a line that ran roughly from Carthage (near where Tunis stands today) to the Balearics. But east of Carthage, the world had been Hellenized all the way to Babylon. Herodotus' language troubles were a thing of the past; Greek would take you anywhere now, and, to make things even easier, the age developed a standardized form, the *koine* 'common tongue', which replaced, or was spoken alongside, the traditional welter of dialects. New ports sprang up to handle the increased movement by sea. This is when Antioch began its long career; it was founded by the Seleucids in 300 B.C. Alexandria, as the name shows, was established somewhat earlier (331 B.C.); the Ptolemies made it their capital and turned it into the greatest entrepôt of the ancient world. From either port you could book passage on big seagoing freighters that sailed over open water to Syracuse and from there on to Marseilles.

The Mediterranean world, bound together as it had never been before by language, trade, and similar way of life, developed an international, cosmopolitan culture. When the Ptolemies established at Alexandria a richly endowed research centre—their famous Museum and Library (258 below)—literary lights and distinguished scholars and scientists flocked there from everywhere: Eratosthenes, the geographer who calculated the circumference of the earth with astonishing accuracy, came from Cyrene; Hipparchus, the astronomer whose concept of the universe with the earth as its centre lasted till the days of Copernicus, from Nicaea, Theocritus, the only first-rate poet the age produced, from Syracuse. There was an international style in art. A middle-class Greek, settling down in the Fayum not far from the age-old Labyrinth, might hire Egyptian workmen to decorate his walls with murals—but the pictures themselves would be crude imitations of what was being painted at Athens or Syracuse or Antioch, and would be done in the same style.

The verve and dash that sent Greeks to seek fame and fortune in the east carried some of them even further, made them into explorers who pushed far back the confines of the known world.

The most dramatic voyage of exploration was one that broke through the clouds of mystery where they were thickest, to the north. About 300 B.C., a certain Pytheas sailed from Marseilles through the Straits of Gibraltar—somehow he managed to slip through the Carthaginian blockade—and was off on the open Atlantic heading north. We have no clue as to what motivated him. Perhaps it was scientific curiosity. Perhaps he was searching for the secret that Carthaginian merchants were keeping so carefully to themselves, the source of the tin they shipped into the Mediterranean. In the event, he accomplished both: he made a number of observations of the sun which enabled later geographers to calculate several parallels of latitude, he determined the true position of the polestar, and he also investigated and reported upon the tin mines of Cornwall. He not only visited Britain but circumnavigated the whole of it and fixed the position of Ireland. From the British Isles he pushed on to an 'island of Thule', six days north of Britain and one day south of the 'frozen' sea, where the sun went down for only two or three hours at night. There has been much clamorous debate about where this distant Thule is. Did Pytheas actually get as far as Iceland? Or did he merely see part of Norway, which he mistook for an island?

From this northernmost penetration he returned to Britain, recrossed the channel to Brittany, and turned leftward to explore the northern coast of Europe to the east. Here he passed an enormous estuary and came to an island where amber was so plentiful that the natives used it for fuel. Again much clamorous debate: some claim he went right round Denmark and into the Baltic, a source of amber, but most that he got no further than the North Sea, that the estuary was the Elbe and the island Heligoland, a way-station for the amber trade.

Two centuries later another important voyage of exploration was made at precisely the other end of the world. Its guiding spirit was one Eudoxus, a native of Cyzicus on the Sea of Marmora. About his motives we have no doubt whatsoever: both he and his backer, Ptolemy VIII, the Pot-Bellied, were solely interested in breaking into the rich trade that flowed from India and Arabia to the Greek world. Whatever Indian spices and Arabian incense came to the Mediterranean by water travelled in Indian and Arab bottoms as far as the Red Sea and in Arab bottoms from there on, and Indian and Arab shippers had every intention of keeping it just that way. Eudoxus happened to be in Alexandria—this was about 120 B.C.—when a half-drowned sailor was brought to the court. Nursed back to health and taught Greek, he gave out the story that he was an Indian, sole survivor of his crew, and offered to prove it by showing the way back to his home to anyone the king picked. He must have been a Tamil-speaking native of southern India where Greeks rarely went; had he come from the north, there would have been plenty of interpreters available, since Alexander had brought the Indus Valley within the Greek orbit.

Indeed, northwestern India by this time was fairly familiar to the Greeks. After Alexander had conquered up to the Punjab, his successors had maintained petty kingdoms there for a while. Some of their expeditions had penetrated as far south as Bombay and as far east as Patna. The Greeks now knew of the Ganges river, of the Himalayas, of the island of Ceylon. They knew that water rather than desert, as Herodotus had reported (61 above), bounded India to the east. But the only way they were able to get there was the way Alexander had, by the long and arduous land route with its exhausting climb through the mountain barrier that closes off India on the northwest. The Arabs controlled the coastal waters of the Indian Ocean and much of the Red Sea and closed the Greeks out as effectively as the Carthaginians did in the western Mediterranean. What is more, they and their Indian colleagues kept to themselves the precious secret of India's monsoons. From May to September the winds blow steadily from the southwest; a skipper can leave the mouth of the Red Sea, stand off the south coast of Arabia, and then strike boldly across open water, and the blustery southwest monsoon, coming steadily over the starboard quarter, nearly astern, will carry him directly to India. By delaying his return until any time between November and March, when the monsoon shifts to exactly the reverse direction, blowing clear and fresh from the northeast, he can make the voyage back just as expeditiously. Indian and Arab seamen had been shuttling back and forth this way for centuries, bringing in pepper, cassia, cinnamon, nard, and other Indian spices. They had maintained so rigid a monopoly that the Greeks believed that some of these products originated in Arabia (60 above), which actually served merely as middleman in the trade.

Eudoxus, with his resuscitated Indian knowledgeable in the ways of the monsoon to guide him over open water safe from Arab attack, made two pioneering voyages from the Red Sea to India, returned safely each time—and each time had the precious cargo of spices he was carrying confiscated by Ptolemy's customs officials. So he decided to reach India by sailing in the other direction around Africa and in that way bypass the king's inquisitive and acquisitive agents. He got together a well-equipped expedition (there were even dancing girls aboard, whether for the harems of Indian rajahs or for whiling away the long days at sea, we cannot be sure), but made it only as far as the Atlantic coast of Morocco, far short of the mark set by Hanno (63 above), where a mutiny turned him back. Undiscouraged, he fitted out a second expedition, set off, and was never heard from again.

On his second return from India, Eudoxus ran straight before the northwest monsoon instead of keeping it on his quarter and, as a result, landed well south on the east coast of Africa. Here, in the best explorer tradition, he made friends with the natives by giving them strange delicacies (bread, dried figs, and wine, the last of which probably helped the most). Again he was not exactly breaking new ground. The trade in frankincense and myrrh from Ethiopia and Somalia was almost as old as Egypt itself (28 above). In Eudoxus' day, it was, like the traffic from India, largely in the hands of Arabs. The Ptolemies, more to aid in capturing elephants for use in the army than in opening trade routes, kept sending out numerous expeditions along the east coast of Africa, and the Greeks gradually acquired a good knowledge of the shoreline up to Cape Guardafui, Africa's easternmost point. Eudoxus must have landed at some obscure spot below the cape, but not far south enough to provide positive information about the orientation of the coast. For two more centuries, map-makers were going to show it making a right-angled turn to the west just below Guardafui.

What Alexander and his successors had begun was brought to its logical conclusion by Rome.

In the last act of Shaw's *Caesar and Cleopatra*, Caesar, about to leave Alexandria for Rome, is told superciliously by Apollodorus a cultivated and artistic Greek, that Rome will never produce any art. 'What!' Caesar answers, 'Rome produce no art! Is peace not an art? Is war not an art?'

Discipline, organization, a gift for administration—these were Roman qualities par excellence, and they brought Rome spectacular triumphs, first in war and then in peace. Roman peasants, fresh off the farm, were swiftly hammered into disciplined and finely organized fighting units, the renowned legions that, within the three centuries from about 500 to 200 B.C., raised Rome from an obscure village on the Tiber to master of the Italian boot and then, after Carthage was humbled, of the entire western Mediterranean. Within two more centuries, the east had been added. When, in 30 B.C., Mark Antony fell on his sword and Cleopatra pressed an asp to her bosom, Augustus, leader of the victorious legions, became sole ruler of an empire that stretched from Spain to Syria.

For the first—and last—time in history, the Mediterranean was politically as well as culturally one world. Along with unification under a single ruler, there came, after centuries of almost continuous bloodshed, the rare and precious gift of peace, close to two hundred years of it. The Roman emperors, with the revenues and manpower of this farflung realm at their disposal, were able to build up a fence of forts and garrisons, in places continuous walls, which cordoned off the empire from barbarian incursions. A permanent navy was founded with units based at strategic points around the

Mediterranean, and it wiped the perennial scourge of piracy from the water.

And so, the first two centuries of the Christian Era were halcyon days for a traveller. He could make his way from the shores of the Euphrates to the border between England and Scotland without crossing a foreign frontier, always within the bounds of one government's jurisdiction. A purseful of Roman coins was the only kind of cash he had to carry; they were accepted or could be changed everywhere. He could sail through any waters without fear of pirates, thanks to the emperor's patrol squadrons. A planned network of good roads gave him access to all major centres, and the through routes were policed well enough for him to ride them with relatively little fear of bandits. He needed only two languages: Greek would take him from Mesopotamia to Yugoslavia, Latin from Yugoslavia to Britain. Wherever he went, he was under the protective umbrella of a well-organized, efficient legal system. If he was a Roman citizen and got into trouble, he could, as St Paul did, insist upon trial at Rome. If he was not a citizen, Rome permitted him to be tried under his own native law, and there were special courts to handle cases where different native codes were involved.

Trade and travel did not stop at the empire's frontiers but stepped past them to traverse areas that had still been *terra incognita* in the days of Alexander's successors. The known world now extended north to Scotland, west to the Canary Islands, south to Zanzibar, east to Indonesia.

The bounds had not been thrust back by eager explorers; there were no Roman Pytheases or Eudoxuses to try their luck on uncharted seas or paths. In Europe it was the legions who did the job. They pushed Rome's frontier steadily more to the north, and in their wake came swarms of traders who hawked their wares deep in the lands beyond and returned with precious information about them. In the Far East and Africa, the traders did the job all by themselves, as they doggedly worked their way towards the source of the ivory, spices, silks, and other oriental luxuries for which, now that Roman society was becoming increasingly affluent, the demand generally outstripped the supply.

Northern Europe had lost much of the mystery that surrounded it when Pytheas made his way there. England was by this time a province of the Roman empire, and traders' reports told much about Scotland and Ireland. Roman troops had operated in parts of the low countries. Germany, which had never been conquered and made part of the empire, was not quite as well known. North of Germany, knowledge grew definitely thin: Denmark was thought to be much larger than it actually is, Scandinavia much smaller and an island to boot. Still further north, the usual fairy stories took over—five days west of Britain was an island where Zeus had exiled his deposed father Cronos, some 500 miles beyond was a great continent whose rivers poured out enough silt to make the Atlantic hard to cross and whose people viewed the known world as a mere island, and so on.

Russia was mostly outside the orbit of travel. The north coast of the Black Sea was known in somewhat more detail than in Herodotus' day, but practically nothing of what lay behind. Even as sober a geographer as Claudius Ptolemy located there the home of the 'Amazons' and a tribe of 'Lice-Eaters'.

The most dramatic advance in knowledge concerns the Far East. Finally the two great civilizations of the ancient world, Graeco-Roman and Chinese, made contact. Sometime after the death of Alexander, Chinese silk, transported by caravan through central Asia and passed along by a chain of middle-men, started to filter through to the Mediterranean, where its superiority to the nearest thing the Greeks had, produced from wild Asia Minor silkworms, was swiftly recognized. In the second half of the second century B.C., the Chinese became more active in the trade, dispatching caravans on a regular basis. Starting from Paochi, centre of a complex of roads, these moved inside the Great Wall by way of T'ienshui,

Lanchou and Wuwei to the western end of the wall and deep
into Chinese Turkistan; by 118–114 B.C., some ten caravans
a year were making the trip. At Anshi between the Gobi desert
and the Nan Shan mountains the route forked into three
branches to avoid the vast salt swamp in the Tarim Basin,
two looping to the north and one to the south. The southern
loop and one of the northern came together at Kashgar, then
forked again to snake through the difficult Pamir mountains;
this stretch was more or less the halfway point to the Mediterranean. All three rejoined at Merv to continue across the
desert and join up with the tracks that led through Persia
and Mesopotamia to the sea. Nobody went the whole distance.
Somewhere between Kashgar and Balkh was a place called
Stone Tower, and here the Chinese turned their merchandise
over to local and Indian traders. The latter carried their share
south to India to send it the rest of the way by boat, the others
plodded on into Persia, where they met up with Syrians and
Greeks who took care of the final leg.

The western world reached the Chinese by water as well,
although only just. Ever since Eudoxus breached the Arab
monopoly of the sea trade with India, that country had become
increasingly integrated into the network of Graeco-Roman
trade. From the beginning of the first century A.D., fleets of
ocean-going freighters, sped by the monsoons, sailed there
yearly, no longer just to the Indus Valley but all along the
coast down to the tip of the peninsula. Agents of Graeco-
Roman trading companies made their homes in India, settling
down, in time-honoured fashion, in separate little foreign
quarters. They exported a variety of Indian products—
cinnamon, nard, cotton, above all pepper—and also some
Chinese, the most important, naturally, being silk. Although
a certain amount of the silk, as we have just noted, came in
overland, the largest part arrived by sea in Indian or Malay
bottoms (the Chinese did not get into overseas shipping until
centuries later). It was inevitable that westerners would move
into this portion of the trade as well; by the end of the second

century A.D. their freighters had ventured into the waters east of India, cutting across the mouth of the Bay of Bengal to trade with Malaya, Sumatra, and Java. Here they discovered cloves, which grow in the Moluccas, to add to the list of spices they dealt in. What drew them on more than anything else was the desire to move nearer the source of silk. A Chinese account mentions that in 'the ninth year of the Yen-hsi period, during the Emperor Huan-ti's reign [A.D. 166] . . . the king of Ta-ts'in, An-tun, sent an embassy which, from the frontier of Jih-nan [Annam], offered ivory, rhinoceros horns, and tortoise shell. From that time dates the intercourse with this country.' Ta-ts'in is the Chinese name for the Roman Empire, and An-tun is Antoninus, the family name of Marcus Aurelius. The account goes on to comment about the very ordinary gifts the embassy had brought for the emperor; there were, for example, no jewels. Most likely it was not an official body at all but a group of shippers who, to get one jump ahead of their competitors, were trying to buy their silk directly from China instead of through middle-men.

Unfortunately, whether by land or sea, the contact between the two great cultures was always tenuous. Shipments of Chinese goods came to the Mediterranean year in and year out, cinnamon-leaf and camphor and jade and other items as well as silk, and Graeco-Roman statuettes and jewellery and pottery made the journey the other way, but rarely was there a direct exchange; in between were merchants from other countries, particularly India, which not only lay astride the sea lanes but was firmly linked by branch roads with the overland silk route. These middlemen had solid information to pass on—it was they who supplied the many place-names in Central Asia and the names of Indonesian islands that the geographers now know—but they were businessmen, not reporters. What filtered back to the man in a Roman or Chinese street was mere fanciful hearsay. The Romans thought the Chinese were all supremely righteous; the Chinese thought

westerners were all supremely honest. Kan Ying, sent as
envoy to Mesopotamia in A.D. 97, describes the people he
met as 'honest in their transactions and without any double
prices'—probably the first and last time that has ever been
said about Near Eastern tradesmen. Kan Ying, the embassy
of An-tun—we can number on the fingers of one hand the
known occasions when westerners and Chinese met face to
face.

In Africa knowledge of the east coast now went a good deal
further than Cape Guardafui. Traders, carrying cheap clothes
and trinkets to exchange for tortoise shell and ivory and
incense, regularly worked down to Zanzibar, and one man
seems to have gone as far as Cape Delgado, eleven degrees
south of the equator. Map-makers consequently no longer
showed the coast abruptly turning west but extended it straight
south, allowing it to end in a vast *terra incognita*. There was
even some new information about the interior, thought not
very much. Hunters or traders had already found out about
the heavy rains in the Ethiopian highlands and discovered
Lake Tana there, enabling geographers to deduce, correctly,
that here was the source of the Blue Nile. The emperor Nero
sent a military expedition into the Sudan which reached the
great mass of floating vegetation that blocks the Nile some
nine degrees north of the equator, a point not to be reached
again until 1839. A trader who had been blown down along
the coast as far as Zanzibar either himself saw, or more likely
heard natives describe, a mighty mountain range of tremendous
height whose melting snows formed two lakes whence the
Nile took its start. It was as close to the truth about the source
of the White Nile as anyone was to come until the mid-
nineteenth century. Other African traders brought back tales
of 'tribes without noses, their whole face being perfectly flat,
others without upper lips, still others without tongues. One
group has the mouth closed up as well as no nose, and they
have just a single orifice through which they breathe and suck
in liquids through oat straws, also oat-grains for food'; the

story is obviously inspired by a description of certain Negro features, but the kernel of fact is almost wholly buried beneath an overlay of fancy.

The Mediterranean world of the first two centuries A.D., then, was bigger than it had ever been before. So was the volume of movement. The roads and sea ways were now thronged with traders in larger numbers than the Greek world had ever known, with armies, bureaucrats, couriers of the government post, and just plain tourists, from the few who travelled far and wide to see the great sights to the thousands who yearly left for nearby beaches or hills to escape the heat of the cities. We learn about these travellers in many and various ways, from the battered remains archaeologists have unearthed of the inns they stayed at to lofty descriptions in Roman poetry of the places they visited. And so we know them far better than their Greek predecessors and can tell of them in some detail—the reasons that sent them off on trips, the way they travelled, where they spent the nights, the sights they saw, and how they were shown them.

7

A Miscellany of Travellers

I built myself five ships, loaded them with wine—which was worth its weight in gold at the time—and sent them to Rome. . . . Every single one of them was wrecked, that's the god's honest truth; Neptune gulped down a cool thirty million in one day. . . . I built myself some more, bigger and better and luckier . . . , got another cargo of wine, added bacon, beans, a load of slaves. . . . The little woman did the right thing by me: she sold all her jewels and clothes and put a hundred gold pieces in my hand. . . . I netted a cool ten million on that one voyage.

The time is the first century A.D., the speaker the celebrated character in Petronius' novel the *Satyricon*, Trimalchio, the ex-slave who became a multimillionaire. Trimalchio was drawn from life, patterned after the thousands who were making their fortune in the booming business of import and export. A certain Flavius Zeuxis, in an inscription on his tomb in Hierapolis in Asia Minor, proclaimed that he 'as a merchant had rounded Cape Malea [in Greece] seventy-two times on voyages to Italy'. He very possibly averaged two trips per summer. Irenaeus, an Alexandrian businessman, writes from Rome to a brother back in Egypt sometime in the second or third century A.D.:

I am well. This is to let you know that I reached land on

6 A Roman merchantman of the early third century A.D. sails into Rome's harbour, passing the lighthouse at the entrance (note the flame at the top). On the afterdeck two men and a woman—probably the captain, owner or charterer, and his wife—conduct a sacrifice to celebrate the safe return.

7 Roman road paved with massive oblong blocks near Aleppo in Syria.

8 Roman mountain road in the Alps (at Donnaz, roughly midway between Turin and Aosta). The road is of solid rock formed by slicing away the cliff and is provided with artificial ruts.

9 The bridge at Narni, built by Augustus. It carried the Via Flaminia over the Nera, a tributary of the Tiber, about fifty miles north of Rome.

Epeiph 6 [30 June] and we unloaded our cargo on the 18th of the same month. I went up to Rome [from the port at the mouth of the Tiber, some fifteen miles away] on the 25th of the same month [19 July] . . . We are daily expecting our sailing papers; up to today not one of the grain freighters has been cleared. Remember me to your wife and dear ones.

There were enough ships in that fleet to transport 150,000 tons of Egyptian wheat annually. During the first century A.D., before Rome's harbour was improved, they used to put in at Puteoli, the port just west of Naples; when they arrived, writes a contemporary, 'the whole mob at Puteoli stands on the docks; they can pick out the ships from Alexandria even in a big crowd of vessels by their sails'. Wheat from Egypt, olive oil from Spain, wine from France, elaborately carved stone coffins from Athens—these and dozens of other products were hauled back and forth across the Mediterranean by a merchant marine larger than any Europe was to know again till the eighteenth century. Certain lines of traffic, as we have seen (123–7 above), went far beyond the Mediterranean. The shippers of Alexandria extended long fingers of trade down the east coast of Africa to Zanzibar and across the ocean to India. Trade was so active that some cities maintained offices in the major commercial centres to help any of their citizens doing business or on visits there. Tarsus, Tralles, Tiberias, and a number of others, for example, had *stationes*, as such offices were called, in Rome right in the middle of the forum. They were, in effect, consulates, providing the services that the *proxenoi* of the Greek city-states had centuries earlier (93 above).

And so a never-ending flow of merchants, shipowners, bankers, buyers, and their various agents kept the ports and sea lanes of the Roman Empire humming. Businessmen were to be found on the roads as well, but in fewer numbers. Transport by land, as already noted (65 above), was prohibitively expensive, and most large-scale hauling, particularly

E

of bulky items, was by water. The roads had been built in the first instance for the government, and the government remained their chief user on a regular basis. Along them was a constant going and coming of government personnel—the couriers of the public post (182 below), tax collectors, circuit judges, district officials, the governors of the provinces (as the administrative units into which the Roman Empire was divided were called), at times the emperors themselves. When a governor took to the road, his retinue of staff and servants made up a sizeable group, and, when an emperor travelled, there was a veritable parade. And neither of them produced anywhere near the numbers using the roads when units of the army were on the march. A single legion, six thousand men strong with a multitude of pack animals and vehicles, the whole line proceeding at the pace of the beasts who drew the wagons carrying the catapults, could stop all other traffic at any point for long hours; an army might stop it for days.

Trade and government no doubt accounted for the lion's share of travel, but far from all of it. There were plenty of people on the go for other reasons.

To begin with, there were those travelling for their health. It was the doctors of antiquity who first thought of the idea of the long sea voyage. 'In the case of tuberculosis . . .', wrote Celsus, the Roman medical authority, in the first century A.D., 'if the patient has the strength, a long sea voyage and change of air is called for. . . . For this purpose, the voyage from Italy to Alexandria is perfect.' Celsus obviously had in mind patients with money. Of the throngs who took to the road for their health, poor and in-between as well as rich, the vast majority were heading not for the deck of a ship but for one of the sanctuaries of Asclepius.

We have spoken of these before (82 above). The earliest were established in Greece in the sixth and fifth centuries B.C., and, by the fourth, were to be found all over the country, on most of the islands of the eastern Mediterranean, in the

Greek cities along the coast of Asia Minor and in those of southern Italy. Asclepius was one of the first foreign gods admitted to Rome, making his debut there in 291 B.C.

In the days of the Roman Empire, three of his sanctuaries stood out above all the rest. One was the foundation at Epidaurus; it achieved great repute early (83 above) and never lost it. A second was the one at Cos (267 below), home of Hippocrates and his school of medicine. The third was at Pergamum, which reached its height in the middle of the second century A.D., when Galen, the most renowned physician of the day, practised there, on and off, for many years. In addition to multiplying, the sanctuaries had prospered mightily. At Pergamum in its heyday, for example, the heart of the complex was a vast rectangular court, 360 feet by 430, entered through a monumental gateway. Along three sides ran colonnades to shelter the patients from sun and rain as they took leisurely walks or sat and rested. At one corner was a library, at another a theatre with seats for 3,500, at a third an impressive rotunda, 86 feet in diameter, for medicinal bathing. Within the court was the temple of Asclepius as well as several others.

The procedure was the same as it had always been (83 above). The patient entered the sanctuary, took a ritual bath to purify himself, entered Asclepius' temple, prayed, spread a pallet, and lay down on it to spend the night there. In his dreams he received the help he sought. Some sanctuaries had a special area for sleeping, but in others, as at Pergamum, people stretched out anywhere in the temple and perhaps other buildings within the precinct. In a few notable cases the cure was a miracle: the patient awoke the next morning hale and hearty. More often he received some prescription, usually spelled out plainly, occasionally enigmatically. There was rarely anything exotic about these. Most of the time they involved the taking—or the not taking—of certain baths or exercises or foods, the application of unguents and salves, the downing of doses of special drugs.

Whatever the reason—and very plausible ones have been suggested—the cures apparently had a fairly high percentage of success or else the sanctuaries could not have enjoyed such favour for so long. Here, for example, is a testimonial drawn up by a grateful Greek who, some time in the first or early second century A.D., visited the establishment which Asclepius shared with the Egyptian healing god Imhotep at Memphis:

It was night, when every living creature was asleep except those in pain; the moment when the divinity used to manifest itself in its more active state. I was burning with fever and convulsed with loss of breath and coughing because of the pain in my side. My head was heavy from my suffering, and I was dropping off half-conscious into sleep. My mother . . . was sitting without enjoying even a brief moment of sleep, distraught at my torment. Suddenly she spied—it was no dream or sleep, for her eyes, though not seeing clearly, were fixed wide open—a divine apparition. It came in, terrifying her and easily preventing her from seeing the god himself or his servants, whichever it was. All she could say was that there was someone of more than human height, clothed in shining garments and holding in his left hand a book; he merely eyed me two or three times from head to foot and then disappeared. When she had recovered herself she tried, still all atremble, to wake me. Finding me drenched with sweat but with my fever completely gone, she knelt down in worship to the divine manifestation. . . . When I spoke with her, she wanted to tell me about the god's unique ability, but I, anticipating her, told her all myself. For everything she had witnessed with her own eyes had appeared to me in my dreams. After these pains in my side had ceased, and the god had given me one more healing treatment, I proclaimed his benefactions to all.

It was not only the uneducated poor who flocked to seek Asclepius' aid and emerged cured—or thinking themselves cured, which would amount to the same thing. His patients covered the spectrum of society. The composer of the above, as we can tell from the way he writes, was a man of considerable culture. Aristides, of whom we shall have much to say later (193 below), a man of very good family, recipient of the best available education, and the greatest public speaker of his age, felt that he owed his life to Asclepius' ministrations. In 142 A.D. or so, he became ill and for the rest of his life was in and out of health sanctuaries, in particular Asclepius' at Pergamum. At the outset of his sickness, which seems to have been some sort of respiratory ailment, he passed two full years there, praying, sacrificing, partaking in the ceremonies, and, of course, dreaming. Some of the prescriptions he received were, no question about it, sheer nonsense. Once, debilitated as he was, he was sent in the dead of winter to take a plunge into the sea. Another time, when burning with fever, he was told to bathe in icy water. Still another time he was sent on a walk out and back in midsummer heat to a place fifty miles away; luckily this was at a moment when he was feeling rather well. None of this, as he more or less admits, did him the least bit of good. But the god also urged him to keep on with his oratorical career—and this was the turning point. Moreover, at the sanctuary he was surrounded by a coterie of like-minded patients, men of culture and learning also there for various cures (one is reminded of the groups to be found in Swiss sanitoria before World War II), and they reinforced the god's orders with their encouragement. The combination did the trick. It restored his purpose in life and sent him forth from the sanctuary, not completely well—he was never that—but able to go on to a dazzlingly successful career and live until he was sixty.

Aristides shuttled back and forth from his estate at Cyzicus or his house in Smyrna to Pergamum (cf. 193 below). The roads yearly saw thousands and thousands like him, people who rose from a sickbed at home to make their way to the nearest sanctuary of the god of healing. The flow went on unabated for hundreds of years, until well into the fourth century A.D., when Asclepius, sharing the fate of his relatives, succumbed to Christianity.

Asclepius' ministrations were for the seriously ill. For the merely ailing, particularly the hypochondriacs who liked to season their efforts in behalf of their health with some pleasures, there were the *aquae*, the mineral springs. These were as well patronized in Roman days as European spas in our own— indeed, in many cases the one is simply the descendant of the other. *Aquae Calidae* has been re-baptized Vichy, *Aquae Sextiae* Aix-en-Provence, *Aquae Sulis* Bath, *Aquae Mattiacae* Wiesbaden, and so on. Italy was particularly well supplied with them. Convenient to Rome were the springs of Vicarello on Lake Bracciano. The ruins have yielded up four silver vessels shaped like Roman milestones and inscribed with the route from Cadiz to Rome; they were gifts to the divinity of the springs from grateful Spaniards who, in Rome on a visit, took advantage of the opportunity to try the waters out. Over 1,500 coins were also found lying on the bottom of the springs—ancient travellers, no less than we, had the super- stition that there was something to be gained by tossing a coin into a fountain; masses of coins have turned up in hot springs elsewhere. Sicily had spas at Segesta, Selinus, Himera— even one on the little island of Lipari and a well-known one at that: 'Many people throughout Sicily', wrote Diodorus, a contemporary of Caesar and Augustus, 'who are troubled with their own peculiar ills go [to Lipari] . . . and by using the baths become healthy again in incredible fashion.' The Bay of Naples, a natural vacation land because of its beauty and climate, is ringed with hot springs. The whole shore, as a consequence, sprouted a line of watering places which became the most fashionable in the Roman world (142 below).

For problems of any kind and not merely health, there were the oracles. People had always patronized them (cf. 84 above) but in this age, marked by incredibly widespread superstition, they did a far more thriving business than ever before, playing somewhat the same role that horoscope casters and readers of tea leaves and palms play today. Apollo, as always, was the fortune-telling god par excellence, and his great oracular seats at Delphi in Greece, Delos in the Aegean, Clarus and Didyma in Asia Minor, answered questions for multitudes yearly. There was the Oracle of Trophonius near Lebadea in Greece, where, to present your query, you had to go down a well-like shaft and slide through a hole at the bottom into a dome-shaped cavern. There was the Temple of Fortuna at Praeneste in the hills back of Rome, where the answer to your question was a marker, drawn by a child at random, which bore an enigmatic line of writing (a fair sample, from another but similar oracle, runs: 'It is a fine looking horse, but you cannot ride on it'). There was the Oracle of Heracles in Greece, where you cast four dice, and the position of the figures on them, appropriately interpreted, determined the reply. All these and any number of others had at least the excuse of antiquity, having been established in most cases in remote times. The superstition of the age, however, even countenanced brand-new ones. A gifted faker named Alexander founded an oracle in a backwater on the south shore of the Black Sea. Here, for stiff prices, a talking serpent he had rigged up answered questions for the local hayseeds and was so successful that:

the fame of the shrine made its way to Italy and descended on Rome. Every soul there, one on the heels of the other, hurried either to go out in person or to send an envoy, particularly the most influential and important personages in the city. The leader and prime figure in this movement was Rutilianus [a prominent Roman] . . . He heard about the shrine and practically threw up his current public office to fly off to Abonoteichos; as next best thing he sent out one envoy after another . . . He got the people at the emperor's court so worked up, most of them promptly rushed out to hear something about their own futures.

Lucian, who reports the above, was a professional satirist and inevitably held a highly jaundiced view of such mumbo-jumbo. Yet even allowing liberally for exaggeration, Alexander must have been responsible for a good deal of traffic on the roads to Abonoteichos.

The traditional Greek international games, such as the Olympics in honour of Zeus or the Pythian for Apollo (76 above), lasted almost as long as the Roman Empire itself. In the first and second centuries A.D., profiting from the peace and prosperity of the age, they were going as strongly as ever—and drawing from far afield not only spectators but many others as well. At the Isthmian Games for Poseidon, for example,

> one could hear crowds of miserable sophists [the ancient equivalent of soapbox orators] around Poseidon's temple shouting and insulting each other . . . , writers reading aloud their silly works, lots of poets reciting their poems while others applauded them, lots of jugglers showing their stunts, lots of fortune tellers telling fortunes, countless lawyers perverting justice, and no lack of peddlers peddling what each happened to have.

The international games were merely the oldest and best known; there were lesser versions going on all over the empire. Cicero mentions in a letter (138 below) his plans to detour to Antrim because his daughter was anxious to be there for the local games. Nero made his debut as a musician on the public stage at the games given in Naples; it was a trial run for the appearances he looked forward to at the great games in Greece. Then there were such events as Sparta's festival in honour of Artemis where the *pièce de résistance* was the ordeal by whipping of the Spartan boys. This grim ceremony, deriving from the city's most primitive days, was carried on for over a millennium, and in Roman times its sadistic delights attracted spectators from many places. Cicero reports seeing it in the first century B.C., Plutarch in the second A.D. (both mention boys dying under the lash), Libanius in the fourth.

But the events that drew the greatest crowds of all in this age were the grandiose spectacles the emperors put on in Rome. By the second century A.D., 130 days out of the year were holidays, given over to lavish public entertainments that featured chariot racing, boxing, theatrical performances, and the like. To celebrate great occasions they gave full scope to the Roman taste for blood-letting with gladiatorial extravaganzas. Augustus, in a document that recapitulates all he had done for the country during his reign, lists the occasions he entertained the public at his own expense:

> Three times I put on contests of gladiators in my own name, and five times in the names of my sons or grandsons; in these some 10,000 men fought. I put on sports events with athletes brought in from all over twice in my own name and a third time in the name of my grandson. I held festivals four times in my own name and twenty-three times in place of the regular officials. . . . I put on hunts of African wild animals in the circus, forum, and amphitheatres in my name and those of my sons or grandsons twenty-six times; in these some 3500 beasts were killed.

When the Colosseum was opened, Titus inaugurated it with 100 days of spectacles. In A.D. 107 Trajan celebrated certain military victories by sending ten thousand gladiators into the ring within a space of four months. All this, to be sure, was aimed primarily at the city mob, was part of the emperors' policy of 'bread and circuses'. But no out-of-town *afficionado* who could afford the travel expense was going to pass by such chances to gorge himself on the finest gladiatorial fare the age could offer.

Then there were the people on holiday—but they deserve a chapter to themselves.

E*

8

On Holiday

'I intend', wrote Cicero to a friend in April, 59 B.C., 'to get to my place at Formiae on the Feast of Pales [21 April] . . . I'll leave Formiae on the first of May so as to reach Antium on the third. There are gladiators at Antium from the fourth to the sixth, and Tullia [Cicero's daughter] wants to see them. Then I'm thinking of going to Tusculum, and from there to Arpinum, reaching Rome on the first of June.' Not only Cicero but all of his neighbours were making such plans. For the coming of spring was the signal that sent Rome's social set forth on their annual *peregrinatio*, as it was called, the moving out of the city to make the rounds of their out-of-town villas.

Cicero's letter mentions the names of three places where he had villas. In the course of his lifetime he accumulated no less than six, to say nothing of the lodges he maintained along the roads to put up at overnight when travelling from one to the other. The villa at Formiae, a seaside resort about two-thirds of the way from Rome to Naples, was one of his earliest acquisitions. (It was also, as it happens, the scene of his death; his servants were hurrying him off in a litter when Mark Antony's soldiers overtook them.) Sometime before 60 B.C. he bought his first along the Bay of Naples, where it was *de rigueur* for all with social ambitions to own a villa. It turned out to be a bit out of the way so, a few years later, he got himself a second at Cumae more to the west. This was *the* fashionable neighbourhood, and Cicero was very pleased at having moved into it (one of his lifelong problems was the way his aristocratic colleagues and neighbours looked down their Roman noses at a *novus homo* 'new man', someone whose place in politics and society came from his abilities and not his exalted lineage). In 45 B.C., just a few years before his death, a friend willed him a third more or less midway between Cumae and Naples, which was convenient for transacting business at Puteoli, a bustling port and commercial centre as well as summer resort. The two others named in his letter were inland. At Tusculum in the cool Alban hills southeast of Rome he had an elegant, handsomely appointed retreat, and at Arpinum, the mountain town where he was born, he kept up the family property.

Cicero's appetite for country and seaside real estate was by no means exceptional. All of Rome's fashionable world maintained the two kinds of villas: along the shore for the cool and pleasant days of spring, and in the hills for the summertime when the Mediterranean sun made the shore an inferno—and several of each so as to avoid the monotony of always going to the same place. It was not only the millionaires who could afford such sybaritic vacationing. Cicero, for example, by the standards of the day, was no more than a moderately wealthy man.

And so villa upon villa dotted the hills about Rome and studded the shoreline down to Naples and beyond. The spot that was far and away the most favoured was the superbly beautiful stretch embraced by the arms of the Bay of Naples, from Cumae and Cape Misenum on the west to the Sorrento peninsula just past Vesuvius on the east. Here the gilded homes clustered so thickly, their terraces and piers thrust so far into the water (cf. Fig. 5), that Horace was moved to observe that the fish were feeling cramped. The aristocracy began to build in the area in the second century B.C., and it never lost its popularity. Among Cicero's fellow holiday-makers here were the greatest names of the Roman Republic—his only rival in oratory Hortensius, the celebrated *bon vivant* Lucullus,

Caesar, Pompey, Mark Antony. Their establishments were all sumptuous and some of them were veritable palaces. Augustus' step-father owned one where he once put up not only Caesar but Caesar's retinue of two thousand. The most stupendous of all was the villa Lucullus built at Naples (he had another, somewhat less grand, about twelve miles west on Cape Misenum); it offered the example *par excellence* of conspicuous spending, a tunnel driven deep through the nearby mountains just to bring in salt water to fill the fishponds. 'Xerxes in a toga', was the way one acidulous visitor, after being shown the place, described his host.

With the coming of the Roman Empire, the emperors and their relatives replaced the potentates of the Republic. Augustus maintained at least four residences in the neighbourhood. Tiberius spent most of the last ten years of his life at a monumental establishment on Capri. Nero was staying at his villa at Baiae the night he attempted to drown his mother; he finally had her assassinated in the bedroom of her own place at Bauli a few miles away. For neighbours the emperors had a new class of villa owner brought into being by the booming prosperity of the early empire, the *nouveaux riches*. Vedius Pollio, who started life as the son of ex-slaves and went from rags to riches, built himself a villa on a height between Naples and Puteoli which he called Pausilypon 'Sans-Souci'; so distinctive was it that it gave its name to the hill, Posillipo as it is known today, where his property once stood. It was the likes of Pollio who provided the model for Petronius' Trimalchio (128 above); the novelist sets the scene of his protagonist's gargantuan dinner party in a de luxe villa near Naples.

Some liked a villa right at the very edge of the shore (Fig. 5), so close that they could fish just by dropping a line from a bedroom window, others one that nestled high on a seaside cliff. On the slopes, where there was plenty of room, the villas were dotted about haphazardly; along the shore, where space was at a premium, they stood, then as now, cheek by jowl. In either case, what determined the location and layout was a view of the water. The preferred style for both was the portico-house, a house that consisted basically of a long porch overlooking the sea on to which opened a series of rooms side by side; each room, thus, commanded a sea-view. A large villa might have four or five tiers of such porches rising one above the other).

The rooms were never very large and windows were small; the object was to keep out the brilliant sunlight rather than let it flood in. Walls were painted, at first with simple and regular patterns, later, from about 90 or 80 B.C. on, with increasingly elaborate and fanciful decor that combined architectural settings with pictures of scenes from mythology, genre scenes, landscapes, seascapes. Outside were prim rows of plane-trees, myrtle, box-wood, and the like. The most lavish villas boasted *piscinae* or fishponds where special breeds, in particular *muraenae*, a type of salt-water eel prized by Roman gourmets, were raised for the master's table. This was *the* status symbol; only multimillionaires were *piscinarii*, to use Cicero's word for them, members of 'the fishpond set'. The parvenu Vedius Pollio, so the story goes, fed his eels on human flesh.

The villa owners spent a good part of their time making leisurely visits to each other, usually capped by elaborate dinner parties. For favoured guests the *piscinarii* would offer eels from their own ponds. Another choice dish were the oysters from Lake Lucrinus, a salt-water lagoon in the western part of the Bay of Naples; they were cultivated here by a method still used in certain places today, by being fastened to ropes hung from horizontal wooden frames (Fig. 19). During Augustus' war to the death with Pompey's son, the lake had been turned into a naval base. When peace came, Augustus had the base transferred to Cape Misenum; it is not impossible that the oyster growers, backed by their influential customers, got him to do it.

Visits were varied with rides along the shore in litters, with excursions on the lake or around the bay in oar-propelled yachts. 'When [the fashionable crowd] goes sailing from Lake

Avernus [a lake next to Lucrinus] to Puteoli in their gaily painted yachts', observed one historian tartly, 'it's a veritable quest for the Golden Fleece, particularly when they venture forth in steaming hot weather. If a fly slips in between the silk-fringed gilded fans, or a tiny ray of sun comes through a hole in the canopies suspended over them, out come laments that they weren't born in the land of the Eskimos.'

The glittering villa folk were only the upper crust of the holiday-makers to be found in season around the Bay of Naples. Particularly during the prosperous first two centuries A.D., people of all walks of life were able to exchange the heat of the city for a room in a boarding house at Baiae or Puteoli or Naples. Finding pleasant ways to pass their time was no problem. The shoreline around the bay is studded with hot springs, so the towns along it were spas as well as seaside resorts. The holiday-maker was able to divide his days between baths and beach, or, if he wished, to rent a small boat and go out on the water. Puteoli had two amphitheatres, so there must have been a good selection of gladiatorial shows for the sports enthusiasts. There there were visits to be made to the fishponds in the emperor's villa, which were open to the public, visits to the oyster beds, strolls through Baiae's *silva* or tree-shaded park, jaunts down to the pier at Puteoli to watch the ships come in, shore dinners in the local restaurants, shopping for gimcrack souvenirs (286 below)—or just the unadorned joys of Mediterranean *dolce far niente*.

Of all the vacation spots along this coast, none was more celebrated than Baiae, lying ten miles or so west of Naples and a mile and a quarter past Lake Lucrinus. It was Rome's first summer resort and forever remained the most popular. Strabo, writing near the close of the first century B.C., reports that here, 'with luxury palaces built one alongside the other, another city as big as Puteoli has grown up'. Being particularly well supplied with hot springs, Baiae became the favoured watering spot. It attracted pleasure seekers of all kinds, and, as will happen, acquired a reputation for impure as well as pure delights. The respectable elements of society sailed decorously about the lake during the day; at night the smart set invited shady women aboard their yachts, went bathing in the nude, and 'filled the lakes with the din of their singing'. 'Unmarried girls are common property, old men act like young boys, and lots of young boys like young girls', snapped Varro, Cicero's learned contemporary. 'Why must I look at drunks staggering along the shore or noisy boating parties?' complained the moralist Seneca a century later. Who wants to listen, he grumbled, 'to the squabbles of nocturnal serenaders?' Cicero in one of his speeches describes a loose woman by listing 'her debauchery, her love affairs, her adultery, her Baiae'—the name by itself spoke volumes. Later on he thunders about her vicious habit of going to dinner parties with men who are total strangers to her not only in Rome, not only in the gardens of her own villa, but 'amid those crowds at Baiae'. Martial, the satirist, composed a sardonic little poem about a certain couple:

> The wife, even worse than her glowering husband,
>   never strayed from virtue's paths,
> until she came to the Lucrine Lake
>   and heated up in Baiae's baths.
> It put her on fire: she left him flat
>   to run off with some young boy;
> she came to town Penelope,
>   she left it Helen of Troy.

The straightlaced Augustus, though he often holidayed in the neighbourhood, never showed his face in town and took a dim view of those who did.

The line of villas carried from Baiae past Puteoli and Naples to Pompeii and Stabiae and out on to the Sorrento Peninsula. Each of the towns that grew up had its own personality. Baiae was spa and seaside resort combined, and the gathering point of the pleasure-seekers. Puteoli was rather more staid, since its resort area rubbed shoulders with one of

Italy's most important commercial harbours; while people on holiday frolicked along the shore, merchants and shipowners bargained, and stevedores sweated around the quays. Naples appealed to the intellectuals. Like most of the great cities in southern Italy, it had been founded by Greeks, and even in the days of the empire, after centuries of Roman domination, a Greek atmosphere reigned: Greek was heard up and down the streets, Greek institutions and ways of life lived on, and visiting Romans doffed their togas to walk about in the *pallium* or *chlamys* (75 above). The traditional Greek contests for poets and musicians were kept up and drew throngs of the culturally minded; it was here, as mentioned above, that Nero made his debut as a musician. This special ambience induced many cultivated people, foreigners as well as Romans, to take up permanent residence and promoted the growth of a thriving literary colony. Schoolmasters found the place well suited for setting up academies, and the elderly for passing their declining years.

Year after year, through all vicissitudes, the Bay of Naples continued to serve vacationers. Romulus Augustulus, the last Roman emperor of the West, when exiled from the capital after A.D. 476, was sent to live out his days in one of Lucullus' villas; it was still in existence over five hundred years after its builder's death. Though the eruption of Vesuvius that destroyed Pompeii wiped out the estates on its flanks, though the convulsive crises that shook the empire through most of the third century A.D. thinned the ranks of the villas, life went on in much the same fashion; the gilded gentry continued to make their decorous rounds or to have a wild time in Baiae. The tart description cited above of luxuriating on the lake was written in the middle of the fourth century A.D. A few decades later, in A.D. 391, the Roman aristocrat Symmachus, who maintained no less than six villas in the area, wrote to a friend:

I've passed a few days on this shore . . . where the healthy air and cool waters are such inducements to linger . . . Now, through mutual invitations, we're transferring either to Bauli or to Nicomachus' villa [i.e., of Symmachus' son-in-law, near Puteoli]. I have a steady stream of friends dropping in on me. I'm not afraid that you'll think of me idling away my time in such delightful surroundings amid such good things. Wherever I am, I lead the life of a Roman consul; I'm serious even on Lake Lucrinus. No carolling in yachts, no gourmet banquets, no going to the baths, none of the young set's nude bathing parties.

Plus ça change, plus c'est la même chose.

In the letter of Cicero quoted earlier listing the moves he planned for the coming of spring, the first, as we have seen, was the traditional one to the shore in April. His next was to Tusculum, his villa in the hills back of Rome. This too was traditional. The culturally minded may have lingered on at Naples all summer, and the ordinary folk at the seaside resorts, but not the *haut monde*. With the onset of the intense heat in May they left their luxurious villas in the hands of their staffs and transferred to the cool of the hills.

The Alban and Sabine hills that ring Rome on the east and southeast are high enough to insure relief from the summer heat and near enough to the capital to enable a senator to leave the stifling senate chamber and refresh himself for a day or two with a minimum of travel. As a consequence, from the first century B.C. on, they were dotted with country retreats. In the neighbourhood of Tusculum alone there were four belonging to various emperors and ten times that many to private citizens. The scene of Cicero's *Tusculan Disputations* is set in the elegant villa he maintained there; he lavished time, energy, and money not only in its construction but in securing just the right works of art for decorating it. In the hill villas the emphasis was on quiet, cool, and shade. The owners liked to have their bedrooms in the interior, sometimes totally cut off from any natural light, the arcaded corridors for their casual strolling were often half-sunk in the ground, and the gardens and courts were laid out with fountains so that the splash and murmur of water was an ever-present sound. A private bath was normally included, complete with cold room, hot room, and swimming pool; some pools were even heated. The greatest villa of this kind was the grandiose complex erected by the emperor Hadrian; for reasons we can only guess at, he put it on the hot plain below Tibur instead of on its cool slopes. Spread over some 180 acres, it included two theatres, three sets of baths, libraries, endless porticoes—a veritable city with the room and facilities to accommodate thousands. The architecture was daring, avant-garde; the effect upon contemporaries must have been like that of World's Fair architecture today. The decor included not only mosaics and wall-paintings but thousands of statues, chiefly replicas of renowned Greek works. And the site was honeycombed with underground passageways so that the army of hard-working slaves who provided the services stayed discretely out of view.

Though set in the heart of the country, these were first and foremost ornamental estates. Growing of farm produce was strictly secondary; many an owner had to load up on supplies in the city on setting out for a stay. Martial describes one whom you could see on the Via Appia in a wagon groaning under a load of cabbages, leeks, lettuce, beets, fowl, hare, suckling pig:

> Is he homeward bound
>   from the country air?
> It's the other way round—
>   he's going there!

In the prosperous first two centuries of the Roman Empire, even the middle class had their country retreats. The farm in the Sabine Hills that Maecenas gave to Horace and to which he rushed gratefully at every possible chance, must have been a relatively modest establishment. Martial, who started his career living in a garret three flights up, eventually got himself a little cottage amid a few acres in the vicinity of Nomentum, some thirteen miles as the crow flies from where Horace's place had been located. And he has a poem about a seedy lawyer who made a poor but sure living off a clientele of rustics who used to pay him in farm produce; then he bought a piece of farm property to retire on, and things were reversed:

> So, Pannychus, you've bought some land,
>   with a ramshackle hut whose roof needs supports,
> with a view on a roadside graveyard, and
>   you've deserted your city estate, the courts.
> Your seedy gown paid steadily, if not well—
>   but the millet, barley, wheat, and rye,
> that when practising law you used to sell,
>   now you're a farmer, you'll have to buy!

The moving about of all these villa-owners with their staffs, provisions, and families must have put long lines of carts, carriages, and litters on the roads, in the spring when the tide flowed to shore and country and again in the fall when it ebbed back into the cities. Around Rome, where the wealth of the nation was concentrated, the traffic must have been especially dense, filling first the Via Appia that led south to the seaside resorts, and later the Via Tiburtina, Via Praenestina, and Via Tusculana that led to Tibur and Praeneste in the Sabine Hills and Tusculum in the Alban Hills.

In the age of the Greek city-states we noted that there were some five basic motives for travel: people left home on business, either their own or the government's, for their health, to go on pilgrimage to an oracle or shrine, to be present at well-known festivals, and, in a very few cases, to see the world. The Romans, as we have just observed, added one more—the holiday—the annual departure from town for the shore or mountains and back.

But far more significant was the Roman contribution to the extent and volume of travel. During the first three centuries A.D., when the Mediterranean had become one world politically as well as culturally, the same motives put infinitely greater numbers on the sea and roads, and their movements extended far further in all directions. Businessmen and government personnel now moved about from Britain to India, Asclepius' sanctuaries catered to an international clientele, the games drew spectators from everywhere—and so many more were able to indulge in the pastime of sightseeing that, as will appear in due course, the topic calls for full-scale treatment.

9

On the Sea

When Pliny the Elder, compiling his encyclopedia in the second half of the first century A.D., turned to the subject of flax he waxed rhapsodic. 'What greater miracle is there', he wrote, 'than this plant which has brought Italy so close to Egypt that Galerius arrived at Alexandria just seven days after leaving the Strait of Messina . . . , which has put Cadiz within seven days of Ostia and the nearer coast of Spain within four?' The ancients used sails of linen spun from flax (cotton, an exotic import from India, was chiefly for fine garments), and Pliny is referring to record runs made by the clippers of his day. To go from Italy to Spain by land would have taken a month, to Alexandria well-nigh two. And, even in cases where the length of a trip was the same over land as by sea, it was infinitely less wearing to pass the days lolling on a deck than walking or riding a mule or mule-drawn carriage. On the other hand, there was the matter of danger to balance against comfort. Rome's efficient administration, at least during the first two centuries A.D., had swept the seas clear of pirates and chased away most of the bandits from the main highways. But the perils of storm were something else again; no matter how careful a skipper was in picking the right season and winds for a sailing, the unexpected could always happen. People on the road trudged or jolted along at a snail's pace, but at least they were spared worries about shipwreck. And the Romans, a lubberly lot in general, were particularly nervous when it came to sea voyages. Time and again their writers fearfully bring up the mere finger's breadth of plank that separates a sailor from a watery death, and the farewell poems they address to friends departing for overseas sometimes read like elegies on their certain death.

There was yet another factor which anyone choosing between land and sea had to keep in mind: ship passages were not available all year round. In ancient times the sailing season was limited by and large to the period from May to October. This was partly because of the severe storms of winter, but even more because of the increased amount of cloudiness that occurs between fall and spring. In the days before the invention of the mariner's compass, sailors plotted their courses by landmarks or the sun during the day and by the stars at night; they gambled on getting good weather, and the odds were with them only in the summer months. Movement by water between October and May did not completely stop, but it was always exceptional—the transport of troops to meet an emergency, the hauling of cargo to alleviate a serious shortage —and could play little part in the planning of itineraries.

Rome, Antioch, Caesarea, Alexandria, Carthage, Cadiz, Cartagena, Tarragona, Narbonne, Marseilles, Arles—these were the chief entrepôts that ringed the Mediterranean. Sealanes crossed from one to the other, while coastal sailings connected each with the neighbouring smaller ports to either side. Rome, the capital and centrally located, was inevitably the best served, with routes fanning out in all directions.

For travellers heading for the eastern Mediterranean from anywhere within the western part of the empire, Rome was far and away the best jump-off point. To get to Egypt there were the fast sailings offered by the Alexandria-Rome grain fleet (158 below). To get to Greece, there were at least two feasible alternatives. The all-water route went from Rome (or Naples) through the Straits of Messina and around the Peloponnese to Corinth and Athens. Those willing to include some travel on land went by road to Brindisi, where they boarded a boat which carried them across the Adriatic and through the Gulf of Corinth to Corinth's harbour on the west side of the isthmus; if headed for Athens, they walked across to the sister harbour on the east side and continued by water. From either Athens or Corinth it was an easy sail across the Aegean to Ephesus or Smyrna, the chief ports of Asia Minor, and from either of these there were coastal craft to carry passengers north or south. Those leaving from Rome for Asia Minor who wanted to bypass Greece could get a direct sailing to Rhodes or the Asia Minor ports.

The time a voyage took depended on the winds and the type of craft chosen, whether a seagoing vessel that went straight over open water or something smaller that stayed close to shore. Ranking government officials occasionally travelled on war galleys placed at their disposal by the Roman navy; since these were little more than oversize racing shells, they necessarily followed the coasts and put into harbour every night. When Cicero left Athens for Ephesus in 51 B.C., en route to the southern part of Asia Minor where he was to assume his duties as a governor, he was put aboard a light naval unit, one of a flotilla. The ships set sail on 6 July, made their way through the Aegean islands (Ceos-Gyaros-Syros-Delos-Samos), with a stop at each one of them, and finally arrived on the 22nd—more than two weeks after departure. His return to Athens, once more on one of a flotilla of galleys, again took two weeks. The distance they covered over the open sea was no more than two hundred nautical miles or so, which even a slow-paced sailing vessel could have done in three or four days. In recompense every night Cicero enjoyed a shore-based meal and a night's sleep in a stable bed.

What principally determined the speed, and at times even the direction, of travel by water were the summer trade winds of the Mediterranean, the Etesians or 'yearly winds' as the ancients called them. These blow consistently from the northern quadrant. Thus the voyage from Rome to Alexandria was apt to be a traveller's dream: with the prevailing wind on the stern, he could generally count on a quick and easy run of ten days to three weeks. But he paid the price on the return, which could take as much as two months or more. The same winds, adverse now all the way, forced vessels into a roundabout course via the south coast of Asia Minor, Crete, Malta, and Sicily, much of which they had to cover beating against headwinds. The voyage from Rome to Corinth or back involved both fair and foul winds and consequently took between one and two weeks. When Pliny the Younger, nephew of the encyclopedist, left the capital to take up his post as governor of the province of Bithynia on the north coast of Asia Minor, he sailed directly from Rome to Ephesus but, from there on, he was compelled for at least part of the way to take to the roads since the Etesians ruled out making the whole trip from Ephesus north to the Hellespont by water.

Ancient ships never had towering tiers of canvas. Their drive was principally supplied by a big square mainsail (Fig. 6). By Roman times a small triangular topsail had been added that was useful for catching upper airs during light winds or calms. Forward was a small squaresail, much like the bowsprit-sail of the eighteenth century (cf. Fig. 16); it served the same purpose, to aid in manoeuvring the vessel; the very largest ships added a mizzen of modest size. It was no rig for developing speed, particularly on the capacious big-bellied hulls the Greeks and Romans favoured. Even before a fine breeze from the right quarter, their ships did no better than six knots. Thus the voyage, say, from Gibraltar to Rome or Carthage never took less than a week. Narbonne was at the very least three days from Rome, Corinth five, Rhodes seven, Alexandria ten. Byzantium (Constantinople) to Rhodes was at least five days, to Alexandria nine. These, we must remember, were optimum voyages; if the return involved sailing from southeast to northwest, against, that is, the prevailing northerlies, it could take twice as long or more.

There were no such things as passenger vessels in the

ancient world. Travellers did as they were to do until the packet ship finally made its debut in the nineteenth century: they went to the waterfront and asked around until they found a vessel scheduled to sail in a direction they could use. 'In Constantinople', writes Libanius, describing his travels in c. A.D. 340, 'I went down to the Great Harbour and made the rounds asking about vessels sailing for Athens.' When St Paul was sent from Caesarea in Palestine to stand trial in Rome, he boarded a ship making for the south coast of Asia Minor, which happened to be on his line of course; arriving at the port of Myra there, he had the luck to find a freighter on the Alexandria-Rome run in harbour and booked passage on it. Rome offered a convenient service which spared people much weary tramping along the waterfront. Its port was located at the mouth of the Tiber. In the town of Ostia nearby was a big piazza surrounded by offices. Of these, many belonged to the shippers of various seaports: the shippers of Narbonne had one, the shippers of Carthage had another, the shippers of Carales in Sardinia still another, and so on. Anyone seeking a sailing had only to check at the offices of whatever cities lay along his route.

Since the vessels were first and foremost for cargo and carried passengers only incidentally, they provided neither food nor services. The crews were solely for working ship; there were no stewards among them to prepare meals or tend cabins. As in earlier times (66 above), voyagers went aboard with their own servants to take care of their personal needs and with supplies of food and wine (the ships did furnish water) to sustain them until the next port of call where there would be a chance to obtain replenishments.

Having selected his sailing, a traveller arranged to book passage with the *magister navis* 'master of the ship', the officer charged with the business side of a voyage, the maintenance of the vessel, and similar matters; on small ships he could be the owner as well, on large he was most often the owner's or charterer's representative. The actual handling of the vessel under way was left to the sailing master, the *gubernator* or *kybernetes* as he was called in Latin and Greek respectively. A booking rarely involved a cabin, since cabin space was at a premium (cf. Fig. 6). The *magister* and *gubernator* most likely each had one of their own, and on big seagoing freighters there were a few available for VIPs or the very wealthy, but the great majority of travellers simply purchased deck passage. They slept in the open or under little tentlike shelters that their servants put up every evening and took down every morning. Most ships, even quite small ones, had a well-fitted galley with a hearth for cooking. The crew very probably had first call upon it, but no doubt hours were set aside when passengers were allowed to send their servants to prepare food.

With his passage arranged, the traveller's next move was to secure an exit pass—or at least in some ports, for we are not sure whether such passes were required everywhere. They certainly were for people departing from Egypt, but Egypt, because of its vital importance as a source of food and revenue, was in many respects under more stringent regulation than the other provinces of the Empire. To leave from Alexandria, for example, one had to apply to the governor who, if disposed to approve, would authorize a port official to issue a pass. These involved a fee, which apparently varied widely according to the trade of the applicant. A price list of A.D. 90 for passes to leave Egypt by way of a Red Sea port has luckily been preserved, and it reveals an amazing range. The captain of a merchant ship paid 8 drachmae, some of his ratings 10, his sailors and ship's carpenter 5. A skilled labourer paid the same as the captain, 8. The government seems to have been out to discourage women from leaving, because common-law wives of army men were charged 20, and prostitutes no less than 108.

When the day of departure drew near, the traveller set about packing his bags (*viduli*, *manticae*; cf. Fig. 13). Like some voyagers right up to the last century, in addition to clothing he took along a battery of things needed for cooking, eating, bathing, sleeping—from pots and pans down to mattresses and bedding. And, as mentioned above, he had to find room for provisions, an item that on certain voyages— the run over open water from Rome to Alexandria, say, a minimum of ten days—could bulk formidably large. He then transferred with it all and his servants to a waterfront inn or to the house of some friend who lived near the harbour. Here he stood by with his ears cocked for the cry of a herald making the rounds to announce the departure of his vessel. He had to do it this way because ships never left on a fixed schedule. First they had to await the arrival of a wind from the right quarter. Then there was the matter of the omens. The Roman Imperial age, as I have mentioned (134 above), was a superstitious one in general, and seamen are a particularly superstitious lot. On many days of the year the religious calendar forbade business of any sort, and this included the departure of ships. Then there were days, like our Friday the 13th, which were ill-omened; e.g., no Roman skipper would shove off from a port on 24 August, 5 October, or 8 November, and the end of the month as a whole was considered no time to be found on the water.

Assuming that the wind was favourable and there was nothing wrong with the date, the ship's authorities would proceed to make a pre-sailing sacrifice (a sheep or a bull; Poseidon preferred bulls), and, if the omens during this were not right, the sailing had to be delayed. If the wind was favourable, if there was nothing wrong with the date, and if the sacrifice had gone off as desired, superstition still left a gamut of bad omens to be run: a sneeze as you went up the gangplank was bad (although if you had sneezed to the right during the sacrifice, that was good), a crow or a magpie sitting, croaking, in the rigging was bad, a glimpse of some wreckage on the shore was bad, the uttering of certain words or expressions were bad. A sailing could also be held up by dreams, if a voyager or the ship's officers took them seriously, as so many of the age did. According to an ancient book on the subject, to dream of turbid waters or a key or an anchor was an unmistakable veto on travel by sea. Goats presaged big waves or storm—and terribly big, if the goats were black. Wild boars meant violent storms. So did bulls, and shipwreck if they gored. Owls and other night birds meant storm or pirate attack, gulls and other sea birds danger but not death. To dream that you saw your face on the moon meant destruction, to dream of flying on your back or walking on water were good omens. In general, encouraging dreams seems to have been far fewer than the other kind.

Omens were not limited to embarkation only; they were equally operative under way. For example, the dreams just listed meant the same whether they came to one in a waterfront inn or under a shelter on deck. Birds settling in the rigging during a voyage was a good sign; it meant land was near, and a skipper who had lost his bearings often found his way by following the flight of a bird. So long as the weather was good, there was to be no cutting of hair or nails; if it turned bad, nail clippings and locks could be tossed to the waves as an appeasement offering. No blasphemies were allowed; it was bad even if they were merely in a letter received on board. Dancing was taboo. If anyone died during a voyage, the body was immediately cast into the sea, since death aboard a ship was the worst possible omen.

Passengers amused themselves as best they could. They had each other for company, and big ships, such as the ones that plied between Rome and Alexandria, could accommodate no small number. Josephus once crossed to Rome on a vessel carrying 600. People of importance were given a chair on the poop where they could chat with the skipper—the equivalent, as it were, of eating at the captain's table on a modern transatlantic liner. Reading to pass the time was for those who could afford books, which, being handwritten, were far from cheap; travellers preferred the parchment codex editions, much like a modern book in form, to scrolls, which not only were bulkier (there was writing on only one side of the sheet) but also less convenient since they had to be held with both hands at all times. Almost certainly gambling must have helped while away many a long hour. There was always the handling of the ship to watch: the helmsman guiding her, not as today by spinning a wheel which controls a rudder at the stern, but by pushing or pulling on tiller bars socketed into enormous steering oars on each quarter (Fig. 6), an apparatus every bit as efficient as a stern rudder; the sailors trimming the lines of the huge mainsail or the triangular topsail or little foresail; the hands in the hold getting rid of bilgewater by walking a treadmill that activated a pump; the hands on the afterdeck hauling in the ship's boat, which was towed astern, to pass some rations to the lonely sailor who stood watch there; the ship's carpenter on the foredeck (Fig. 6) fashioning spare oars, shells for blocks, belaying pins, and what not; in short, all the miscellaneous chores that go on day in and day out aboard sailing ships no matter what age they belong to. There was no problem about keeping occupied when trouble was in the offing. Then everybody aboard, passengers as well as crew, were put to work. When a storm hit St Paul's ship, he and the other passengers helped jettison the tackle. In any blow, the yard, an enormous spar which could be almost as long as the vessel itself, had to be lowered to the deck and either secured properly or cast adrift, a job that needed all the muscle aboard. Later, when the danger grew even worse, Paul and the others pitched in to help dump the cargo of grain. The alternative to keeping the ship afloat was death, since ancient vessels carried no lifeboats; the ship's boat, which might accommodate a dozen people at best, was for harbour service not saving lives.

As the vessel sailed into its port of destination, the captain gratefully performed a sacrifice on the poop (Fig. 6). A harbour tug—a heavy dory manned by husky rowers pulling extra-long oars—came out and, taking a line from the ship, got it under tow, brought it up to a dock nose first, and here it was securely moored to a huge stone ring on the quay. The gangplank was lowered, stevedores swarmed aboard to start unloading the cargo, and the passengers with a sigh of relief walked down to terra firma. A sigh of relief because, among other things, the tension had been greater than ever from the moment the harbour had been sighted: from then on it was of crucial importance that no one utter any word, or commit any act, of ill omen.

The comfort and speed of a sea voyage depended upon the ship—and ancient ships, like modern, ran the gamut from lordly long-distance freighters to humble local coasting craft.

When the Jewish princeling Agrippa was planning to leave Rome for Palestine, the emperor Caligula advised him not to take the coastal route: 'from Brindisi to Syria, which was long and tiring but, waiting for the Etesian winds, to take a direct sailing to Alexandria'. He added that, 'the ships are crack sailing craft and their skippers the most experienced there are; they drive their vessels like race horses on an unswerving course that goes straight as a die'. Caligula was referring to the mighty ships that plied between Alexandria and Rome bringing Egyptian grain to feed the capital. By a lucky coincidence, we happen to know what they looked like. One day about the middle of the second century A.D., one of them ran into a particularly bad stretch of weather, was blown far off course, and ended up in the Piraeus, Athens' port. The arrival of a unit from the famous grain fleet in what was at this time a commercial backwater created a sensation. Everybody in town turned out to see it including, fortunately for us, Lucian. He and his friends walked the five miles from Athens to the waterfront to get a look at what was causing all the excitement. He was astonished. He wrote:

What a size the ship was! 180 feet in length, the ship's carpenter told me, the beam more than a quarter of that, and 44 feet from the deck to the lowest point in the hold. And the height of the mast, and what a yard it carried, and what a forestay held it up! And the way the stern rose up in a gradual curve ending in a gilded goose-head, matched at the other end by the forward, more flattened, sweep of the prow with its figures of Isis, the goddess the ship was named after, on each side! Everything was incredible: the rest of the decoration, the paintings, the red topsail, even more, the anchors with their capstans and winches, and the cabins aft. The crew was like an army. They told me she carried enough grain to feed every mouth in Athens for a year. And it all depended for its safety on one little old man who turns those great steering oars with a tiller that's no more than a stick! They pointed him out to me; woolly-haired little fellow, half-bald. Heron was his name, I think.

More than 180 feet long, more than 45 wide, with a hold 44 feet deep—it *was* a mighty vessel, probably able to hold over a thousand tons of grain, or three times as much cargo as any merchantman that plied between Europe and America before 1820. And probably able, too, to squeeze aboard a thousand passengers. 'And we were in all in the ship two hundred three score and sixteen souls', said Luke of the vessel used on the same run that he boarded with Paul at Myra, and that was during an off-season sailing.

The *Isis* represents one end of the scale, the queens of the Roman merchant marine, the biggest and finest vessels a voyager could book passage on. It is not surprising that the emperor Vespasian preferred them to the naval galleys available to him. At the other end of the scale were the modest vessels that tramped along the coast. And we have some idea of what these were like thanks to a description by Synesius. This aristocratic Greek intellectual, who was converted to Christianity and eventually became Bishop of Ptolemais, took one in A.D. 404 to go from Alexandria along the Egyptian and Libyan coast to Cyrene and wrote up his experiences in a lively, chatty letter to his brother back in Alexandria. Though we must take a good deal of what he relates with a large pinch of salt—Synesius is as much interested in entertaining the reader as in informing him—it provides an amusing and illuminating picture of what a trip on one of these humble craft was like:

Our shipowner was being crushed to death by a load of debt. There were twelve in the crew all told, with the captain making thirteen. Over half were Jews, including the captain, a race of non-conformists who are persuaded that piety consists in arranging to kill as many Greeks as possible. The rest were ordinary farm boys who up to last year had never touched an oar. The one thing they all shared in common was having some bodily defect. And so, so long as we were in no danger, they made jokes about this and called each other by their misfortunes instead of their real names— Cripple, Ruptured, One-Arm, Squint; each and every one had his nickname. All this rather amused us. But, in time of need, it was no laughing matter; we had reason to groan over these very defects, since there were more than fifty passengers, about one-third of them women and mostly young and pretty. Don't be envious: a curtain walled us off, a good strong one, a piece of sail that had recently ripped, a veritable wall of Semiramis in the eyes of decent temperate men. And even Priapus himself would have been decent and temperate if he had been a passenger on Mr Amarantus' ship. There wasn't a moment when he let us relax from the fear of mortal danger.

To start with, after rounding [the cape] near you with the temple of Poseidon, he decided to make straight for Taposiris with all sail flying and take a try at Scylla, the one in the story books we get so scared at. When we realized this and, a hair's breadth from disaster, let out a shout, we just managed to force him to give up doing battle with the rocks. Then, spinning the vessel about as if having a change of mind, off he went for the open water, for a while struggling against the sea as best he could but later helped along by a good breeze from the south.

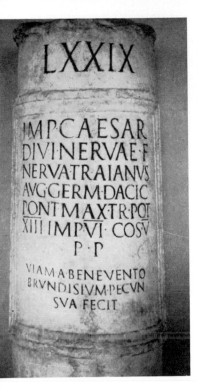

10 Milestone marking the 79th mile of the Via Appia Traiana, the extension of the Via Appia from Benevento to Brindisi built by Trajan. The inscription reads: IMP(erator) CAESAR DIVI NERVAE F(ilius) NERVA TRAIANUS AUG(ustus) GERM(anicus) DACIC(us) PONT(ifex) MAX(imus) TR(ibunicia) POT(estas) XIII IMP(erator) VI CO(n)S(ul) V P(ater) P(atriae) VIAM A BENEVENTO BRUNDISIUM PECUN(ia) SUA FECIT 'The Emperor Caesar Nerva Trajan, son of the Divinized Nerva, Augustus, Victor in Germany, Victor in Dacia, Pontifex Maximus, holding the tribunician power for the thirteenth time [i.e. in 108 A.D.], Imperator for the sixth time, Consul for the fifth, Father of the Fatherland, built the road from Beneventum to Brundisium at his own expense.'

11 Roman wagon of the early second century A.D. drawn by a mule. It is a relatively unusual type being fitted with shafts for a single animal instead of a draught-pole for a team.

12 Roman covered wagon, perhaps a *carruca dormitoria*, of the Imperial period.

13 Gravestone of the second to third century A.D. showing a dispatch carrier of the Roman *cursus publicus* in a light carriage. See page 183.

Had Synesius known anything about the handling of a sailing ship, he would have realized what was happening. The skipper had started with a long tack landward, extending it just as far as he possibly could, as a good skipper will. He then 'spun the vessel about'—but not because of any change of mind; he simply wore ship to go on the opposite tack, where, as even Synesius became aware, he was helped along by the offshore wind. As he extended this tack, he left the shore further and further behind, and Synesius, suspicious of the crew's competence and getting more and more nervous, began to complain bitterly. Amarantus patiently explained what was going on, but Synesius remained only half convinced.

Toward evening, the wind started to make up and by midnight they had run into a storm:

The men groaned, the women shrieked, everybody called upon god, cried aloud, remembered their dear ones. Only Amarantus was in good spirits, thinking he was going to get out of paying his creditors. . . . I noticed that the soldiers [a large group of the passengers were members of an Arab cavalry unit] had all drawn their swords. I asked why and learned that they preferred to belch up their souls to the open air, on the deck, rather than gurgle them up to the sea. True descendants of Homer, I thought, and approved of the idea. Then someone called out that all who had any gold should hang it around their neck. Those who had, did so, both gold and anything else of the value of gold. The women not only put on their jewellery but handed out pieces of string to any who needed them. This is a time-honoured practice, and the reason for it is this: you must provide the corpse of someone lost at sea with the money to pay for a funeral so that whoever recovers it, profiting by it, won't mind giving it a little attention. . . .

The ship was rushing along under full canvas because we couldn't shorten sail. Time and again we laid hands on the lines but gave up because they were jammed in the blocks.

F

And secretly we began to be equally afraid that, even if we escaped from the raging sea, we would be approaching land in the dead of night in this helpless condition. Day broke before this happened, and we saw the sun—and never with greater pleasure. As the heat of day came on, the wind moderated, and, with the wetness out of the ropes, we were able to use them and handle sail. To replace with a stormsail was impossible—it was in the pawn shop. We took the sail in like the folds of a tunic, and within four hours, we, who had been expecting death, find ourselves disembarking in a remote deserted spot with not a town nor farm nearby for fifteen miles around. The ship was tossing in the open roads (for the spot was no harbour), held by one anchor—the second anchor had been sold, and Mr Amarantus did not own a third. When we touched beloved land, we embraced it like a living mother.

IO

Roman Roads

The web of roads that Rome spun the length and breadth of the territory she administered was not only a magnificent achievement, but one of profound significance. It enabled her rulers to establish and maintain the most durable empire in European history; it set the lines along which traders, priests, and soldiers would carry the seeds of change in western civilization; it determined where many of the great urban centres of Europe were to be. Only a rich and powerful state whose authority stretched unchallenged far and wide could have carried out the task, could have built so many thousands of miles of highway, maintained them more or less in good order, fitted them with the appropriate facilities, and given them the essential police protection. When the Roman Empire broke up into a number of independent states, its great road system broke up with it, and, since no nation in the Middle Ages had the necessary organization or money, the fragments gradually degenerated. Spanish and French and English coaches jounced painfully or got bogged down on stretches where, fifteen hundred years earlier, Roman *redae* and *carrucae* had clipped along on smooth all-weather paving.

The Romans learned the art of roadbuilding from excellent teachers, the Etruscans. This mysterious people, who settled in what is today Tuscany in the ninth century B.C. and flourished there for half a millennium, has left striking witnesses to their ability as engineers, particularly hydraulic engineers. They taught Rome how to make sewers, aqueducts, bridges, and—

more to our present point—properly drained roads. The Etruscans never went beyond well-graded, drained, and carefully surfaced dirt roads. The Romans went one key step further: they added paving. It had long been known, for the Near East had used it for centuries for short distances in special areas (50 above). Rome used it for mile upon mile of her major highways.

The first of the great Roman thoroughfares was the Via Appia, the *regina viarum* 'queen of roads', begun in 312 B.C. under Appius Claudius, commissioner of public works for that year. It went to Capua, and then later was carried on to Brindisi, the gateway for travel to the east (150 above). A century later two highways leading to the north end of the peninsula were laid down. The Via Flaminia, named after Gaius Flaminius, public works commissioner in 220 B.C., the year construction was started, ran from Rome to Fano on the Adriatic coast, snaking across the Apennines so ingeniously that there were few times in the year when snow closed the passes; some decades later the consul Marcus Aemilius Lepidus added the Via Aemilia, which carried the Flaminia on to Piacenza (it was eventually extended to Milan). The second, the Via Aurelia, which was begun in 144 B.C. or even earlier, took traffic from Rome along the west coast, reaching, with various prolongations, as far as Genoa.

Thus, by the end of the second century B.C., the Italian boot had a set of first-class highways traversing its entire length. The next step was to extend these further, as Rome acquired territories outside of Italy, to permit an uninterrupted flow of soldiers and dispatches from the capital to all points in the Roman sphere of authority. These splendid thoroughfares, we must remember, though used by traders and travellers in plentiful numbers, were built primarily by and for the army.

The East claimed the road-builders attention first. Just across the Adriatic from Brindisi, terminus of the Via Appia, was the town of Durazzo. Shortly after 148 B.C. they began to lay the Via Egnatia from here across Macedonia to Saloniki, where it met up with the roads leading to the city-states of Greece. Later it was prolonged to Byzantium, on the site occupied today by Istanbul. From this point on Rome's engineers did not have to bother with new construction so much as improve and consolidate what the Assyrians, Persians and Greeks had built long before. By the first century A.D., the traveller who had taken the Via Egnatia to Byzantium and been ferried across the Bosporus could count on good roads right across Asia Minor and down the length of Syria to Alexandria in Egypt.

In the west, there were the tracks used by the Gallic tribes to follow, but much work was needed to bring them up to Roman standards. From Genoa the coast road was steadily extended till eventually it carried traffic through Marseilles, Narbonne, and Tarragona as far as Cadiz on the Atlantic coast of Spain. More than a dozen routes straddled the Alps (cf. Fig. 8): over the Mont Genèvre Pass, the Little and Big St Bernard, the Splügen and Julier into France and Switzerland, and from Aquileia over a number of low passes into the Danube valley. For some reason, Rome's highway engineers ignored some of today's favourites: there was no carriage road over the Brenner until late in the second century A.D., and none during all of ancient times over the Mt Cenis or Simplon or St Gotthard.

In North Africa a long ribbon ran from Alexandria all the way to Algeria.

So, by the first century A.D., the Mediterranean was girdled along its various coasts by a nearly continuous ring road. Trunk roads and branches radiated from it deep into Europe and Asia, somewhat less deeply into North Africa. In each of Rome's provinces two or three cities came to serve as nodal points for the road web within it. Most have continued to serve, first as road and then as rail centres, and along their approaches Roman paving can often be found under the asphalt or the railway ties. In Spain there was Zaragoza, Cordoba, and Merida, of which only Merida has been left in the lurch and is now but an archaeological site. In France there was Lyons and Rheims, both of them still busy road and rail centres. In Britain it was London, in Italy Rome and Milan and Aquileia; the last, after the fall of Rome, was overtaken by its rising neighbour, Venice. In Asia Minor, from among the many well-established Greek cities there, Rome chose Pergamum, Ephesus, and Apamea as hubs for her road pattern, and, in North Africa, Carthage in Tunisia, and Tebessa and Constantine in Algeria. The ebb of the tide of civilization in both Asia Minor and Africa has reduced most of them to ghost towns or backward villages today.

'The roads were carried straight across the countryside without deviation, were paved with hewn stones and bolstered underneath with masses of tight-packed sand; hollows were filled in, torrents or ravines that cut across the route were bridged; the sides were kept parallel and on the same level—all in all, the work presented a vision of smoothness and beauty.' So wrote Plutarch describing the construction programme carried out by Gaius Gracchus between 123 and 121 B.C. Plutarch's language is fulsome, but he does not exaggerate: he is describing main highways, and by and large this is the way they were built. The hallmark of a Roman road is the directness of its course. Over the flat it runs like an arrow shot, and even where the terrain is not perfectly level, as in Britain, a stretch can go twenty or thirty miles with only a half-mile deviation. When driving in Europe today you often can tell you are going over what was once a Roman thoroughfare by the way it rolls on and on without a curve.

Rome's prime concern was to have through routes that were usable at all times of year and in all kinds of weather. In other words, they had to be laid on a firm foundation, to be properly drained, and, where traffic was heavy, to be surfaced with a durable paving. This was a tall order for Roman engineers who disposed of limited manpower—the work on main thoroughfares was done by the army which often could not

spare troops for the time-consuming job of building roads—
and the simplest of tools: pick, hammer, mattock, spade. Rock
obstructions had to be painfully picked away, earth obstructions spaded away, and the chips from the one and dirt from
the other carried off in baskets, since that superbly useful
instrument, the wheelbarrow, though long used by the
Chinese, did not reach Europe until the Middle Ages. The
feats Rome's road builders were able to perform with this
meagre equipment are impressive (Fig. 8). There is a point
along the coast at Terracina where a huge slice of rock
measuring 126 feet from top to bottom was removed from a
sheer cliff in order to squeeze the Via Appia in between the
cliff and the sea; we know this because the construction gang
carved numbers in the rock, starting at the top, to record how
many feet they chopped off, and the road ran along at the
level of the CXXVI mark. The modern road laid over the
Via Flaminia still passes through a forty-yard tunnel that was
hacked out in A.D. 77, and there are other tunnels extant
(though no longer in use) that measure up to 1,000 yards in
length. But the Romans went in for such works only when
absolutely unavoidable. Their standard procedure was to take
advantage of the terrain rather than fight it, and they did this
with great skill.

When building over plains, as in the Po Valley, they laid
their roads straight across, sometimes raised slightly above the
level of the land. This not only helped drainage but, in regions
that saw snow, enabled the road to stand out even after a
heavy fall. In rolling or hilly terrain, rather than putting roads
on the floor of the valleys, they favoured running them along
the sides, even though this made for curves and added length.
At times a modern highway will proceed straight over a valley
floor, while its Roman predecessor will be high above, following the twists and turns of the slopes. The point was to avoid
laying a bed on marshy or even just damp soil, to avoid the
problem of spring floods, and to cross streams high in their
course, where they are easy to ford, rather than at their full

width where they would have to be bridged. Moreover we must always remember that these roads were built first and foremost for the army, and a slope along one side of a road protected marching troops from attack in that direction. To the Roman planners, extra curves were little enough to pay for these many advantages.

Having determined where a road was to go, the engineers then surveyed its track, a procedure that often taxed their primitive instruments. Roads were laid in segments, and frequently, because of imprecise surveying or imprecise determination of gradients, segments meet each other unevenly or vary in level. Their next step was to make a careful study of the terrain and the soil to see what kind of road-bed they would put down.

We commonly read in handbooks that the Romans, in building major highways, dug to a depth of $2\frac{1}{2}$ to $3\frac{1}{2}$ feet to lay a bed of three different courses, one of which was sealed with cement. We are also given the impression that roads were built in this fashion for the whole, or nearly the whole, of their length. Nothing could be further from the truth. The error goes back to a wrong set of conclusions arrived at by a French scholar early in the seventeenth century and repeated uncritically by one writer after another ever since. In the past decades, scholars have examined the actual remains of Roman roads in many parts of western Europe, and particularly in Italy and France, and have discovered two striking features. The first is that the Romans never used cement in road-building, the second that they never stuck doctrinairely to one type of bed but let the choice depend on soil and terrain.

A major road had to have an all-weather surface. Where traffic was light, as in the provinces, the engineers made do with a gravel surface; we will have more to say about this in just a minute. Where traffic was heavy, as along the Via Appia or Flaminia or any of the great highways that fanned out from Rome, they laid a first-quality road, a *via silice strata* 'road paved with silex', i.e. with polygonal paving stones of durable igneous rock, such as basalt (silex), granite, or porphyry. The stones were massive, not uncommonly measuring a foot and a half across and eight inches deep and sometimes much bigger, and were fitted together as cunningly as a jigsaw puzzle to form an absolutely smooth surface. Since igneous rock can be quarried to break off in polygonal chunks, one simple way of getting perfect joints was to put stones together on the road-bed just as they had come out of the quarry; presumably contiguous pieces were marked in the quarries and shipped in a batch. The key problem was to prepare a bed that would not allow any of the stones to sink and form depressions. These were fatal since, over and above the jolts they gave to the passing traffic, they held rainwater which would eventually seep through and undermine the road. As a Roman poet, who had watched the building of a road through soft sandy terrain west of Naples, put it, the engineers had 'to prepare the underbody for a pavement in such a way that the ground would not give, that the foundation would not prove treacher-ous, that the bed would not prove unstable when the paving blocks pressed down on it [sc. under the weight of traffic]'. Sometimes a road went over land so firm that there was no need whatsoever of a bed and all the gangs had to do was level a track and place the paving stones right on the ground; there is a beautifully preserved stretch of the road that ran from Antioch to Chalcis in Syria laid this way (Fig. 7). Where the ground was not that resistant, the gangs trenched until they came to a firm enough layer. Into the trench they set the bed, usually of more or less naturally rounded stones in a mass of clay or clayey earth; the thickness of the bed depended entirely on how deep the trench had to go. When a raised road was called for, as often happened, the bed was built up until it overtopped the ground level to the desired height. The one thing Rome's engineers were finicky about was that the earth or clay used as binder come from elsewhere, not from any trenching done for the road. The sides of the embankments were prevented from being washed away by the addition of

F*

terrace walls of either fieldstone or, where a more decorative effect was sought, of squared stone.

Sometimes the surveyors simply could not avoid cutting across marshes or over sand, and then the road gangs had to go to great lengths to prepare a proper bed. One way was to open a deep trench and simply toss in rock until so ponderous a load of stone had been laid down that a firm bed resulted. Where this would not work, they drove in wooden piers, brought in the carpenters to fashion a grillwork of wood, and then laid a gravel road over the wood.

Once the bed was ready, the masons set about fitting the paving blocks. These were laid so as to leave the road with a pronounced crown, i.e. higher in the middle than at the sides, in order to shed rainwater. In roads running along slopes the same purpose was achieved by tilting the whole surface toward the lower side. Lastly—or at least on the great thoroughfares—a raised stone border was put along each side, and outside the border an unpaved track, some two feet or so wide, was levelled for pedestrians and pack-animals. At intervals high stones were set along the sides to help a traveller mount a horse—most welcome in an age that did not use stirrups (181 below)—or climb into a high-wheeled carriage. And all highways, whether fitted with borders and paths or not, had channels (*fossae*) along one side or both to carry off rainwater.

Not only the bed, but the surfacing as well varied with soil and terrain. In North Africa, even major routes were simply tracks marked out in the sand. In mountainous or other stony areas a road was often made by cutting into the rock a level surface of the appropriate width (Fig. 8); artificial ruts, like those the Greeks and Etruscans had used centuries earlier (69 above), might be added along certain spots to enable carts to move along without danger of skidding (Fig. 8). Sometimes the kind of road had more to do with the facts of life than the facts of construction. Every now and then, for example, we find a piece of road of first quality followed by a long unpaved tract of mediocre workmanship; it looks very much as if expert army engineers did the first part and then, called away for some reason, left the locals to finish off.

The width of roads varied. The Via Appia, Rome's first large-scale road-building project, is in places ten Roman feet wide (about three and a half inches short of ten English feet), in other words, a comfortable two-lane road where carriages could pass abreast with ease. Elsewhere it measures eight feet, which was the minimum the Romans allowed for a two-lane road. Between major points highways were sometimes given three lanes, that is a width of fourteen to eighteen feet. Most of the roads that led into Rome spread to thirty feet or more just before the city gates. All these figures are for the road proper, the part used by horsemen and vehicles. Borders and footpaths would add at least five feet.

In mountainous areas, where road-building was painfully slow work and traffic relatively light, widths were held to a minimum. Through narrow passes roads sometimes slimmed down to a single lane, about six feet wide, with occasional bypasses to enable traffic meeting from opposite directions to get through. Along stretches where neither cutting away the rock nor tunnelling was feasible, the road-builders would pin wooden scaffolding to a cliff to support a wooden road, a rather dangerous expedient since it demanded continuous surveillance and maintenance. Grades were carefully adjusted, but were rather steep by our standards, going as high as 15 per cent. At the Maloja pass between Italy and Switzerland, for example, the modern road uses twenty-two curves to get up a slope that the ancient took in three.

The Romans set their roads high above valley floors in order, among other things, to cross a stream where it could be forded—and they had no compunction about using fords. On occasion they unbent sufficiently to pave the stream bed with flat stones. Where they had to they made bridges, in remote areas with timber, along the main highways with durable structures of stone, or of concrete faced with stone, in the form of an arch or series of arches resting on massive piers. The Via Flaminia crosses a river near Narni over a bridge (Fig. 9) whose central arch stood more than sixty-two feet high and spans more than one hundred feet. A Roman bridge built under Trajan still carries traffic over the Tagus near Merida in western Spain; its six arches rise some 245 feet above the normal level of the water. Roman engineers designed their bridges with long access ramps on either side in order to keep the approaches as nearly horizontal as possible.

As highways rolled on out of populated or active zones into the hinterland, they gradually lost their amenities, the footpaths, the borders, and eventually the elegant surface of polygonal paving stones. Now they were paved only along the approaches to towns, at crossroads, or other important points; the rest was no longer a *via silice strata* but a *via glarea strata* 'road paved with gravel'. The bed was still made in the careful Roman manner, by trenching until firm ground was reached and putting down a thick course of naturally rounded stones packed in clay or clayey earth; where needed, the bottom of the trench received a reinforcing floor of flat stones. The upper part of the bed, worked smooth and given a crown to throw off rainwater, formed the surface; ditches alongside carried the rainwater away. Secondary roads were all made in this or even more primitive ways, down to the *via terrena*, the simple dirt road.

The government's set-up for administering the road system was calculated to favour Italy at the expense of the provinces. In Italy each highway had its own *curator* or commissioner, charged with keeping it in repair and adequately policed. In the provinces the governor had the responsibility for roads along with everything else, and he simply passed along orders to the local communities: they were to keep the army-built highways in repair and to construct from scratch whatever additional roads were needed. How well or how quickly the orders were executed is another matter; communities were often too hard pressed by taxes and the upkeep of other services to do much about roads.

The last step in building a road was to put up *miliaria* 'milestones'. These were placed every Roman mile (1,000 five-foot paces, hence some ninety-five yards shorter than our mile). In Italy each was inscribed with a figure giving the distance from Rome or from the city where the road started (Fig. 10). In the provinces they showed sometimes the distance between towns, sometimes from the roadhead—e.g. roads fanning out from Lyons would carry the number of miles from that city. Occasionally they gave even more information, the distance from either end of the road or from three or four principal points along the road. In Rome itself, at one end of the Forum stood the *miliarium aureum*, the 'golden milestone', which, in letters of gilt, indicated the mileage from Rome along the trunk roads to key points in the empire. Road centres in the provinces had their local equivalent. To the voyager, plodding along on foot or in a slow-moving cart and wondering how long he had to go to get a meal or bed or change of animals, milestones were a godsend, so much so that many a settlement took its name from the stone it was nearest. Some have kept such names right up to the present day. On the road from Marseilles to Aix, four Roman miles out of Marseilles one comes to a village with an area called Cars or Carts, surely a derivative of *quartum*; in Roman times it was *ad quartum lapidem* 'At the Fourth Stone'. Three miles further along, or seven out of Marseilles, is the village of Septèmes, from *septimum* 'seventh'; nine miles out there was in the Middle Ages a *villa de nono*; and fourteen miles out is the town of Milles, which probably got its name from the *miliarium* planted there.

Lining the roadsides along with the milestones were religious monuments, particularly in honour of Mercury, or his Greek equivalent Hermes (cf. 71 above), the patron saint of wayfarers. They ranged from full-fledged roadside sanctuaries through single statues, often simple and rough, down to mere mounds of stones, 'Mercury's heaps'; these somehow symbolized the deity, and passersby carried on the age-old practice of making an obeisance by tossing an additional stone on the pile.

As it happens, the Romans were not the only skilled road-builders of antiquity. On the other side of the world the powerful lords of the Han dynasty of China (c. 200 B.C.– A.D. 200) ruled an equally farflung empire, which they too knit together by means of a comprehensive system of highways. Their engineers, like Rome's, laid the tracks as straight as possible, cutting through forests and bridging streams, and even outdid Rome's when it came to hacking out roads in China's towering mountains or running them over trestles at dizzying heights. They went in for greater width than Rome; fifty feet is mentioned for major routes, wide enough for nine chariots abreast. We cannot confirm the figure since the Chinese never used paving—gravel surfaces satisfied their needs—and accordingly hardly a trace of their ancient roads has survived. We have only contemporary or near contemporary descriptions to go on, and these cannot always be taken as gospel truth.

In Europe during the Middle Ages wherever possible traffic passed over the roads that Rome had built. But by now the horse collar had been invented (181 below), and a vehicle could carry a far heavier load. This put a burden on them that they had never been intended to bear, and the surfaces gradually came to be chewed up as a result. Any new roads that were laid were surfaced with a jumble of stones bound only by what dirt the traffic brought and ground in. In one respect the road-builders of the Middle Ages did surpass the Romans: thanks perhaps to their experience in raising Gothic cathedrals, they put up finer bridges—but allowed them to be approached by grades that were almost impossibly steep.

The Renaissance brought in improved surveying instruments, the seventeenth century the use of earth embankments (rather than stone with an earth binder as was the Roman practice), but Rome's road-building efforts were not really surpassed until the beginning of the nineteenth century, when J. L. McAdam introduced his revolutionary technique of minimizing the road-bed and surfacing with a layer of small cut stones of approximately equal size.

II

On the Road

To travel by land was more time-consuming than by water and infinitely more tiring but, as we saw earlier, there were compensations. For one, storms were rarely a matter of life and death. For another, the season of the year did not have to make a difference. There was no obstacle to starting a trip at any time along the major roads ringing the Mediterranean. Even in mountainous areas travel was merely reduced during the winter months; only periods of heavy snowfall brought it to a complete halt.

A trip by land might involve more baggage than by sea. In addition to the inevitable kitchenware and tableware, towels, bedding, and the like, the traveller probably had to have more changes of clothing, as well as special wear adapted to the rigours of the road: heavy shoes or heavy sandals, broad-brimmed hat (cf. 75 above), and a selection of capes (cf. Fig. 13)—a short light one for milder weather (the Greek *chlamys* or the Roman *lacerna*), another for rainy days (e.g. the Roman *paenula*, made of wool or leather, fitted with a hood, and reaching to the knees), still another for cold days (e.g. the *birrus*, a long wool garment with hood, rather like an Arab burnous). Money and valuables were carried in a purse on a belt about the waist (*zona*) or in a little bag on a cord about the neck (*crumena, ballantion*). Travellers who insisted on knowing the time could equip themselves with a pocket sundial, a little round gadget of bronze (the specimens that have been found range from $1\frac{3}{8}$ to $2\frac{3}{8}$ inches in diameter);

some were designed for use anywhere in the Roman Empire, others in limited areas. Women on the road wore more or less the same clothes as men, though of greater length, reaching to the ankles. If they took along jewellery, they kept it out of sight. 'Bring your gold jewellery with you, but don't wear it!' cautions a soldier writing to his wife who was to join him at his station.

We happen to have—they were by great good fortune unearthed in Egypt—the account books kept by a high Roman official named Theophanes during a trip he made from upper Egypt to Antioch sometime between A.D. 317 and 323. Theophanes took along practically a miniature household. The inventory of his clothing lists three types of tunic (light, ordinary, sleeved), light and heavy capes, various mantles and hoods, a rain-wrap, light felt shoes as well as heavy sandals, numerous changes of underwear, and several pairs of riding breeches. Then there was the kitchen equipment: cooking utensils, tableware, napkins; also oil lamps, both standing and hanging. For washing and bathing he carried olive oil, alum, and natron (a natural compound of sodium carbonate and sodium bicarbonate abundant in Egypt), and myrrh as an after-washing lotion, and a supply of wash-cloths, hand towels, face towels, and bath towels. For sleeping he had mattresses, sheets, blankets, pillows, rugs, and a selection of cushions.

Since a traveller put up with friends or family wherever he could, inevitably there were gifts or things they had requested to cram into the bags. 'When you come,' the soldier mentioned above instructs his wife, 'bring ten wool fleeces, six jars of olives, four jars of honey, my shield—just the new one—and my helmet. Bring my lances too. And bring the fittings for my tent.' Luckily for the poor lady, the projected trip was down the Nile and would be done comfortably by boat. If a traveller was heading for areas where inns were few and poorly stocked, he had to make room for food and drink on top of everything else. Theophanes' party, for example, when crossing the desert between Palestine and Egypt laid in extra supplies of bread, eggs, and wine; the wine alone amounted to 150 litres or more. More baggage inevitably meant more servants to oversee, pack, and unpack it; Theophanes had so many that their upkeep accounted for well-nigh a third of his daily expenditures.

In Italy or along the great routes that linked major centres the roads were good enough to permit hauling baggage in carts or wagons as well as on pack-animals, which in the Near East now included camels (cf. 54 below), in addition to the ubiquitous donkeys and mules. Off the main roads pack-animals or porters were the rule, with porters favoured over animals in mountainous or heavily forested areas.

As the date for departure approached, the superstitious anxiously thought over their dreams. For a journey by land, no less than by sea, was subject to the proper omens. To dream of quail presaged being tricked or meeting bandits en route, owls meant meeting storms or bandits, wild boars meant meeting storms. A gazelle foretold an easy or hard trip, depending on its physical condition. Donkeys meant a safe trip but slow. Garlands of narcissi or marshes were bad omens, clear bright air or stars good. Certain gods, such as Hermes or Aphrodite, augured a good journey, others, such as the Dioscuri or Dionysus, a bad one. A dream in which statues of the gods seemed to move was favourable.

If his dreams were favourable, or if he was not the kind to take such things seriously, the voyager proceeded to get himself and his baggage from house or inn to a convenient town gate. Since in many cities wheeled traffic was not allowed to circulate within the walls during daylight hours (263 below), this could mean leading a parade of servants and hired bearers or pack animals, all loaded down with gear. Those who had the money were able to rent litters or sedan chairs to carry themselves and whoever went along with them.

Once at the city gate, the voyager had several possibilities to ponder over. If he was alone he might choose to go on foot—if poor, he had no alternative—trudging stolidly on his way; along some of the very first-class Roman roads there were pavements to accommodate such traffic. En route he might hitch an occasional ride on a ponderous *plaustrum*, a farm or work wagon. These were hauled at a snail's pace by a team of oxen and announced their coming from afar by the tortured creaking of their wheels; the only lubricants available, dregs of olive pressings or animal fat, were too expensive to be used very liberally. For those who could afford to hire a carriage, there were livery stables conveniently located at the city gates and offering a wide range of choice. Couples or single persons with little baggage might take a *birota*, a two-wheeled passenger cart (Fig. 15), perhaps an *essedum*, large and elaborate and therefore preferred by the emperors and their like, perhaps a *covinnus* or a *cisium*, both of which were lighter and simpler and hence a much commoner sight on the roads. All were almost always pulled not by one but by a pair of horses or fast-stepping mules, for reasons to be explained in a moment. They accommodated two to three passengers. A larger party, or anyone following a route that led over slow secondary roads, would hire a *reda* (Fig. 13), a robust open four-wheeled wagon drawn by one or two pairs of mules. The *covinnus* was so light and handy, it could be driven by one of the passengers; other carts and wagons had not only a driver (*mulio*) but a man at the bridle (*cursor*) who led the animals along at a swift walking pace (cf. Fig. 15). More comfortable and better suited for family travel was the *carruca*, the Roman descendant of the age-old covered wagon (25 above) with an arched leather or cloth canopy (Fig. 12); certain types were fitted for sleeping (*carruca dormitoria*). People of wealth, particularly ladies of the court, frequently used the *carpentum*. This was a heavy two-wheeled de luxe carriage with a sub-stantial roof supported by ornamental columns; the sides could be closed off with draw curtains, often gaily decorated, often of expensive fabrics such as silk. The differences between a homely *reda* and an elegant *carpentum* were solely for the eyes of the beholders; their riding qualities were the same. Both had wooden wheels with iron tyres and were innocent of springs; the occupants jounced along feeling every bump in the road. The way to avoid such discomfort was to go in a litter (*lectica*) rather than a carriage; there was no longer any prejudice against them (67 above), and they were also available for hire at the city gates. The travelling litter consisted of a couch fitted with canopy and draw curtains; the rider lolled at his ease as six or eight husky slaves bore it along on their shoulders. For long journeys, the men could be replaced by a pair of mules harnessed to the carrying poles, one ahead and one behind. A bearer-borne litter was the most painless way of travelling, but inevitably the slowest.

The emperors and others of high society or of wealth took to the road in the grandest imaginable style. They packed a veritable household to spare them the ignominy or discomfort of stopping at any inns save those able to accommodate a royal party: tents and commodes as well as the usual cooking utensils, bedding, and tableware; some of the last could be so precious and fragile it had to be carried by hand and not trusted to a jolting wagon. An army of attendants was *de rigueur*. Horace ridicules one Roman worthy who, for the short trip from Rome to his villa at Tibur, took along no less than five slaves, even though he was so tight-fisted that the only gear they were called on to handle were the two items he refused to be without—wine jug and commode. A lavish spender's entourage could include not merely the customary maids, valets, chefs, scullions, and so on, but exotic Moors and Numidians in eye-catching costumes to run ahead and make sure no traffic encumbered the way, or mincing pages with their faces masked so that the sun or cold would not hurt their delicate complexions. Matched teams of mules or horses, covered with embroidered or purple cloths and fitted with gilded trappings, pulled the vehicles, which were themselves gorgeous affairs adorned with gold and silver statuary and upholstered in silk. The emperor Claudius, who liked to play dice, had a travelling carriage fitted as a gaming room. Commodus had one with seats that swivelled, so that he could adjust them to catch the sun in cool weather or a breeze in hot, and others rigged with a gadget that recorded the miles covered. The Elder Pliny, a compulsive writer, always made room for a stenographer who had pen and tablets at the ready.

Some travellers went on muleback or on a slow-gaited cob, with their servants trudging in their wake. Few rode fast saddle horses, since horses, as in times past (52 above), were chiefly for cavalrymen, hunters, or dispatch-riders. Expense was one, but not the only, reason for this. Riding a horse in ancient times, particularly for long distances, was a wearisome business: stirrups were unknown—this crucial piece of equipment did not come into use in Europe until the ninth century A.D.—and saddles were rudimentary, often consisting of little more than a cloth on the horse's back. In fact, as we noted earlier (24 above), the ancients never realized the full potentiality of the horse either as mount or draught animal. As mount they limited its usefulness not only by riding without stirrups or a proper saddle but also by leaving it unshod; they did have certain sandal-like devices of metal, leather, or straw, which slipped over the hoof, but these, made for mules and camels as well as horses, apparently were only temporary expedients for special circumstances, to protect a sore hoof or to provide a grip on slippery ground. The iron horseshoe fastened permanently with nails found general acceptance only from the eighth century A.D. on. And, as draught animal, the ancients insisted on putting it in a harness basically designed for oxen, setting a pair of horses on either side of a draught-pole, and harnessing them by means of a breast-band to a yoke at the front end (Figs. 12, 13, 15). The breast-band had an unfortunate tendency to slide up the throat and press on the windpipe; the harder the pull, the greater the choking effect. The padded horse-collar, which made the point of pressure the shoulders instead of the neck, did not come into being until the Middle Ages. From the beginning of the second century A.D. on, there are examples of wagons fitted with shafts (Fig. 11), which permitted the use of a single horse instead of a pair, but it seems to have found limited acceptance despite its advantages of cheapness and convenience, particularly on narrow country roads.

The voyager, having picked a conveyance or riding and pack animals, having loaded up and got under way, next faced the problem of where to stop for the night, and, if he was travelling with hired gear, where to find a change of animals and equipment. As it happened, his choices were often determined by the network of inns and hostels that belonged to the *cursus publicus*, the government post.

Rome's *cursus publicus* was created by Augustus, but the idea of such a service was hardly original with him; it is an essential tool for any government that rules extended areas. The earliest examples we know of go back to the third millennium B.C., when the city-states of Mesopotamia first began to build miniature empires (36 above). Five centuries before Augustus' day the Persians were using the highly developed service that Herodotus admired so (53 above); on the other side of Asia, at just about the same time, China's Chou dynasty had built up an equally efficient system. And, by the third century B.C., China's Han dynasty and the super-centralized administration that the Ptolemies had set up in Egypt were running the nearest thing to a modern postal system that the ancient world was to know. The carriers were all mounted. In China the post-stations were some eleven miles apart, with two or more substations in between. In Egypt they were sparser, at intervals of six hours by horse-back or roughly thirty miles apart. Some records of one of these Egyptian post offices have been dug up by the archeologists, so we have a fair idea of the way they worked. Thanks to Egypt's geography, mail had to go only north and south, along the ribbon of inhabited land bordering the Nile. The offices handled at least four deliveries daily, two from each direction. For packages and other heavier matter there was an auxiliary camel-back service.

When Augustus conquered and annexed Egypt in 30 B.C., the system was right at hand to serve as a model. He, however, was interested neither in speed nor regular delivery. What he sought was a facility which would forward dispatches when necessary and permit him to interrogate the carriers as well as read the papers they brought. So he fashioned a service in which there were no relays: each messenger went himself the whole route, and since time was not of the essence, travelled in carriages rather than on horseback. As the system developed, the couriers were more and more drawn from the army, especially from the elite unit called *speculatores* 'scouts'; instead of scouting the situation of an enemy, they scouted, as it were, the situation at the headquarters they were delivering to. A gravestone of a *speculator* has survived which bears a relief picturing the deceased in the course of his duties (Fig. 13). We see a *reda*, an open four-wheeled carriage, drawn by three horses, two in the yoke and a trace-horse. On the box is a driver who, plying the whip, keeps the team stepping smartly along. On a bench behind is the courier wearing a hooded travelling cloak and holding what seems to be a riding crop. Behind him, facing rearward, is his servant, who sits on the baggage and clutches a lance with a distinctive head, a special insignia of office showing that his master was attached to the staff of the local governor.

In Egypt the Romans may well have maintained the Ptolemies' mail service, since it was so feasible a system there. But everywhere else the Roman post operated as Augustus had designed it, making sporadic deliveries according to need —or rather the emperor's need, since officially only men carrying dispatches from him or for him were entitled to the privileges of the *cursus publicus*. Every user had to have a *diploma*, as a post warrant was called, signed by the emperor or, in his absence, his authorized agent; governors of provinces could also issue them, but they disposed of a limited number only, rationed out by the emperor. A *diploma*, entitling one to travel with the use of government maintained facilities, was a prized possession, and inevitably some fell into hands which did not deserve them (188 below). When the emperor Otho was defeated in battle in A.D. 69, with the inevitable consequence that warrants bearing his name would no longer be honoured, an interested party hushed up the news and spread word of a victory in order to keep the precious documents alive.

At the beginning of the third century A.D., Septimius Severus altered the system radically: he added the *cursus clabularis*, a transport service charged with the duty of purveying provisions for the army. Overnight the organization swelled in size and became more complicated. The administrative staff had to be expanded, there was more intensive use of all facilities, there had to be an increase in the size and number of the post stations, and wagons and heavy duty draught animals had to be added to the couriers' light carriages and fast-stepping teams. The *diploma* now took two forms, the partial warrant (*evectio*) which authorized transport only, and the full (*tractoria*) authorizing both transport and subsistence.

We know the operations of the *cursus* best in the fully developed form it achieved by the second half of the fourth century A.D., when it had long been in use as a transport as well as dispatch service. All along the routes at strategic intervals were more or less well-equipped inns (201 below) called *mansiones* or *stationes*; the first term originally applied to places with the facilities to handle an imperial party, the second to posts maintained by the road police, but by this time the two had gradually merged. In between the *mansiones* or *stationes* were very simple hostels (202 below), *mutationes* 'changing places' as they were sometimes called, which could supply the minimum of a traveller's needs—a bite to eat, a bed, and, as the name implies, a change of beasts or vehicle. The distance from one *mansio* to the next depended on the terrain and how thickly an area was populated, but in general an effort was made to keep them twenty-five to thirty-five miles apart, that is, the length of an average day's travel. In densely settled districts, such as around the capital, they tended to be a good deal closer. There might be one or two hostels between a pair of *mansiones*, again depending on the terrain. For example, a traveller setting out from Aquileia at the head of the Adriatic to cross the Alps into Yugoslavia, which was the main route from northern Italy to the east, came to a simple hostel at eleven miles, a second one twelve miles further on, and then, after another twelve miles to make thirty-five in all, arrived at an inn (*mansio*). Next day he climbed twelve miles to the top of the pass, where he found a hostel, and then ten miles down the other side to an inn.

The inns varied widely in the range and quality of what they could provide, from the so-called *praetoria* with accommodations to put up a royal party down to modest establishments that were but a cut above the hostels. A fully equipped inn offered practically everything a traveller might possibly need: meals and sleeping quarters; change of clothing for the drivers and postilions; change of animals (big stations stabled as many as forty horses or mules), carriages, and drivers (*muliones*); grooms (*stratores*); escorts for bringing back vehicles and teams to the previous station (*hippocomi*); porters (*bastagarii, catabolenses*); veterinarians (*mulomedici*) to put to rights animals in trouble; cartwrights (*carpentarii*) to put to rights equipment in trouble.

The inns and hostels of the *cursus publicus* were not built specifically for it, nor did they service only those travelling on official business, although these had an ironclad priority. The post, despite the fact that it was run wholly for the benefit of the central government, was largely maintained by the communities along the routes. The emperors simply selected given existing inns of the required quality and incorporated them into the system, requiring them to put up without charge any holder of a *diploma* who came along. Only in remote areas, as on mountain passes or along lonely tracts of road, did they have to build from scratch (202 below); such places, too, to help meet expenses put up all voyagers, private as well as official. Vehicles, animals, drivers, stablehands—all were requisitioned, wherever possible, from local citizens. With the passage of time these found the upkeep of the post a galling burden, since its demands grew steadily, not merely the legitimate demands but those of unscrupulous officials who would arbitrarily seize horses and equipment or barefacedly bed down unauthorized travellers in the inns. Every now and then, the emperors tried to do something about the situation. Severus, for example, shifted a good part of the costs to the government treasury; by Constantine's time, however, all expense was again on the backs of the locals. Emperor after emperor enacted stringent laws to eliminate abuses and to keep the service up to the mark. There were regulations governing the number of wagons or animals that could be requisitioned, the size of the wagons, maximum permissible loads, numbers of drivers to be used, routes to be followed, weight of saddles and saddlebags, even the size and nature of the whips. One regulation stated that 'no person shall remunerate any driver, cartwright, or veterinarian employed on the public post, since . . . they obtain subsistence allowances and clothing, which is believed sufficient for them'—in other words, no tipping allowed. Rarely have no-tipping rules been made to work, and all signs indicate that neither it nor very many of the other well-meaning statutes on the books were adequately enforced.

Anyone using the *cursus publicus* had to know exactly where the various inns and hostels belonging to it were located. Handlists called *itineraria* were available, which detailed for a given route the stopping places along it and how far each was from the next. There were also maps designed specifically to show not only the location of such places but what they had to offer. By good fortune a copy made in the Middle Ages of one of these has survived, the so-called Tabula Peutingeriana (Fig. 14). Done on an elongated piece of parchment that is no more than thirteen inches wide but over twenty-two feet long, it presents a map of the Roman empire as distorted as if seen in a trick mirror. This was done on purpose: the cartographer's sole aim was to give a schematic picture of the Roman road system in a form suitable for ready reference. He put in just about the same information we find on a modern automobile map: lines showing routes; names of cities, towns, and other stopping places; numbers indicating the distance in Roman miles between them. In addition and most interesting, alongside many of the names there stands a little coloured picture-symbol. These serve the same purpose as the surprisingly similar symbols used in the *Guide Michelin* or other modern guide books, to show at a quick glance the nature of the facilities available for spending a night. A schematized picture of a four-sided building with a court in the centre stands for a town or country inn of some consequence, one that could offer a considerable range of services. A picture of the front of a house with a twin-peaked roof stands for a less pretentious country inn. Twin cupolas instead of peaks means the same grade of inn but with ample water available. A single-peaked boxlike cottage stands for a very modest inn. Names with no picture alongside probably indicate the simplest form of hostel, places that could furnish little more than water, shelter, a bare meal, and a fresh relay of animals. For example, a traveller leaving Rome by the Via Aurelia, which ran north along the west coast, could see by the map (cf. Fig. 14) that his first convenient stopping place would be Alsium, eighteen miles from the capital, with minimum facilities (no picture) and that from here it was ten miles to Pyrgi, with minimum facilities; then six miles to Punicum, with minimum facilities but close to Aquae Apollinares, with first-rate facilities (four-sided building); then nine miles to Castrum Novum, with quite good facilities (twin-peaked building); then four miles to Aquae Tauri, with the same facilities as Aquae Apollinares, and so on.

Government couriers hustled along from station to station at an average of five miles an hour for a total of fifty miles in a normal day's travelling. Thus, a dispatch from Rome would reach Brindisi in about seven days, Byzantium (where Constantinople was later founded) in about twenty-five, Antioch in about forty, Alexandria in about fifty-five. During emergencies, travelling night and day, they could treble this speed. When the legions mutinied at Mainz on the Rhine in A.D. 69, the news reached Rome in some eight or nine days; the messenger had averaged better than 150 miles per day.

The traveller charged with government business, and hence with the facilities of the *cursus publicus* at his disposal, had few problems: he would present his *diploma* to the nearest authorized inn and be issued an appropriate conveyance. He would consult his handlist or map for the stopping places available along his route, and at these he would eat, sleep, and pick up changes of animals and equipment until he reached his destination. Private voyagers were officially barred from the *cursus publicus*, but, human nature being what it is, exceptions were inevitable. 'My lord,' wrote Pliny, governor of a province in the north of Asia Minor in A.D. 109–111, to the emperor Trajan, 'up to this moment, I have never accommodated anyone with a *diploma*. . . . However, my wife heard that her grandfather died, and since she wanted to run to see her aunt, I thought it unnecessarily severe to deny her the use of a *diploma*'. Libanius, scion of one of Antioch's leading families, arriving at Constantinople in A.D. 336 with his own mules exhausted, was chagrinned to discover that 'the man I had hopes would send me on to Athens with a team from the Imperial Post . . . had fallen from power, and . . . , said he, this was the one thing he could not do'. The aristocrat Sidonius Apollinaris, who went from his home town in southern France to Rome in A.D. 467, reports that, as soon as he emerged from the town gate, he 'found the government post at my disposal, like someone summoned by a letter from the emperor'. These cases involve the time-honoured relaxing of the rules in favour of the highly placed; more serious and frequent were the cases involving political influence, bribery, even the blatant sale of post warrants. The regulations on the books against unauthorized use of the *cursus publicus* steadily increased, the penalties became stiffer (selling a *diploma* was punishable by death), but how effectively they were enforced is an open question.

The private voyager who had no access, legitimate or illegitimate, to the government post would still find himself putting up at inns and hostels that formed part of the network, because in many areas they were the only ones available and elsewhere were presumably the best. Moreover, if not travelling in a carriage or with animals of his own, he would find himself applying to them for what was available for hire. Along the open road, if he reached a station just after an official party had come through and had requisitioned everything in sight, he had no alternative except to wait. In any event, he inevitably moved along more slowly than the government couriers. In normal terrain, with no toilsome slopes to negotiate, he did about fifteen to twenty miles a day on foot, some twenty-five to thirty in a carriage. Forty, even forty-five, was possible but it meant an exhaustingly long and hard day's travel. The stopping places along the open roads were spaced to accommodate such speeds. For example, an itinerary of the fourth century A.D., prepared for use by pilgrims going from Bordeaux to Jerusalem, lists for the stretch of sixty-two Roman miles from Toulouse to Carcassonne: nine miles to a *mutatio* (hostel) at Nonum, then eleven miles to a *mutatio* (hostel) at Vicesimum, then nine miles to a *mansio* (inn) at Elusione, then nine miles to a *mutatio* at Sostomagus, then ten miles to Vicus Hebromago (a village), then six miles to a *mutatio* at Cedros, then eight miles to Carcassonne. Carriages, in other words, were expected to do the trip in two days, covering twenty-nine miles the first to spend the night at Elusione, and thirty-three the next. The *mutationes*, the modest roadhouses in between, were set eight to ten miles apart on the average. In difficult terrain, as we would expect, the stopping places were closer together. Between Arles and Milan, for example, a journey that included crossing the Alps, the average distance between them diminished to six miles.

To get some idea of what it was like to journey along the roads during Roman times, of what were the traveller's day to day experiences, let us follow three very different men making very different kinds of trips. The first is the Roman administrator Theophanes, mentioned several times above, who was sped by the government post on official business from upper Egypt to Antioch and back. The second is the Greek intellectual Aristides, a private citizen travelling on his own along more or less back-country ways in Asia Minor. The third is the poet Horace, who accompanied one of Augustus' great ministers of state down the Appian Way in the days before Augustus had brought the government post into existence.

On 12 April in one of the years between A.D. 317 and 323, Theophanes left Pelusium (not far from the modern Port Said) on the edge of Egypt proper. He was accompanied by at least two subordinate officials, a steward, a clerk, and a host of servants. We have, as it were, a worm's eye view of his trip, one derived not from a formal description but from some preserved pages of the ledger in which his clerks recorded the points reached and the daily expenses incurred at each. Since nowhere are there entries for lodgings or the hire of animals, it is clear that Theophanes and his party were enjoying the privileges of the public post. On the other hand, his daily outlays for food show that he did not have a courier's full warrant, but one that authorized only transport and lodging.

Details are lacking for the voyage out, and about all we can do is reconstruct his itinerary and speed. The party took four days to plod across the desert between Egypt and Palestine, never doing more than twenty-six miles in a day and one day doing as little as sixteen. Once in the land of milk and honey, however, they stepped up the pace sharply to average forty a day for six days, which brought them right to Tyre. Here they let up a bit, averaging under thirty a day for the next eight days to Laodicea. From Laodicea to the final destination at Antioch was a good sixty-four miles but, like horses smelling the stable, they reeled it all off in a single day, arriving on 30 April. The trip had taken eighteen days in all.

On 19 July Theophanes readied his party for the return. A load of food supplies was purchased in anticipation for departure the next morning: fine bread for Theophanes and the others who shared his table, cheap bread for the servants, jars of local wine, 2 lb. and 1 oz. of beef or veal for the master's dinner, fruit (grapes, apricots, watermelon), cabbage, olive oil, the special strong cooking sauce called garum, honey for sweetening, and wood for the cooking fire. The following day, after adding a purchase of sausages and apples, the party got under way; probably it was late in the morning, since they stopped for the night at some village only fourteen miles along. On the 21st, however, they put all of fifty miles behind them to reach Laodicea. Theophanes must have had business here because they stayed in town all of the 22nd, using some of the time to lay in more supplies: the usual two grades of bread, 1 lb. 6 oz. of beef for the master's dinner, and more fruits and wine. Theophanes was particular about his wine: at Laodicaea the pint he had for his lunch cost him almost as much as all the vin ordinaire he bought for his squad of servants.

On the 23rd they were back on the road and by the 25th were in Byblos, having covered a respectable 140 miles in three days. Our connoisseur must have treated himself to a particularly good wine here, since the ledger records an expenditure for snow, which must have come from the heights of the Lebanon that rears up behind the city, to cool it. This luxury was not very expensive, considering the trouble it took to get it; the wine for dinner cost 700 drachmas, the snow only 100. They came to Beirut, twenty-four miles further on, on the 26th, where they were able to lay in a variety of fruits (grapes, figs, peaches, apricots) and re-stock on cleaning materials (natron, bath oil, soap). The next day's stop was Sidon, thirty-four miles along, and here eggs were bought in for the master's dinner (safer no doubt than meat in the height of summer). The entries for the following few days are fragmentary, and all we can do is trace the party's progress: thirty-six miles to Tyre on 28 July, forty-five to Ptolemais on the 29th, and forty-four to Caesarea on the 30th, with a stop for lunch at a *mutatio* on the way. The next day they also lunched at a *mutatio*, one that had an animal available to slaughter for them, since an entry records the purchase of 4 lb. 2 oz. of beef or veal here. They stopped for the night at Antipatris, having covered thirty-three miles. Lunch at Gebala the next day (1 August) included lamb and pork rather than beef or veal, and at a fraction the cost. By evening they had done the forty-three miles to Ascalon, where Theophanes had eggs for dinner and everyone enjoyed a wide variety of local fruits: peaches, plums, grapes, figs, apples. The second of August brought them thirty-nine miles to Raphia, where dinner was cheese and goat's meat, and the fruits melons, grapes, and mulberries. Another thirty-eight miles on 3 August and they were at Rhinocoloura, the jump-off point for the desert crossing. Here they stocked up. Theophanes had eggs for dinner, and laid in some extra for the following day. They bought in triple supplies of bread and, since the desert is a thirsty place, no less than 140 to 160 litres of the local wine. And the master prepared for the austerity ahead by treating himself and some guests at lunch to a wine that cost exactly one-half of what the 140 litres cost. At the desert hostel the next day (4 August) they were able to pick up some cheese for lunch and dinner and some grapes and water-melon for dessert, but the hostel they stopped at for lunch on 5 August apparently had nothing at all to offer. By nightfall they were at Pelusium in Egypt and back, so to speak, in civilization. They celebrated by buying not only eggs and cheese but also dried fish, while some of the party had snails for lunch. And the next day, for the first time in the eighteen since leaving Antioch, they had fresh fish.

In the summer of A.D. 165 or perhaps a few years later, Aristides, a well-known public lecturer, was stricken by a fresh attack of illness after a span of fairly good health and decided to leave his sick bed at Smyrna and go to the famous sanctuary of Asclepius at Pergamon, where he had enjoyed some near miraculous recoveries before. He describes the trip in detail in one of his essays. The morning of the day of departure he had the baggage loaded on carts or wagons to be sent ahead with the servants and wait for him at Myrina, a town along the way. When the preparations had all finally been completed, it was noon and too hot for him to be out on the road. He waited around a few hours until the sun lost some of its bite, and about half past three in the afternoon he and his party got into their carriages and started off. By seven that evening, they had covered fourteen Roman miles and arrived at an inn a short distance from the point where the road crossed the river Hermus. He debated whether to pass the night there, but decided against it—there was no sign of his baggage, the inn was pretty bad, and, as darkness set in, a cool invigorating wind was springing up. They crossed the river and by about 10 P.M. had covered ten more miles to the next town, Larissa. The inn here was just as discouraging, still no sign of the baggage, so he was just as pleased to keep moving. By midnight or a little later he was at Cyme, only to find everything shut. Aristides again was not unhappy: the party had covered thirty-five miles, the cool evening had turned into a chilly night, all the others were begging for a halt, but he by now had the bit in his teeth, and there was no stopping him. About four in the morning they clattered wearily into Myrina—and there, sitting in front of one of the inns were the servants with

G

the baggage still all packed: they had arrived so late they found everything closed for the night. With forty-two miles behind them and no sleep for almost twenty-four hours, the whole party was dropping with fatigue. There was a pallet lying in the vestibule of the inn and they wasted time trying out places to set it, but to no avail, there was no getting comfortable on it. The only thing left to do was bang on likely doors; they did, but could not wake a soul. Finally they found a way to get into a friend's house—but the gate porter had let the fire go out, so they had to grope their way through in the dark. While a fire was being started, dawn broke. Aristides refused to let up at this point and waste the daylight in sleep; he roused the company and grimly made them push on. After stopping to offer sacrifice to Apollo at a sanctuary along the way, they finally bedded down at Elaea, twelve miles beyond Myrina. The following day they covered sixteen more to the final halt at Pergamon. It had been a gruelling grind for a well man, let alone one hurrying to a sanatorium.

In 38 or 37 B.C., the poet Horace travelled from Rome to Brindisi as member of an embassy headed by one of Augustus' great ministers, Maecenas. On his return, he wrote up his experiences in chatty, lighthearted verses. He set out with a friend—they were to meet up with the rest later—along the Appian way, most likely in a carriage. The first day they covered sixteen miles and stopped at Aricia at a 'modest inn', the second day twenty-seven to Forum Appii—'we divided into two days', remarks Horace, 'a journey that faster stepping travellers than ourselves make in one; the Via Appia is easier on those who don't take it in a hurry.' Forum Appii was 'full of boatmen and nasty tavern keepers', chiefly because of a barge service it offered: travellers could, toward evening, board a little barge there which, towed by a mule down a canal through the Pontine marshes, would bring them while they slept almost to Terracina, the next major stop, thereby saving them a day on the road. At Appi Forum Horace's troubles started:

Because of the water, which was horrible, I declare my belly a public enemy and wait, not very happily, for my fellow travellers to finish dinner. When it was time to board, the sailors hollered at our servants, and our servants at them: 'This way with the boat! You're jamming three hundred people aboard—hey, that's enough!' By the time the fares are collected and the mule hitched up, a whole hour has been lost. Then there was no sleep for anyone, thanks to the murderous mosquitoes, the frogs in the swamp, and the sailor and one of the passengers—soused on stale wine, they were taking turns serenading absent girl-friends. Finally the passenger gets tired out and falls asleep, and our shiftless sailor unhitches the mule to let it graze, tethers it to a stone, stretches out on his back, and snores away. By now it's dawn, and we notice that the boat is standing still. A hothead jumps up, flails away at sailor and mule on flanks and head with a willow branch, and finally, about 10 A.M., we dock.

They stayed the night at Terracina; here they met up with Maecenas and the main body of the party, and Horace took a moment off to get some black salve for his eyes, which were bothering him. The next day brought them to Formiae, twenty-six miles further along, where a local aristocrat extended them the hospitality of his villa. The following morning a number of others including Vergil joined them, and the party was complete. The next day they did twenty-seven miles to a very simple inn for the night, and 'from there the mules put down their loads in Capua in good time. Maecenas goes off to play, Vergil and I to sleep.' They had arrived early since they only had seventeen miles to cover in getting to Capua. The day after, twenty-one miles further along, they had the best accommodations of the trip at a sumptuous villa owned by one of the notables in the party. They lingered long over dinner, being amused no end by a time-honoured and timeless form of entertainment, a pair of professional comics flinging insults at each other ('I'd say you look like a horse. With horns.' 'You talking—with that scar? What happened, somebody cut off the ones on your forehead?'). Maybe they slept late as well, because all they made the following day was eleven miles to Beneventum. Here the innkeeper was so anxious to do the right thing by his distinguished guests that he almost burned down his kitchen while barbecuing some scrawny fowl for their dinner. By now they were going through the Apennines, and the next night's stand was at a little hostel well in the mountains. Horace had a bad time here. The firewood was damp and the chimney smoked, which made his sore eyes water. And he 'stupidly stayed up till midnight waiting for a liar of a girl'; she never came, he had an erotic dream, and soiled his bedclothes. The next day they did twenty-four miles in wagons (*redae*) to another mountain town where the water was the world's worst but the bread was superb; smart travellers, Horace comments, usually carry off an extra supply since the bread at Canusium, the next stop, is hard as rock. From Canusium they arrived at Rubi dead tired; it had been a long twenty-four miles, and constant rain hardly helped. The day after they made twenty-three miles from Rubi to Bari; the weather was better but the road poorer. By now they were on the coastal plain and the end was almost in sight; they stepped up the pace, reeling off thirty-seven miles to Egnatia on their next to last day (where they got a good laugh when shown the local miracle, an altar that burned incense without fire) and all of thirty-nine to Brindisi on the last—'the end of a long journey as well as scroll' quips Horace in the closing line of his poem. It had taken him about two weeks to do some 375 miles, and he had had his taste of the typical ups and downs of travel: some sunny weather, swift travel on major highways, first-rate accommodations, good company, lots of fun; some rain, slow going over bad roads, primitive hotels, traveller's tummy, nights without sleep, and a rendezvous with a girl who never showed up.

12

Inns and Restaurants

Where to stay? It was a crucial question as a traveller walked off a dock, or neared the gate of a town, or noted night darkening the sky while on the open road.

If he was in the service of the government, he would go to the nearest facility maintained by the *cursus publicus*. If he was well-to-do or noble or both, there were a number of equally simple alternatives. He might have a house or estate at the intended destination (195 above), and all he need do was alert the servants to his arrival. Here, for example, is the text of a letter sent in A.D. 256 by a wealthy landowner to one of his caretakers:

> God willing, expect us to come to you on the 23rd. As soon as you receive this letter of mine, do your best to have the bathroom heated, having logs brought in and collecting chaff from everywhere, so that we can bathe in warmth since it is now winter. . . . See to it that we have everything we need, especially a nice pig for my guests—but let it be a good one, not like the last time, skinny and worthless. And send word to the fishermen to bring us some fish.

The writer lived in Egypt, and the estate he intended to visit was in the Fayum; letters like this must have been received day in and day out by bailiffs and caretakers all over the Roman Empire. Owners of villas that lay more than a day's travel from town often maintained lodgings at strategic points to provide shelter during the journey there and back (138 above).

When people of means had no establishment of their own to put up at, they did the next best thing: they arranged to stay with friends, family, business associates, or other acquaintances; a rich man's mansion often included for the use of guests a whole separate wing complete with its own street entrance, bedrooms, and dining rooms. Where such hospitality was unavailable, as on trips through relatively remote areas, they would pack tents in addition to the usual traveller's gear and camp out—in elegant style to be sure, waited upon by the omnipresent staff of servants. Finally, if all else failed, they could always turn to the local authorities. When Cato the Younger, after finishing his military service, toured through parts of Asia Minor he used, Plutarch reports,

the following procedure. At daybreak he would send ahead his baker and cook to the place where he planned to put up. These, very decorously and quietly, would go into town and, if Cato did not happen to have acquaintances or friends of the family there, would prepare for his reception at an inn, without bothering anybody. Where there was no inn, they would turn to the local officials for hospitality, gratefully accepting whatever was offered.

Cato, who liked to project an image of himself as a man of simple tastes, as one who asked for no more than any of his fellows, was an exception. The average highly placed Roman on the road expected the purple carpet. A letter like the following, which was excavated in Egypt and was no doubt the work of a clerk in the Ptolemies' foreign office, must have been typical. Dated 112 B.C., it is addressed to an official in the chief city of Egypt's Fayum, Arsinoe or Crocodilopolis 'Crocodile town' as it was also called from the presence there of a sacred crocodile, the local god:

Lucius Memmius, a Roman Senator in a position of considerable importance and honour is sailing [up the Nile] from Alexandria to the district of which Arsinoe is capital to see the sights. Receive him in the grand style, and see to it that, at the usual points, lodgings are prepared and landing facilities to them are completed, . . . and that the gifts, a list of which is attached below, are presented to him at the landing places. Also provide furniture for the lodgings, the special food for feeding to Petesouchos [the crocodile god] and the crocodiles, whatever is needed for a visit to the Labyrinth, offerings, sacrifices. . . . In general, remember to do everything possible to please him; put forth all your efforts.

Memmius, in other words, was to get specially prepared housing, gifts, and guided tours to the two key sights in the neighbourhood, the sanctuary of the sacred crocodiles and the Labyrinth (101 above). Still another letter, dealing with a visit that took place a century earlier, shows how elaborate such preparations could be. This one is from a local official who has been asked to get things in order for the arrival of some notable. He writes:

In accordance with your letter, we have made ready for the visit of Chrysippus, Secretary of Finance and Chief of the Bodyguard, 10 white-head fowl, 5 domestic geese, 50 fowl; of game birds, 50 geese, 200 birds, 100 pigeons. We have borrowed 5 riding donkeys, and have in readiness 40 pack donkeys. And we are getting on with building the road.

It sounds as if Chrysippus and his fellow travellers totalled five (exclusive of servants, who would walk), and that their gear needed no less than forty beasts of burden; they were not exactly travelling light. They must have come by way of the Nile, and the poor locals, on top of supplying the animals to transport the entourage from the river to their town, had to fix up the road to take a pack train this size. The distinguished guests were obviously going to eat well and plentifully—if they happened to like fowl. Another document of this kind reveals that, when the governor of Egypt stopped at the town of Hermopolis in A.D. 145 or a few years later, the combined resources of dozens of local worthies had to be called upon to furnish a proper menu, which, over and above the domestic and wild fowl that Chrysippus had been served, offered veal, pork, dried and fresh fish, cheese, olives, lentils, and vegetables. Obviously playing compulsory host in this fashion could become a burden. In one of his best-known letters Pliny the Younger tells how a certain coastal town was forced into taking drastic action when it suddenly became a tourist attraction thanks to a remarkable dolphin that one day joined the children swimming off the beach and from then on desported with them daily. 'All the government officials poured in to see the sight, and the unexpected expense of their arrival and staying around wore down this modest community. And, in the last analysis, the place itself was losing its peace and privacy. So the decision was taken to kill off surreptitiously what was causing the influx.'

The ordinary traveller, with no claim on official hospitality, no well-to-do friends to put him up at their various abodes or provide letters of recommendation that might secure him such accommodation, and no staff of servants and pack train to handle elegant camping equipment, had no alternative—he put up at an inn.

Anyone making his way along major routes or through populous districts had no problem: he could choose where to stop, in places even have a choice of inns. If, for example, he had left Rome to follow the Appian Way he could, as Horace did (194 above), put up at Aricia—or he could end his day's journey some four miles short of there at Bovillae and stay at the inn where Cicero's bitter enemy Clodius was taken when wounded and near which he was eventually murdered. Seventeen miles further along was Tres Tabernae, where the Disciples met St Paul on his way to Rome; the place must have derived its name from the presence there of 'three inns'. Another ten miles on was Forum Appii, which was 'full of nasty tavern keepers', as Horace reported (194 above), and most taverns had rooms for travellers.

If, on the other hand, he was making his way through open country, he had to bed down at whatever lonely lodging house he managed to reach by nightfall. They were available along most highways, strategically placed, as we have seen (189 above), a day's travel apart. Often, in the course of time, such solitary inns sparked the growth of settlements about them which came to bear their names. This is the only way to explain such place-names as Rufini Taberna, 'Rufinus' Inn', a Roman hamlet in north Africa, or Ad Stabulum, 'By the country inn', a Roman village near Narbonne in southern France, or the Tres Tabernae on the Appian Way, or a host of others. Quite a few modern place-names can be traced back to ancient village names that arose in this fashion. Zabern, between Strassbourg and Metz, is simply a version of Tabernae 'The inns'; the same word is the ultimate source of such French place-names as Saverne, Tavers, Tavernières, Tavernolles.

Archeologists have uncovered a few isolated country inns (cf. Fig. 15) in western Europe that must have belonged to Rome's comprehensive public post. In Styria, a district of Austria, they brought to light what was very likely a standard-sized Roman roadhouse, a *mansio* (184 above); built in the reign of Augustus, it remained in continuous use for the next three hundred years. It was a two-storey oblong structure, measuring roughly 40 feet by 70, set with one of the short sides fronting the road. Paralleling one of the long sides was a court for wagons and carriages. The ground floor included a stable that could handle a dozen or so animals, a repair shop complete with blacksmith's forge, an office, a kitchen measuring some 6½ feet by 19½ feet, and a dining-room of about the same size. Office, kitchen, and dining-room all faced south, and the last in addition had hot-air ducts under the floor, the usual Roman system for heating a chamber. The upper floor, now entirely gone because it was probably of wood, must have contained the bedrooms (cf. Fig. 15).

A much more elaborate *mansio*, also built in the first cen-
G*

tury A.D. and used until the fourth, has been laid bare at the top of the Little St Bernard Pass, which carried over the Alps one of the main routes between Italy and France. It was a complex of stables and court and buildings that covered a total area of some 60 feet by 216. One half of this oblong was given over to a court approximately 36 feet by 75 surrounded on three sides by two floors of chambers; most of those preserved measure roughly 16½ feet by 16½, and a few are much longer. The rooms on the second storey were entered from an outside gallery, which, projecting over the court, provided a certain amount of covered space below. The lower storey must have included the public rooms and some bed-rooms, the upper only bedrooms. The other half of the building was given over to stables, repair shop, and so on. There are no traces of heating ducts, so the rooms must have had fireplaces or braziers.

Even an example of what was probably a *mutatio* (184 above), a simple hostel, has been found, near the top of the pass that brought the road from Aquileia over the Alps to Yugoslavia. Again we have a rectangular building, although this time much smaller than the two others, only about 47½ feet long and 21 wide. It was divided into three rooms, a central chamber flanked by a kitchen on one side and a bedroom on the other. The kitchen was of modest size (5 feet by 12½), and the bedroom tiny (3 feet by 7½), leaving the lion's share of the available space to the central hall. All three rooms were well heated, as we would expect in an Alpine lodge, the kitchen by its hearth, the bedroom by a fireplace, and the long chamber by a floor fitted with hot air ducts. The bedroom was perhaps for the landlord, to be surrendered, when occasion called, to exalted or well-heeled guests; the long chamber probably took care of the ordinary clientele, serving as refectory during the day and dormitory during the night. The stables, forge, and other facilities must have been in sheds back of or alongside the main house.

In the Greek world, the traditional inn of earlier times

(88 above) was a square or oblong courtyard for accommodating animals and vehicles, on all sides of which was a line of more or less identical rooms for their owners or drivers. In the Greek-speaking eastern half of the Roman Empire this type apparently lived on to become the spacious khans of the Near East, for these are laid out in just that way. In the barren region east of the Dead Sea there still stand the imposing ruins of a building erected in late Roman or Byzantine times, that is exactly like a khan and has its generous proportions. It is square, with each side measuring about 150 feet, and embraces a yard roughly 100 feet square, providing plenty of space for unloading, feeding, and stabling pack-animals. The rooms along each side were also generous, averaging some 20 by 13 feet or better, and there were even some two-room suites.

The only other type of inn known from the Greek east is represented by a pair at Olympia for housing distinguished visitors to the games; one was put up in the first half of the second century A.D. and, when this was turned to some other use, a replacement was put up in the second half. Like the inn that stood on the grounds five hundred years before (90 above) for the same purpose, these consisted of a gracious patio surrounded by public rooms and by bed chambers of ample size; in the earlier of the two buildings, for example, the smallest bedrooms were $10\frac{1}{2}$ feet square, and most were larger, many of them considerably so.

There is much more known about inns in the Latin-speaking part of the empire. As we have just seen, excavators have brought to light several examples of inns maintained for the *cursus publicus* along the open road; what is more, they have uncovered in the ruins of Ostia and Herculaneum and Pompeii any number of the kind to be found along city streets. And, in addition to such physical remains, Roman writings, especially of the jurists, tell a good deal about the facilities and personnel of inns in general.

The country inn furnished the traveller the basic minimum:

food, a night's lodging, and, if he was using hired vehicles or animals, a change of either or both. But even in a major centre, as it happens, he could not look for very much more.

We are told that a series of resort hotels or nightclubs lined the canal linking Alexandria with Canopus. Perhaps Rome or other great metropolises boasted similar facilities. But even if they did, such establishments were rare exceptions. The average public house in town was a workaday no-nonsense place for housing the rank-and-file traveller overnight, the equivalent of our commercial railway hotels. People who had to spend more than a few days in a place and had no friends or associates to offer them hospitality, nor any letters of recommendation, took hired lodgings, as St Paul did during his stay in Rome. Owners of private houses used to rent out rooms, just as they do today—and the problems were the same, to judge from a plaque which one resigned owner displayed; in Latin verse he announced:

> If you're clean and neat, then here's a house
>   ready and waiting for you.
> If you're dirty—well, I'm shamed to say
>   it, but you're welcome too.

The transient, however, most often put up at an inn, and even respectable inns, the ones the Romans generally dignified by the neutral terms *hospitium* 'place for hospitality' or *deversorium* 'place for turning aside', included prostitutes among the services offered, while the kind they called a *caupona* was distinctly low class: it catered to sailors and carters and slaves; its dining-room had more the atmosphere of a saloon than a restaurant; and the *caupo* (or *copo*), as one who ran a *caupona* was called, was of the same social and moral level as his establishment. Indeed, *caupones*, along with ships' captains and owners of livery stables, were the subject of special legislation, since a traveller was completely at their mercy, and the law was aware that, as a group, they were hardly noted for scrupulous honesty. Ordinarily Roman law allowed a person who had been robbed to look for satisfaction only from the thief—which admittedly made things hard since a thief first had to be caught. However, a guest at an inn or a passenger on a ship whose baggage had been stolen had the right to institute proceedings against the innkeeper or the ship's captain; the one was legally responsible for the acts of his maids and servants, the other for those of his sailors. There must have been some bounds set to their liability; after all, if the victim happened to be a courier entrusted with, say, a bagful of gems, this could be disastrous for a poor *caupo* whose only mistake was to assign to bedroom cleaning a slave who was not proof against temptation. Roman law allowed a proprietor of general storage facilities to post notices to the effect that 'he did not receive gold, silver, or pearls at his risk'; probably inn-keepers, then as now, could do the same.

The one clear advantage of spending a night in a town as against a country inn—at least in a fair-sized town—was that it could offer a selection of accommodations and, as we shall see in a moment, a choice of entertainment as well. The traveller would come upon inns even before he reached the town proper; they lined the roads outside the city limits just as rows of lodgings catering to motorists do today. Most of these would be the kind the Romans called a *stabulum*, an establishment which, like its country cousin, had a courtyard for handling vehicles and a place to stable animals for the night. Just inside the gates would be more inns, and there were still others in and around town centre.

Inns in town were not hard to identify. Even a traveller arriving late at night could spot them, by the lamp they kept lighted over the door. During the day there were the street-front bars, the standard eating facility of an inn in town, to distinguish them or a sign with an appropriate picture to illustrate the establishment's name. The names have a familiar ring, since they belong to a tradition that has lasted in Europe to this day: there were inns named after animals (The Elephant, The Camel, The Little Eagle, The Hind, The Cock, The

Serpents), after things (The Wheel, The Sword), after deities (The Diana, the Mercury and Apollo). Often the facade was gaily decorated with relevant murals, such as wine jars, or, depending on the trade the owner catered to, erotic scenes. In addition to the nature and general condition of the external decor, posted notices helped the potential client make his choice. A plaque that once stood outside The Mercury and Apollo in Lyons reads 'Here Mercury promises you wealth, Apollo health, and Septumanus [the inn-keeper] room and board. Whoever comes will be the better for it afterwards. Traveller—keep an eye on where you will put up!' One uncovered at Antibes announces, 'Traveller, listen. If you like, come inside; there is a bronze plaque which will tell you everything'—in other words, a posted list of prices (they must have been fairly stable to have been engraved on bronze). A most elaborate notice has survived which was carved in Greek on the portico in front of some inn in Egypt. Written in heroic verse à la Homer, it proclaims:

> The walls of Thebes were razed and destroyed.
> But this wall of mine has never known either Ares,
>   who with hate raises the din of war, or the
>   deeds and cries of enemies.
> Here flourish banquets with grand talk, and
>   crowds of youths gathered from all over;
> Here is heard the call of the flute, not of the bugle;
> Here the soil is drenched with blood of butchered
>   cattle, not men;
> Here we dress ourselves in white robes, not armour.
> Not the sword but the cup is what our banqueters use.
> All night long with good cheer we sing the Sun-God's
>   praises, our heads wreathed with garlands.

No doubt in many an establishment the owner or manager stood in the doorway and did his best to hawk customers in. In a lively little poem attributed to Virgil, a lady innkeeper, to tempt a tired and weary traveller, raves about the charm and cool of her place, reels off the *plats du jour*, and assures him he will find not only Ceres and Bromius, i.e. bread and wine, but also Amor. A relief found in a town in southeast Italy amusingly summarizes the range of services an ancient inn provided. It pictures an innkeeper, female as in the poem just mentioned, talking with a departing guest, and above the figures is inscribed the dialogue they are carrying on:

'Innkeeper, let's reckon up the bill.'
'One *sextarius* of wine [about a pint] and bread,
    one *as*. Food, two *asses*.'
'Correct.'
'Girl, eight *asses*.'
'Correct again.'
'Hay for the mule, two *asses*.'
''That mule will be the death of me!'

The wine, so cheap it was reckoned in with the bread and not separately, was surely local stuff. No mention is made of a room; since the guest could hardly have had a girl without one, maybe the eight *asses* covered both.

A *stabulum*, an inn at the edge of town with accommodation for vehicles and animals, could not afford to spread itself the way those in the open country could. One found at Pompeii had on the ground floor facing the street an antechamber, flanked on either side by modest-sized rooms for kitchen, restaurant, and reception, and, tucked in a corner, the latrine. Going through the antechamber, you came out at the back into a court-yard where wagons could be unharnessed and left; at the rear was a shelter that served as a stable. A second storey was given over to bedrooms; there were some bedrooms as well on the first floor opening onto the court. The inns within town, intended for lodging only guests, lacked the antechamber and court; on the ground floor were kitchen, restaurant, reception, latrine, and perhaps a few bedrooms, with most of the bedrooms on the second floor. The restaurants generally had a separate street entrance of their own since, as we shall see shortly, like the grill-rooms of modern hotels, they catered to the general public and not just the inn's clients.

The inns found at Pompeii are all small, rarely with more than a dozen or so rooms to rent. But Pompeii was just a provincial town, and larger and more active centres could well have supported, at least in desirable locations, bigger facilities. In the heart of Rome, just a few steps from the forum, a building has been uncovered which had more than thirty nearly identical rooms, windowless little cells—they measured as a rule a scant five to six and a half feet by six—that were entered from narrow low corridors. The place was either a cheap rooming-house or brothel. It lasted in its choice location until, along with everything else nearby, it was demolished to make way for the grandiose park Nero laid out around his sumptuous new palace, the Golden House.

As far back as the earliest days of travel, innkeeping was often a woman's job (37 above), and this continued right on into Roman times. If she ran a *caupona*, she was called a *copa*, even as the male equivalent was called a *copo*. The keeper of a *hospitium* or *deversorium* was a *hospes* 'host'. Frequently owners of inns, instead of running them personally, used an *institor*, a manager, either a freedman or a slave. The rest of the staff—the doorman (*atriarius* or *ianitor*), bellboys and porters and waiters (*ministri, pueri*), barmaids (*vinariae*; cf. Fig. 16), cleaning girls (*ministrae, ancillae*)—were usually slave. The boys and maids would shoulder the luggage and accompany the guest to his room (*cella*), most often of very modest size and to be shared with as many fellow guests as the innkeeper could cram in. The furniture was minimal: bed (*lectus* or *lectulus* 'cot'), mattress (*matella*), and candle-holder (*candelabrum*). Experienced travellers would look the mattress over carefully since bedbugs were so common they were known as *cauponarum aestiva animalia* 'the summertime creatures of the inns'. The apocryphal *Acts of John* tells a story of how the Apostle dealt with these nuisances during a trip he took from Laodicea to Ephesus. He and his companions spent the night at an abandoned inn. Perhaps it had been abandoned for the very reason that the bedbug population had increased beyond the tolerance point, because, during the night, John, who had been given the only bed, was heard to call out, 'I say unto you, O bugs, behave yourselves, one and all, and leave your abode for this one night and remain quiet in one place, and keep your distance from the servants of God.' The others who, stretched out on the floor, were spared the problem, giggled at their leader's discomfiture—yet, thereafter, the Apostle slept in utter peace, and the next morning they found all the bugs dutifully lined up outside the front door.

The decor of the average inn was minimal, with some of it not infrequently contributed by previous guests who had vented their feelings by scribbling on the bedroom walls. 'Vibius Restitutus slept alone here and yearned for his Urbana' wrote one faithful lover or husband who had spent the night at an inn in Pompeii. 'Innkeeper, I pissed in the bed. I did wrong, I admit it. Want to know why? There was no mattress!' is the snarl another has left. One homesick traveller scrawled his fond goodbyes to his home town, Puteoli. Some, in the Kilroy tradition, simply inscribed their names.

Having deposited his baggage in the room, the traveller would probably be interested in washing. This was hardly a problem: no town of any size was without that ubiquitous feature of Roman life, well-equipped public baths. Here he would find a swimming pool and all that is provided in a modern turkish bath—indeed, these were given their name by early British visitors to Constantinople who, seeing the old Roman baths still in operation, jumped to the conclusion that they were a Turkish invention. He might spend long leisurely hours there, inasmuch as the ordinary Roman public bath offered much more than just bathing facilities: gymnasiums, beauty treatments, concerts, art exhibitions, lectures, promenades, and the chance of meeting and chatting with practically everybody in town. If he was hungry, he could pick up a bite from a food vendor (*lixa*) or at one of the bars in the bath complex.

There were usually a few inns located conveniently near the public baths, but they were not for guests seeking peace and quiet. The Roman philosopher Seneca once hired lodgings over a bath, and his description of the noise that came up from below is hair-raising:

I live right over a public bath. Just imagine every kind of human sound to make us hate our ears! When the muscular types work out and toss the lead weights, when they strain (or make believe they're straining), I hear the grunting, and whenever they let out the breath they've been holding in, there's the whistling and wheezing at maximum pitch. If it's a lazy type I'm up against, someone satisfied with the cheap massage given here, I have to hear the crack of the hand as it hits the shoulders, one sound when it's the flat of the hand, another when it's the cupped hand. But if a ball-player arrives on the scene and begins to count shots, then I'm done for. Add the toughs looking for a fight, the thieves caught in the act, and the people who enjoy hearing themselves sing in the bath-tub. Add also the people who dive into the pool with a deafening splash. On top of all these, who at least make ordinary sounds, don't forget the hair-removal expert forever forcing out that thin screech of his to advertise his services and only shutting up when he's plucking a customer's armpits and can make someone else do the yelping for him. Then there's the drinkseller with his various cries, the sausage-seller, the cake-seller, and all the managers of the restaurants, each hawking his wares with his own special intonation.

When night fell, no inn within the city limits could guarantee its guests quiet since, with sunset, there began the creaking of cart wheels, cracking of whips, and swearing of muleteers. This was because any number of towns and cities, Rome included, banned almost all wheeled traffic from the streets during daylight hours, and heavy transport had to take place between dusk and dawn.

If the traveller, having sampled all the baths had to offer, still felt in the mood for diversion he could try one of the local brothels; he might even be lucky enough to find a new one in town, its presence announced by an oil lamp over the door burning all day as well as all night. If he preferred a more restful *ambiente*, he could return to his room and send down for one of the maids, who doubled as prostitutes; in a lonely country inn, this was just about the only entertainment available. When dinnertime came, his servants would buy food and serve it in the room. There was also room service— the inn's kitchen could on request send up a meal. Or he could eat at a restaurant, if he did not mind the atmosphere— which brings us to the subject of ancient restaurants.

The traveller who elected to eat out would sally forth in search of a satisfactory *kapeleion* or *potisterion* as it would be called in a Greek-speaking city, *popina* or *taberna* in a Latin-speaking one. If he wanted to go further afield than the facility run by his own inn or any of those nearby, he could find an ample selection almost anywhere in town: near the city gates, around the baths, theatre, gladiator barracks, forum, and so on. At Pompeii, for example, the main street, which was a little over 600 yards long, boasted as many as twenty of various kinds and grades, an average of one every thirty yards.

If he was in a hurry and wanted just a quick bite, but something more than he could pick up from a street vendor, he would stop at the simplest form of *taberna*, which was the ancient equivalent of a snack bar (Fig. 17). It had a marble-topped counter opening on to the street, which ran from the side wall to the doorway, generally a distance of some six to eight feet or so. Often the counter, after running its distance to the doorway, made a right-angled turn into the shop to provide a few more feet of counter space. At Pompeii the surface of the marble tops was broken every few feet by the gaping mouth of a big clay wine-jar embedded in the masonry that supported the counter, and, near the end, by an emplacement for a little charcoal-burning furnace where a kettle of hot water was kept simmering. Against the wall at which the counter ended was a series of marble-topped shallow shelves, rising in steps like a miniature staircase, on which glassware, plates, etc. were kept. The shop proper was a tiny cell accommodating the counterman, who was usually the owner, his assistants—who would normally be his wife and grown children or his slaves—a clutch of big jars of wine for replenishing those set in the counter, a basin for washing tableware, and a narrow staircase which led to a little mezzanine where the family slept. The customer would stand in the street, and what he ordered would be slapped down on the counter in front of him: wine, ladled from one of the jugs, bread, a cut of sausage, and the like. An ancient Roman, planted in front of the bar of such a *taberna*, munching his piece of meat and guzzling his glass of wine, is the forbear of the clients of today's espresso bars.

If a traveller was tired of being on his feet and wanted to sit down, or was looking for entertainment as well as a meal, he would go to a *popina* (Fig. 16). Its streetward aspect was little different from a snack bar's; it had the same counter and set of stepped shelves. However, adjoining would be at least two small rooms, a kitchen with a charcoal fire for cooking, and a dining-room fitted with tables and chairs. More elaborate *popinae* had several dining-rooms, a few private rooms for dalliance as well as eating, and latrines. The dimensions were always modest. In a typical *popina* at Pompeii, the main dining-room measures $6\frac{1}{2}$ feet by $14\frac{3}{4}$, while the two private rooms are cells roughly $6\frac{1}{2}$ feet square. Some *popinae* had an open court for eating *al fresco*, and this could offer some elbowroom. Near the amphitheatre at Pompeii was a *popina* with a grape arbour 60 feet long and 30 wide; on days when games were scheduled and the weather was good, it must have been thronged with customers who, seated under the vines, enjoyed a cool glass of wine in refreshing shade.

The ancients preferred to eat reclining rather than seated, and there generally were a few better class *popinae* in town whose dining-rooms had tables surrounded on three sides by couches rather than chairs. To dine seated was for the poor or hurried, the equivalent of our eating perched on a bar stool.

The emphasis in every one of these establishments, from the street-counter snack bar to the restaurant with couches, was on drink as much as food: they were all bars as well as cafés. Their stock-in-trade was presumably cheap local wine, but even a very modest establishment could usually satisfy customers who were interested in something better. One *popina* in Pompeii has a picture of a servant pouring out wine and the caption reads, 'A cup of Setian, too', i.e. wine from Setia, a town in the hills north of Terracina that produced a fine quality. Another shows a picture of a girl identified as *Vinaria Hedone* 'Hedone, the barmaid', and the caption goes on to say: 'Drinks served for one *as*; if you pay double, you will drink better; if you pay quadruple, you will drink Falernian'; Falernian, famous through Horace's loving references to it, was Italy's prize wine. Even imported wines of Spain and France and Greece were available in the *popinae* of Italy; very likely Italian and other western wines could be had in the *kapeleia* and *potisteria* of the cities in the eastern part of the empire. And, to the north, in Gaul for example, taverns served beer.

The ancients never drank wine straight; they always added water. This is one reason why a simmering kettle was so standard a feature on a wineshop's counter: customers often ordered hot toddies, wine with warm water. (In poor neighbourhoods, the wineshop's kettle performed a further service: it helped out the many local inhabitants whose quarters were so cramped they had no facilities for heating their own water.) Cooled drinks, on the other hand, were only obtainable at a *taberna* or *popina* that had a well in which jugs could be stored suspended at the end of a line (91 above), or at a country inn on a brook, where the jugs could be kept submerged in the cooling waters. At the banquets of the high and mighty, wine was sometimes chilled with snow (191 above), but this expensive procedure was not for the likes of ordinary inns or restaurants. Bartenders also served more complicated drinks than merely the standard mix of wine and water, types of wine punch involving seasoning with various spices and sweetening with honey (sugar was practically unknown to the ancient world). The drinks were served in ample cups which often bore inscriptions that presumably tickled the fancy of the customers: 'Give me a drink!', 'Fill it up, bartender!', 'Fill it up again!', 'Another!', or, more specifically, 'Let's have some punch, bartender!', or still more specifically, 'Spare me the resinated stuff! Give me Amineum!' (Amineum was a fine Italian wine).

In mixing wine with water, there was always a precise amount to be added depending upon the wine, more with heavy wines, less with light. The ancients complained about the adulteration of wine by crooked innkeepers or owners of *popinae* as much as we do about the watering of mixed drinks by unscrupulous bartenders. One irate customer scribbled on the wall of a tavern at Pompeii, taking the time to put his outburst into quite respectable verse:

> May you soon, swindling innkeeper,
>   Feel the anger divine,
> You who sell people water
>   And yourself drink pure wine.

The innkeeper who 'watered wine'—i.e. watered the stuff that he was selling as presumably pure wine—appears in literature from at least the seventh century B.C. on: 'Your wine is watered', railed the prophet Isaiah, addressing the city of Jerusalem. The satirist Martial, who spent his fair share of time in the *popinae* of Rome and elsewhere, directed the following shaft at one offender:

The rains this year left sopping wet
　　the grapes on every vine.
So, barman, don't you try to say
　　there's no water in your wine.

At Ravenna, Martial ran into the reverse of the coin. In this
marshy area good drinking water was so scarce it cost more
than wine. Martial complains that:

A Ravenna barman did me in.
　　He well knew how to cheat:
I order up a standard mix,
　　And he serves it to me neat.

Cheating apparently could go on in the kitchen as well as
the bar, though not nearly to the same extent. The Roman
physician Galen, for example, in describing human flesh as
tasting very much like swine's, adds that he 'knows of many
innkeepers and butchers who have been caught selling human
flesh as pork, and the diners were totally unaware of any
difference.' The perpetrators of such frauds were no doubt
helped by the fact that the meat at a *popina* ran to the poorer
cuts well roasted or well stewed and probably highly seasoned.
The exotic creations of Roman cookery that we hear so much
about were for the *haut monde*, not the clientele of restaurants.
　Wining and dining was only part of a *popina*'s function; it
was also a place of entertainment, affording at once the facilities
of a night-club, gambling den, and brothel. You went there to
spend the whole evening or, if you were a *popino* 'barfly', to
spend the day as well, since *popinae* opened for business about
eleven A.M. or earlier. Many an establishment offered music
and dancing; in the poem attributed to Virgil mentioned
above, the innkeeper, a Syrian girl, put on some of her native
oriental shimmies for the customers. Most had prostitutes
available. The preserved remains of *popinae* at Pompeii reveal
that frequently one or more rooms were decorated with the
phallus erectus or with erotic scenes, clear enough indication

of their use; some customers proudly noted in scribblings on the wall that they 'had had intercourse with the proprietress' herself. And all offered gambling. 'Serve him wine and the dice', says the Syrian innkeeper in Virgil's poem; the two went naturally together.

A *popina* at Pompeii has the walls of a room decorated with scenes, complete with captions, which give a good idea of the activities carried on there. In one, we see a serving girl bringing a jug and a glass to two seated customers. 'This way!' says one of the two. 'No! It's mine!' says the other. And the girl, exasperated, retorts, 'Whoever wants it, take it! Hey, Ocean [this addressed to a fanciful third person to whom she gives an appropriate name], come on and drink!' Two other of the scenes follow in sequence. In the first we see two customers seated around a table playing dice. One has just thrown and says triumphantly, 'I'm out!' The other replies, 'No! It's three 2's.' In the next scene there are three figures, all on their feet. The first two are our pair of gamblers and one is saying, 'So strike me dead—I swear I won!' The second replies by calling him a filthy obscenity and shouts, '*I* won!' And the third, the proprietor, pushing the two toward the door, says, 'Go on outside to do your fighting.'

It follows from all we have said that ancient restaurants catered to a clientele of no very high level. If you went to one, your fellow diners would be muleteers, sailors, pedlars, and the like. Juvenal, the mordant Roman satirist, sneers at a certain wealthy aristocrat who frequented a *popina* at Ostia, the port town of Rome: 'You will find him at table with some thug, mingling with sailors, crooks, and runaways in a crowd of hangmen, low-class morticians' assistants, and eunuch priests too drunk to beat their tambourines.' Many a *popina* must have been a low dive of this sort, the ones that Cicero claims Mark Antony haunted, or those that, according to Nero's biographer, the emperor made the rounds of as soon as night fell. To the very lowest level must belong a *popina* of the first century A.D. discovered at Catania in Sicily. It can be identified by the messages scratched on the wall of what was probably the dining-room, one of which reads: '16 August, Festival of Lady Ceres. Here three young fellows—read their names: Onesimus, Lucius Valerius Ersianus, Filumenus—had a good time, one of them, the last named, with a woman'— and the other two presumably with each other. The adding of the date was important: it showed they deliberately chose the solemn holiday when women were supposed to observe nine days of chastity to carry on this way. The names reveal that two of the men were Greek slaves and the third a freedman. The woman is unnamed since she was just hired for the occasion.

It was establishments of this ilk that the aediles, the city officials in charge of, among other things, inns and restaurants, had to crack down on so often. In the first century A.D. the Roman emperors were still interested in attempting to improve the moral tone of the capital, and one of their devices was to try to cut down the activity of Rome's *popinae* by limiting the foods they could serve. Tiberius banned bread and cakes, Claudius banned cooked meats and hot water and shut down completely those places that sold only wine and no food, Nero allowed only the sale of vegetable dishes, Vespasian only peas and beans. That each emperor had to institute a new decree reveals how much more these regulations were honoured in the breach than the observance, and, after Vespasian, we hear of no further efforts in this direction.

Since *popinae* serviced the lowest ranks of society, the decor could not help but reflect this. Wall paintings ran to the scatological, as well as the erotic. In a *popina* at Ostia, one room is decorated with a series of portraits of impressive looking men, pictures of first-rate quality done by a skilled professional artist. They represent the 'Seven Sages of Antiquity', and each sage's portrait is accompanied by a line of writing purporting to summarize his philosophy—his philosophy, in this case, with regard to the actions of the bowels: 'To promote a good movement, Solon used to rub his belly';

'Thales advises the constipated to push hard'; 'The subtle Chilon taught the art of breaking wind silently'. Below the portraits appear a line of men obviously manning the seats in a latrine, and each figure has an appropriate caption: 'Put some effort into it and you'll get there quicker'; 'I'm hurrying'; 'Friend, you're forgetting the proverb: "Have a good movement and screw the doctors".' It was inevitable that the Church, when it achieved power, would pass a rule allowing priests to eat at restaurants only when on the road, where there was no alternative.

So, a traveller, having filled in his daylight hours pleasantly at a public bath, could while away equally pleasant evening hours at a *popina*, chatting or taking an occasional turn at the dice, or, if the spirit moved him, having a session in a back room with one of the girls. If the last piqued his appetite for further diversion of this sort, he could move on to a fully equipped brothel.

13

Mail

As early as the third millennium B.C., the city-states of Mesopotamia had devised a government postal system (36 above).
Assyria worked up an expanded form to meet the needs of
her far-flung empire, and Persia further refined this to create
the service that so impressed Herodotus (53 above). Even
Persia's minuscule neighbours, the city-states of Greece, had
their organized means of communication, staffs of 'day-
runners' or 'herald-runners' who, tirelessly reeling off mile
after mile at a steady trot, delivered the formal messages that
one state addressed to another. And, of course, from Augustus'
time on there was the sophisticated *cursus publicus* of the
Roman Empire.

But all these were for government use only—or for the
favoured few who managed to avail themselves of the facilities
through bribery or influence. Private citizens did not get a
service specifically intended for their own needs until as late
as the seventeenth century, when Charles II of England
established the London 'Penny Post'. Before then all they
could do was improvise.

Well-to-do Greeks or Romans were better off in this as in
so many other respects: in effect they supplied their own postmen. Among their slaves they included a certain number
whose prime duty was to serve as couriers, *grammatophoroi*
'letter carriers' as they were called in Greek, *tabellarii* 'tablet
men' in Latin. Family and friends living near to each other
used to pool their couriers in order to increase the opportun-

ities to get off or receive a letter. But it was basically a catch-as-catch-can arrangement; there never were enough carriers to meet the needs, and delays were inevitable. 'For many days I have had a letter on my hands waiting for a courier', laments Cicero in a note to his brother. The opposite side of the coin was to have to dash off some lines at breakneck speed to take advantage of an available carrier. We find Cicero complaining to a correspondent that:

> you have preposterous couriers . . . , they clamour for a letter when they leave me—yet when they come they bring none. Anyway, they'd oblige me more if they'd only give me a moment to write something, but in they come, hat on head, and tell me their mates are waiting for them at the gate.

When, under the emperors, the official government post was in operation, even the wealthy found it convenient to pull strings and have their correspondence travel in the government pouch.

The vast majority of letter writers, of course, had neither couriers nor the pouch available to them. Their only recourse was to find some traveller who happened to be heading in the right direction. This is what correspondents did whether writing in the second millennium B.C. (37 above) or the second century A.D. 'Finding somebody going your way from Cyrene, I felt I had to let you know I was safe and sound', writes a young Greek en route to Rome from Egypt in the second century A.D. 'I was delighted to receive your letter', writes a Greek living in Egypt in the third A.D., 'which was given to me by the sword-maker; the one you say you sent with Platon, the dancer's son, I haven't got yet.' 'I sent you two other letters,' writes another in A.D. 41, 'one by Nedymos and one by Kronios, the armed guard. I've received the one you sent with the Arab.' Cicero himself at times could do no less. 'Have Acastus [a servant] go down to the waterfront daily', he writes while en route to Italy to his secretary, who was then in Patras, 'because there will be lots of people to whom you can entrust letters and who will be glad to bring them to me. At my end I won't overlook a soul who is headed toward Patras.' Travellers, we gather, had no objections to filling the role of postman—it was, after all, the only way they could get word to anyone themselves.

Not only delivery but the very writing of a letter was a much more complicated business than now. There were no such things as pencils, nor convenient types of pen. The only writing instrument was a reed pen, and ink was of lampblack, gum, and water that normally had to be mixed for the occasion. The Greeks and Romans usually used papyrus for letters, a kind of paper made up of razor-thin slices from the pith of the papyrus reed, which was almost as good and convenient as the heavier types of modern paper. It was, however, vastly more expensive; ancient correspondents did not as a rule go in for lengthy missives. There were no envelopes, so, when the writer had put down all he had to say, he rolled the sheet up, or folded it, keeping the message on the inside surface, addressed it, tied it about, and, to seal it, fixed a blob of clay or wax to the tie and impressed his seal on it. The address was usually very simple, e.g. 'To Apollinarius from his brother Irenaeus'; there was no need for anything more, since the person who agreed to make delivery was going to the addressee's town or village and would be told by the sender just what street and house to go to.

Mail moved quite fast over short distances. Cicero, in his villas near Naples, used to get letters from Rome in four or five days on the average; the Italian post office does not do much better today. But long distances, particularly when crossing water was involved, was another matter. The courier checked the waterfront to see if any ships were sailing in his direction and, if none were, all he could do was sit around and hope. A letter Cicero wrote from Rome to his son in Athens took over seven weeks, while another from Rome to Athens took only three. In the first case the carrier had to wait for a ship, in the second he had the luck to find one right away—which must have been unusual, since Cicero comments that the letter arrived *sane strenue* 'mighty quickly'. Cicero's secretary once wrote to him from Patras, and the letter arrived at Brindisi fifteen days later, even though the distance involved could have been covered, all things being equal, in three. From Africa to Rome was a three-day trip, yet it once took twenty for a letter from there to reach Cicero. Some letters from Syria to Rome arrived in fifty days, others needed double that time.

A number of letters sent home by random travellers or tourists have been preserved. They were all addressed to people living in Egypt, where they were unearthed in the last hundred years; the recipients tossed them into the rubbish heap, and, since the valley of the Nile in places gets practically no rainfall, there they remained intact, or nearly so, until the archeologist's spade brought them to light. They are written in Greek, the language of the middle and upper class living in Egypt in the days of the Roman empire. Most do just what travellers' letters do in any age—report safe arrival. 'Having arrived on Italian soil', writes someone in the second century A.D., 'I felt it essential to let you know that I and all with me are fine. We had a slow voyage but not an unpleasant one.' 'Dear Mother,' writes a young naval recruit also sometime in the second century A.D., 'greetings! I hope you are well. I'm fine. . . . I beg you to know, Mother, that I arrived in Rome on Pachon 25 [20 May] in good health, and was posted to [the naval base at] Misenum, though I don't know the name of my ship yet. . . . I beg you, Mother, take care of yourself and don't worry about me; I've come to a fine place. Please write telling me you're all right, and how my brothers are, and your whole family. And whenever I find someone [going your way] I'll write you—I won't put off writing to you. Remember me to—' and here follows a long list of names of friends and family. Another recruit in telling that he had arrived safely mentions his giving 'grateful thanks to the god Serapis who came right away to my rescue when I was in danger on the sea.' And I have already cited (128 above) the letter of an Alexandrian businessman informing a brother of his arrival at Rome.

On occasion a letter announced a safe arrival that very nearly wasn't. In the latter part of the third century A.D., when the long years of the *pax romana* were at an end and the empire was plagued by frequent breakdowns of law and order, a certain Psois, who had just come back from a trip, writes to a friend in Hermopolis: 'Just as we were rejoicing at being about to arrive home, we fell into an attack by bandits at Mt Maro, and some of us were killed . . . Thank god I escaped with just being stripped clean. I wanted to come your way to tell you what happened to us, but I couldn't and went directly to Oxyrhynchus . . . God willing I'll come for the festival in Phaophi [October]. I hope you are well.' And here is a letter, also of the third century A.D., from a lady who, held up not by bandits but by such time-honoured traveller's troubles as missing connections and running short of funds, never arrived at all:

Dear Mother,

First and foremost I pray to God to find you in good health. I want you to know that on Tybi 13 [8 January] I went to Tyrannis but I found no way I could get to you, since the camel-drivers didn't want to go to Oxyrhynchus. Not only that, I also went up to Antinoe to take a boat, but didn't find any. So now I've thought it best to forward the baggage to Antinoe and wait there until I find a boat and can sail. Please give the bearers of this letter 2 talents and 300 drachmas in compensation for what I asked and received from them in Tyrannis to pay for transportation. Don't delay them even an hour . . . If you know you don't have it at hand, borrow it . . . and pay them, since they can't wait around even an hour. See to it that you don't fail me and hold up these people who have been so nice to me. My regards to [and here follows a series of names].

Many letters reveal the traveller's traditional hunger for news from home. 'Dear Mother', writes a particularly anxious son sometime in the third or fourth century A.D.,

I am writing to you via our Heliodorus [i.e., the family servant who carried the letter] from Caesarea, where I intend to go off to Cappadocia, in good health and praying to find you well and in good health. I pray for you to the local gods here. I have already written many times about your well-being, and you haven't thought it worth your while to write to me. If you'd just send a note telling me if you're well or how you are, so I can stop worrying! Up to now I've been troubled about you since I haven't had any letters from you. Perhaps I'll ask permission from my patron and come to you quickly so I can greet you after so long a time. My news you can get from our people, from Neilos and Eudaimon and those who've come your way. Many greetings to my dear sister Taesis and my brother Zoillos and all my friends. May they all stay well for a long time!

Ancient travellers, like so many of us today, could not resist sending streams of instructions on what to do about things back home. 'Dear Zenon,' writes an associate of his in 252 B.C., 'I am writing just after our arrival in Sidon. . . . Please take care of yourself and write me if you want anything done that I can do for you. Would you please buy in time for my arrival three jars of the best honey, six hundred bushels of barley for the animals . . . , and take care of the house in Philadelphia so that it has its roof on when I arrive. Try to keep an eye as best you can on the oxen, pigs, geese, and the rest of the stock there . . . And see to it that you somehow get the crops harvested, and if there are any expenses to meet, don't hesitate to take care of them.'

Egypt has preserved as many letters written to travellers as by them. A loving wife, for example, writes to tell her husband how much she misses him: 'Send for me—if you don't, I'll die without seeing you daily. How I wish I could fly and come

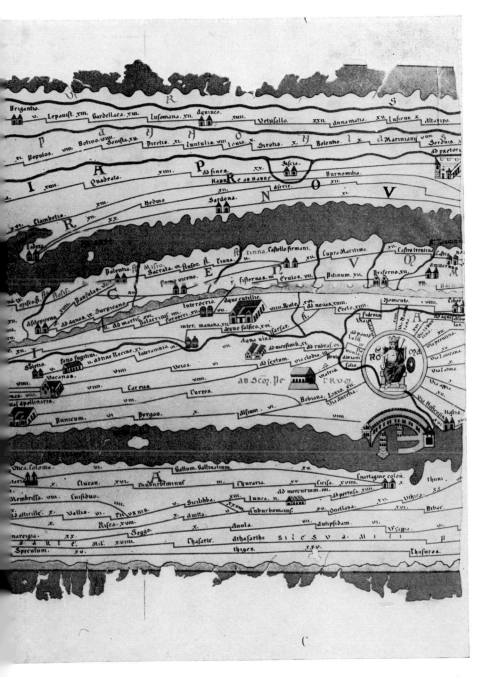

14 Detail of the Tabula Peutingeriana showing the area around Rome.
See page 186.

15 Travellers arriving at a country inn. The inn with its peaked roof
and balcony across the front rather resembles an Alpine chalet. The
travellers are in a carriage drawn by horses. The *cursor*, the servant who
walks leading the horses, is being greeted by the personnel of the inn.
Fourth century A.D.

16 Travellers in a restaurant at the port of Rome. Third century
A.D. On the left is the vessel arriving at the port symbolized by the
lighthouse. On the right the travellers are seated in a restaurant. One
already has a drink, the other is being served by a barmaid. Behind her
is the bar with the usual three tiers of shelves on the wall beside it.

to you . . . It tortures me not to see you.' Another wife, whose husband had obviously settled down for a long stay at Alexandria, writes in quite another vein:

I'm disgusted at your not coming home, when all the others . . . have. Here I've steered myself and the child through a time like this, and been driven to the last resort because of the price of food, and now, when I'm thinking I'll get some relief with you coming back, you haven't given a thought to coming back, haven't given any regard whatsoever to our situation, how I had nothing when you were still here, not to mention how much time has passed and all these crises and you've sent us nothing. What's more, Horus, who brought me your letter, reports that your stay is over and you've been released, so I'm completely disgusted.

And some of us will surely feel a fellow sufferer's sympathy for Theon who, toward the end of the second century A.D. or the beginning of the third, received the following from his son, Theon Jr:

A fine thing you did! You didn't take me with you to the city! If you don't want to take me with you to Alexandria, I won't write you a letter, I won't talk to you, I won't say Hello to you even. If you go to Alexandria [sc. without me], I won't shake hands with you or greet you ever again after this. If you don't want to take me, that's what will happen. Mother said to Archelaus [probably the boy's tutor], 'He upsets me—take him away!' A fine thing you did, all right. Big gifts you sent me—chicken feed! They played a trick on me there, the 12th, the day you sailed. Send for me, I beg you. If you don't, I won't eat, I won't drink. There!

H

PART THREE

TOURISTS AND TOURING IN ROMAN TIMES

14

The Sights to See

At the end of the summer of 167 B.C., Aemilius Paulus, commander-in-chief of the Roman army, was in northern Greece resting on his laurels as victor in a bitter struggle against Macedon. The historian Livy recounts that at this time:

he decided upon a tour of Greece, to see those things which, through their fame and reputation, had been magnified by hearsay into more than what the eye beholds. . . . With no great retinue, . . . he travelled across Thessaly to Delphi, the celebrated oracle. Here he sacrificed to Apollo. . . . Then he went to the Temple of Zeus Trophonius and saw the mouth of the cave which those who consult the oracle enter to put their question to the gods. . . . Next he went to Chalcis to see the Euripus and Euboea, an island of enormous extent yet yoked to the mainland by a bridge. From Chalcis he crossed to Aulis, three miles away, the famous harbour that once upon a time was the gathering point for the thousand ships of Agamemnon's fleet and the site of the temple of Artemis, where that king of kings sought a fair wind for Troy by sacrificing his daughter on the goddess' altar. From there he came to Oropus in Attica, where an ancient seer [Amphilochus] rather than any god is worshipped; the sanctuary is very old and a pleasant spot because of the springs and streams all about. Then to Athens, also renowned for its hoary antiquity but still with many sights to see—the Acropolis, the port town, the walls joining the Piraeus to the city, the naval base . . . , the statues of both gods and men, outstanding for every kind of workmanship and material. He left the city after sacrificing to Athena, patron goddess of the Acropolis, and proceeded to Corinth, arriving on the following day. The city was then a splendid one; this was before its destruction. The Acropolis and the Isthmus were also sights to see—the Acropolis, set on an immense height, girdled with walls and flowing with springs; the Isthmus splitting with its narrow span the neighbouring seas to east and west. Then he visited the splendid cities of Sicyon and Argos, and after that Epidaurus, far less wealthy but celebrated for the splendid temple to Asclepius; it stands five miles from the city, and now is rich only in the traces of votive gifts that were carried off as plunder; once it was rich with the actual gifts, which the sick gave to the god as payment for their cures. Then to Sparta, with no magnificent buildings but memorable for its institutions and educational methods, and to Pallantium. Then via Megalopolis to Olympia. Here he saw many sights, but what touched him profoundly was the Zeus—he felt he beheld the god in person.

Paulus' choice of places to visit illustrates to the letter the interests of the vast majority of tourists who came after him. He was no Herodotus, poking into the ways and manners of men, picking up conversations with sacristans and businessmen. He was interested, almost to the exclusion of all else, in the past. And, of the monuments of the past, he gave precedence to those that commemorated the presence of gods; next came those that recalled mythology and history. Thus he saw the great temples and sanctuaries at Delphi, Athens, Oropus, Epidaurus; he also visited the harbour where Agamemnon gathered the fleet for the legendary attack upon Troy, and the base that served the navy which, two and a half centuries

before his time, had made Athens' name great in history. He
included Phidias' statue of Zeus at Olympia, not so much for
art's sake as for its renown and the solemn religious effect it
had on the beholder (according to report, his reaction was,
'Phidias has sculpted the Zeus of Homer!'). And he took in
one of nature's marvels, the Euripus, the narrow channel—
only forty yards wide—between the mainland of Greece and
the island of Euboea, where the current whips through at four
to five miles an hour and seems to switch direction with
bewildering irregularity.

Among the sights Paulus included in his itinerary only one
had to do with nature—the channel of the Euripus. And he
went there not for aesthetic or emotional reasons but to see a
curiosity. We today take long trips for the pleasure of viewing
a varied terrain, or make laborious ascents to enjoy a superb
panorama, and we particularly like wild and savage prospects
untouched by man's hand. The ancients went to the trouble of
climbing a mountain for a specific reason, to investigate the
possibility of a practicable route across it, or in quest of some
natural marvel on the summit. They were not at all interested
in beholding serrated files of snow-capped peaks, they were
untouched by the austere beauty of boundless wasteland.
What enjoyment they found in a landscape generally was its
amoenitas 'charm'. So far as nature was concerned, they were
mainly interested in places where one felt the presence of
divinity—but not on mountain tops or in deserts, where we
tend to seek it, but rather in more intimate spots. They visited
springs, for, in the inexplicable perpetual bubbling forth of
the water they saw the hand of a god; they erected shrines and
chapels nearby and honoured the deity by tossing into his
waters the offering of a coin (cf. 134 above)—thereby starting
a long-lived tradition. They visited grottoes, for, groping in
the gloom and hearing only remote mysterious sounds such as
the muffled roar of underground streams, they imagined themselves near to supernatural beings. They visited groves and

forests, where the chiaroscuro and quiet gave them the same feeling.

Certain natural features became attractions because of their literary fame, the way the English lake country has for us. A typical case in point is the Vale of Tempe in northern Greece, whose virtues were sung by poet after poet and a replica of which, a triumph of landscape gardening, was one of the wonders of Hadrian's grand villa at Tibur. The ancient tourist also liked to visit rivers which had made a mark in literature— the Nile, the Danube, the Rhine, the winding Meander in Asia Minor.

Lastly there were the impressive curiosities nature offers, like the Euripus that Paulus went to see. The one mountain the ancients did climb willingly was Etna—to gape in awe at the crater of an active volcano. The hot springs at Hierapolis in Asia Minor were famous not only for the waters but also for a special sight, a fissure in the ground, only large enough to admit a man, which gave forth a noxious gas so strong it killed birds that flew through it or even bulls dragged up for a sniff; a protective guard rail surrounded it, and a viewing stand was nearby. The Lake of Avernus near Naples, where similar exhalations took place (as they do now in the nearby Solfatara), was turned by Virgil's fancy into an entrance to the underworld.

Sometime in the third century B.C., an unknown scholar who probably lived in Alexandria worked up a list of seven wonders of the world. They were not tourist meccas in any sense, but they give a good idea of what the ancients considered noteworthy. All were works of man, not nature, and most were of considerable age: the Pyramids, the Hanging Gardens at Babylon, Phidias' statue of Zeus at Olympia (which so affected Paulus), the Temple of Artemis at Ephesus, the Mausoleum. Only the Colossus of Rhodes and the Lighthouse at Alexandria were modern, of the compiler's own times.

In preferring the past to the present, the ancient tourist was not unlike his counterpart of today who travels to see the glories of Greece, the grandeur of Rome, the hoary cathedrals of the Middle Ages, and so on. The key difference is that the ancients did not distinguish as carefully as we do between the legendary and historical past; for them history began in the earliest ages recalled in mythological tales. And so, among the prime tourist sights were concrete memorials of those remote days. At Salamis, the visitor was shown the stone where old Telamon sat and watched his sons, Ajax and Teucer, sail off to Troy; near Sparta, the point in the road where Penelope made up her mind to marry Odysseus; at Troezon, the spot where Phaedra used to spy on Hippolytus while he exercised in the nude; not far from the mouth of the Tiber, the site of Aeneas' camp (as late as the sixth century A.D. an 'Aeneas' ship' was still on display in Rome; its timbers had presumably held up for a thousand years); at Panopeus in central Greece, remains of the clay from which Prometheus moulded the first humans; and those intrepid enough to make their way into the Caucasus mountains could look up to the cliff where Zeus once had the Titan chained. Tourists could see the hewn stone at Troy to which Cassandra had been tied (the front side when touched or rubbed gave out milk, the back side blood—or so the legend went); the plane-tree in Phrygia in Asia Minor where Apollo strung up Marsyas for flaying; the olive tree at Troezon where Hippolytus' chariot crashed, and the one at Mycenae under which Argos sat as he guarded Io; the cave in Crete where Zeus was born, and the one on Pelion where Chiron lived. At Agyrion in Sicily they could examine certain prints in the rock which were supposed to have been made by the cattle of Geryon, the triple-bodied monster slain by Heracles. At Athens they climbed to a point on the Acropolis from which the sea was visible and were told how Aegeus had plunged to his death from there when he saw Theseus' ship approaching under black sails (Theseus had forgotten to raise white ones, the agreed signal for his safe return).

H*

There were, as we would expect, no end of graves of heroes and heroines to visit. You could see Helen's on Rhodes, Achilles' and Ajax' at Troy, Iphigeneia's at Megara, Nestor's at Pylos, Phaedra's at Troezon, Orestes' at Sparta, Oedipus' at Athens, Medea's children's at Corinth. To complicate matters, the same personage sometimes turned out to have been buried in two different places. Both Troezon and Athens claimed Hippolytus' grave, both Argos and Cyprus Ariadne's, Parium and Crebrene Paris', Mycenae and Amyclae Agamemnon's and Cassandra's. There were dwelling places of mythological times to visit as well as graves: Menelaus' house at Sparta (still standing, indeed still in use, 1,500 years later), Nestor's house at Pylos (also the cave where he kept his cattle), Hippolytus' house and Orestes' hut at Troezon, the site of Aegeus' palace at Athens, the ruins of Amphitryon's house at Thebes (guides were even able to identify the room that served as Alcmene's bridal chamber).

Though the notables of mythology seem to have had first claim on the tourist, he by no means neglected those of history. Xenophon's grave was shown at Scillus, the town near Olympia where he spent many years in retirement. Themistocles' was shown in the market place at Magnesia in Asia Minor. Pindar's could be visited at Thebes, Solon's at Athens, Demosthenes' at Calaureia (the island near Troezon where he committed suicide), and Virgil's north of Naples. Among the sights of Rome were the tombs of the emperors: the moundlike mausoleum where Augustus and Tiberius and Claudius were buried; Trajan's column, whose base housed a gold urn with the emperor's ashes; Hadrian's grandiose monument, big and massive enough to be converted into a fortress, the present Castel Sant' Angelo. In Athens one could see Socrates' house, Demosthenes' house with the underground chamber where he used to shut himself up for months at a time to practise oratory, the house where Alcibiades had scandalously parodied certain very secret rites, the tomb of an Indian who left Augustus' entourage to burn himself alive in the approved Indian manner. At Thebes was the house of Pindar, spared by Alexander when he razed the rest of the city. At Heliopolis near Cairo was the house where Plato allegedly stayed while imbibing ancient wisdom from the Egyptian priests; at Metapontum in southern Italy the house where Pythagoras lived and died; on Capri the cliff from which Tiberius tossed into the sea people he suspected of treason; at Rome a chapel on the Capitoline marking the spot where Augustus was born, and the 'tiny dark room in a squalid house' where Titus was born; at Babylon the house where Alexander the Great had died.

Alexander, as a matter of fact, was well-nigh a cult. Trajan was able to go through the house at Babylon almost four hundred years later. At Alexandria, the most famous of the many cities named after him, a stately tomb sheltered his corpse, which was enshrined in a sarcophagus of gold (when Egypt fell on hard times in the first century B.C., one of its rulers made off with the precious casket, and the remains had to be transferred to a coffin of glass or alabaster). Mithridates once spent a night in a certain lodge simply because Alexander had slept there. Outside Tyre visitors were shown the spring besides which he had had a dream that portended the capture of the city. In a town in Macedon near the capital they saw the school where Aristotle gave instruction to his prize pupil. At Chaeronea they were taken to 'Alexander's oak', a tree where his tent had been pitched during the crucial battle in which he and his father defeated Athens and Thebes and ended Greece's days as a collection of independent cities. The four statues that used to support the tent ended up in Rome, two in front of the temple of Mars the Avenger, two in front of a building in the forum. And a handbook for Greek shippers doing business with the Indus valley in far-off India reminded them about the 'remains of Alexander's army in the area, ancient altars, foundations of camps, and enormous wells'.

Another feature of the historical past that drew tourists were memorials of great battles. Visitors to Athens often included an excursion to Marathon, twenty-two miles away, site of Athens' spectacular victory over the Persians in the First Persian War. They were shown, among other things, the mound marking the common grave of the 192 Athenians killed in action (the Persians lost 6,400). Then there was the battlefield of Chaeronea just mentioned. Here a mound surmounted by a stone lion commemorated the spot where the 500 soldiers of Thebes' elite guard died to a man and were buried; visitors today still see the lion, for it was unearthed in the last century and re-erected. The quarries at Syracuse were one of the chief sights the city offered; quite likely many people went mainly to see the gelid caves which killed off 7,000 Athenian prisoners penned there after their disastrous defeat in 413 B.C.

Lastly, then as today, art stood high on the tourist's agenda. Paulus' visit to Phidias' statue of Zeus at Olympia turned out to be one of the highpoints of his tour—not too surprising since this masterpiece had been included in the list of the Seven Wonders and competed with Praxiteles' Aphrodite for the distinction of being the most famed work of art of the ancient world. The latter was in Cnidus, a city on the southwest coast of Asia Minor, and the story goes that one of the wealthy Asia Minor kings once offered to pay off the city's entire public debt in exchange for it. The Cnidians turned him down, and there could have been hard-headed calculation as well as sentiment in the decision: the statue, displayed in a special open pavilion so that spectators could view it from all sides, attracted droves of tourists to the island yearly. A third renowned sculpture was a bronze cow by Myron that stood on the Acropolis at Athens; poets scribbled ecstatic verses about its being so realistically made that it could fool not merely a herdsman but even calves and bulls. Cicero, in a speech written about 70 B.C., mentions in passing some half-dozen works of art of outstanding reputation, pieces that people made pilgrimages to see. These included, in addition to Praxiteles' Aphrodite and Myron's cow, a statue of Europa on the bull at Tarentum done by Pythagoras of Rhegium; a marble Eros at Thespiae in Greece executed by Praxiteles; a painting at Cos of Aphrodite, shown rising from the sea, by Apelles, who was considered by the ancients to be their greatest painter (Romans were spared any travel to see this masterpiece because, a half-century or so after Cicero wrote, the emperor Augustus bought it and installed it in a temple dedicated to Caesar in the forum); a portrait at Ephesus of Alexander, also by Apelles; a picture of Ialysus, the legendary founder of Rhodes, on Rhodes (but moved to Rome after Cicero's day) and a picture of the *Paralos*, one of Athens' flagships, in the great gateway to the Acropolis at Athens, both by Protogenes, a contemporary of Apelles. Cicero's list is illuminating: all are sculptures or paintings done 200 to 400 years earlier (Pythagoras, Myron, and Phidias lived during the fifth century B.C., and Praxiteles, Apelles, and Protogenes during the fourth). The ancient art lover, in other words, was interested first and foremost in old masters.

But he could not see them conveniently collected in a Louvre or Uffizi; the best he could do was make his way from temple to temple. And how the ancient temple came to serve as museum and art gallery is the subject we must turn to next.

15

Museums

The tourist in Europe today goes from cathedral to cathedral. His counterpart in the ancient world went from temple to temple. Like a cathedral, a temple was a good deal more than a specimen of architecture. It was, to begin with, the house of a god, which raised it above the level of all other of man's works, gave it a very special distinction. And it had full measure of that ingredient so precious to the Greek or Roman tourist, the past. For one thing, the temples people went to see—like most churches we go to see—were themselves places where men had worshipped for centuries. For another, they offered glimpses of manifold phases of the past, for they were the nearest thing to museums that the ancient world had to offer.

In 1160 B.C., Shutruk-Nahhunte, king of Elam, campaigned triumphantly through Agade, Sippar, Eshnunna, and other towns of Babylonia. He returned to his capital at Susa with a rich haul of loot, which he offered up to the god who had led him to his victory (it included among other things two price-less pieces that archeologists unearthed there three thousand years later, the stele of Naram-Sin, a chef d'oeuvre of Near Eastern art, and the monument inscribed with Hammurabi's law code). In all probability many a conquering monarch before him had done likewise; it was an appropriate gesture, and, indeed, becomes just about standard procedure in later ages. Shutruk-Nahhunte's instance is notable only because it is the first we are sure of: ancient records report that he presented his booty to the Elamite deity In-Shushinak and placed it on exhibition in his temple.

The next such dedications we know of were made by that nation of soldiers par excellence, Assyria. In the ninth century B.C. there was a chamber in the western gateway at Assur where the Assyrians stored captured mace-heads and cudgels dedicated to their war god Nergal. Two centuries later Assurbanipal's records mention statues looted from Susa after his destruction of the city, and obelisks brought back from Thebes after his campaign against Egypt; he must have dedicated it all somewhere in his capital, though the exact spot is unknown.

Since a museum is by definition any 'room, building, or locale where a collection of objects is put on exhibition', the display areas in In-Shushinak's temple at Susa or the gateway at Assur—if it was open to visitors—qualify as museums, but only just. For a museum that begins to approach what we generally mean by the term we must go down in time to the first half of the sixth century B.C., the reign of Nebuchadnezzar II of Babylon. He and his successor were particularly interested in the past. They studied archaic inscriptions, they restored old buildings, they even conducted archeological excavations to locate the foundation stones of ancient temples. So it comes as no surprise to discover that Nebuchadnezzar II installed in an area of his palace a collection of objects stemming from bygone times.

We have a fair idea of what it was like, for excavators have unearthed a good part of the contents. Its earliest piece went back over a millennium and a half, an inscription from Ur of 2400 B.C. Then there was a statue of a ruler of Mari in upper Mesopotamia of 2300 B.C., a clay spike from Isin in lower Mesopotamia of 2100 B.C., a club of 1650 B.C. which had once been wielded by some Kassite, one of the people who ruled Babylon until the Elamites took over. There were Assyrian pieces dating from about 900 to 650 B.C.: inscriptions, reliefs, stelai, clay cylinders. There were a few Aramaic pieces—a statue of a weather god and some stone bowls—dated c. 700 to 600 B.C. And there were contemporary things, some clay cylinders of Nebuchadnezzar himself. The collection was kept up after his death since it included cylinders of his successor Nabonidus and a stele from the time of Darius the Great of Persia, who suppressed a revolt in Babylon around 520 B.C. Obviously Nebuchadnezzar was following in the footsteps of Shutruk-Nahhunte and the others before him who had amassed displays of spoils of war. But his collection, though acquired for the most part in the same way, shows deliberate selection to illustrate a long span of time and a wide variety of objects. He named it the 'Wonder Cabinet of Mankind', and opened it to the general public. It was for all intents and purposes a museum of historical antiquities.

If the birthplace of the museum was the ancient Near East, its coming of age took place among the Greeks. Certain important Greek sanctuaries, like Apollo's at Delphi or Zeus' at Olympia, gradually accumulated objects of special value donated as thank-offerings for services rendered—or as bribes for services that hopefully would be rendered. Some of the gifts were of value for their historical associations, like the inevitable spoils of war, but others for their own sake, for their costliness or beauty, the precious metals or workmanship that had gone into them. The Greek gods commanded a considerable following among non-Greeks, and a number of these turned out to be particularly generous donors. Delphi, for example, was a veritable Fort Knox, thanks to the reputation the oracle enjoyed among the kings of Phrygia and Lydia, lands blessed with fabulous gold deposits. When Herodotus made a visit in the fifth century B.C., in the building called the Treasury of the Corinthians he saw a throne dedicated by Midas of Phrygia (c. 700 B.C.) whose very name conjures up visions of gold, six gold mixing bowls dedicated by Gyges of Lydia

(678–652 B.C.) that weighed in the aggregate some 1,730 pounds, and a gold lion from Croesus, the last king of Lydia (560–546), that weighed 375 pounds (it was originally 575 but a destructive fire left it considerably slimmed down).

Herodotus singled these pieces out for mention because of what they had cost; the workmanship in them was incidental. For aesthetic quality we have to look to the offerings of the Greeks themselves, inhabitants of a land poor in precious metals but rich in artists. The temple of Hera at Olympia is a good case in point. During the seventh and sixth centuries B.C., this venerated spot acquired, among other dedications, a two-hundred-year-old cedar chest that was intricately carved with scenes from mythology, and some twenty-odd statues of major and minor divinities, stately figures done in the archaic style of the times. As the years passed, these hoary pieces were joined by others from the hands of Greece's best known contemporary artists. In the fourth century B.C., it received a particularly prized donation, a marble statue by Praxiteles of Hermes holding the infant Dionysus; unearthed by archeologists excavating the temple in 1877, this has once again become one of the sights to see at Olympia. Other notable votives were a bronze by Cleon, and two gold and ivory figures by Leochares; both men were contemporaries of Praxiteles and not far behind him in repute. By the third century B.C. there had been added a gilded statue of a naked child by Boethus, a ranking sculptor of the time. In short, thanks to centuries of dedications, any who came to the temple of Hera could see a sculpture collection of scope and quality.

Nor was this an exceptional case. All over the Greek world, through generous gifts of statues and paintings from the hopeful or the satisfied, temples became art galleries as well as houses of worship—exactly as Europe's cathedrals and churches were destined to become through the offerings and grave monuments of pious Christians. And they drew visitors the same way that art-laden churches do today, to see the treasures and only incidentally say a prayer. A skit by

Herondas, a Greek poet of the third century B.C. noted for his skilful little genre sketches, portrays a visit by two ladies to the temple of Asclepius on the island of Cos; the author has the ladies hastily dispose of their offering to the god and then settle down to the real business of their visit, a careful viewing of the stellar collection of paintings and sculpture that the place boasted.

One reason why Greek temples became museums of art rather than of war trophies was the practice the Greeks had of cashing in their spoils and purchasing offerings in the form of statues to dedicate. At the very entrance to the sanctuary of Delphi, for example, the visitor passed a series of figures erected by Tegea from the spoils of a victory against Sparta, a series erected by Sparta from the spoils of a victory against Athens, and a series by Athens from the spoils of the Battle of Marathon.

This is not to say that the Greeks banished war trophies from their shrines; they had their displays of historical antiquities no less than the Near East. The Athenians filled a colonnade at Delphi with ships' figureheads and shields taken in the naval battles of the Peloponnesian War, while at Athens itself, in the Erechtheum on the Acropolis, was the sabre of Mardonius, commander-in-chief of the Persian land forces during the Second Persian War, and the breastplate of the officer who headed the Persian cavalry in a crucial engagement. In addition to mementoes of war, the Greeks enthusiastically dedicated mementoes of the great names of bygone days. Some of these came from the historical past: at Delphi, for example, was preserved the iron chair of the poet Pindar, in a temple on Rhodes the personal jewellery of King Artaxerxes of Persia and the linen corselet of Pharaoh Amasis of Egypt, in a temple in Arcadia the breastplate and lance of Alexander the Great. Others came from the mythological past, since the ancients did not distinguish between history and mythology (cf. 233 above). As a matter of fact, the heroes of mythology, being mightier and more numerous than those of history, supplied by far the larger number and the most cherished. An inventory of the contents of a famous temple to Athena at Lindos on Rhodes happens to have survived; it reveals that the building had been a storehouse of such relics. There was a pair of bracelets that once graced the white arms of Helen of Troy and the cup from which she drank (it was in the shape of one of her breasts); various drinking vessels that once belonged to Minos, Cadmus, Telephus, and other mythological notables; weapons and armour from Menelaus, Teucer, Meriones, and Heracles; nine complete suits of armour deposited by members of the contingent that Rhodes had sent to the Trojan War; a set of tiller bars left by the helmsman of Menelaus' galley. All were presumably on display until the fourth century B.C., when a disastrous fire wiped out the best part of the collection.

Mythological bric-à-brac of this sort was to be seen the length and breadth of the Greek world. Helen's mementoes, for example, were by no means all in Rhodes. Delphi had a neck adornment and the stool she sat on, while one of her sandals was in southern Italy. Zeus had visited her mother in the form of a swan, and legend had it that she had been hatched from an egg; the egg was in a temple at Sparta, suspended by cords from the roof. Visitors could see Aeneas' shield on the island of Samothrace, Menelaus' in a temple to Athena in south Italy, Diomed's in Athena's temple at Argos (though the rest of his armour was in her temple at Luceria in south Italy), Achilles' spear in her temple at Phaselis in Asia Minor, the tools Epeius used for building the Trojan horse in a temple in south Italy. Orpheus' lyre was in Apollo's temple on Lesbos, Marsyas' flute—he was the one who dared to challenge Apollo to a music contest—in Apollo's temple at Sicyon. Marsyas of course lost, and he was punished for his insolence by being flayed; the skin was on display in the town in Asia Minor where Apollo had it hung up. Relics of the wandering Odysseus were not confined to the Greek world: a remote town in Spain had a shield and the prow of a ship; Circei, on the Italian coast where Circe was reputed to have lived, had a goblet; Djerba, the island off Tunisia which claimed to be the land of the Lotus-Eaters, offered as proof an altar set up by the hero; even remote Scotland had a memento, an altar inscribed in Greek which he was supposed to have dedicated.

Inevitably, as happens today, the same relic sometimes turned up in more than one spot. Thebes as well as Delphi offered the visitor Helen's stool. The hair that Isis tore out in her grief at the death of Osiris could be seen either at Coptos or Memphis. A pair of towns in Asia Minor both displayed the true sword with which Iphigeneia slaughtered victims during her enforced service as priestess of Artemis among the barbaric Taurians in the Crimea. Orestes, her brother, when he rescued her from there, stole and brought back a famous image of the goddess; Athens, Sparta, Aricia in Italy, and several other places all claimed to have it in their local sanctuaries of Artemis (one ancient writer in desperation suggested that perhaps Orestes stole more than one copy). The Palladium, the image of Athena that kept Troy safe until Odysseus made off with it, was on display in Argos, Rome, and three Italian towns.

Temples preserved not only mementoes of the heroes of mythology but even their physical remains, as churches preserve those of saints. Tantalus' ghost may have been in the underworld vainly trying to drink the water at his feet and eat the fruit out of reach above his head, but his bones, or what passed for his bones, were in a bronze jar at Argos. His son Pelops' were in a bronze chest at Olympia, Orpheus' were in a stone jar in a small town in northern Greece, the head of the gorgon Medusa was in an earth mound at Argos, and the bones of giants were to be seen in any number of temples. Thebes, for example, claimed to have Geryon's, the triple-bodied monster who was killed by Heracles.

'Giants' bones' brings us to another purpose Greek temples served: in addition to art and historical or pseudo-historical memorabilia, they housed curiosa of all kinds. Such bones, it has plausibly been argued, were really mammoth's bones, which not infrequently turn up in Greece. Similarly, Helen's egg has been explained as an ostrich egg. A temple at Tegea in the Peloponnese displayed the hide and tusks of the Calydonian boar that was hunted down by Meleager, and a temple near Naples the tusks of the Erymanthian boar whose destruction was one of the labours of Heracles; both exhibits were probably the remains of boars of exceptional size.

In all these instances the objects had earned their exalted posts at least in part by virtue of their alleged mythological associations. There were, however, plenty of others treasured purely and simply as curios. A rib or jawbone of a whale was on view in the temple of Asclepius at Sicyon. Until Carthage was destroyed in 146 B.C. one could see in its temple to Astarte the skins of the 'three women with hairy bodies', the chimpanzees or baboons that Hanno of Carthage had brought back from his epoch-making voyage down the west coast of Africa (63 above). Quite a few temples had elephant tusks, and one near Naples a whole skull. These may have come from India rather than Africa, since India supplied a good many cherished oddments. A temple in Asia Minor offered examples of Indian armour and Indian amber as well as elephant tusks. Pliny reports that 'Indian reeds' as big as tree trunks were a common sight in temples; they must have been specimens of bamboo. 'Indian nuts', also reportedly a common sight, probably were coconuts. Pliny is also our source for what surely was the most remarkable Indian curiosity of all: the horns of one of the monster gold-digging ants of India (111 above), he informs us, could be seen in the temple of Heracles at Erythrae in Greece. Even technological curios were put on display, such as an archaic flute with but four holes, a mirror that gave a distorted image, a special dental forceps made of lead for testing extractable teeth (the dentist was to go after only those which could be pulled by this relatively feeble instrument). The list of items enshrined in temples reveals a wildly haphazard miscellany, yet they were a significant beginning, they represent the seeds that would eventually blossom into our museums of natural history, ethnology, geography. Even the mythological bric-à-brac played its part. The various objects ascribed to Achilles, Odysseus, and the others were no doubt genuine examples of strange or obsolete weapons, armour, utensils, and adornments—museum pieces, as we would call them.

And, of course, temples had marvels to offer. There was a temple with an altar that consumed victims placed on it without fire, and one with a cluster of candles kept in the open which never went out. A sanctuary of Zeus had a fountain or spring with the power to rekindle torches which had been extinguished in it, while a sanctuary of the wine-god Dionysus had one that ran with wine during the seven days of the god's annual festival (the wine had to be consumed on the premises because, if carried out of sight of the temple, it reverted to water). Two statues of the goddess Artemis in two nearby towns, though completely exposed, were never touched by wind or rain. A temple at Pergamum, to protect a set of valuable murals by Apelles, paid a pretty penny for the skin of a basilisk which had the power to keep away spiders and birds.

When the world of small city-states gave way to great empires after the death of Alexander the Great (115 above), quite a few of the new monarchs turned out to be men of culture ready to spend the wealth that a crown commands in the cause of the arts. In Alexandria, Egypt's recently founded capital, Ptolemy I created an institute of advanced study (258 below). In Pergamum, the Attalids, particularly Attalus II (160–139 B.C.), collected art to adorn the impressive new buildings they were putting up. Pieces available on the market for purchase, they bought; what they could not buy, they had reproduced. Their sculpture included, for example, a replica of the renowned Athena by Phidias that stood in the Parthenon. They sent a team of painters to Delphi to copy a set of famous paintings there. The result of their efforts was an extensive private art gallery, the first to be created by deliberate selection and not haphazard dedications.

While the Attalids were acquiring art for their gallery with taste and discrimination, off in the west the nation which was soon to create the nearest thing to public museums that the ancient world would know was gathering it in like fishermen netting a catch. Rome, before the Punic Wars of the third century B.C., was a rough-hewn town, unsoftened by the presence of any Greek art. In 211 B.C., during the Second Punic War, the Roman general Marcellus captured the rich city of Syracuse and, as spoils of war, brought back a multitude of statues and paintings which he proceeded to dedicate in various parts of Rome. It was the opening of a floodgate: for the next 150 years, as the legions made their way through Greece and the Near East, the city was deluged with Greek art. When Marcus Fulvius Nobilior in 189 B.C. occupied Ambracia, a provincial capital in western Greece, he returned with no less than 285 statues in bronze and 230 of marble. In the victory procession that Aemilius Paulus held in 167 after defeating Perseus, king of Macedon, the parading of the looted statues and paintings took a whole day. The climax came with Mummius' sack of Corinth in 146; the booty produced 'the greatest number and the best of the public monuments of Rome', to use the words of Strabo, who visited the city a century later. What these conquerors acquired went to adorn their capital, not their private town houses or country mansions. As a matter of fact, some, like Mummius, had little taste for art; the story goes that he only learned of the value of one of his captured paintings when Attalus II, always on the lookout for masterpieces, offered a fabulous price for it.

In the next century, the looting of art was joined by its extortion—but the collectors were out for themselves rather than their city. Verres, the scoundrelly Roman governor of Sicily from 73 to 71 B.C. who was successfully prosecuted by Cicero, outdid even Hermann Goering. Some works he extorted, like the statue of Eros by Praxiteles that he made the owner sell to him for the equivalent of a measly £200 (or $500). What he could not extort, he confiscated, and what he could not confiscate, he robbed. Others operated legitimately, like Cicero himself; his letters are full of his enthusiastic search to buy art treasures for decorating his various country houses. Indeed, the mania for collecting had grown so among Romans of power and wealth that it became *de rigueur* to include in the plans for a villa special rooms for mural paintings and special areas for the display of sculpture.

With the fall of the Republic and the founding of the Roman Empire, works of art ceased being 'banished as exiles to country villas', as Pliny put it, and once again returned to the city's temples and other buildings. Caesar, then Augustus, and then most of the emperors of the first and second centuries A.D. continued to adorn Rome with Greek art. Soon the city had any number of temple-museums that boasted some of the ancient world's finest works. The collections emphasized old masters; a Roman emperor would readily use a contemporary artist to decorate a public building or do his portrait, but for the display of art he preferred time-honoured pieces, sculptures by Polyclitus, Myron, Phidias, Praxiteles, Scopas and Lysippus, paintings by Polygnotus and Zeuxis and Apelles—in short, the recognized greats of the sixth to the third century B.C. Their *chef d'oeuvres* were on view all over the city. The visitor could see a Zeus by Myron on the Capitoline hill, a Heracles by him in the Circus Maximus. The temple of Fortune had four pieces by Phidias, the 'Key Bearer', an Athena, and two statues of figures in Greek dress. Praxiteles' 'Success' and 'Good Fortune' were on the Capitoline, and an Eros by him in the Portico of Octavia. Scopas was represented by an Ares and an Aphrodite in the Circus Flaminius, an Apollo in one temple of Apollo, the Children of Niobe in another. Lysippus' Apoxyomenos was in front of the baths built by Agrippa, a Heracles by him on the Capitoline, and twenty-five bronze figures he had made of Alexander's leaders in the Portico of Octavia. Paintings by Apelles were to be seen in the Temple of Diana, the Temple of the Deified Julius, the Temple of Mars the Avenger; paintings by Zeuxis in the Portico of Philip or the Temple of Concord. The last-named building was fitted with big windows, an unusual feature in a temple; presumably they helped visitors see the art inside.

The location of several of the works just mentioned shows that, in their enthusiasm for decorating their city, the Romans did not limit themselves to temples. Public buildings of all sorts were adorned with statues and paintings, the porticoes, the theatres, the monumental public baths. As a matter of fact, by the third century A.D., after ruinous fires, like the one during Nero's reign, had destroyed the rich collections in many a temple, the Baths of Caracalla became one of the principal museums of Rome.

The Romans by no means limited their collecting to art. Every bit as reverent as the Greeks about relics from mythological times, even more liberal in treasuring historical mementoes, and just as enthusiastic in preserving miscellaneous oddments, they did their fair share of filling temples with curiosa of all sorts. Julius Caesar's sword was in the temple of Mars, a dagger from one of Nero's would-be assassins in the Temple of Jupiter, the royal robe of the early king Servius Tullius in the Temple of Fortune, the famous ring of Polycrates—he had tossed it into the sea only to have it turn up again in the belly of a fish brought to him as a gift—in the Temple of Concord. In the Temple of Eros at Thespiae in Greece the emperor Hadrian deposited a she-bear he had killed and in Zeus' temple at Athens an Indian snake. During the First Punic War, Roman soldiers campaigning in Tunisia had killed with a catapult shot a 120-foot serpent; the skin and jawbone were exhibited in some temple at Rome. A century and a half later soldiers on campaign there came across certain animals resembling wild sheep which were named 'gorgons' because their looks could allegedly kill; after a number of men had been lost trying to get near enough for a sword thrust, cavalrymen picked off a few specimens with well-aimed javelins, and the hides were deposited in the Temple of Hercules. There was a stuffed crocodile on display in Isis' temple in Caesarea in north Africa, a large cinammon root— which must have come from India—enshrined in a gold dish in a temple on the Palatine, an extraordinary chunk of crystal that weighed over 100 pounds in a temple on the Capitoline, a breastplate of British pearls in a temple in Caesar's forum. The Romans were the first to put precious stones on public view. Pompey, after the defeat of King Mithridates, looted the latter's collection and dedicated it on the Capitoline, and Caesar put into his favourite temple of Venus Genetrix no less than six different collections.

With statues and paintings acquired haphazardly by the looting of conquerors or the whim of emperors, and standing cheek by jowl with exotica gathered from here and there, did not a Roman temple look like somebody's old attic? Not necessarily. Thanks to a description written in A.D. 95, we know the contents and arrangement of a small collection in the temple of the Deified Augustus near the forum (Fig. 18). It was a model of careful judgement and taste. The works of art were set out in the front porch of the building under the projecting gable. After climbing the staircase to the level of the porch, as the visitor stood on the top step, he saw on the wall to his left a painting of Hyacinthus and a relief in marble of an hermaphrodite; on the entrance wall facing him, he saw, on one side of the door a painting of Danae and, on the other, a painting of Europa; on the wall to the right, he saw a marble relief of Leander. As he walked down the middle of the porch toward the entrance door, he passed between two files of three free-standing statues each. In the file to his left stood a gold statue of a Victory, behind that a clay statuette of a boy, and behind that a bronze of Apollo by Praxiteles, the *pièce de resistance* of the collection. To his right was a silver statue of Athena, behind that a clay statuette of Heracles, and behind that a bronze of Heracles as an infant strangling a pair of serpents. The exhibit was subtly arranged: a marble relief on either side wall; a gold statue to the left balanced by a silver one to the right; behind each of these two, to right and left, a clay statuette; behind each statuette, to right and left, a bronze. Though but a small collection, it was admirably comprehensive. It included three major art forms: painting, free-standing sculpture, relief. It presented a variety of materials—precious metals, bronze, clay, stone. And it illustrated at least three periods of art: Praxiteles' work and the paintings were of the mature classical style of the fourth century B.C.; the infant Heracles exemplified the baroque-like style of the next two centuries; and the two marble reliefs were 'modern'.

Statues, paintings, armour, snakeskins, dental forceps—all were on display for the art lover and curiosity seeker, yet all were in buildings whose prime function was something else, most often a house of worship. They were museums, but only incidentally, and as such all they usually did was to give house room to objects at which people were expected to gape in wonder without making any particular sense out of them. And this situation continued for well-nigh a millennium after the fall of Rome. The products of the minor arts that the Middle Ages had such a fondness for—enamels, wood carvings, ivories, fabrics—found their way into the cathedrals and the churches, as did the Arab glass and armour and rugs that flooded back to Europe in the wake of the Crusades. And churches took over the role of ancient temples in becoming repositories for oddments: the cathedral at Arezzo sheltered the jawbone of a whale, St Stephen's in Vienna some bones of mammoths, St John's at Lüneburg the shoulder bone of some sea monster, a church at Ensisheim in Alsace a meteorite, the cathedral at Merseburg a large tortoise shell, the cathedral at Seville a stuffed crocodile as well as a few elephant tusks and the bridle used by El Cid. As time went on, wealthy nobles caught the fever and began to amass private collections of such curios. The brother of Charles VI of France toward the beginning of the fifteenth century had a 'cabinet of wonders' that boasted ostrich eggs, snakeskins, porcupine quills, boars' tusks, whalebone, polar bear hides, mammoths' bones, and coconuts. It was a primitive museum of natural history—but it was strictly for his eyes and those of his friends, not the general public.

And then, on 15 December, A.D. 1471, Pope Sixtus IV took an epoch-making step: he set aside certain rooms in the Palazzo dei Conservatori on the Capitoline Hill for a display of ancient sculptures and appointed a board of four men to take charge of them. By this act he brought into existence the world's first true museum of art. Very soon thereafter, alongside the wealthy amateurs with their ragbag agglomerations of curiosities, arose a new type of collector, the professional scholar. Georg Agricola of Saxony (1494–1555), for example, a physician who worked in the mining areas of his country, gathered specimens of minerals, published codified descriptions of them, and by his writings induced his sovereign, Augustus of Saxony, to found at Dresden a 'Chamber of Art and Natural History' that eventually grew into the city's fine museums. Andrea Cesalpino (1519–1603) was a passionate botanist who headed a botanical garden at Pisa; his pupil, Michele Mercati (1541–1593), became keeper of the botanical garden of Pope Pius V and founded at the Vatican Italy's richest collection of minerals and fossils. These are but a few names out of many. By the sixteenth century the day of the modern museum had without question dawned.

16

The Itinerary

We travel long roads and cross the water to see what we
disregard when it is under our eyes. This is either because
nature has so arranged things that we go after what is far off
and remain indifferent to what is nearby, or because any
desire loses its intensity by being easily satisfied, or because
we postpone whatever we can see whenever we want, feeling
sure we will often get around to it. Whatever the reason,
there are numbers of things in this city of ours and its
environs which we have not even heard of, much less seen;
yet, if they were in Greece or Egypt or Asia . . . we would
have heard all about them, read all about them, looked over
all there was to see.

So wrote the younger Pliny around the beginning of the
second century A.D. Like the New Yorkers who have climbed
the Eiffel Tower but never the Empire State Building, the
ancient tourist hankered after what was exotic and remote.
And he went to find it, as Pliny reveals, chiefly in three areas:
Greece, Asia Minor, and Egypt.

In the fifth century B.C., Herodotus had gone all the way to
Mesopotamia; in the second A.D., Pausanias, a lifelong traveller
(292–9 below), remarks that he never saw the walls of Babylon
himself nor ever met anyone who had. The tourist's passion
for the past clearly had its limits. Even Syria and Palestine
were not included in the normal itinerary, although the day
was not far off when, with the Holy Land sites to offer, they

would become the tourist attraction nonpareil. Voyages farther afield, to Africa or India, were for businessmen.

If Romans fanned out eastward to tour what was to them the old world, people living in the provinces flooded in to Rome itself. So many were there that, as we have seen (129 above), cities maintained offices in the forum to aid their citizens when they came to visit or do business in the capital. There was plenty of the past to be seen in Rome: the fig-tree at the foot of the Palatine Hill where the cradle holding Romulus and Remus overturned; the shepherd's hut on the hill, complete with cradle, where the twin infants were raised; the Temple of Vesta in the forum where the Virgins kept the sacred flame burning eternally; the door of Janus' temple, which was left open in times of war and closed only in times of peace; the rich collections of art (248 above). But the citizen from the provinces was there to see the new Rome just as much as the old, the grandiose monuments the emperors had built testifying to the wealth and power of the state to which he belonged as well as to their own generosity. He gaped at the palaces on the Palatine Hill; these housed not only the emperor's quarters but the central administration too, and, as the business of government and its paperwork grew, so did the number of palaces. He passed leisurely hours enjoying the superb facilities of the huge public baths. If he had timed his trip right, there were programmes at the arenas or circuses to keep him busy for days (137 above). From the original forum he walked through a series of new forums, each donated by a different emperor—Caesar's, Augustus', Vespasian's, Nerva's, Trajan's. All were splendid places, lavishly decorated with expensive imported stone. Augustus boasted that he found a city of brick and left it a city of marble, and his successors carried on in the same tradition.

Those who started from Rome for Greece, Asia Minor, or Egypt, had to make a fundamental decision: whether to go by sea or land (149 above). The sea route, which involved embarking at Ostia, the port of Rome, or at Puteoli, the port of

Naples, and sailing to Athens or Alexandria, was not only the most comfortable way to go but, since the vessels all passed through the Straits of Messina, passengers had an opportunity to see Sicily, which had a good deal to offer the tourist. First, there was Syracuse itself with temples to Artemis and Athena that sheltered famed works of art, the quarries where the Athenian prisoners had been kept (236 above), and the fountain of Arethusa, a vast spring of sparklingly clear water teaming with fish. Then there was the ascent of Etna to see the crater, a must on many itineraries. Still another curiosity of nature that drew visitors was the Lacus Palicorum, a small pool about forty to fifty miles northwest of Syracuse, where twin jets of volcanic acid from fissures in the bottom kept the water moving agitatedly as if boiling.

In Greece tourists followed, by and large, the itinerary that had been in vogue for centuries (229 above): Delphi, Athens, Corinth, Epidaurus, Olympia, Sparta. Much had changed since the days of Classical Greece. Olympia, for example, now had some of the amenities Roman engineering could supply, such as running water brought in by an aqueduct (78 above). The Corinth earlier Greek travellers saw had been wiped out by the Romans in 146 B.C. and replaced by a thriving new town—but that meant little to those who came primarily for a look at the acropolis and the isthmus with its two ancient harbours, one on either side, and its *diolkos*, the paved way over which warships and other relatively light craft were hauled from one to the other. Epidaurus, after a period of decline (230 above), had got a new lease of life, and splendid new votives thanking Asclepius for his cures had replaced the ones that had been plundered. Much of Greece, however, unlike Epidaurus and Corinth, had fallen into decay by Roman Imperial times, enabling tourists avid for mementoes of the past to enjoy the added dimension of picturesque abandonment. Site after site offered the romantic combination of ruins in a serene pastoral setting that we see in Piranesi's prints of the remains of Rome and that so ravished eighteenth-century travellers to Italy. The visitor to famed Thebes found the greater part of it deserted. The city of Pisa, which a thousand years earlier had owned the land where the Olympic games were held and had taken charge of them, was now a vineyard. The walls of an erstwhile thriving town in Euboea now encompassed only farm land; its gymnasium had been turned into a wheat field where statues of deities and worthies peeked out amid the stalks, and sheep grazed in the agora surrounded by the ghosts of buildings that had once housed public offices.

The tour of Greece also included some of the islands. Visitors went to Delos with its venerable sanctuary of Apollo; to Samothrace, home of certain mysterious divinities whose worship, immensely popular, involved various secret rites; above all to Rhodes, which, like Athens, still had impressive witnesses to its days as an independent and rich nation. The Colossus, a brobdingnagian bronze statue of Apollo that stood at the harbour, had collapsed during an earthquake around 224 B.C., but there were still thousands of other statues, broad streets, and a circuit of formidable walls.

From Rhodes it was but a hop and a step to Asia Minor. And Asia Minor offered the greatest tourist attraction of all— the site of the Trojan War, 'Homer Country', so to speak. Priam's Troy, after the sack, had more or less lain neglected in ruins for a long while. Around 700 B.C. or so, Greek settlers raised a new town on the site, a second Ilium. This remained a relatively modest place until the Romans turned their attention to it. Rome had been founded, the legend went, by a handful of Trojan survivors who managed to escape from the burning city and, under the leadership of the hero Aeneas, sailed to Italy. Julius Caesar, whose family claimed to be descended from Venus, Aeneas' mother, felt himself personally involved in the legend and viewed the site as a sort of national shrine. As a consequence, he heaped honours on the little town, granting it additional territory, independence, and exemption from taxes; his successors confirmed all his favours and thought up some new ones. To its privileged status, Ilium

17 A restaurant at Herculaneum. First century A.D. Note the counter
with jars sunk into it and the three tiers of shelves on the wall beside it.

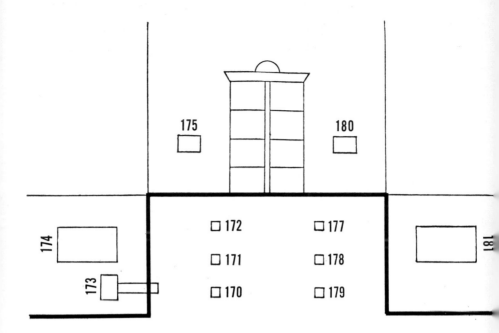

18　Arrangement of the art on display in a small Roman temple museum:
173 painting of Hyacinthus, 174 marble relief of an hermaphrodite, 175
painting of Danae, 180 painting of Europa, 181 marble relief of Leander,
170 gold statue of a Victory, 171 clay statuette of a boy, 172 bronze of
Apollo by Praxiteles, 179 silver statue of Athena, 178 clay statuette of
Heracles, 177 bronze statue of Heracles.

soon added a thriving business as the official custodian of Homer Country. It supplied guides who made sure that every significant place or feature mentioned in the Iliad was identified. They showed the tourist the strip of beach where the Greek ships had been pulled up, the plain where the battles had taken place, the two rivers that occur in so many scenes, the fig-tree outside the Scaean gates, the tombs of Achilles and Patroclus and Ajax (Protesilaus, the first Greek to jump ashore and the first to be killed, was buried just across the Hellespont), the cave where Paris gave his fateful judgement, even the spot from which Zeus' eagle carried off the Trojan princeling Ganymede. In a temple on the site, they pointed out a lyre allegedly belonging to Paris and armour allegedly of the Homeric heroes. Asia Minor had other sites to offer the visitor—Cnidus, the home of Praxiteles' world-famous statue of Aphrodite, flourishing cities such as Ephesus and Smyrna; the venerable oracles of Apollo at Colophon and Didyma— but none had the appeal of the site of the Trojan War; this was the *pièce de resistance*.

Next came Egypt, and getting there from Asia Minor was no problem at all. Those who were satisfied with seeing no more of Asia Minor than Homer Country could push on some twenty miles to Alexandria Troas ('Alexandria at Troy') and take a boat from there directly to Alexandria in Egypt. Those who went on to Smyrna or Ephesus could get a sailing from either place.

Egypt was a tourist's paradise. It offered an exotic landscape, an exotic way of life, exotic monuments and, on top of all this, relatively easy travel. Almost everybody went there by sea, and those who came directly from Rome made the crossing on the big comfortable grain ships that plied between Alexandria and Rome (158 above). Once in Egypt, the visitor was able to continue to do his moving about by water, since the inhabited portions of the country were strung out along the river. To make things ideal, the Nile was a particularly easy stream to sail on. It is blessed with a prevailing wind that

I

blows opposite to the direction of flow; a boatman can drift effortlessly downstream (or help his progress along with the oars if he is in a hurry) and, when it is time to go back, hoist sail and be wafted up-river. That very special traveller, Apollonius of Tyana, the miracle-working sage of the first century A.D., preferred to go by land and see every village instead of sailing by them; he and his party padded along the bank on camels from Alexandria to the pyramids.

The visitor's first thrill came even before he landed—while he was still some thirty miles out at sea, he could make out the top of the lighthouse of Alexandria, one of the Seven Wonders of the World. The city itself offered practically everything. There were famed monuments such as the tomb of Alexander, the temple of Serapis, the sanctuary of Pan (which was built on the top of an artificial hill and afforded a fine view of the entire city), the Museum. This last was a 'museum' in the ancient sense of the word; we would call it a research institute or institute of advanced study. It included four faculties: literature, mathematics, astronomy, and medicine. It had a great hall that served as commons room, where the faculty members ate together, a cloister for walks or ambulatory lectures, a theatre for public discussions, studies and quarters for the individual professors, library, botanical garden, and menagerie. Then there was the bustling life of the city itself. Alexandria was the greatest port in the Mediterranean, handling traffic from India and Africa as well as from most of the provinces of the empire, and offered all the features of a booming international entrepôt: a waterfront where you saw not only Mediterranean types but Arabs, Persians, Ethiopians, and Indians as well; various foreign quarters; an entertainment district lined with nightclubs. *Unus illis deus Nummus est,* 'They worship only one god there—Cash', someone once grumbled. It was not completely true. If Alexandria was the Marseilles of the ancient world, it was also the Vienna, a city of passionate lovers of music; at cithara concerts, for example, it was said that even humble listeners who could not read or write had so keen an ear they were able to spot every false note.

Alexandria was a Greek city with a cosmopolitan overlay. For the real Egypt, the tourist had to go up the Nile. He took a boat and sailed along the Canopic arm until he reached the site of modern Cairo near the apex of the Delta. Here he disembarked for a look at Heliopolis, where the most ancient temple to Re stood. By Roman times Heliopolis was a ghost town, the temple was partly in ruins (around 10 B.C. Augustus had carried off two of its obelisks to Rome, where they stand today), and of the once great population of learned priests only a handful were left to perform routine sacrifices and show visitors around. But the buildings were still impressive and legend made them more so; the guides took pains to point out where Plato and Eudoxus, a well-known Greek astronomer, lived during their apocryphal thirteen-year stay with the priests to learn from them the secrets of the heavenly bodies.

A little further upstream was Egypt's greatest claim to fame, Memphis. Here was the venerated temple of Ptah and the building that housed the sacred Apis bull; you were allowed a peek through a small window in the stable or, at a fixed time, the chance to see him take his exercise in an interior courtyard—as a matter of fact, the exercise period was largely for the benefit of tourists. Notable as these sights were, Memphis had something far better to offer: it was the starting point for a visit to the great pyramids. We marvel at their size; the tourist of those days was able to marvel at their superb finish as well, for he saw them still wrapped in the smooth skin of their revetment and adorned with numerous hieroglyphic inscriptions. All that is now left of the revetting is a scant cap about the apex of the pyramid of Khafre.

Back aboard the boat to sail on to Lake Moeris and get a look at a monument that the ancients ranked with the pyramids—the Labyrinth (101 above). Nearby was Crocodilopolis where tourists were encouraged to feed the sacred crocodile that incarnated the god Suchus (199 above, 271 below). Before

27 B.C., when, as we shall see in a moment, Thebes gained precedence, these sights stood highest in the list of Egypt's tourist attractions—at least it seems that way from the pains the Ptolemies took to invite junketing VIPs to visit them. I have already cited (198 above) the letter, written in 112 B.C., alerting the officials of Crocodilopolis to the arrival of a Roman dignitary. Here is another from a much earlier time, 254 B.C., which instructs one of the minister of finance's agents that he:

> upon receipt of this letter send the light chariots and other conveyances and the pack-mules to Ptolemais for the ambassadors from Paerisades and the envoys from Argos whom the king has sent to see the sights of the Arsinoite nome . . . At this moment of writing, they have already set sail upriver.

Paerisades was ruler of a far-off kingdom in the Russian Crimea, Argos is the well-known Greek city-state, and the king referred to is Ptolemy II (285–246 B.C.). The party had been put aboard a boat at Alexandria and were to get off at the river port of Ptolemais, a convenient point for anyone going to the Arsinoite nome. This was the district of which Arsinoe was capital, and Arsinoe was Crocodilopolis, renamed by Ptolemy II in honour of his queen, whose contribution to the success of his reign he was well aware of. The Labyrinth was no more than seven and a half miles away from it.

Having finished with this area, the tourist took to the river again, this time for a long ride upstream to Abydos to see the temple of Seti. Once again aboard ship to proceed further southward to Thebes. Thebes' renown had reached Greece as early as Homer's day, for the poet sings of its many houses and its hundred gates. For many centuries visitors ventured there, as they do now, chiefly to see the underground tombs in the Valley of the Kings (278 below). Then in 27 B.C., the city leaped into the forefront of Egyptian tourism when the so-called statue of Memnon, which had been standing there quietly since c. 1400 B.C., suddenly began to 'talk' and its unique performance became the acknowledged highlight of a visit to the country (272 below).

Those who were determined to leave nothing out continued on upriver to Syene (Aswan) at the First Cataract, which for thousands of years marked the southern border of Egypt. After sailing as near to the cataract as they could, they would go along the bank for some miles to get past the rapids, and, just beyond, be ferried out in a tipsy Egyptian canoe to see the temple on the island of Philae. And that was the end of the road for most visitors. Only the most determined of sightseers went past this point to brave the barren stretches of the Sudan, and they did not go very far.

So, in the days of the Roman Empire, tourists concentrated on these points above all: Rome; certain parts of Sicily; Greece, Delos, Samothrace, Rhodes, and perhaps a few other islands of the eastern Mediterranean; Asia Minor, particularly Troy and its environs; and Egypt.

17

Sightseeing

When plane, train, and car replaced sail, hoof, and foot, one key aspect of travel, the getting to a place, underwent revolutionary change. But the equally important aspect of what the traveller did when he got there—that is another story. Here in many respects time stood still; the ancient Roman, say, who landed in Greece for a holiday went about things not too differently from the thousands who have flocked there ever since.

If he arrived at Olympia or Delphi or Athens, he probably did as tourists have done in all ages, embarked as soon as he could on an investigatory walk about the place. At Olympia or Delphi, if he arrived late in the day, he had to wait until the next morning—just as the visitor does today. At Athens, or any sizable town, he could, if he wanted, take an evening stroll. Along the main street, light was no problem, since the oil lamps in the open-fronted shops provided plenty of illumination. At Pompeii, for example, excavation has revealed that one main avenue some 500 yards long had forty-five shops on either side; since each kept at least one lamp burning, there was a light every ten yards or so. Another street, some 700 yards long, had a total of 170 shops on both sides, so here the lamps were even closer. Street lights—as distinct from casual lighting from shops—were limited to main intersections, and there was a tendency to emphasize not illumination but effect, by, for example, setting up street lamps behind stone masks with gaping holes in the eyes and mouth, like jack-o'lanterns. Side streets were in total darkness, and anyone who planned to wander there had to hire linkboys to light the path either with torches, which just blazed the way, or with oil-burning lanterns which, when fitted with razor-thin sheets of horn or mica, could be adjusted to throw a shaft of light. And he had to be sure he knew his way back. Street signs and house numbers were as unknown to Roman as to Greek times (86 above), and the stranger's only recourse, stopping some local and asking, was hardly feasible in the small hours of the night.

In addition, pedestrians roaming after dark had to keep a sharp eye out for traffic. Many ancient cities had the good sense to ban most wheeled vehicles during daylight hours, limiting their movements to between late afternoon and sunrise. People on the streets then often found themselves squeezing into doorways in order to avoid getting crushed under some massively loaded, precariously swaying oxcart.

The daytime too had its perils for leisurely strolling. Though there may have been no wheeled traffic to worry about, a careless walker could easily be bowled over by a litter on the shoulders of a team speeding along at a brisk trot and with no means of braking to a fast stop. And then there were the dangers that in all ages confront the stranger on the street. 'There are shysters', warns a travel writer of the late second century B.C. in his description of Athens, 'who run about the city and swindle the well-to-do strangers who come to town. When the authorities catch them they hand out stiff penalties . . . But what you must guard against with all your might are the prostitutes; they're a pleasant way of getting ruined without realizing it.'

When the time came for serious sightseeing, the ancient tourist sallied forth stripped for action, with servants at his heels to carry any food or gear he took along. He was not even burdened with a guidebook. Not that this most useful form of literature did not exist. From at least the fourth century B.C. on, guides to individual places or monuments were available, and, between A.D. 160 and 180, a period when tourism was flourishing, Pausanias published his excellent *Guidebook of Greece* (292 below). But all these were for preparatory reading, not for use on the spot like ours. Moreover, ancient books, handwritten on relatively thick papyrus or leather sheets, were too bulky for casual carrying around, to say nothing of being too valuable.

Some ancient tourists must have been as interested as their camera-carrying descendants in having a pictorial memento of what they saw. If they had an aptitude for sketching, they could take along papyrus, pen, and ink, or perhaps merely wax tablets and stylus, much as travellers of the last centuries packed their boxes of watercolours. If not, they almost certainly were able to find, lined up waiting for business, any number of quick-working miniaturists, who could dash off, say, a bravura portrait with, at Athens, the Parthenon as background, at Delphi the temple of Apollo, at Olympia the temple of Zeus, and so on.

In setting forth to see a site, the ancient visitor's first problem was the same that so often confronts his counterpart today—to run the gauntlet of local guides lying in wait for him, the *periegetai* 'leaders around' or *exegetai* 'explainers', as they were called in Greek. 'I was going around the colonnades in the sanctuary of Dionysus,' says a character in one of Lucian's satirical sketches, 'examining each one of the paintings . . . , and right away two or three people ran up to tell me all about them for a small fee.' Many of us, willy nilly, submit to these tyrants; it saves the energy spent in lugging maps, plans, and a tourist handbook, and the time spent pouring over them. The ancients, with no such literature at their disposal, did not even have this alternative. And, from all accounts, local guides have not improved very much in the course of two thousand years.

To begin with, they were everywhere; the sightseer could not avoid them even if he wanted to. They were not only at the great tourist sites, such as Athens or Troy, but even in small towns that boasted but few attractions of no great dawing power. Lucian, in a spoof of the Baron Munchausenesque travel writers of his day, tells how he took a group of intrepid voyagers on a trip that included a visit to the Underworld, and there, when they reached Purgatory, 'guides showed us around and, for each victim, filled in the biographical data and reasons for punishment'. Another satirist has a character in one of his pieces utter the fervent prayer: 'Zeus, protect me from your guides at Olympia, and you, Athena, from yours at Athens.'

Next, the ancient guide shared with modern descendants the inability to stop, once he was launched on his patter. 'The guides went through their standard speech', grumbles one of the characters in a sketch Plutarch wrote about a party that was seeing the sights of Delphi, 'paying no attention whatsoever to our entreaties to cut the talk short and leave out most of the explanations of the inscriptions and epitaphs.' When the party managed to seize a few moments to discuss among themselves the point that particularly interested them, the patina on a certain bronze statue, the very moment their conversation came to an end, the guides were dinning their ears again.

It was not only that guides never stopped talking; it was also what they talked about. Much of their information, of course, was useful, even essential. They led a tourist over a place, they identified and filled in the historical background of buildings and monuments and statues, they explained the subject matter of paintings, they described local ritual and custom. At a site such as Olympia, where there was a veritable forest of statues and votive offerings, the accumulation of hundreds of years of dedications by or in honour of victorious runners, wrestlers, jumpers, racing teams, etc., a tourist was helpless without a guide. But useful information was not their only stock in trade. For example, they liked to discourse on the monuments they could not point out as much as those they could. At Delphi they held forth on the barbecue spits a

I*

celebrated courtesan had once dedicated there but which had disappeared ages ago; at Syracuse they held forth on the numerous works of art that Verres (247 above) had made off with (Cicero, in a prosecuting speech against the scoundrel, observed that the guides at Syracuse had turned 'their tours around. Before, they used to show where each piece was. Now they show where each piece was stolen from'). Even worse, whatever facts they did offer they liked to embroider with fancy, knowing that the average hearer had no way of checking up. 'Your guide', remarks Aristides, 'amid practically obliterated traces points and tells you "Here's Semele's marriage chamber, here's Harmonia's, here's Leda's"', and all that sort of thing.' The guides who took Herodotus around the pyramids fed him a tall story about the fabulous amounts paid out for supplying the workers with radishes, onions, and garlic (101 above); six centuries later, their descendants were telling Aristides that each pyramid extended downward into the earth the same distance it did upward. The priest who showed tourists around a certain temple at Ephesus, as he approached a famous statue carved out of particularly luminous marble, would stop and make each person cover his eyes—they might be damaged, he warned, by the intense reflection from the stone. When a small town in Asia Minor was hit by a severe storm, the rain and wind laid bare a skeleton on a nearby hillside; the local guides immediately began passing it off as Geryon's, the mythological triple-bodied monster slain by Heracles. Pausanias on his visit to the site could not resist pointing out that Geryon had lived, died, and been buried at Cadiz, at the opposite end of the Mediterranean. At Argos, the guides told him that one of the treasures of their city was the celebrated image of Athena which had once been Troy's sacred possession; 'But', comments Pausanias in exasperation, 'everybody knows that the Palladium, as the statue is called, was taken to Italy by Aeneas.' And he adds sorrowfully, 'The guides at Argos know very well that not all the stories they tell are true, but they tell them anyway.' Much of the embroidering of fact came from the guides' passion to connect whatever they could with the heroic days of mythological times, a passion no doubt nourished by the eagerness with which the customers lapped up such nonsense. 'Abolish fabulous tales from Greece,' snickered Lucian, 'and the guides there would all die of starvation, since no tourist wants to hear the true facts even for nothing.'

Having picked his guide, the ancient sightseer then began dutifully following him about. Knowledgeable tourists went soberly about their business trying, like the party Plutarch describes at Delphi, to shut the guides up or, like Pausanias, to keep them from too wild flights of imagination. The gullible dogged the guide's footsteps, eagerly drinking in every word, like the Caius Licinius Mucianus whom Pliny quotes so often. Mucianus, who spent a long time in the Near East—he was governor of Syria in A.D. 68—and travelled widely, though a ranking statesman and soldier, apparently swallowed whole everything he was told; it was from him that Pliny got the story of a spring in a temple of Dionysus that could flow with wine (246 above), of a temple in Lycia that preserved a letter written by one of the heroes of the Trojan War, of the people on Mt Tmolus in Asia Minor who lived to be one hundred and fifty years old, of a certain elephant that learned to read Greek and could write, of all things, 'I myself wrote this and dedicated these spoils won from the Celts.'

Most of the tourists were neither particularly knowledgeable nor particularly gullible, but went about being properly impressed by what they were seeing. The clearest proof we have of this is the skit by Herondas mentioned before (242 above). It concerns a trio right out of tourist life: Phile, the kind of female who bubbles enthusiastically about whatever she is shown; Kynno, her friend, serious and so knowledgeable that she is able to act as guide; and an unctuous sacristan. The two ladies go to make an offering at the well-known temple of Asclepius on the island of Cos, the site of the famous school founded by Hippocrates, father of medicine.

The place was also a museum of considerable renown, since some of the walls had been decorated by Apelles, perhaps the greatest painter of the ancient world, and the votive offerings that were all about included a number of celebrated sculptures (one was Boethus' statue of a boy struggling with a goose, a work so popular that innumerable copies of it were made, and no less than four have survived to this day). While waiting for the sacristan to report on how the god had reacted to their offering—it was only a rooster; that was all the poor ladies could afford—they decided to look over the collection. The impressionable Phile starts gushing immediately:

PHILE   Kynno, my dear! What beautiful statues! What sculptor did this one? Who paid to set it up?

KYNNO   Praxiteles' sons. Don't you see the inscription on the base? And a Euthies, son of Prexon, had it set up.

PHILE   May the god bless them and Euthies for such beautiful things.

KYNNO   Phile, see the statue of that girl, the one looking up at an apple.

PHILE   Wouldn't you say she'll simply faint if she doesn't get that apple? And, Kynno, that old man—and, in heaven's name, that boy choking a goose! If it weren't in stone, as you can see close up, you'd say that piece could talk!

KYNNO   I tell you, one of these days men will be able to bring even stone to life.

PHILE   That's right, Kynno. Just look at the way this one shows that hussy Batale standing, the statue of that pimp's daughter [*presumably a portrait dedicated by some local in honour of a cure the god had affected*]. Anyone who didn't know her, could just look at this image and never need the real thing.

KYNNO   Follow me, my dear, and I'll show you something beautiful, the likes of which you've never seen in your

whole life. (*To her maid*) Kydilla! Go call the sacristan
out. You there, looking every which way with that stupid
expression, I'm talking to you! (*To Phile*) Look at that!
Doesn't pay a bit of attention to what I say. Just stands
there staring at me worse than a crab! (*To the maid*) You
heard me, go call the sacristan! . . . Kydilla, as god's my
witness, I don't want to lose my temper, but you are
making me furious! I tell you, as god's my witness the
day will come when you'll be rubbing that damned skull
of yours!

PHILE   Don't be so quick to take everything to heart,
Kynno. She's only a slave. Laziness plugs the slave's ears,
you know.

KYNNO   But it's getting on, and the crush is getting bigger.
(*To the maid who had finally started to go off*) Hey, wait!
The door opened. We can go into the sacristy.

PHILE   Kynno! My dear! Look at these! Wouldn't you say
Lady Athena carved them herself? (*Turning and suddenly
seeing a statue of Athena*) Why, hello, my lady! (*Looking
at a painting of the sacrifice of an ox*) Why that naked boy,
if I were to scratch him, wouldn't he just bleed, Kynno? The
flesh is painted on him so that it's warm, it beats with life
in the picture. And that pair of silver tongs—if any
Mr Lightfingers saw it, wouldn't the eyes pop out of his
head! He'd think it's really silver. And the ox, and the
fellow leading it, and the girl attendant, and that hook-
nosed fellow and the one with his hair sticking up—aren't
they all the image of life? If I didn't think it was unlady-
like, I'd have screamed out loud that that ox might do me
harm. The way he looks at me sideways, Kynno, with
that one eye!

KYNNO   Phile, Apelles' hand is true in everything he paints.
You can't say, 'There's a man who took up one thing and
disregarded another.' No, whatever came to his mind, he
was eager to jump up and try. If anyone looks at him or

his works without being overwhelmed—why let him be strung up by the heels in a laundry [*i.e. the place* par excellence *for squeezing, wringing, beating*]!

SACRISTAN (*coming forth to greet them*)   Ladies, your offering is perfect; it looks as if better things are in store. No one has pleased our lord more than you. (*Praying*) O Lord, for these fair offerings of theirs, thy blessings on these ladies and whoever be their spouses and near of kin, O Lord. Amen.

KYNNO   Amen, great Lord, and grant that we come back in good health to bring you a better offering, along with our husbands and children. (*To a maid*) Kokkale, don't forget to cut a nice drumstick off the bird and give it to the sacristan.

To do the collection of an ancient temple was somewhat easier than, say, an art-laden church, since many of the treasures were out of doors, in full sunlight and never barred by lock and key. War trophies, such as shields, were often hung on architraves and along friezes. Statues in marble or bronze were set up in the porches at either end (Fig. 18) or between the columns along the sides. Or they might be placed at various points in the sanctuary grounds; two favoured solutions were to put them under colonnades or in niches in the perimeter wall. Objects of intrinsic value, like pieces in silver or gold, or objects that could not take the weather, like statues of wood or of gold and ivory, were generally within walls. To see these, one faced the problem that has plagued tourists through the centuries, of knowing the hours of opening or of finding someone to unlock the doors. In Herondas' sketch, Phile and Kynno started with the statuary, which must have been dotted about the sanctuary, but then, for the paintings, which were inside, they had to wait until the sacristan opened up. Praxiteles' masterpiece, the Aphrodite at Cnidus, was in a special building which enabled visitors to view the figure from all sides—but, to see it from the rear, they had to go through a back entry, and that involved locating a lady who had the key. There was no question that temples had to be kept locked, for they were robbed as ruthlessly as churches are today. At Rome thieves made off with a hoard of gold stored in the temple of Jupiter on the Capitoline, the sword of Caesar that was kept in the temple of Mars the Avenger, even the helmet from the statue of Mars there. The situation got so bad at times that the Roman authorities made the guardians of temples with particularly valuable pieces responsible for them with their life.

The opportunity to see great works of art or historical buildings and monuments is what draws a tourist to a site. However, once there, he is glad to have some diversion; even the confirmed lover of art and antiquities can lose interest after hours of plodding around, particularly during the heat of a Mediterranean summer. And so, in ancient times as now, the the locals had special performances to offer which provided a welcome change of pace for a footsore sightseer. One of the high points of the tour of the pyramids, for example, was to watch men from the nearby village of Busiris, who had made a specialty of the feat, shinning up from the ground to the very tip—a bravura display of agility in those days when the sloping faces, with the revetment still intact, were absolutely smooth. Further up the Nile were the sacred crocodiles; the priests had taught them to come when called and, on command, open their jaws and let their teeth be cleaned and then wiped dry with cloths. At Arsinoe, where the crocodile who incarnated the god Suchus dwelled, a tourist could enjoy an even better show. If he came to the temple provided with an appropriate food offering for the god—a kind of pastry, some roasted meat, and a pitcher of wine sweetened with honey—he could watch while the priests called the beast, opened its mouth, stuffed in the pastry and meat, and flushed it down with the wine. Suchus must have been uncommonly well fed because, if a second tourist came up to make an offering, the priests would forthwith go through the whole routine again. At Syene (Aswan) on the First Cataract, the local boatmen would put on a special act they had perfected: working their way upstream to a point beyond the cataract, they turned around, set their craft drifting downstream, and then shot the rapids; this, however, was for the delectation of distinguished visitors only.

The most renowned performance of all, one that attracted tourists from all over the ancient world, was put on by nature and not man. At Thebes in Egypt, not far from the Valley of the Kings, stands a pair of colossal statues, each consisting of a base and a throne with a seated figure upon it. They are as tall as a six-storey house; the feet alone are three yards long. But it was not their size that drew the crowds; it was that one of them 'talked'.

Today we know that the singularly gifted statue represents Amenhotep III, who reigned about 1400 B.C. and was one of Egypt's greatest pharaohs. The Greeks and Romans, however, were convinced it was a likeness of the mythological Memnon, child of the Goddess of Dawn, who figures in the legend of Troy; he was king of the Ethiopians, and met an untimely death at the hands of Achilles when he led an army from his native land through Egypt to help the beleaguered Trojans. At some time, probably about 27 B.C., an earthquake broke the statue across the torso, and the upper part fell to the ground. The remainder developed a unique feature—the ability to utter sound. At daybreak—not any other time of day, only daybreak—it made a sharp cracking noise which somewhat resembled the snapping of the string of a musical instrument. The conviction arose, no doubt ably fostered by the local guides, that these sounds were Memnon's way of talking to his bereaved mother.

The earliest to report the phenomenon is the learned geographer Strabo, who wrote in the last decade of the first century B.C., not too long, therefore, after the statue had started to 'talk'. Strabo was not convinced. Mentioning that the upper half of the colossus had fallen, reportedly as the result of an earthquake, he goes on to say:

It is believed that, once a day, a noise like a blow of no great force is produced by the part of the statue remaining on the throne and base. I myself was present on the spot along with Aelius Gallus [governor of Egypt] and a group of his companions and soldiers and, an hour after sunrise, I heard the sound—whether it came from the base of the statue or was deliberately made by one of the people standing around and near the base, I cannot say for sure. Indeed, because the source is indeterminate, any plausible idea that occurs to one is easier to believe than that the sound was sent out by stones fixed that way.

When Pausanias was compiling his *Guidebook of Greece* sometime about the middle of the second century A.D., the statue was still talking. Pausanias includes a description of it, and, though not an out and out sceptic like Strabo, is definitely guarded. He writes:

What surprised me far more than anything else was the Colossus of the Egyptians. At Thebes in Egypt . . . you come to a seated statue that gives out a sound. Most people call it Memnon . . . The Thebans, however, say that the image represents, not Memnon, but a native with the name of Phamenoth [probably a garbling of Amenhotep]. I have also heard some claim that it represents Sesostris [a quasi-mythological Pharaoh]. . . . Every day at sunrise it cries out, and the sound can be best compared to the snapping of the string of a lute or lyre.

But Strabo with his scientific doubts and Pausanias with his caution were voices in the wilderness. For all who flocked there, the statue was Memnon conversing with his mother. And they kept flocking right up to the beginning of the third century A.D. when for some reason Memnon stopped talking. It was just about this time that the emperor Septimius Severus had the piece which had fallen down replaced, and it may have been this that struck Memnon dumb. It has been suggested, with some plausibility, that the sound was caused by the sudden increase of temperature at sunrise, which heated the air trapped in holes in the broken surface causing it to expand and, in escaping, produce a sound. Thus, when the reconstruction covered up this surface, the miraculous voice was abruptly silenced.

Since Memnon during his vocal period had performed daily, he was able to gather far more witnesses to his unusual powers than, say, any of today's miracle-working statues of saints which perform only annually on the appropriate saint's day. We know of these witnesses and their steadfast faith in the talking statue thanks to yet another tourist characteristic that has not changed one whit during the course of two thousand years—the compulsion to scribble one's name in the places one has been, to leave, as it were, a calling card for all subsequent visitors to see.

We can trace this compulsion back at least four thousand years, to the days of Egypt's Eleventh Dynasty around 2000 B.C. Henu, a high official under pharaoh Mentuhotep III, had been entrusted with an expedition of some sort down the Red Sea; as he made his way back through the gorge that leads from there to the Nile, the Wadi Hammamat, he chiselled on its walls his name and accomplishments. This, to be sure, was a carefully carved inscription, a rather formal version of the calling card. More familiar are the informal ones, the random scribblings or graffiti 'scratchings', as they are called. These too are of hoary antiquity; we have already encountered examples that date from the thirteenth century B.C. (33 above). The next oldest specimens we have were written in 591 B.C. In that year Egypt's pharaoh dispatched deep into the Sudan an expedition of Egyptian troops stiffened with a foreign legion, a contingent of Greek mercenaries. As the combined army made its way upriver it passed the spectacular temple of Ramses II at Abu Simbel with its four colossal seated figures in front (this is the temple that was recently cut away and raised to the top of a cliff to avoid being submerged under the waters backing up behind Egypt's new high dam). On the legs of the statues the commanding officers and some of the men scratched things like: 'When Pharaoh Psammetichus came to Elephantine [near the First Cataract], this was written by those who sailed in the flotilla commanded by Psammetichus, son of Theocles. . . . Potasimto commanded the foreign legion, Amasis the Egyptians. This message was inscribed by Archon, son of Amoibichos, and Pelekos, son of Eudamos.' Others, presumably from the ranks, just put down their names. 'Telephos of Ialysus [a city on Rhodes] wrote this', says one inscription; it was an ancient Greek soldier's way of saying 'Kilroy was here'. Some four centuries later troops dispatched by one of the Ptolemies added additional signatures, including that of 'Krateros, son of Leukaros, elephant-hunter'. Elephants were the tanks of the Ptolemaic armies, and expeditions were sent regularly into Africa to catch them; we find a graffito recording 'the soldiers of the elephant hunt' on a temple wall in Abydos; it was scribbled no doubt when the men were passing through en route to or from a foray. The names at Abu Simbel go right down the centuries; even Ferdinand de Lessups, builder of the Suez Canal, left his there.

The monument whose surfaces the tourist found absolutely irresistible was Memnon. Over one hundred graffiti cover practically the whole of his legs and base; they range in time— about a third of them are dated—from the reign of Tiberius (A.D. 14–38) to A.D. 205. Most, as it happens, are no casual scribblings but veritable inscriptions carved with care; they were probably done by professional stonecutters who were available for hire in the vicinity. Apparently only the *élite* were allowed to leave these elegantly engraved mementoes. Heading the list of notables who did so is Sabina, wife of the Emperor Hadrian; she accompanied her husband on a trip to the famed monument in A.D. 130 and attests that 'during the first hour

[i.e., after sunrise] she twice heard Memnon'. Her husband
has left no record; perhaps he was piqued because, as we
gather from some verses indited by a voluble poetess who
accompanied the royal entourage, Memnon had the bad taste
to fail to perform for his distinguished visitor. Before Hadrian's
time the marvel had drawn quite a few high-ranking officials—
no less than five governors of Egypt—and any number of
army officers, probably from units stationed in the neighbourhood or passing through. As the years passed, its attraction
grew steadily, among intellectuals as well as officials, reaching
a climax with the emperor's own visit. While Hadrian was on
the throne Roman officialdom felt it was almost *de rigueur* to
go there and inscribe their names. Among the graffiti that date
from his reign are three left by governors of Egypt, three by
district governors, a scattering by lesser officials, one by a
judge, and at least three by self-styled 'poets'. After Hadrian,
the inscriptions fall off sharply. By this time, with the total
going past the hundred mark, space was running short. The
latest that bears a date was done around A.D. 205. Septimius
Severus' restoration presumably took place the next year or so.

These messages, left by wellnigh two centuries of visitors,
make it plain how thin were the ranks of the sceptics and how
full those of the true believers. For the writers attest not only
to their presence there but to their faith in the miracle as well.
Officials are curt and to the point; one has the feeling that they
say what they have to say in the verbiage they use in their
formal reports: 'I, Lucius Funisulanus Charisius, mayor of
Hermonthis and Latopolis [two nearby villages], heard
Memnon twice, before the first hour and at the first hour,
along with my wife Fulvia. 8 Thoth, 7th year of Hadrian, our
lord [i.e. 5 September A.D. 122].' The intellectuals who flocked
there, poets and poetesses, professors, the literary-minded in
general, found prose too bald to express their feelings. They
turned to verse, usually archaic verse done in the style of
Homer—after all, was not Memnon a character from the legend
of Troy? One of the Roman governors of Egypt, obviously a

man of culture, combines both styles, the bureaucratic and the poetic. 'On the day before the Ides of March,' he writes in terse Latin, '16th consulship of Emperor Domitian Caesar Augustus Germanicus [i.e. 14 March A.D. 92], Titus Petronius Secundus, Governor of Egypt, heard Memnon at the first hour and honoured him with the Greek verses inscribed below:

> Lord Memnon, thou spake loud and shrill
> When struck by the rays burning hot
> Of Apollo (for much of thee still
> Sits in majesty here on this spot).'

Another official, who signs 'poet and procurator', is responsible for what is probably the best metrical effort on the monument:

> O Thetis, nymph of the sea, know that Memnon
> Still lives, still speaks to his mother aloud,
> When warmed by her light, on the bank by the mount
> Which the Nile cleaves from Thebes, gated city so proud,
> While the voice of Achilles, thy battle-crazed boy,
> Can no longer be heard either in Greece or at Troy.

Most of the versifiers rarely rise above the level of doggerel à la Homer. Here, for example, are the words penned by a certain Falernus who calls himself 'professor and poet' and has no humble opinion of his talents:

> He has learned to orate, he has learned to keep quiet;
> The force both of words and of silence he knows.
> At the sight of the dawn, of his saffron-robed mother,
> He utters a sound, and more sweetly it flows
> Than the clearest of speech ever voiced by another.
> This poem did Falernus, Professor and Poet, infuse
> With a quality worthy of a Grace or a Muse.

And Paeon, poet in attendance on Mettius Rufus, governor of Egypt from A.D. 89 to 91, is hardly better:

> Thou still hast thy voice, O great Memnon, e'en though
> By destroyers thy body was smitten,

For Mettius heard it, and can say it is so.
This poem by Paeon was written.

Of the sixty-one graffiti in Greek, no less than thirty-five are in verse. (Of the forty-five in Latin, only four are—but we must remember that Homer's language was Greek.) The prose messages, though not always as bare as the examples in quasi-officialese cited above, rarely went in for more than a brief allusion to the quality of the experience. Thus a certain Artemidorus, a village clerk who paid a visit with his family, writes: 'I heard the wonderful Memnon, along with my wife Arsinoe and my children Ptolemaios and Ailurion, also called Quadratus, 11 Choiak, 15th year of Hadrian Caesar, our lord [i.e. 7 December A.D. 130].'

Memnon, with only legs and base available for inscriptions, had to be selective about who was to sign on him. In another set of monuments nearby of rather lesser note there was space galore for tourists to relieve themselves of the itch to scratch—the underground tombs of the pharaohs in the Valley of the Kings. Long before Greek and Roman times, these had been broken into by robbers, stripped of their riches, and left open. By the end of the first century B.C., at least forty were known. And, in ten of these, six centuries of visitors have left their mark.

The earliest graffiti go back perhaps to the third century B.C., but there are not many this old. The big tourist influx began in the first century A.D. and reached its height in the second, the great years of the Pax Romana. Visitors kept right on coming until the Arab conquest of Egypt in the seventh century finally put an end to the traffic. Unlike Memnon's carefully engraved and often lengthy messages, we find here the short hurried notes that are typical of graffiti. The tombs are all in the form of a long series of underground corridors and chambers hacked out of the living rock—the Greeks called them *syringes* 'pipes' because they resembled pipe-like galleries—and this meant that writing had to be done under little or no natural light, which did not encourage lengthy or careful composition. Most of the graffiti are clustered near the entrances, where the sun penetrated, but there are quite a few deep in the bowels, and these could only have been done under the flare of torches.

There are over 2,100 inscriptions in the tombs. Inevitably they are able to tell us much more than Memnon's select one hundred-odd about the nature and ways of sightseers in ancient times. They show that, even as now, tourists liked to go about in company. Families travelled together, as we see from the many instances in which fathers sign for their wives and children as well as for themselves. People of like interests travelled together; there are graffiti, for example, left by a group of Neoplatonist philosophers who paid the site a visit *en masse*. Officials went with their entourages: a certain Tatianus, governor of the district of Thebes, left signatures in three different places, and nearby are those of at least two secretaries, two assistants, and a friend. Many graffiti include mention of a home town, and these reveal that the fame of the tombs was world-wide. The major districts of Greece are represented, all the main islands of the Aegean and eastern Mediterranean, many parts of Asia Minor, the Levant, Italy, Sicily; one visitor came from as far east as Persia, two from as far west as Marseilles. As we might imagine, the tourists were largely from society's upper crust, people who had time and money for travel. No royalty ever took the trouble to see the tombs, but at least six governors of Egypt did, quite a few district governors, and the inevitable ubiquitous army officers. For intellectuals the 'pipes' seem to have had even more appeal than Memnon: calling cards were left by judges, lawyers, poets, prose writers, public speakers, professors, doctors (no less than twenty-eight of these), and philosophers of various persuasions—one Aristotelian, a number of Cynics, and the contingent of Neoplatonists just mentioned. There was a special reason for these last, revealed by one of their number, a lawyer named Bourichios from Ascalon on the southwestern coast of Palestine, who pointedly says that 'he made his visit because of Plato'. It was a commonplace among Greeks that Egypt was the fount of much ancient wisdom, and the man in the street would take it for granted that so profound a philosopher as Plato had spent long years there. On top of this, one of the most famous Platonic passages is the Allegory of the Cave in the *Republic*; conceivably people like Bourichios thought they were beholding the very place the master had written about. Though plenty of intellectuals are recorded, there is not one manufacturer or merchant, but this is hardly surprising: business was not a career one often boasted about in the ancient world. Of the hundreds who signed without indication of profession, a few at least must have been merchants; the two who came from distant Marseilles, which carried on a good volume of trade with Egypt, almost certainly were. The others no doubt represent the spectrum of the middle-class folk who lived in the neighbourhood or no great distance away.

A number of the graffiti are precisely dated, giving even the month and day, and these indicate that the ancient 'tourist season' in Egypt was just about what it is today, from November to April, when the weather is relatively cool. Only locals braved the midsummer sun, and not very many of them. The itinerary seems to have started with a pre-dawn trip to Memnon. He was the sight *par excellence* and, standing in the level fields along the bank, was easy to reach. After he had gone through his act, the ranks no doubt thinned, and only those sufficiently enticed by the fame of the 'pipes' to tackle the climb involved, followed the guides on to the Valley of the Kings. Artemidorus, for example, the village clerk who signed for his wife and two sons on Memnon, mentions only his wife in the tombs; quite possibly he spared the children the rugged walk and sent them back with an attendant. The guides took all visitors to the feature attraction, the tomb of Ramses VI. Not that it was so much more impressive than the others; it owed its popularity solely to the widespread belief,

which had somehow sprung up, that it was Memnon's. Of
the more than two thousand known graffiti, almost half were
inscribed here. A good many people also saw the tomb of
Ramses IV, conveniently located near the entrance to the
royal cemetery. About a third of the graffiti are here, including
many left by Christians; for some reason the place seems to
have become a Christian cult centre in later centuries. The
tombs of Ramses X and Merneptah ran a poor third with 132
and 121 graffiti respectively. Six other tombs have a mere
sixty-odd signatures each or less. The rest apparently were
never or hardly ever visited. Most tourists were satisfied with
a tour through 'Memnon's', quite a few did at least two—
'Memnon' and Ramses IV—while some did three or even
four. A certain Jasios and Synesius hold the record—in the
tomb of Ramses X they scribbled 'This is the sixth "pipe" we
have seen'. Jasios had come all the way from Neocaesarea
near the south shore of the Black Sea, and he obviously was
not going to miss a trick. His name occurs in other tombs,
once with a note mentioning that he had also heard
Memnon.

At the entrance to a tomb the guides stopped to let the
visitors accustom their bodies to the cool and their eyes to
the semi-darkness after the glare of the sun. Very likely many
took advantage of these moments to whip out reed pen and
ink or a pointed instrument and leave their name; as mentioned, many graffiti are clustered near the entrances, including
the better part of the ones done in ink. Of these, about three
hundred are in black ink, some forty in red, and a scattered
few in green or brown; all the rest of the graffiti, some 1,750,
are scratchings. The guides then lit torches and led the way
into the depths. Disregarding the parts of the walls that were
covered with rows of hieroglyphs, they would stop in front
of the mural paintings to explain them. This was another
convenient time for writing, and many used it to scribble on
the blank spaces surrounding the figures in the pictures.

The visitor to the tombs felt compelled to record not merely that he had been there but that he had been 'amazed'. 'I, Palladius of Hermopolis, judge, saw and was amazed'; 'I, Alexander, Governor of the District of Thebes, saw and was amazed—and I, Isaac of Alexandria, his secretary, was more than amazed at the wonderful work.' Some are more expansive: 'I, Antonius, son of Theodorus, of Heliopolis in Phoenicia, Honourable Minister of Finance, who have long resided in Rome and gazed on the marvels there, have seen these here too.' Some were even ecstatic: 'Unique, unique, unique!' one burbled. A Roman officer who writes in Latin apparently wanted to be absolutely certain his amazement was noted, for he recorded it no less than four times: in the tomb of Ramses IV with the words, 'I, Colonel Januarius, saw and was amazed at the place along with my daughter Januarina. Greetings to all'; in a corridor and an inner chamber of 'Memnon's' tomb with the words 'I, Colonel Januarius, saw and was amazed at the place'; and in the room that held the sarcophagus with the customary minimum 'I, Colonel Januarius, saw and was amazed'. A 'Marcus Volturius, Roman', who signed himself in Latin in the two favoured tombs, both times repeated the message in Greek to make sure that all comers would be able to read it. The record for scribbling goes to a certain Amsouphis who visited four tombs and left a total of nine signatures. Once he 'was amazed', once he left his 'homage', once he signed his name with his profession—'magician', no less—and six other times he just left his name. Some were so impressed by the mystery all about them, particularly the baffling hieroglyphic characters on the walls, that they elected to go in for mystery themselves and inscribed their names in anagrams. 'Onipsromse', wrote one, which unscrambles easily enough to Sempronios; 'Onaysisid' wrote another, which unscrambles to Dionysias. Neoplatonist and lawyer Bourichios, presumably adept at unravelling the secrets of the law or of philosophic thought, was depressed in front of the inscrutable hieroglyphs. 'Having made my visit,' he laments, 'I blame myself for not understanding the writing.' 'I did not accept that reproach from you, Bourichios!' scribbled a sympathetic friend right below.

Understandably, 'Memnon's' tomb drew the most extravagant expressions of amazement. 'I saw the other "pipes"', writes Hermogenes from Amasis in northern Asia Minor, 'and was amazed, but, when I visited this one of Memnon, I was more than amazed.' It even moved some to verse although, working by dim light, they restrained their effusions to a few lines:

Everyone of the 'pipes' held Heraclius in thrall
But he says that King Memnon's is most wonderful of all.

Not every visitor was quite so awestruck. In two places someone, tongue in cheek, scratched the children's age-old challenge: 'Does your mother know you're out?' A certain Ephiphanius records grumpily that he 'made the visit but was amazed at nothing except the stone'—presumably the feat of hacking so great a structure out of living rock. 'I saw the madness, and I was amazed', writes Dioscurammon. These noncomformists made their visits in later centuries, and, despite the name Dioscurammon (the Dioscuri were the Greek gods Castor and Pollux, and Ammon was the chief Egyptian deity), both may have been Christians, which would account for their attitude. Christian visitors to the tombs, reluctant to admit the achievements of pagans, rarely mention amazement and simply sign their names, often with an indication of their faith such as a cross or the abbreviation for Christ.

The most accessible of Egypt's noted tourist attractions was the complex of pyramids and the great sphinx outside Memphis, and it goes without saying that the ancient sightseers left their mark here. Many must have scratched messages on the smooth outer skin of the sloping faces. However, since the slabs that made it up were cannibalized over the centuries for use elsewhere, the inscriptions have almost all been lost. We have the text of only a few, copied down by pilgrims who visited the site in the fourteenth and fifteenth centuries when some of the skin was still in place. The most elaborate is a six-line poem in Latin epic verse, the work of some melancholy Roman lady. 'I saw the pyramids', she writes, 'without you, dearest brother. Sadly I shed tears here—which was all I could do for you—and mindful of our sorrow do I inscribe this lament.' A number of tourists scribbled on a paw of the sphinx, and their words have survived, including a few effusions in poetry. One, in the archaic Homeric verse that was *comme il faut* for such messages, runs:

> This sphinx who lacks naught is a vision divine.
> If you ponder her shape you will note the sure sign
> That her form is all made like a sacred apparition:
> Above is she holy, her face of heaven's rendition,
> But a lion, king of beasts, in limbs, body, and spine.

Most, however, were satisfied just to record their respects to the deity: 'homage from Harpocration', 'homage from Hermias', and the like.

This formula and other similar ones are found also at the temple of Isis on Philae, a tiny island in the Nile just above the First Cataract. The temple still stands, but, after a dam was raised at Aswan between 1899 and 1902, was submerged by the waters that backed up behind; it can now be seen only during the early summer months when the level of the Nile drops to its lowest. Philae was remote—foreigners who disembarked at Alexandria had to sail upriver the length of Egypt to reach it—so visitors, other than locals or officers and men from the troops stationed roundabout, were not too common. Yet a few made it there in one way or another. A certain Heliodorus, native of a town in Syria, who left an inscription on Memnon, went on to leave one at Philae, probably in the early years of the second century A.D. An intrepid traveller of roughly the same time who records that he came to Egypt just to see the sights, and who included even the far-off sanctuary of Ammon in the Libyan desert in his itinerary, paid a visit to Philae. Two Roman senators who travelled through Egypt in 2 B.C. signed the walls there. Envoys from the King of Meroe deep in the Sudan to the governor of Egypt at Alexandria had to pass through Philae; some who were *en route* in the mid-third century A.D. took advantage of the occasion to visit the temple and scratch a message. Like Memnon, Philae inspired many of its beholders to verse. There are, for example, no less than three poems from a Catilius who paid his visit in the last decades of the first century B.C. In recording their respects to the deity of the temple, the graffiti writers liked to include a plea for blessed remembrance of others who could not be there or to record the performance of a ceremonial act in their behalf. Thus an Ammonius, son of Dionysius, who visited on 6 June A.D. 2, writes that he, 'made his prayer to Isis and Serapis and the other gods dwelling here and rendered homage in the name of my brother Protas and his children, of my brother Niger, of my wife, of Demas and her children, of Dionys and Anoubas'. And a certain Demetrius, who was there probably on 4 February, 28 B.C., effuses in Greek verse:

> I, Demetrius, having coursed the fruit-giving Nile,
>   Came to Isis, whose power knows no end,
> To ask of her blessed remembrance for my every
>   Child, brother, sister, and friend.

Such messages were not peculiar to Philae. They are found in Hatshepsut's temple at Deir-el-Bahari, in the Memnonion at Abydos—indeed, they must have been an ubiquitous nuisance, since Plutarch, in a blast against all who scribble in public places, singles them out for special mention. 'There is never anything useful', he storms, 'or charming in what they write, just things full of nonsense such as "So and so asks for blessed remembrance for so and so".'

Having visited a spot, watched whatever performances the locals had to offer, perhaps added his name to the others, scratched there, the tourist had one thing left to do: find an appropriate souvenir.

Not very much information about shopping for souvenirs is available from the ancient world, just enough to reveal that only the objects of the hunt have changed, that the tastes and desires and purposes involved were much the same as now. The religious-minded Roman lady touring in Egypt brought back a container of Nile water to use in the service of Isis, just as the visitor to Italy today returns with a rosary. The amateur art lover came home from Athens with a replica in miniature of the great statue of Athena by Phidias, just as we come back from Florence with one of Michelangelo's David. The wealthy did not content themselves with miniatures; they ordered full-scale reproductions to adorn their town houses and country villas. Hadrian, most widely travelled of the Roman emperors, not only filled his monumental villa outside Rome with masterful copies of famous statues he had seen, but, as we noted earlier (232 above), devoted whole areas of it to reproductions of entire sites that he had enjoyed, such as Greece's Vale of Tempe or the sanctuary of Serapis at Canopus near Alexandria.

Inevitably the ancients had their versions of the cheap, gimcrack souvenir. Thanks to the archeologists, we have quite a few samples to show what these were like. In Afghanistan there was unearthed a glass vessel decorated with a scene of the harbour of Alexandria; it must have arrived at that far-off place in the luggage of some local who wanted a memento of his long trek to the great metropolis. In the second century B.C. shops in Alexandria sold a distinctive type of cheap faience pot with a figure in relief on it of one of the Ptolemaic queens; though intended primarily for the local folk—most examples have turned up in Egypt—it also appealed to visitors, who carried them off as souvenirs. The Bay of Naples area, Rome's favoured holiday area (139 above), offered a typical tourist item, little glass vials (Fig. 19) bearing pictures of the chief sights in the region identified by labels:

'Lighthouse', 'Palace', 'Theatre', 'Nero's Pool', 'Oyster Beds', etc. At Antioch, which boasted one of the most popular statues of the ancient world, a figure representing the city's Tyche or goddess of good luck, one could buy glass bottles about six inches high made in the shape of the statue. Lucian, in his recounting of the founding of an oracle by a quack (135 above), avows that, as soon as visitors began to flock in, the quack had his bogus deity reproduced in 'paintings and models and statuettes, either in bronze or silver' for ready sale. In a sketch describing a visit to the famed Aphrodite by Praxiteles at Cnidus, Lucian has one of his characters remark that he could not help 'laughing at the obscene pottery; this was, after all, Aphrodite's town'; one probably had to run the gauntlet of shops displaying such pieces all along the approach to the building that housed the statue. When St Paul came to Ephesus he had some uneasy moments because a certain Demetrius, a silversmith who specialized in 'silver temples of Artemis', called upon his fellow artisans to protest at the way Christianity was hurting their business; his 'silver temples' were miniature models intended for the throngs who came to see the temple of Artemis at Ephesus, which ranked among the Seven Wonders; customers bought them to offer as dedications, the way we offer plaques, candles, or the like. Demetrius must have catered to the well-to-do, but cheap terra-cotta versions were no doubt available for humbler visitors; terra-cotta models of temples frequently turn up in excavations.

Serious buyers would press past the pedlars and push-carts with their tawdry gimcracks to make their way to where the best shops were to be found. Here is a graphic picture, drawn by the Roman satirist Martial, of shopping, particularly for *objets d'art*, in a row of Rome's fanciest shops toward the end of the first century A.D.:

> Along the shops in the old voting hall,
> the places where Rome with the wherewithal

puts its money to work, Mamurra made
a long and leisurely promenade.

First call was at the slave blocks where
with expert eye he stopped to stare—
not at the cheap goods all can see,
displayed for the likes of you and me,
but the luscious boys for sale inside,
and feasted his eyes till satisfied.
Next, tables and chairs—he had legs hauled down,
had tops uncovered, and with a frown,
after four times measuring, bemoaned his fate
that a tortoise-shell inlaid couch for eight
was a little too small, just wouldn't be good
with his precious table of lemon-wood.
He consulted his nose in order to tell
the authentic Corinthian bronze's smell;
took Polyclitus' work to task;
got outraged because a crystal flask
had a tiny flaw; selected with care,
to be held aside in his name, five pair
of rare bowls; appraised old goblets and
anything he found from Mentor's hand;
counted the emeralds on enamelled gold things,
and the oversize pearls on pendant earrings;
on each and all counters assayed every stone,
and put in his offer for the biggest ones shown.

At five P.M., all tired and hot,
he ended up buying a five-penny pot.

Mamurra was, to be sure, a native and not some wide-eyed
stranger. But, during the course of his day, he doubtless
rubbed shoulders with any number of the latter on the lookout, like himself, for bargains in antiques; Rome, capital of
the world and its wealthiest city, was the centre of the art

trade. It is a trade that has not changed much in two thousand years; a Roman poet is bitter about those 'artists . . . who contrive to get bigger prices for their latest works by writing Praxiteles' name on their sculpture, Mys' on their polished silver, Zeuxis' on their paintings'.

In other cities there were the locally available products or local specialties to shop for. Alexandria, lying at the end of the sea routes from the Far East and Africa (129 above), was middleman for all the exotic wares that came from there. Anyone visiting Egypt had to pass through Alexandria, and confronting him on all sides would be irresistible buys: silks from China and cottons from India; spices, such as pepper and ginger and cinnamon, from India and Indonesia; perfumes derived from African myrrh. At the very least he would lay in a supply of the paper manufactured from papyrus (221 above), a plant that grew only along the Nile and its branches and hence ensured for Egypt an unassailable monopoly over this cheapest and most convenient type of ancient writing material. The traveller to Syria could pick up Syrian glass or Near Eastern carpets and embroidered textiles; Far Eastern imports were available here too, since many of the caravan routes that led from Asia passed through Syria. In Asia Minor he could get fine woollens and linens. In Greece there were the excellent fabrics woven at Patras. If he got no further than Athens, he could settle for a jar of the prized Mt Hymettus honey, or, if he happened to be in a sombre mood, with thoughts of the inevitable future on his mind, he might make the rounds of the coffin-makers; one of Athens' specialties during the Roman Imperial period was the production of elaborate stone coffins, which could be ordered either fully carved or with the carving just roughed out so that the detail could be put in after delivery under the buyer's own eye. We have only few and vague references to the shopping habits of the Greek or Roman traveller but they seem to indicate that he—or his wife—could no more pass by a local bargain than we can. 'If my health improves', writes a Greek living in

K

Egypt to a friend, in the mid-third century B.C., 'and I go abroad to Byzantium [the modern Istambul], I'll bring you back some fine pickled fish.' Both tunny and turbot were caught there, and either made as welcome a gift to someone living in Egypt then as caviar to any of us today.

There was one factor which must have held shoppers' enthusiasm somewhat in check: the *portoria* or customs charges. The Roman Empire maintained stations not only at all ports and frontiers but also at the boundaries between provinces, since duty was payable even on goods crossing from one province to the next. The traveller's *instrumenta itineris* 'materials for the voyage'—that is, beasts of burden, carriages, wagons, luggage containers, and the like—and objects *ad usum proprium* 'for personal use' during the voyage were exempt. Everything else was dutiable, right down to corpses being transported for burial elsewhere. On most items the rates were not stiff, only two to five per cent *ad valorem*, but on the very things that tourists would find most enticing, such as silks, perfumes, spices, pearls, and the other prized luxuries imported from the Far East, it was twenty-five per cent. Certain people, such as recognized benefactors of the state, members of the armed forces, from about A.D. 100 on even veterans of the armed forces, had the privilege of exemption from customs. This was, of course, only for goods for their own use; it by no means gave them *carte blanche* to bring in things for resale.

The customs agents, called *portitores* or *publicani* in Latin and *telonai* in Greek, began by asking for the *professio*, or customs declaration, on which a traveller put down in writing everything he had with him. They were strictly business. When the celebrated wonder-worker and sage Apollonius, on being asked the routine question of what he was taking with him, answered loftily, 'Continence, Justice, Virtue, Self-Control, Valour, Discipline', all words feminine in gender, the inspector snapped, 'Let's have the list of those slaves!' (at which point Apollonius observed that they were more his mistresses than his slaves). With declaration in hand they went methodically through all effects. 'We get irritated and upset', writes Plutarch philosophically, 'at the customs agents . . . when they go through gear and baggage that is not their own, searching for hidden items, yet the law allows them to do this.' Even things worn on the body were subject to scrutiny; lawyers wrangled over the issues involved if a married woman —who by law could not be touched—was carrying four hundred pearls in her bosom and the inspector insisted on examining them and all she was willing to do was give him a look. If an agent uncovered any objects that were *inscripta* 'undeclared', he confiscated them on sight. The culprit could buy them back—but at the price the agent reckoned as their value, and, even if he set a reasonable figure, it meant at least a doubling of the cost. Some things could not even be bought back. If someone tried to sneak in a young slave by dressing him up in citizen's clothes and passing him off as, say, a member of the family, and the slave revealed the truth, the customs officer gave him his freedom on the spot. Whatever irregularities a traveller could prove were genuine mistakes and not attempts at fraud were treated leniently; he got off with a fine equal to double the normal amount of duty.

As always, it helped to know the right people. 'Send . . . a bathing costume as quickly as possible,' writes a certain Hierocles in 257 B.C. to Zenon, trusted agent of the Minister of Finance of Egypt, 'preferably of goatskin or, if not, of light sheepskin. Also a tunic and cloak and the mattress, blanket, pillows, and honey. You wrote me you were surprised that I didn't realize that all these items were subject to duty. I'm aware of it, all right, but you are perfectly able to arrange to send them without any risk whatsoever.'

18

Baedeker of the Ancient World

Wit, style, a keen and original mind, an eye for the unusual—
these are what delight us in the travelogue writer. The compiler
of a guidebook, on the other hand, must be a totally different
kind of person. His job is to report the location, dimensions,
age, and life-history of monuments, and only incidentally, if
at all, the emotions or associations they arouse in his breast.
Wit and originality have no place in such an assignment; in
fact, they might very well get in the way. What he requires
above all are the matter-of-fact virtues of thoroughness,
diligence, and accuracy.

And these were the virtues *par excellence* of a certain
Pausanias who, between roughly A.D. 160 and 180, wrote a
Guidebook of Greece, the sole guidebook that has survived from
ancient times. We know about him only what we can glean or
deduce from his work. He obviously was a man of means; no
other would have had the leisure for travel and writing. His
politics, conformably, were safe and sound: he was content
with Rome's autocratic form of government (he lived under
Hadrian, Antoninus Pius, and Marcus Aurelius, all, it so
happens, particularly able emperors), was convinced of the
beneficial qualities of Roman rule, and had the distrust of
democracy so commonly found in conservative members of
the upper class. He was godfearing. He believed in all the

traditional deities, piously made sacrifices, and was so devoted a member of the mystery cult at Eleusis—it was open to initiates only and worshipped Demeter and Persephone in a secret ritual—that he utters not a word about the rites, not even a word about the precinct and its buildings. He believed in oracles, in the gods' power to intervene in the lives of mortals, and especially in their power to reward the good and punish the evil (inevitably he cites far more examples of sinners than saints). The only thing he will not swallow whole are the Greek myths. He is enough the child of his age to draw the line occasionally. For example, he refuses to believe that the Hydra, the serpent slain by Heracles, had many heads, or that every time a sacrifice was made to Zeus on Mt Lycaeus 'Wolf Mountain' some man was transformed into a wolf (it happened the first sacrifice only, he holds), or that Actaeon's dogs turned on him because of Artemis' command (they were suffering from rabies, he suggests).

His artistic tastes were, like his politics and religion, thoroughly conservative. In painting his favourite was Polygnotus, an old master if there ever was one, since he lived in the second half of the fifth century B.C., some six hundred years before Pausanias' day. In sculpture his favourites went even further back, to the early fifth century B.C. Of the masters of the fourth B.C., he has a few nice things to say about Praxiteles, and he mentions Scopas and Lysippus—and that just about ends it; all who come later hardly count.

He was born in Asia Minor, probably in Lydia; we do not know this for certain but it seems a reasonable conjecture considering the intimate knowledge he reveals of those parts. We can only guess at the extent of his travels from remarks that he drops. In the east he had been as far as Syria and Palestine; he had seen Lake Tiberias, the Jordan River, Jerusalem, and the Dead Sea. He did not get to Babylon—but then again, as he informs us, he never met anyone who had. He had visited Egypt, going all the way up the Nile to Thebes to hear the miraculous Memnon and even making the trek across the western desert to the Oasis of Ammon in Libya. It goes without saying that he had been all over Greece and the Aegean islands. In the west he had seen Rome (where he was most impressed by Trajan's Forum and the Circus Maximus) and some of the cities of the Campania, such as Capua. He did not venture further west than Italy; after all, a typical ancient tourist, principally interested in monuments of the hoary past, would find little to engage his attention in the relatively new centres that had sprung up in the wake of Rome's conquest of Gaul, Spain, and Britain.

The idea of writing a guidebook was certainly not original with Pausanias (very little was); he had any number of examples to follow. Unfortunately none of these have survived; indeed, in most cases we know of them only through someone's casual mention of their titles. Toward the end of the fourth century B.C., one Diodorus (not the historian of the same name) wrote on the towns and monuments of Attica. A century or so later, the beginning of the second B.C., a certain Heliodorus drew up a long guide to the works of art on Athens' Acropolis. The most prolific writer of guidebooks was a younger contemporary of Heliodorus, Polemo of Ilium. *The Athenian Acropolis*, *The Pictures in the Monumental Gateway* [to the Acropolis], *The Sacred Way* [from the sanctuary at Eleusis to Athens], *The Painted Portico in Sicyon*, *Spartan Cities*, *The Treasure Chambers at Delphi*, *Settlements in Italy and Sicily*, *Guidebook to Troy* are some of the titles credited to him. Polemo was particularly enthusiastic about stelae, the slabs of stone with official inscriptions carved upon them that were to be seen in public places. He went about so assiduously copying them that he was nicknamed *stelokopas* 'inscription-swallower'.

Though Pausanias owes the idea of a guidebook to these various predecessors, he towers above them as a mountain above a plain. They had written monographs on single places, even single monuments; he had the grandiose notion of compiling a guidebook for all the memorable places and monuments throughout the whole of Greece. It turned out to be, as he probably knew it would, a lifetime's work. He published the first section—there are in all ten sections, or books as we generally call them—soon after completing it. The other nine took him at least ten years more, perhaps longer than that.

'There is but one entrance to the Acropolis: it admits of no other, being everywhere precipitous and fortified with a strong wall. The monumental gateway has a roof of white marble, and for the beauty and size of the blocks it has never yet been matched. . . . On the right of the gateway is a temple of Wingless Victory.' So begins Pausanias' description of the approach to Athens' Acropolis; the visitor today can follow it as easily as the comparable description in any contemporary guidebook.

Pausanias' next words are:

> From this point the sea is visible, and it was here, they say, that Aegeus cast himself down and perished. For the ship that bore the children to Crete used to put to sea with black sails; but when Theseus courageously sailed off to fight the bull called the Minotaur, he told his father that he would use white sails if he came back victorious over the bull. However, after ridding himself of Ariadne he forgot to do so. Then Aegeus, when he saw the ship returning with black sails, thought that his son was dead; so he flung himself down and was killed.

This mythological digression, appended to the description of the imposing entry to Athens' finest sight yet running longer than the description itself, brings into sharp relief the fundamental difference between the modern and Pausanias' conception of a guidebook.

His aim was to identify and describe all the memorable places and monuments of Greece. So far so good; this is what any Baedeker or Guide Bleu aims to do. Pausanias, however,

considered it equally his task to report the various mythological, historical, religious, or folk-loric traditions and stories
associated with each. Furthermore, the places and monuments
that he—and doubtless the bulk of the tourists for whom he
wrote—considered memorable were those that bore witness
to Greece's great past, and, of them, in his eyes the sacred
were infinitely more memorable than the profane. He could
not help, in guiding his readers through a city, but note the
marketplace, colonnades, law courts, government offices,
fountains, public baths, and so on, but he spends scant time on
them. It is when he gets to the sanctuaries and temples that
he lets himself go, telling us with lavish detail about the
buildings and their decoration, the altars, the votive statuary
and other offerings. Consider, for example, his description of
Acro-Corinth, the citadel that defends the city of Corinth. A
spectacular mass of grey limestone that rises sheer from the
plain, it is the greatest natural fortress in Greece, and the
Corinthians aided and abetted nature in impressive style by
running their city walls up its slopes to embrace the summit.
From the top one gets a breathtaking view that includes
the city at the foot, the gleaming waters of the gulf on
which Athens lies in one direction, the snowclad peaks of
Mt Parnassus and Mt Helicon in another. All of this Pausanias
passes over without a word. What he feels called upon to
report is the mythological story connected with the hill (it was
awarded to the Sun-God, who resigned it to Aphrodite) and
the various religious monuments located there.

As a matter of fact, when Pausanias includes a feature of the
countryside, it is almost always to point out some religious or
mythological association, hardly ever its natural beauty. He
will mention a mountain only to tell us which god is worshipped on the top, a cavern to explain that it is the haunt of
Pan, a river to relate the mythological stories in which it
figures, a lake because through its waters one descends to the
underworld, a great cedar tree because it has an image of
Artemis hanging amid its branches. It is on the rarest of

occasions that he will refer to nature for its own sake, and then in but a casual phrase.

The first section of the work describes Athens and Attica. The detail is thinner in this portion and the arrangement of the material somewhat haphazard; you get the impression that Pausanias was feeling his way, had not yet found a satisfactory scheme. By the second book, devoted to Corinth, he is in his stride, revealing an eminently workable plan for taking the reader around the sights. He begins with an outline history, long or short as the case may be, to introduce you to the area. Then he takes the shortest road from the frontier to the capital, noting whatever there is of interest along the way. He continues straight to the centre of the city—in most cases the marketplace—describes what there is to see there, and then works through the various streets that lead out from it. Having finished with the capital, he turns to the rest of the territory within its jurisdiction. He follows out and back each chief road that radiates from the capital to its borders with neighbouring city-states, pointing out the notable villages, towns, and monuments that one passes on the way. When he has followed the last such road to the frontier, he steps across and begins all over again with an adjacent city-state. This is the procedure he uses for Corinth and Argos in Book 2, Sparta in Book 3, Mantinea and Megalopolis and Tegea in Book 8, and Thebes in Book 9.

Inevitably the sites that bulk the largest in his narrative are the three where the most and greatest monuments of the past were clustered: Athens (Book 1), the great sanctuary of Zeus at Olympia (Books 5, 6), the great sanctuary of Apollo at Delphi (Book 10). Pausanias lingers longest over Olympia; in the standard translation of his work his description covers some seventy pages, while that of Athens fills forty-two and Delphi forty. As always, identification and description of the memorabilia form only a part of the text, the rest being made up of his recountings, often at exhaustive length, of their mythological, historical, and religious associations.

K*

So extensive is this added material—and sometimes so peripheral—it leaves the impression that Pausanias introduced it in the hope of interesting a wider circle of readers than just tourists who needed a guidebook. At the very outset, for example, in his description of the Senate House at Athens, mention of a picture there portraying the Athenians resisting an invasion of Gauls sends him off on a two-page history of the Gauls. A little further along, a casual reference to two kings of the Hellenistic period triggers a twelve-page survey of Hellenistic history. There are disquisitions on natural curiosities such as earthquakes, ocean tides, and the frozen vastnesses of the north; there are allusions to exotic birds and beasts—parrots, camels, the ostrich, the rhinoceros, India's huge serpents. Such digressions, together with the endless mythological and historical notes, often seem to overweigh the guidebook proper. This is deceptive, however. If we were to print Pausanias' text in the manner of a modern guidebook, with the historical introductions and lengthy descriptions set off in small type and subordinate matter relegated to notes and appendices, the sturdy skeleton of its arrangement and its inherent consistency would be amply visible.

And it is a good guidebook, as accurate as could be expected of a pioneering work compiled with the help of relatively rudimentary research facilities. His mythological material came from the older poets, especially Homer. For the historical facts, he consulted all the available authorities, Herodotus, Thucydides, Xenophon, Polybius, and many others whose works have not survived, including writers of local histories. When confronted with contradictory accounts, he compared them and judiciously picked the one he considered the most plausible. Some information he drew from the inscriptions set up in or about public buildings or sanctuaries; these, too, he compared and analysed before arriving at conclusions. Other information, such as measurements of buildings or little-known local traditions, he must have obtained from guides. Despite his healthy distrust of their chatter (cf. 266 above), he now and then let down his guard and accepted as gospel what manifestly could not have been the case. But the heart of his work, after all, are his descriptions of monuments and places, and the vast majority of these he almost certainly visited in person. Here he passes on to us what he saw with his own eyes, and he was a keen and careful observer.

Undistinguished as writer or thinker but staid and sober and thorough, tirelessly industrious, and with a deepseated respect for accuracy, Pausanias marks a milestone in the history of tourism. He is the direct ancestor of the equally sober and unimaginative, painstakingly comprehensive and scrupulously accurate Karl Baedeker, who, in turn, spawned the Guide Bleus, and other guides that we clutch as we make the rounds of sights today. And for Greece's archeologists and historians of art and architecture, his work is of indescribable value. As his translator, J. G. Frazer, puts it: 'Without him the ruins of Greece would for the most part be a labyrinth without a clue, a riddle without an answer. His book furnishes the clue to the labyrinth, the answer to many riddles. It will be read and studied so long as ancient Greece shall continue to engage the attention and awaken the interests of mankind.'

19

To the Holy Lands

As Constantine approached Rome in A.D. 312 to struggle with Maxentius for mastery of the city, he received a sign from heaven, the sight of a gleaming cross in the sky. Victory followed swiftly—and equally swiftly followed the victory of Christianity over its various competitors; during Constantine's reign Rome was converted from a pagan to a Christian state.

Under paganism Rome had had no organized clergy. There were, to be sure, professional priests, like those at Apollo's oracles or Isis' shrines, but they and their like were relatively few. Most liturgical duties were performed by part-time clergymen, civil magistrates, lay appointees and volunteers, and so on. Christianity's elevation, first to a recognized religion and then to *the* religion, brought in its wake a vast clerical structure, a sister bureaucracy to that which ran the government.

And the new bureaucrats, like the old, did a good deal of moving about. Governors of provinces, circuit judges, soldiers, imperial dispatch riders and all the other traditional users of Rome's highways and sea-lanes were now joined by prelates headed for the court at Constantinople, by junketing bishops, by the Church's financial agents and letter-carriers. The travel itch seems to have particularly affected bishops. They cavalierly left their flocks in the lurch to go off for politics, business, or simply relaxation so often that the church was forced to take action. An ecumenical council held at Sophia in 343 decreed that no bishop was to appear at the emperor's court unless in answer to a summons, and added that 'those of us who live near a public road and see a bishop en route will ask him the purpose of and reason for his voyage.... If he has been impelled by frivolous reasons ... one must refuse to sign his letters [i.e., those authorizing travel facilities] or communicate with him.'

What drew the greatest number away from their thrones at any one time were the councils themselves. When Constantine called the first in 325, there descended on Nicaea from all over the empire some 300 bishops, each accompanied by a staff of priests, deacons, acolytes. The council at Sophia brought out 170, one at Rimini in 359 no less than 400. The delegates did not have to put up with the ordinary discomforts of travel. Constantine extended to them the right to use vehicles belonging to the public post (182 above); he shrewdly played no favourites, granting the privilege impartially to members of schismatic sects as well as the orthodox. Subsequent emperors went even further, issuing warrants not only for transportation—saddle horses for riders, the customary *reda* (183 above) for nonriders—but also lodging and meals. Inn-keepers were called upon to supply the travellers with bread, eggs, vegetables, various meats (beef, suckling pig and pork, lamb and mutton) and fowl (goose, pheasant, chicken), cooking ingredients (olive oil, fish sauce, and a battery of spices—cummin, pepper, cloves, spikenard, cinnamon, gum mastic), desserts (dates, pistachio nuts, almonds), the inevitable salt, vinegar, and honey (for sweetening, in lieu of sugar, which was virtually unknown), and wine or beer to drink. Obviously no cleric on the move was expected to mortify the flesh—if the supplies were available and the personnel of the public post were not out to make trouble. When Melania the Younger was en route from Jerusalem to Constantinople in 436 with authorization to use the *cursus publicus*, a functionary at Tripoli in Syria refused to issue her all the animals she needed on the grounds that her warrant covered her alone and not the rather sizable party she had along; it took a bribe of three gold pieces to change his mind (later, thanks to prayers offered to the local saint, he saw the light, and ran seven miles to catch up with the party and return the money).

Just as clerical over-indulgence in travel became a nuisance, so did clerical over-use of the public post. Gregory of Nyssa in the spring of 380 B.C. got a carriage from the *cursus* and not only kept it during the whole of a voyage from Pontus in northern Asia Minor as far as Palestine and Arabia but lived in it, turning the vehicle into a sort of travelling chapel. 'The *cursus publicus* has been prostrated by the immodest presumption of certain people', snarled Julian the Apostate in a decree he issued in A.D. 362 to curb abuses; no doubt a good many of the 'certain people' he had in mind were clergy. Basil even tried to talk the authorities into letting a group of Christians use the public post for bringing back the body of a relative who had died in some remote spot. And there was a story about a chap with influence at court who, convinced he was possessed by a demon, did not hesitate to ask the emperor for a warrant so that he could get to St Hilarion and have the offender exorcized.

In addition to clerics going to the court or councils or off on other church matters, the intelligentsia of the Church, a small but highly important group, restlessly moved from centre to centre in their search for education. Basil studied at Caesarea in Cappadocia, Constantinople, and Athens; Gregory Nazianzen at Caesarea in Palestine, Alexandria, and Athens; Jerome at Antioch, Constantinople, Rome, and Alexandria; Origen at Antioch, Caesarea in Cappadocia, Caesarea in Palestine, Athens, Nicomedia, Bostra, and Tyre.

Sharing the roads and sea-lanes with the prelates and intellectuals, but far outnumbering them, were the Church's business agents and letter-carriers, particularly the latter; they were for ever shuttling back and forth from church to church, bishop to bishop. The clergy had access to the *cursus publicus* for travel only; except on rare occasions, the government pouch was closed to their letters. So they had to use their own personnel for carrying their mail, at first lectors and sub-deacons, then, by the fourth century, when the job had gained some status, deacons and priests and monks. These had the advantage of being enough abreast of events to fill out by word of mouth the bare lines of a communication—or to supply them in case the missive itself got lost. When no Church personnel were available, Christian correspondents did as the pagans had done (220 above): they used anyone they could find going in the right direction. Augustine entrusted a letter to a Roman procurator, John Chrysostom to a member of the Praetorian Guard, Paulinus of Nola to a Roman soldier, several of Jerome's correspondents to a shipowner, Eusebius and Ambrose and Basil to Roman officials of various grades, high and low. Jerome, when living in the Holy Land, could look forward to a batch of mail brought by the pilgrims who flooded in at Easter time.

The informal postal service, though useful, was too hap-hazard for comfort, and so the Church supplemented it with *tabellarii*, professional letter-carriers—reluctantly, for these were far from ideal. They made a poor impression right on arrival since they dressed as they pleased. Paulinus of Nola could hardly bear to look at some he had to deal with: they had wild hair-does and clothes that belonged on a swaggering soldier; if only all letters, he laments, could have been delivered by monks with their reassuringly pale faces, sober garments, and shaven heads! What is more, they grumbled about going to far or difficult places, lingered at attractive places, and seemed always to be in a hurry. Paulinus opens one of his letters with the remark that 'the bearer of this is right now running for the boat' (but then proceeds to indite no less than ten well-packed pages). Even worse, they read communica-tions that were intended to be confidential. Ausonius suggests to a correspondent with an over-inquisitive wife that 'you write your letters with milk. The paper, on drying out, will conserve the characters invisibly, and ash will make them reappear', i.e. use invisible ink. Ecclesiastics might very well have used it to circumvent over-inquisitive postmen.

The multifarious business and professional moving about of the clergy was one new aspect of travel ushered in by Rome's conversion to Christianity. A second was a new form of tourism.

Greeks and Romans had beat a path to Troy to visit 'Homer country'; now the pious flocked to Palestine to see 'Bible country'. 'Everywhere in the world we venerate the tombs of martyrs . . . ,' writes Jerome, 'how can anyone think we should neglect the tomb in which they placed the Lord!' He felt that the Christian scholar had to see Jerusalem even as the Greek scholar had to see Athens or the Latin scholar Rome. At times he elevated a pilgrimage almost to a sacred duty. 'It is part of the faith', he proclaimed in one letter, and in another pointed out that the great figures of the church felt they had less religion if they had not been to Jerusalem.

Even before the time of Constantine, a trickle of Christians had voyaged to the venerable city to pay their respects to the birthplace of their religion. In the second century, Melito, bishop of Sardis, made a tour of the holy places, and, in the third, Alexander and Firmilian, both bishops of Cappadocian towns, Origen, and a growing number of humbler visitors. The sights accessible to these pioneers were limited. They had to be satisfied with the mementoes of Christ's birth at Bethlehem, for those of his death at Jerusalem, along with many another hallowed spot, were buried under the ruins left by the sacking of the city in A.D. 70 or under the structures raised by Hadrian when he built a new Palestinian centre, Aelia Capitolina, upon the remains of the old.

In 326 Constantine turned his energetic attention to the Holy Land, and the picture changed overnight. The rubble was cleared from the hill of the Crucifixion uncovering the cave where Joseph of Arimathea had laid Christ's body to rest, and masons started work on erecting over it the round structure that the pilgrims called the Anastasis. In the same year Helena, Constantine's mother, made the celebrated trip to Palestine that culminated in her discovery of the True Cross, and she joined enthusiastically in the programme of building and restoring. The basilica which the pilgrims refer to as the Martyrium began to rise over the site of the Crucifixion and the spot where the cross had been found. In 331 or 332 we hear of visits to the Holy Land by Eusebius of Caesarea, father of ecclesiastical history, Eusebius of Nicodemia, first bishop of Beirut, and Theognis, bishop of Nicaea at the time of the great council. By the end of the century the yen to make the *peregrinatio ad loca sancta* had spread to the four corners of the Roman empire. Some of the most dedicated pilgrims were women. Paula, a wealthy widow from one of the best Roman families, left Rome in 385; among other places she visited Sareptah to see Elijah's dwelling, Bethlehem to see Rachel's grave and Constantine's new church over the cave of the Nativity, Hebron to see the tree alleged to be Abraham's oak and the hut, supposedly Sarah's, where what passed as Isaac's swaddling clothes were on display. She eventually settled down at Bethlehem and financed there the erection of a monastery, convent, and hospice for pilgrims. Melania the Younger, another Roman lady of the highest connections, left Rome for a sojourn of seven years in Africa. Unable to resist the allure of the Holy Land she continued on to Jerusalem, stopping off at Alexandria on the way for a brief visit. From Jerusalem she returned to Egypt for a comprehensive tour of the holy men living in the northern part of the country. She eventually made her home on the Mount of Olives, leaving it only once, to go to Constantinople in order to convert her ailing pagan uncle before he died. The most energetic sightseer of all, male or female, was a certain Etheria, a lady of means and position like the others, but not from Rome, from some western province probably Gaul. From her home she took the long slow overland route to the east. After visiting Jerusalem and other parts of Palestine, she pushed on to Egypt, going up the Nile as far as the district around Thebes to visit the monks in their desert habitat. This was just a preliminary for her next foray, into the blazing heat of the Sinai peninsula, where she conscientiously did the sights of 'Moses country'. She made the climb to the very peak where he received the tablets, and then descended to the valley; on the way down she notes such memorabilia as the spot where Aaron stood while Moses was being given the law, the burning bush (apparently still alive and flourishing), the site of the Israelite camp, the place where the golden calf had been made, the rock on which Moses smashed the tablets, the place where it rained manna, and so on. From Sinai she returned to Clysma (Suez) and, after a much needed rest, set out to trace in reverse the route of the Exodus. Somehow she talked the Roman authorities into giving her an escort of Roman soldiers, since the trip lay through a no-man's land where anybody on the road was fair game for bandits. Once back on the Nile, she dismissed her guard, made her way to Pelusium, and then took the age-old coastal highway from Egypt (26 above) back to Palestine and Jerusalem. She now made Jerusalem into a base for a series of excursions into eastern Palestine and Jordan. First she took off for the Dead Sea and a visit to Mt Nebo to stand on the very point from which Moses got his view of the Promised Land. Back to Jerusalem and off again northward up the Jordan valley to Salem for a look at Melchizedek's church and city and a pool nearby where John the Baptist performed his ministrations; then to Tishbe, Elijah's birthplace, where she saw the cave in which he used to sit; and then across the Jordan to Karnaim to visit the burial place of Job. Again back to Jerusalem, this time to start the long trek home. After getting as far as Antioch, the temptation of a side trip to Edessa with a chance to pray at St Thomas' tomb and examine the letters that Abgar, the city's ruler at the time, had exchanged with Christ, was too much to resist. Off she went, and was taken about Abgar's palace, was shown the city gate by which the postman had entered, and had Abgar's letter and Christ's reply read to her. From Edessa she pushed on into the Haran. This was 'Abraham country', and here she visited the church built upon the site of Abraham's house, Rebecca's well, and the well at which Jacob had watered the flocks of Laban. By now even this indefatigable tourist had had enough and finally set a course for home.

Constantine's handsome new churches and other buildings only enhanced the Holy Land's allure. Its prime attraction, as Etheria's itinerary reveals, were the sites, monuments and buildings, real and fancied, that were hallowed by their association with the Bible.

For the main lines of the tour we have a precious source of information, a guidebook for Christian pilgrims drawn up by an anonymous citizen of Bordeaux who paid his visit in 333. As Etheria was to do a half-century or so later, he took the overland route to the east, traversing southern Gaul, climbing the Alps, and passing through northern Italy and the Balkans to get to Constantinople. From here he went south across Asia Minor to Syria and then followed the Phoenician coast to Caesarea. Up to this point he gives scant attention to sightseeing; he merely lists the towns, *mansiones* and *mutationes* (184 above) one passes through, pausing no more than four times or so to point out special sights: between Chalcedon and Nicomedia he indicates the spot where Hannibal was buried, at Tarsus he mentions that it was the birthplace of Paul, at Sareptah he shows where Elijah had asked the widow for food and drink, and at Mt Carmel where the prophet had sacrificed. At Caesarea he left the shore and turned inland to follow the road to Jerusalem, and here his guided tour of the Holy Land really begins, the sights now come thick and fast. Stradela (Jezreel) is where King Ahab's palace stood, where Elijah prophesied, and where David slew Goliath (in point of fact, the battle was fought nowhere near here but miles further south in Judah); Shechem (Nablus) offers Joseph's tomb, Jacob's well, and a row of plane trees that Jacob had planted;

308   TRAVEL IN THE ANCIENT WORLD

Mt Gerizim is the site of Abraham's sacrifice of Isaac (only according to the Samaritans, who inhabited the region; the Israelites liked to place it on the holy rock covered by the temple in Jerusalem); Bethel is where Jacob had his dream and the fight with the angel.

Twelve miles from Bethel and we are at the gates of Jerusalem. Notable are a pair of grand pools, built by Solomon, that once flanked his temple, and, further inside the city, the twin pools of Bethesda whose water is ever in motion and has the power to heal the sick. The remains of Solomon's palace include the room where the great king composed the Book of Wisdom (actually written some eight centuries after he died). In the temple, on the marble before the altar is the blood of Zachariah and, as if imprinted in wax, footprints of the soldiers who killed him. Near the temple there still stand statues of the Roman emperors Hadrian and Antoninus; Helena had allowed them to remain there. Not far from them is a 'pierced stone' where the Jews come yearly on the anniversary of the destruction of the city to lament and rend their garments—in other words, the 'wailing wall' of the day.

At the mouth of the valley that runs through Jerusalem is the pool of Siloam; it flows, we are told, only on weekdays, miraculously switching off on the Sabbath. The sights of Mt Zion include the site of the house of Caiaphas, the column of the Flagellation, remains of the house of David, ruins of the praetorium where Pilate interrogated Christ, and the most awesome sight of all, Golgotha, now adorned with the nearly completed churches Constantine had ordered to be raised over the cave of the Entombment and the site of the Crucifixion. Leaving the city by the eastern gate we cross the Valley of Jehoshaphat for the Mount of Olives where we see 'the rock where Judas Iscariot betrayed Christ', the palm tree that was stripped for fronds to cast in Jesus' path as he entered Jerusalem in triumph, and, a stone's throw away, tombs allegedly of Isaiah and Hezekiah (they belong to neither, and the one of them that is today called Absalom's no more covers his bones than it does Isaiah's). The Mount of Olives boasts another of Constantine's new churches. A mile and a half to the east lies Bethany, site of the resurrection of Lazarus.

Next, an excursion to the Jordan. En route to Jericho we see the sycamore that Zacchaeus climbed to get a look at Christ during his triumphal entry and the fountain that Elisha cured of making women sterile. In Jericho is Rahab's house. The tour continues to the Dead Sea and to the point, five miles up the Jordan, where John baptized Christ and where there is on the bank a little mound from which Elijah was raised to heaven.

Another excursion, this time to Bethlehem and beyond. Nearing the town we pass the tomb of Rachel. In town is still another Constantinian church, one marking the site of the Nativity, and a multiple tomb containing the remains of 'Ezekiel, Asaph, Job, Jesse, David, and Solomon, whose names can be read in Hebrew characters on the walls of the staircase leading to the funerary crypt'. There surely was a tomb there which had a Hebrew inscription, and surely the guides were giving this their own free translation. From Bethlehem we push on to the terebinths near Hebron where Abraham spread his tent (another Constantinian church here), and then to Hebron itself for a look at the common grave, marked by a square tomb of stone, of Abraham, Isaac, Jacob, Sarah, Rebecca, and Leah. Here the tour of the Holy Land comes to an end. From this point on our guide, as he had done on the way out, simply lists the names of the towns and stopping places along the route back to the west, with a very occasional gloss for the sightseer (e.g. Philippi is noted as the spot where Paul had been imprisoned, the '*mutatio* of Euripides' as the poet's resting place, Pella as Alexander's birthplace).

As time went on, the number of tourist attractions burgeoned. At Bethany pilgrims saw not only Lazarus' tomb but also the house shared by Mary and Martha and Simon the Leper, at Hebron not only the house of Sarah but David's as well, at Nazareth not only the house of the Annunciation but also a cave where Christ had lived. The list of hallowed caves in particular grew steadily longer: where Moses had once dwelled, where the angels had appeared to the shepherds to announce the birth of Christ, where Christ had washed the Apostles' feet, where he had taught the Apostles. Imaginative guides no doubt played the major role in multiplying the number and extending the range of sacred memorabilia. A certain Antoninus of Piacenza, who made his visit in 570, two and a half centuries after the Bordeaux pilgrim, gives a starry-eyed report of the wondrous things he was shown: at Nazareth the bench on which Jesus had sat as a schoolboy and the very copybook in which he had written down his ABCs; outside Jericho the ashes of Sodom and Gomorrah, still covered by a dark cloud smelling of brimstone, and the pillar of salt that Lot's wife had been turned into—not in any way diminished by the licking of animals as reported, but in its pristine condition; in Jerusalem the dried blood of Christ on the rock where the Crucifixion had taken place, the imprint of his palms and fingers on the column of the Flagellation, the lance, the crown of thorns, a clutch of the stones that had been used in the stoning of Stephen, and the column that supported the cross on which Peter had been executed (how it was supposed to have got to Jerusalem from Rome is anybody's guess).

The guides in Egypt were even worse—they had the effrontery to pass the pyramids off as Joseph's silos. And there were plenty of people to hear their outrageous tales, since Egypt was second only to the Holy Land in attracting pilgrims. Here the appeal was not biblical associations but something equally holy and a good deal more dramatic—the monks who dwelt in the deserts flanking the valley of the Nile.

As early as the first half of the third century, a trickle of Egyptians had left their homes to escape either grinding poverty or the equally grinding Roman exploitation and had settled down to a hermit's life in the lonely lands roundabout. One of these, Anthony, became the most renowned hermit of the day and a founding father of Christian monasticism. He retired to the desert at the early age of twenty or so, at first living in partial solitude and then totally alone in an abandoned fort near Arsinoe in the Fayum. When, after two decades, he finally emerged, the fame of his holiness drew other solitaries to settle down in some caves nearby. By 305 or so a community had grown up with Anthony acknowledged as head. Soon similar groups sprang up elsewhere, the members living either by themselves or in twos and threes but forming a definite society under the leadership of a particularly venerated member. The barren Wadi Natrun, roughly one hundred miles west-northwest of Cairo, became a favoured location; in 330 Macarius retired to the wastes here to found one important community and, in 352, Ammonas another.

What drove the Egyptian anchorites together was, more than anything else, the kind of regimen they pursued. Over and above denying all the pleasures of the senses, the solitary insisted on limiting himself to the barest minimum of food and drink, frequently fasting for days on end, and, as if this was not enough, added injury to hunger with self-inflicted physical torments. In a famished, often half-delirious state, opening his eyes either to the gloom of a cave or the blinding glare of the desert, he inevitably was visited by hallucinations, saw apparitions—and these he held to be the most awful ordeal of all, for he was convinced they were the fiendish snares of the Devil. In his ceaseless combat not to weaken, not to be tricked into going astray by the arch-enemy's temptations, he found it a towering comfort to have a comrade-in-arms nearby. By the end of the fourth century, there were thousands of solitaries clustered in the Wadi Natrun alone. The movement overflowed the borders of Egypt into Palestine, Syria, and other parts of the Near East. In Syria it spawned its most bizarre version, the pillar saints, who took refuge from the everyday world by retiring not to a cave but the top of a column. The most famous of them was Simeon Stylites 'Simeon of the pillar'. In 423 he set up residence about thirty-five miles from Antioch on a stone block about three feet high. As time went on he kept gaining altitude until he finally settled on a platform six feet square atop a sixty-five-foot pillar. Here he lived for thirty years, praying and performing so many continuous obeisances that one observer who tried to keep count gave up after 1,244.

The pillar saints and other anchorites outside of Egypt never matched in numbers the veritable armies within. The scorched wastes on either side of the Nile valley apparently offered the most appropriate setting for their chosen way of life. The solitaries for some reason favoured north and middle Egypt. The south, however, was not neglected. Here arose a different form of monasticism, considerably less dramatic but destined to be far more significant in the history of Christianity.

It began in 320 to 325 at Tabennisi near Denderah in upper Egypt. A hermit named Pachomius, abandoning the life he had been carrying on until then, brought together a group of kindred spirits who, though living separately, agreed to take their meals in common. As time went on they expanded their shared activities until they became a genuine cenobitic community. Eventually Pachomius put into flourishing operation no less than nine monasteries and, with the aid of his sister, two convents. Anthony's or any other anchorite group needed only a cluster of contiguous caves or the like; Pachomius' required a complicated assemblage of buildings. Normally there were several dormitories each housing about twenty monks in cells that accommodated one to three, a church, refectory, kitchen, cellar, garden, and hospice for guests. And, since barbaric tribes from the Sudan were constantly spilling over the border to maraud, the whole was encircled by a powerful wall. Anthony's followers spent all their days in prayer, meditation, and similar religious pursuits; Pachomius' spent a good part of the time in useful work, such as cultivating gardens or weaving reed baskets.

The pilgrim to Egypt was usually content with a visit to the communities of the north, particularly those in and around the Wadi Natrun. The anchorite monks there were not only more spectacularly holy with their gauntness, nondescript clothing, unkempt hair and beards, they were also a good deal more accessible; visitors were spared the rigours and dangers of a journey into the blistering and bandit-ridden upper reaches of the Nile. Etheria, Paula, Rufinus, Melania the Elder and Younger, Jerome—of all these distinguished visitors to Egypt, only the intrepid Etheria ventured south to the Thebaid. The rank and file of the anchorites generally extended guests a warm welcome; the gruff and crusty senior members, on the other hand, who were the 'fathers' were not always quite so charming. When Archbishop Theophilus visited a community near the Wadi Natrun and arrived ill, the monks there asked their 'father' to say something which would help the invalid. 'If he doesn't get any benefit from my silence', was the retort, 'he'll get even less from my talk.' By and large, however, the reception was so cordial and the way of life so uplifting that many a pious visitor elected to stay on for a spell. One of the best contemporary accounts we have of the monks of the Nile was written by a certain Palladius who, arriving in Egypt in 388, spent more than a dozen years in monasteries in the Wadi Natrun and around Alexandria. John Cassianus put in seven years in them, Rufinus six, Melania the Elder half a year.

Another prime Egyptian tourist attraction was the grave of Menas, a martyr who fell during Diocletian's persecutions in 295 and was buried at a spot about midway between Alexandria and the Wadi Natrun. People went there only secondarily because of the saint's fame; the main attraction was the magical healing powers attributed to the local water. 'Take the all-beneficial water of Menas—pain flees', is the pregnant message scratched by some visitor on a wall not far from the crypt. Toward the end of the fourth century an imposing basilica was erected near the grave. In the fifth, still another was added and, along with it and connected to it, a bath complex complete with cisterns, pools, dressing-rooms, and so on, where pilgrims could immerse themselves in the miraculous water; for those who merely wanted to drink or carry some off, pipes supplied two fountains in the nave of the church. People flocked here right up to the ninth century, when the Arabs destroyed the sanctuary.

The *peregrinatio ad loca sancta*, then, for the truly devout involved Egypt as well as the Holy Land proper. In both places most moving about was perforce done by land. For the long voyage out to the Near East, however, the pilgrims took advantage of the choice open to them of travelling by land or by sea.

As always (149 above), the sea offered the quickest and most comfortable transportation. This is the way Jerome elected to go in 385. His vessel, setting sail from Ostia at the mouth of the Tiber, passed through the Straits of Messina and then shaped a course across the Aegean through the Cyclades and Ionian islands; after a stop at Cyprus, he finally docked at Antioch, the major port in the Levant for direct overseas traffic. Paula, following a month later, took a commercial galley that more or less stayed close to shore. She too went south to the Straits of Messina, then crossed the Ionian sea to Methone, coasted south of the Peloponnese, threaded a way through the Cyclades to Rhodes and then from there to the coast of Asia Minor at Lycia, stopped at Cyprus, and eventually put in at Seleuceia and Antioch, where she joined forces with Jerome. From here they went in a party to Jerusalem by land, Paula riding donkeyback. Similarly, in 372 Melania and Rufinus chose to go by sea from Ostia to Alexandria, a well-established run (158 above), and by land from there to Jerusalem. Melania the Younger went by ship from Sicily to the African coast opposite, and eventually continued by ship to Jerusalem, with a stop en route at Alexandria. Antoninus of Piacenza sailed from Constantinople to Syria, with a stop at Cyprus.

Others, like the Bordeaux pilgrim or Etheria, preferred to stay away from boats despite their speed and comfort. The land route followed major highways used by the *cursus publicus*, so presumably the traveller had no great trouble finding food, lodging, animals, and vehicles along the way. Moreover, pilgrims who were either highly placed or knew the right people could count on the services of the *cursus*. With or without its help, the going was slow. The Bordeaux pilgrim reckoned that he covered about 3,400 Roman miles between Bordeaux and Jerusalem, and it took him 170 days; this works out to twenty a day, which was a good average for travel by land (189 above). Melania the Younger, leaving Constantinople at the end of February and anxious to reach Jerusalem in time for Easter, pushed on relentlessly and, despite bitter cold and mountainous terrain, managed to do twenty-six miles a day. The trip took her forty-four in all; she might have made it in no more than ten, had she been willing to risk a winter sailing. She was not alone in preferring land to water for travel between Constantinople and Syria; for some reason a good many others also did and not merely in winter.

A third way was to combine land and water (cf. 150 above). One could leave Rome by the Appian Way, travel its length to Brindisi, take ship there for Corinth, cross the isthmus, take another ship for Ephesus, and go on from Ephesus either by ship or foot. All sorts of similar combinations were possible and no doubt used.

From the last decades of the fourth century on, when pilgrimage to the Holy Land was in full swing, the critical problem for the traveller was more danger than hardship. The emperors of Rome no longer wielded the strong military and naval arm they had during their halcyon days. In the west, Vandals, Visigoths, and others were tearing great rents in the fabric of the empire. All over the Mediterranean pirates were back in operation; the navy had been one of the casualties of the tumultuous third century, and the well-organized flotillas that used to conduct regular patrols were a thing of the past. On land the main highways by and large were safe enough. Libanius, for example, who conducted an extensive correspondence from Antioch during the middle of the fourth century, appears serenely confident that all his letters will reach their destination, and, as a matter of fact, he never once mentions the loss of any through attack by bandits. Yet there were times when even here armed guards were advisable. John Chrysostom, for a trip from Antioch to Constantinople, had a soldier as escort supplied by the local governor. And the back country was a veritable no-man's-land. Chrysostom's movements there were often menaced by Isaurian brigands, and Etheria had to be wary of marauding Arabs. The last were a particular threat, to judge from an incident that Jerome puts into the mouth of the monk Malchus:

When you go from Beroea (Aleppo) to Edessa, near the highway is a wasteland where Arabs are forever on the prowl, camping now here and now there. Travellers in the area, anticipating this, gather in groups so as to reduce the menace by standing by each other. My party included men, women, young, old, children, about seventy in all. Lo and behold, suddenly Arabs riding on horses and camels swooped down on us. They had long hair bound with headbands, were half naked, and trailed cloaks and long sandals. Quivers hung down from their shoulders, and they brandished unstrung bows and carried their long spears—they had come, you see, not to fight but to rob. We were captured, split up, and carried off in different directions. I . . . along with one other, a girl, fell to the lot of one master. We were led off—or rather carried off—atop camels. We hung more than sat on our way across the vast desert, in constant fear of destruction. Our food was half-raw meat, our drink camel's milk.

The story is fiction, not fact, but it still reflects well enough the sort of thing a traveller could encounter in deserted parts.
    One excursion that brought a pilgrim deep into such parts

was to Mt Sinai to see 'Moses country'. By the end of the fourth century, when Etheria visited it, communities of monks were already in existence there, and in the sixth century Justinian founded St Catherine's, which still flourishes today. Arabs as well as Christians regarded the area as sacred, so it inevitably became a site that, despite the remoteness and dangers, drew a steady stream of visitors. We know this not only through the reports of Etheria and others but also through a rather uncommon source of information, a few casual lines in some matter-of-fact business papers; in their way, they are more eloquent than the rhapsodies of pious pilgrims.

In 1936 by great good fortune a batch of papyrus documents was discovered in the ruins of Nessana (Auja), a town in the Negeb which stood on the main ancient road to the south. It was the last community of any size that travellers passed on the way from Palestine to Sinai; beyond it stretched more or less open desert. From the middle of the fifth century, the Roman government, followed subsequently by the Arabs, maintained a fort and garrison in the place to protect the borders of southern Palestine from inroads by marauding bands of Bedouins. Three of the documents in the find furnish precious details about the trip to the 'Holy Mountain', a term used at the time for either Mt Sinai and its neighbouring hills in general or the monastery of St Catherine in particular. One is an account of expenses, business transactions, and other similar matters kept by the agent of a caravan of camels and donkeys that, sometime in the last half of the sixth century or the first of the seventh, made a trip across the Negeb. Their route took them to the Sinai peninsula, for, in the middle of the account we come across the following entries:

Paid to the Arab escort who took us to the
  Holy Mountain $3\frac{1}{2}$ solidi
Turned over to us by Father Martyrius $270\frac{1}{2}$ solidi

We went to prayers in the Holy Mountain and made an offering of	1 solidus
Expenditures for you [i.e. the principals of the parent company of the caravan], also purchase of fish and almonds	1 solidus
Donation to the monastery on behalf of the group from your town	10 solidi

The agent, in other words, hired an Arab to guide them to Mt Sinai—not just any country bumpkin but a skilled professional, as we can tell from his fee; a comparison with other entries shows that it amounted to half the cost of a camel. At the monastery a Father Martyrius, very likely the abbot, entrusted to the agent a sizable sum of money; perhaps it was to be deposited with his principals for purchasing supplies which the caravan would bring on a return trip. The agent and his staff took advantage of their presence in this sacred area to attend a service and put a modest donation in the collection box. They also made some purchases for the company's account, including provisions for the next leg of the journey. On departure they left a quite generous contribution in the name of the company.

Later in the account, after the guide had presumably been dismissed, we come across an entry that reads 'reimbursement for the camel which the Arabs, the bani al-Udayyid, took'. Was it a raid or just a theft? Did the caravan pay the guide so large a fee because he not only led the way but also guaranteed safe-conduct, i.e. ensured proper behaviour on the part of his brethren? The two other documents that mention Mt Sinai seem to confirm this. One, dated 5 December, 683, reads:

In the name of Almighty God!
Abu Rāshid, Governor, to the people of Nessana.

Thanks be to God, etc. When my wife Ubayya comes to you, furnish her a man who is to guide her on the road to Mt Sinai. Also furnish the man's pay.

The other, dated March 684 and couched in almost the same language, is addressed to the chief administrative officer of Nessana rather than the people in general, and the guide is required for a certain Abu 'l-Mughīra, a *mawla* or convert to Islam. We are now well into the age of the Arab conquest—Nessana and its environs were probably over-run as early as 633—and so the area is under the jurisdiction of Arab officials; the Abu Rāshid who issues these orders was very likely the local governor resident at Gaza. The first, dated in December, is for his wife, and she must have been just a sightseer, taking advantage of one of the coolest months of the year for her trip and of her husband's position to travel at government expense. The Moslem convert of the second may have been a tourist or perhaps an agent on government business. In both instances one gets the feeling that the guide was needed to ensure safe-conduct as much as to show the way.

So much for the hazards Christians met on the road. Let us turn to a second problem they had, where to put up for the night.

When on the open highway, they had no alternative: like the Bordeaux pilgrim, they stopped at whatever *mansio* or *mutatio* they had managed to reach by nightfall. However, once they found themselves in a place where the church enjoyed strong local support, things looked up considerably. There travellers of wealth or position, as their pagan counterparts before them (197 above), could count on elegant accommodations in the homes of friends or of the local authorities. Melania the Younger, for example, during her stay in Constantinople, lived in the palace of Lausus, chamberlain to Theodosius II, even though it meant abandoning much of her customary austerity (and no doubt blushing every time she passed the nudes in his collection of Greek statues; his piety, though outstanding, was not quite up to getting him to renounce his artistic treasures). Paula was invited by the governor of Palestine to put up at his mansion in Jerusalem, but she turned down the offer in favour of a tiny humble cell in Bethlehem. Bishops had a reciprocal understanding: each could count on a room in a fellow bishop's palace whenever he passed through.

The rank and file, on the other hand, had to stay at inns—and the average ancient inn, as we have seen (204 above), was hardly a proper place for the godfearing. Paulinus of Nola, a man of understanding and sympathy for human failings, could not help flying into a rage at the sight of the row of *tabernae* that stood in a line near the basilica of St Felix and disgorged a constant procession of drunks to stagger past the martyr's tomb. The Apostolic Constitutions forbade the use of inns except in cases of urgent necessity. However, when the Council of Laodicea met in 363 it was able to ban their use absolutely, for, by that time, the Church could pride itself on having provided proper accommodations just about wherever they were seriously needed.

It was the great Basil of Caesarea who conceived and promoted the idea of setting up hospices for Christian travellers. In fact, such a foundation was at first called a *basileias* and only later by the name that was to become standard in the Greek-speaking world, *xenodocheion* 'place for receiving strangers'. The Council of Nicaea gave what Basil had begun the force of law, and not long afterwards every Christian community of any consequence was able to boast a hostelry. Their size and style varied from place to place. In big centres, particularly where bishops took pride in the service and even gave up some of their perquisites to put money into it, they were ample and very good. If we may take the word of Antoninus of Piacenza, who is rather given to exaggeration, by 570 Jerusalem had a pair of hostels—one for men, the other for women—whose combined capacity totalled 3,000. Monasteries were in the forefront of taking care of travellers: each had at least some beds available for guests, and eventually a full-fledged hospice became an indispensable feature of almost every complex. Private citizens here and there added their bit.

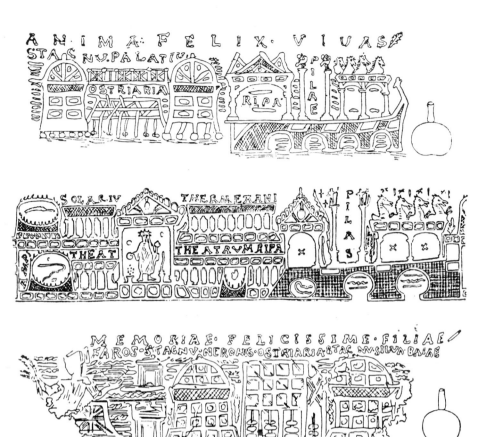

19 Pictures on glass vials sold as tourist souvenirs in Baiae and Puteoli. The first was found at Populonia on the northwestern coast of Italy. The left half shows Baiae with an artificial pool (*stagnum*), a palace (*palatium*) with oyster beds (*ostriaria*) in front, and beyond the palace another pool. The right side shows the pier (*ripa*) at Puteoli built on arches (the squiggles represent water running through them) and bearing a building, two columns (*pilae*) topped by statues, and an arch topped by a monument with four seahorses. The second, found near Lisbon, shows only Puteoli: its two amphitheatres, *solarium* or arcaded promenade, theatre (*theatrum*), a temple with its god portrayed before it, baths (*thermae*—or *therme* as spelled here), arcades (*jani*), the pier. The third, found near Rome, shows Baiae: its lighthouse (*faros*), artificial pool built by Nero (*stagnum Neronis*), oyster beds, another artificial pool, wooded park (*silva*).

20 Pilgrim souvenirs. Above, clay flask with the Annunciation scene; the Greek letters give part of Luke 1.28: 'Hail, thou that art highly favoured, the Lord is with thee.' Below, a Menas flask (see p. 327).

At Der Siman, for example, near the site of Simeon's pillar and a mecca for tourists after the saint's death in 459, several locals founded and maintained hostels; these were no vast complexes, to be sure, but they were able to put a roof over at least dozens of pilgrims' heads, and, to judge from the remains, no humble roof at that. Even the state helped out. In Constantinople a whole succession of rulers—Theodosius II, Justin, Justinian and Theodora—established *xenodocheia*. The story is told that at Oxyrhynchus in Egypt, a town swarming with monks, the local magistrates, eager to do their share, used to post men at the city gates to buttonhole and take in any stranger who looked down at the heels and, for extra consolation, underwrite all his expenses.

The *xenodocheia* existed to receive only members of the faith, not travellers in general. Consequently some reliable system had to be devised to screen out imposters. As early as Apostolic times Christians on the move were armed with letters of recommendation which enabled a stranger in town to introduce himself to his local co-religionists and request lodging or other assistance. Paul prided himself on being so well known that, as he reported to the Corinthians, he had no need of such documents. Later, during the years of the persecutions, they were more important than ever as a means of identifying authentic seekers of refuge or bearers of messages. By the fourth century, when Christianity was the reigning religion, they retained their usefulness as a way of keeping the unauthorized, heretics as well as pagans, out of the hospices.

The ordinary traveller carried a simple 'letter of peace', as it was called, one that presumably entitled him to the standard hospitality available. Clerics were given an actual letter of recommendation, a document of a higher order that brought its possessor favoured treatment. At first priests were permitted to give them out, but this led to abuses; too often nonclerics were able through money or position to get their hands on letters of recommendation. By the fourth century only bishops could issue them.

L

With a letter in his hand, a traveller could knock on the door of any hospice, day or night, and be assured of a reception. Each arrival was greeted with the 'sacred kiss', and hustled off to have his feet washed, in some places even anointed with oil. The sexes, as we have seen, were lodged separately. Meals were simple, varying with the means of the establishment or the degree of austerity it affected. In the Wadi Natrun, a visitor shared the Spartan menu of bread and water. Elsewhere he could usually count on getting some local fruit (cf. 193 above) in addition, and, in certain well-to-do places, even fish, vegetables, and a cup of wine. The quarters must have varied even more widely, although so few examples have survived that it is hard to be sure. A few sanctuary or monastery hospices are preserved in northern Syria, and, as it happens, these are quite different in design from the traditional ancient inn with its central courtyard surrounded on all sides by a line of individual chambers (203 above). They are oblong structures, two storeys high, without any court and with most of the space on each floor given over to a large dormitory; adjacent are a few smaller rooms which must have served for dining, for offices, and the like. At Turmanin there was a single large hospice whose dormitories, measuring forty feet by seventy-six, could pack in some 400 guests. At Der Siman there were two moderate sized hospices which together could accommodate just about a third of that number. All three were impressive stone buildings surrounded by high porticoes of massive piers.

Hospices offered a whole range of services in addition to bed and board. If the traveller arrived sick, they furnished medicines and a doctor; if in worn clothes, they furnished replacements. They gave him guides to show him around the sights. They even gave him money if he had run short, although here there was the sticky problem of weeding out those who were seeking it *sub specie peregrinationis* 'on the pretext of being a pilgrim'. Above all the traveller's soul was well cared for; even the poorest monastery, whatever it may have lacked to satisfy his bodily needs, provided richly for his spiritual, offering him ample opportunity for meditation and prayer.

For all this physical and mental sustenance there was no formal charge. However, it was assumed that those who could afford it would leave donations, as the caravan from Nessana did at St Catherine's in Mt Sinai, and these were gratefully accepted. In the Wadi Natrun visitors who stayed for long periods were expected to work. The contributions of guests, whether in money or gifts or labour, inevitably covered only a fraction of the costs; the lion's share fell on the foundations themselves. In Egypt the monks turned over surpluses from their work to the abbot to help support the hospices; elsewhere monasteries budgeted a tenth of their income. Charitable bequests were a great help; Justinian's Code contains a provision that if a will names 'the poor' as legatee with no further qualification, the sum is to go to the local hospice.

Not only was a considerable amount of money required, but of time and effort as well. Though hospitality was a Christian virtue which prelates and monks undertook unquestioningly, it is clear that they often smarted under the strain of entertaining a steady stream of guests. Jerome resignedly used to put off his work until the still hours of night, particularly the long winter nights, but he could not resist a brief aside, to the effect that receiving pilgrims was a job for the young and not the old, who no longer had the energy for such doings. The monks of the Wadi Natrun insisted on silence in the guests' quarters until noon. Some solitaries kept visiting hours, like Simeon on his pillar; he received only after 3 P.M.

Hospices were located with an eye to keeping possible inconvenience to a minimum. Monasteries, for example, often put them by the entrance and away from the rest of the complex. At the Wadi Natrun, the quarters were hard by the church so that guests could quietly step in for prayers without distracting the community. In sanctuaries where martyrs and saints were buried, the hospice stood as close to the tomb as possible, since having a saint as near neighbour, being his guest as it were, was a crowning joy for a pilgrim. Melania the Younger, on her first visit to Jerusalem, stayed in a chamber in or near the Anastasis, the church over the cave of the Entombment. When Paulinus settled down at Nola he moved into one of the cells reserved for pilgrims visiting the burial place of the martyr Felix. Pilgrims waiting to board ship at Carthage used to take shelter in a waterfront church near the grave of St Cyprian. Many a pilgrim preferred sleeping under an open portico that surrounded a venerated tomb to a more comfortable night in a hospice. The experience was exalting, and no donations were expected.

The monastery hospices were generally run by selected monks responsible to their abbot, the church hospices by priests responsible to their bishop. The arrangement, as it worked out, left much to be desired. These clerical hotel managers, in the nature of the case operating independently of the organization to which they belonged, tended to create a state within a state and, as will happen, resented attempts at supervision or control. The bishop or abbot's only recourse was to pick the right men for the job, men of particularly saintly reputation. For the rest of the staff—clerks, doctors, cooks, maintenance personnel—they favoured bachelors or spinsters, people who, free from family ties, could be expected to devote full attention to their work.

The Christian tourist, after dutifully following his guides about and eagerly lapping up what they had to say, tall stories and all, felt no less than his pagan brother the irresistible compulsion to leave his mark, to scribble somewhere an eternal record of his fleeting presence. 'We came to Cana', writes Antoninus of Piacenza, 'where our Lord attended the wedding, and we sat down on the very couch, and there—I'm ashamed to admit it—I wrote the name of my parents.' He must have inscribed the sort of message found so often in the

tombs of the pharaohs and elsewhere, one that lists for remembrance relatives and friends who are not present (285
above). I have already mentioned the pilgrim who scratched
his accolade to Menas' magical waters on the wall of a building
in the saint's sanctuary on the way between Alexandria and
the Wadi Natrun. In the Holy Land itself, pilgrim graffiti
have survived only on rather remote monuments; well-known
monuments have either disappeared or were protected against
such defacing. An artificial grotto at the foot of Mt Carmel
that was considered sacred—it was first a church and then a
mosque—has on the soft rock of its walls a vast tangle of
scribbled signatures left by its myriad visitors over the years.
The remains of the church on the site of Abraham's oak at
Mamre near Hebron still retain a few out of what must have
been a mass of pilgrim scratchings. 'O Lord God', reads the
best preserved, 'help . . . Paregarios your servant.'

Lastly, again like his pagan brother, the Christian visitor
could not leave without acquiring a suitable memento. But in
his case no tawdry gimcrack would do. It had to be something
that in a tangible way partook of the sanctity of the places he
had visited. Pilgrims enthusiastically carried off pebbles or
pinches of dirt from hallowed areas, pieces of fruit or twigs
from sacred groves, bits of wax from the candles that burned
in sanctuaries, drops of water from a stream where a saint
had refreshed himself or blades of grass from where his feet
had trod, and so on. At the Sanctuary of the Ascension on the
Mount of Olives, for example, where a portion of the floor
was left unpaved to recall Jesus' last footprints before his
miraculous departure, so many visitors helped themselves to
the earth and sand that the custodians had to shovel in replacement continually. Some went after bigger game such as the
ingenious souvenir-hunter who came away with the prize of
all time, a splinter of the True Cross: on Good Friday, when
worshippers were allowed to kiss the wood, he managed to
bite off a mouthful. Henceforth sharp-eyed deacons stood
guard there—and presumably anywhere else that offered

a similar temptation—to make sure that it never happened again.

In a monastery at Farfa some ten miles north of Rome there is a whole collection of typical Holy Land mementoes, very likely deposited by the monks who founded the place, a group that migrated from the orient about A.D. 700. The various items are now in little silk sacks but originally they were wrapped in pieces of white cloth and carefully tied and labelled. Some of the labels are still preserved, and we can read on them such inscriptions as 'From Mount Calvary', 'From the Rock of the Mount of Olives', 'From the Table Where He Ate with the Disciples', 'From the Tomb of Our Lord', 'Twig of the Tree That Furnished the Branch with Which Moses Divided the Red Sea'. One sack contains some reddish earth which is identified as 'Soil Drenched with the Blood of Christ', another some particles of plaster or the like which came 'From the Spot Where the Angel Announced Death to the Virgin Mary' (presumably from the house at Gethsemane that was supposed to be hers), still another a few scraps of wood 'From the Wood of Paradise'. One sack encloses a glass vial about four inches high which held 'Oil of the Holy Saturday from Jerusalem', i.e. from the lamp at the Holy Sepulchre which was reputed to light up by itself each year on Holy Saturday.

This last is an example of what was a favourite Holy Land souvenir, a few drops of oil from the myriad lamps that burned about the tombs of the various saints and martyrs. To hold the precious liquid visitors could purchase special containers, miniature flasks decorated with appropriate illustrations and inscribed with appropriate sentiments. For the well-to-do pilgrim there were flasks of silver some seven inches in diameter with both faces displaying scenes from the New Testament tastefully done in relief. He had an ample selection of subjects to choose from: Annunciation, Visitation, Nativity, Adoration of the Shepherds and Magi, Baptism, Crucifixion, Resurrection, Ascension, Christ Walking the Waters, Doubt-

ing Thomas. The inscriptions were more limited. A flask
with a relief of the Annunciation reads 'Blessing of the Mother
of God', one showing the Resurrection with the Church of
the Holy Sepulchre beneath reads 'Blessing of the Lord of the
Holy Places', and so on.

But flasks of silver were hardly for everybody. The economy-
minded were able to purchase more modest containers of
glass. Dozens of little jugs and bottles, a standard type some
three to seven inches high, hexagonal in shape and decorated
with crosses, have been found; they were manufactured for
the pilgrim trade by a shop in Jerusalem that was in operation
about A.D. 600. But even glass was too expensive and fragile
for the rank and file of pilgrims. For them there were available
cheap crude flasks of terra cotta that could be turned out from
moulds by the thousands (Fig. 20). One big centre of production was in Alexandria, another near Smyrna, and there
were active workshops in Jerusalem and other Palestinian
centres. Though intended primarily for lamp oil, the flasks
could of course take any liquid that was valued as a souvenir,
and, as it happens, those we know best, because so many
specimens have survived, held water. They were sold at the
sanctuary of Menas, described above, whose springs were
thought to have curative powers. For carrying off the precious
fluid souvenir flasks were available in two grades. The more
expensive was larger—some $5\frac{1}{2}$ to $6\frac{3}{4}$ inches high and 4 to
$6\frac{1}{4}$ broad—and generally was more elaborately decorated; the
cheaper was smaller—$3\frac{1}{2}$ to $4\frac{1}{4}$ high and $2\frac{3}{4}$ to $3\frac{1}{4}$ broad—and
could bear as decoration no more than a flower or a cross or
at most a head of Menas. The preferred decoration for both
sizes (Fig. 20b) was a full-length picture of the saint with
arms outstretched in an attitude of prayer and with camels
kneeling near his feet to recall that, according to the tradition,
when facing martyrdom he had asked that his corpse be put
on a camel and buried wherever the animal stopped. Both
sizes were sometimes inscribed 'Blessing of St Menas'.

The word 'Blessing' here and on the silver flasks is

significant. It reveals that these were much more than just
containers for mementoes, that they were amulets as well:
carried on a string about the neck, they ensured by virtue of
the saint's benediction the bearer's good fortune. Some of
the Menas flasks have on the back a picture of a boat; they
were probably for pilgrims who returned by sea. For those
who wanted an amulet more compact than a flask, medallions
with a 'Blessing' inscription and appropriate picture were
available made of pressed earth. For those who wanted a
compact amulet-cum-memento, there were 'Blessing' medallions made of hallowed materials such as earth from the Holy
Sepulchre.

Lastly a word about Jewish pilgrims. Before the destruction
of Jerusalem by the Romans, Jews had always flocked there,
particularly during the Passover season. Numbers of them
continued to do so, making the pilgrimage like their Christian
brethren. Indeed, the very shop that manufactured glass
souvenir jugs and bottles put out a line for Jewish customers,
the identical containers decorated with the seven-branched
candlestick instead of the cross. And synagogues, like the
Christian foundations, maintained quarters to accommodate
Jewish travellers.

So, each year thousands of pilgrims, their medallions or flasks
about their necks, left the sacred soil for the long trek home,
probably so exalted by the experience that they gave scant
thought to the rigours that lay ahead—or the reality that lay
behind. To those with eyes to see, it was sadly apparent that
tourism was no respecter of sanctity, that it was giving the
cities of the Holy Land more the air of Sodom and Gomorrah
than of Eden. 'Do not imagine that your faith is in any way
lacking because you have not seen Jerusalem', wrote Jerome
in a bitter moment to Paulinus of Nola in 394–95, almost a
decade after his first sight of it, 'and don't think us better off
because we live here. . . . If the site of the Cross and the
Resurrection were not in a terribly crowded city which has its

government building, its barracks, its prostitutes, troups of actors, clowns, and all the rest just like any other town, or if it were reserved for bands of monks alone, then surely all the monks in the world should try to settle down here. But now it is the height of stupidity to renounce the world, leave your fatherland, abandon the cities, and take the vows in order to live far from your home amid denser crowds than you would in your own country! They flock here from the four corners of the universe. The city is full of all sorts of people, there is such a packed mob of men and women that, whereas elsewhere you can escape certain things, here you have to put up with everything'.

It is a pity that others did not share Jerome's view. The world would have been spared much bloodshed.

L*

Abbreviations

AJPh: *American Journal of Philology*

AM: L. Casson, *The Ancient Mariners* (New York 1959)

Anderson: J. Anderson, *Ancient Greek Horsemanship* (Berkeley and Los Angeles 1961)

AP: *Anthologia Palatina*

Ath. Mitt.:   *Mitteilungen des deutschen archäologischen Instituts, Athenische Abteilung*

Balsdon: J. Balsdon, *Life and Leisure in Ancient Rome* (London 1969)

Behr: C. Behr, *Aelius Aristides and the Sacred Tales* (Amsterdam 1968)

Breasted, *ARE*:   J. Breasted, *Ancient Records of Egypt* (Chicago 1906)

Cabrol-Leclerq: F. Cabrol and H. Leclerq, *Dictionnaire d'archéologie chrétienne et de liturgie* (Paris 1907–53)

Cary-Warmington: M. Cary and E. Warmington, *The Ancient Explorers* (New York 1929)

Chr. d'Eg.:   *Chronique d'Égypte*

CIG: *Corpus inscriptionum graecarum*

CIL: *Corpus inscriptionum latinarum*

Crook: J Crook, *Law and Life of Rome* (London 1967)

D'Arms: J. D'Arms, *Romans on the Bay of Naples* (Cambridge, Mass. 1970)

De Ruggiero: E. de Ruggiero, *Dizionario epigrafico di antichità romane* (Rome 1886—)

DS: C. Daremberg and E. Saglio, *Dictionnaire des antiquités grecques et romaines* (Paris 1877–1919)

Edelstein: E. and L. Edelstein, *Asclepius* (Baltimore 1945)

Enc. Arte Ant.:   *Enciclopedia dell' arte antica* (Rome 1958–66)

ESAR: T. Frank and others, *An Economic Survey of Ancient Rome* (Baltimore 1933–40)

Evans, *PM*:   A. Evans, *The Palace of Minos at Knossos* (London 1921–35)

Fliche–Martin: A. Fliche and V. Martin, *Histoire de l'Église* iii (Paris 1936)

Forbes: R. Forbes *Studies in Ancient Technology* ii (Leiden 1965)

Frazer: J. Frazer, *Pausanias's Description of Greece* (London 1898)

Friedländer: L. Friedländer, *Darstellungen aus der Sittengeschichte Roms* i (Leipzig 1922)

Fustier: P. Fustier, *La route* (Paris 1968)

Gardiner: A. Gardiner, *Egypt of the Pharaohs* (Oxford 1961)

Geyer: P. Geyer, *Itinera hierosolymitana, saecula iii-viii* (Corpus scriptorum ecclesiasticorum latinorum, vol. 39, Vienna 1898)

Gorce: D. Gorce, *Les voyages, l'hospitalité et le port des lettres dans le monde chrétien des ive et ve siècles* (Paris 1925)

Gorce, Melanie: D. Gorce, *Vie de Sainte Melanie* (Sources chrétiennes 90, Paris 1962)

Grenier: A. Grenier, *Archéologie gallo-romaine*. Deuxième partie: *l'Archéologie du sol, les routes* (Paris 1934)

Homo: L. Homo, 'Les musées de la Rome impériale', *Gazette des Beaux Arts* 61 (1919) 21–46, 177–208

Homo, *Urb.*:   L. Homo, *Rome impériale et l'urbanisme dans l'antiquité* (Paris 1971²)

How and Wells: W. How and J. Wells, *A Commentary on Herodotus* (Oxford 1912)

IEJ: *Israel Exploration Journal*

IG: *Inscriptiones graecae*

IGRR: R. Cagnat and others, *Inscriptiones graecae ad res romanas pertinentes* (Paris 1911–27)

ILS: H. Dessau, *Inscriptiones latinae selectae* (Berlin 1892–1916)

Jahres.:   *Jahreshefte des österreichischen archaeologischen Instituts*

JDI: *Jahrbuch des deutschen archäologischen Instituts*

JEA: *Journal of Egyptian Archaeology*

JHS: *Journal of Hellenic Studies*

JRS: *Journal of Roman Studies*

Kaibel: G. Kaibel, *Epigrammata graeca* (Berlin 1878)

Kleberg: T. Kleberg, *Hôtels, restaurants et cabarets dans l'antiquité romaine* (Uppsala 1957)

Levi: A. and M. Levi, *Itineraria picta. Contributo allo studio della Tabula Peutingeriana* (Rome 1967)

Liebeschuetz: J. Liebeschuetz, *Antioch. City and Imperial Administration in the Later Roman Empire* (Oxford 1972)

Meissner: B. Meissner, *Babylonien und Assyrien* i (Heidelberg 1920)

Muller, *FHG*:   C. Muller, *Fragmenta historicorum graecorum* (Paris 1841–70)

Needham: J. Needham, *Science and Civilisation in China*, vol. 4, parts ii-iii (Cambridge 1965, 1971)

Not. Sc.:   Accademia dei Lincei, Rome: *Notizie degli scavi di antichità*

Oppenheim, *Letters*:   A. Oppenheim, *Letters from Mesopotamia* (Chicago 1967)

Pfister: F. Pfister, *Der Reliquienkult im Altertum* (Religionsgeschichtliche Versuche und Vorarbeiten, v. Band, Giessen 1909)

Pflaum: H. Pflaum, *Essai sur le cursus publicus sous le haut-empire romain* (Mémoires présentés par divers savants à l'Académie des inscriptions et belles-lettres xiv, Paris 1940)

PG: J. Migne, *Patrologia graeca*

P. Giss.:   *Griechische Papyri im Museum des oberhessischen Geschichts-vereins zu Giessen* (Leipzig 1910–12)

P. Iand.:   *Papyri Iandanae* (Berlin and Leipzig 1912—)

PL: J. Migne, *Patrologia latina*

P. Lips.:   L. Mitteis, *Griechische Urkunden der Papyrussamlung zu Leipzig* (Leipzig 1906)

P. Lond.:   F. Kenyon and H. Bell, *Greek Papyri in the British Museum* (London 1893—)

P. Mich.:   H. Youtie and others, *Michigan Papyri* (Ann Arbor 1931—)

P. Oxy.:   B. Grenfell, A. Hunt, and others, *Oxyrhynchus Papyri* (London 1898—)

Pritchard, *ANET*:   J. Pritchard, *Ancient Near Eastern Texts Relating to the Old Testament* (Princeton 1955², Supplement 1969)

P. Ryl.:   A. Hunt and others, *Catalogue of the Greek Papyri in the John Rylands Library at Manchester* (Manchester 1891—)

PSI: *Papiri greci e latini* (Florence 1912—)

P. Strass.:   F. Preisigke, *Griechische Papyrus der kaiserlichen Universi-täts- und Landesbibliothek zu Strassburg* (Strassburg and Leipzig 1906–1920)

RA: *Revue archéologique*

Ramsay: W. Ramsay, 'Roads and Travel in the New Testament', in Hastings' *Dictionary of the Bible, Extra Volume* (London 1904)

RE: *Paulys Real-Encyclopädie der classischen Altertumswissenschaft*

REA: *Revue des études anciennes*

REG: *Revue des études grecques*

RhM: *Rheinisches Museum für Philologie*

Röm. Mitt.:   *Mitteilungen des deutschen archäologischen Instituts, Römische Abteilung*

Salonen, *Hippologica*:   A. Salonen, *Hippologica Accadica* (Annales Academiae Scientiarum Fennicae, Ser. B, Tom. 100, Helsinki 1955)

Salonen, *Landfahrzeuge*:   A. Salonen, *Die Landfahrzeuge des alten Mesopotamien* (Annales Academiae Scientiarum Fennicae, Ser. B, Tom. 72, 3, Helsinki 1951)

SB: F. Preisigke, F. Bilabel, and others, *Sammelbuch griechischer Urkunden aus Ägypten* (Strassburg, Berlin and Leipzig 1913—)

SEHHW: M. Rostovtzeff, *The Social and Economic History of the Hellenistic World* (Oxford 1941)

SEHRE: M. Rostovtzeff, *The Social and Economic History of the Roman Empire* (Oxford 1957²)

Sel. Pap.:   A. Hunt and C. Edgar, *Select Papyri* (Loeb Classical Library 1932–1934)

SHA: *Scriptores historiae augustae*

Singer: C. Singer, *A History of Technology* i-ii (Oxford 1954, 1956)

Spano: G. Spano, 'La illuminazione delle vie di Pompei', *Atti della reale accademia di archeologia, lettere, e belle arti di Napoli* 7 (1920) 3–128

SSAW: L. Casson, *Ships and Seamanship in the Ancient World* (Princeton 1971)

TAPA: *Transactions of the American Philological Association*

Thomson: J. Thomson, *History of Ancient Geography* (Cambridge 1948)

TLL: *Thesaurus linguae latinae*

Tobler: T. Tobler, *Itinera hierosolymitana et descriptiones Terrae Sanctae* (Geneva 1879)

Vermeule: E. Vermeule, *Greece in the Bronze Age* (Chicago 1964)

Vigneron: P. Vigneron, *Le cheval dans l'antiquité gréco-romaine* (Annales de l'Est, publiées par la Faculté des Lettres et des Sciences de l'Université de Nancy 35, Nancy 1968)

Wachsmuth: D. Wachsmuth, *Pompimos Ho Daimon: Untersuchung zu den antiken Sakralhandlungen bei Seereisen* (Doctoral Dissertation, Berlin 1967)

Warmington: E. Warmington, *The Commerce between the Roman Empire and India* (Cambridge 1928)

W. Chrest.:   L. Mitteis and U. Wilcken, *Grundzüge und Chrestomathie der Papyruskunde*. Erster Band (Leipzig and Berlin 1912)

Wilkinson: J. Wilkinson, *Egeria's Travels* (London 1971)

Notes to Chapter 1

21–2 First seagoing vessels, *SSAW* 17, 20–2. Seagoing commerce in the late third millennium B.C., W. Leemans in *Journal of the Economic and Social History of the Orient* II (1968) 215–16; he argues (225) that the ships in the Mesopotamia–India trade were Indian since, among other things, Mesopotamia had no ship-timber whereas India had its abundant supplies of teak. 'When the Nile', Herodotus 2: 97. Egyptian and Mesopotamian rivercraft, *SSAW* 16–24, 29. Buoyed rafts and coracles, 4–6. 'Aboard a live donkey', Herodotus 1: 194.

22–5 Donkeys known in Mesopotamia as early as 3000 B.C. and horses and mules about 2300, Salonen, *Hippologica* 12, 46, 71. Earliest four-wheel and two-wheel vehicles, Salonen, *Landfahr̄zeuge* 155–6, 160–1. Drawn by oxen, 29. Remains of wagons, 157–8. Horse as draught-animal, *Hippologica* 22–4. Chariots, Evans, *PM* iv, 807–25; Salonen, *Landfahr̄zeuge* 163–4; Singer i, 724–8; Needham iv, 2, 246. Construction of chariots, Vermeule 261–2; A. Lucas and J. Harris, *Ancient Egyptian Materials and Industries* (London 1962⁴) 436, 438 (a surviving Egyptian chariot with yoke and handrail of elm, pole of willow, axle of ash, spokes of plum; all except the willow had to be imported). Diomed, *Il.* 10: 504–5. Harness, Singer i, 719–21. Indian bronze models, Singer i, 719, fig. 518B; S. Piggott, *Prehistoric India* (London 1950) 178–9. Piggott suggests on the basis of bronze models of oxen which have been found that oxen were put into the shafts; if so, that would round out the circle: the Near East used horses in a harness suitable for oxen, and India oxen in one suitable for horses. Shafts in China, Needham iv, 2, 246–50. Covered wagon, J. Pritchard, *The Ancient Near East in Pictures* (Princeton 1954) no. 169. Joseph's wagons, Genesis 45: 17–19, 46: 5. Travellers' use of donkeys, Meissner 338. Litters, Salonen *Landfahr̄zeuge* 144–5 (mention of light litters of fibres or reeds; the clay model of a palanquin of c. 1700 B.C. found on Crete [Evans, *PM* ii, 157–8] reproduces a heavy type probably used in processions).

25–7 Shulgi's hymn, Pritchard, *ANET* 584–6. Hammurabi's letter, A. Ungnad, *Babylonische Briefe aus der Zeit der Hammurapi-Dynastie* (Leipzig 1914) no. 15. 'Way of the land', Exodus 13: 17. Processional way of the Hittites, W. Andrae, *Alte Feststrassen im Nahen Osten* (Leipzig 1941) 15–16 and plate 1. No bridges in Mesopotamia, H. Schmökel, *Kulturgeschichte des alten Orients* (Stuttgart 1961) 84. Ferries: cf. the scenes on later Assyrian reliefs of chariots being ferried across streams, e.g. R. Barnett and W. Forman, *Assyrian Palace Reliefs* (London 1960) nos. 16–20 (BM 124540). Very likely body, axle, and wheels were so put together that they could swiftly and easily be taken apart; cf. Singer i, 717–18. Road on Crete, Evans, *PM* ii, 60–92, esp. 62, 71; viaduct, 93–102. Roads in Greece, 91, note 1; Vermeule 263. Wall painting from Tiryns, 261–2 and 192, fig. 33c. See also *AJA* 77 (1973) 74–7.

28–9 Travelling functionaries, J. Yoyotte, 'Les pèlerinages dans l'Égypte ancienne', *Les pèlerinages* (Coll. 'Sources Orientales' iii, Paris 1960) 24, 37–8, 52. 'I reached Elephantine', 38 (= Breasted, *ARE* i, nos 611–13). Travellers to Sinai, Pritchard, *ANET* 229–30. Harkhuf, Breasted, *ARE* i, nos 333–6, 353. 'To open up', Gardiner 99–100. Extent of Harkhuf's travels, Gardiner 100–1. Egyptian voyages down the Red Sea, *AM* 9–14.

29–31 Levantines leading donkeys, Singer i, 706. On the well-organized caravan trade between Mesopotamia and Asia Minor, see M. Larsen, *Old Assyrian Caravan Procedures* (Istanbul 1967); Leemans, *op. cit.* (334 above) 171–215. 'Thirty years ago', Oppenheim, *Letters* 74. Hammurabi's regulations, Pritchard, *ANET* 170. Mesopotamian cargo financing, A. Oppenheim, 'The Seafaring Merchants of Ur', *Journal of the American Oriental Society* 74 (1954) 6–17. 'The Egyptians', Herodotus 2: 59–60.

32–4 Egyptian tourism, Yoyotte, *op. cit.* (see 28–9) 49–53. 'Hadnakhte', C. Firth and J. Quibell, *The Step Pyramid*. Vol. i, *Text* (Cairo 1935) 82–3. 'Came to contemplate', Yoyotte 57. 'Scribe So-and-So' and 'in the view', 53. Pennewet and Wia, Firth-Quibell 84–5. 'The scribe of clever fingers', 81. 'Hurry and bring', Gardiner 58–9. 'I have never', Oppenheim, *Letters* 87.

35–8 'Commands have been sent', Breasted, *ARE* i, no. 354. Shulgi, Pritchard, *ANET* 585. On the nature of travel in Mesopotamia, cf. A. Oppenheim, *Ancient Mesopotamia* (Chicago 1964) 119–120. Government post of Lagash, T. Jones and J. Snyder, *Sumerian Economic Texts from the Third Ur Dynasty* (Minneapolis 1961) 293–302. Minoan hostel, Evans, *PM* ii, 103–39. On private hospitality in Mesopotamia, cf. Oppenheim 78. Town inns in Sumer and Babylon, T. Jacobsen, *Toward the Image of Tammuz* (Cambridge, Mass. 1970) 349; G. Driver and J. Miles, *The Babylonia Laws* i (Oxford 1952) 202. Female tavernkeepers cited in the recently published fragments of the law code of Ammisaduqa (1646–1626 B.C.), Pritchard, *ANET* 528. Tavern regulations, 170 and Driver-Miles i, 202–8; J. MacQueen, *Babylon* (New York 1965) 71–2. 'If a man urinates', I. Gelb and others, *The Assyrian Dictionary* (Chicago 1964—) s.v. *astammu*. 'I am now sending', Oppenheim, *Letters* 86.

38–9 'This land was reached', Pritchard, *ANET* 229. On dangers in Mesopotamia, cf. Meissner 338–9. Compensation, 338. 'Men sit', Gardiner 109. Guard stations in Crete, Evans, *PM* ii, 66, 78. Wenamon, Pritchard, *ANET* 25–9.

Notes to Chapter 2

44–6   For a convenient recent summary of the end of the Bronze Age in Greece, see M. Finley, *Early Greece: The Bronze and Archaic Ages* (London 1970) chapters 1–6; for the age that Homer describes, see pages 81–9. Phoenicians, *AM* 67–72. 'Phoenicians, famed for their ships', *Od.* 15: 415–16.

46–8   Odysseus' return to Ithaca, *Od.* 13: 70–6. Telemachus' voyages, *Od.* 2: 414–18, 15: 282–6. Pylos to Sparta, *Od.* 3: 478–4: 2. Sparta to Phthia, *Od.* 4: 8–9. Mules, *Il.* 23: 115–23 (hauling wood from Mt Ida). Priam, *Il.* 24: 266–7. Nausicaa, *Od.* 6: 72–88. Telemachus' gifts, *Od.* 15: 114–29. Gifts from king and queen of Thebes, *Od.* 4: 126–32. Sleeping accommodations, *Od.* 3: 397–403, 4: 296–305, 7: 344–47. 'Stranger', *Od.* 14: 56–8. 'Pay no heed', *Od.* 9: 275–6.

48–9   'You're out of', *Od.* 18: 327–9. Lot, Genesis 13: 13, 19: 1–11. Levite, Judges 19. Jacob, Genesis 28. Shunammite, II Kings 4: 24. Kings and nobles on mules, II Samuel 13: 29; I Kings 1: 38. Return of the ark, I Samuel 6: 7–12.

50–1   Xenophon's Greeks, *Anab.* 3: 4: 10–11. 'I took my chariots', D. Luckenbill, *Ancient Records of Assyria and Babylonia* (Chicago 1926) i, no. 222. Assyrian chariots, Salonen, *Landfahrzeuge* 166–67. Battering rams, Barnett-Forman, *op. cit.* (334 above) no. 23 (BM 124536). Assyrian roads, Meissner 340–41. Paved sanctuary roads at Assur and Babylon, Andrae, *op. cit.* (334 above) 19–43. Paving at Babylon, R. Koldewey, *Das wieder erstehende Babylon* (Leipzig 1913) 25. Bridge at Babylon, Herodotus 1: 186. Remains, Meissner 342. Assyrian post, Meissner 339.

51–2   Horse as riding animal, J. Wiesner, *Fahren und Reiten* (Archaeologica Homerica, Band i, Kapitel F, Göttingen 1968) 110–28; Anderson 10–14. 'Mounted the horses', *Il.* 10: 529–31. Chariots in China till the Han period (200 B.C.–A.D. 200), Needham iv, 2: 247–8. Bit and bridle, Anderson 40–78.

53–4   Persian 'royal road', Herodotus 5: 52–3 and How and Wells ad loc. Persian post, Pflaum 4–17. 'There is nothing', Herodotus 8: 98. *Harmamaxa, DS* s.v. 'Well, first', Aristophanes, *Ach.* 68–71. Alexander's hearse, Diodorus 18: 26–8. Camels, Salonen, *Hippologica* 84–90; Forbes 193–208.

Notes to Chapter 3

59–61   Carthaginian blockade, *ESAR* i, 6–8. Greek knowledge of the Mediterranean, Thomson 47. The Atlantic, Cary-Warmington 30. Celts and Danube, Thomson 52. Russia, Thomson 56–64. India and Arabia, Thomson 78–82; Cary-Warmington 61–2. Africa, Thomson 65–7.

61–3   Circumnavigation of Africa, Thomson 71–3; Cary-Warmington 87–97. Hanno, Thomson 73–7; Cary-Warmington 47–52.

Notes to Chapter 4

65–6   'Frogs', Plato, *Phaedo* 109b. Figures preserved show how astronomically high were the costs of land transport. Stones, for example, which sold for 61 drachmae in Corinth were worth over ten times that much—705 drachmae—when delivered to Delphi. The construction records of a building at Eleusis, near Athens, show graphically why: to haul a single column drum from a quarry just fifteen to twenty miles away took three days and required thirty-one span of oxen. See H. Michell, *The Economics of Ancient Greece* (New York 1957²) 252; C. Roebuck, ed., *The Muses at Work* (Cambridge, Mass. 1969) 14; W. Burford, 'Heavy Transport in Antiquity', *Economic History Review* Second Series 13 (1960) 1–18, esp. 14. Greek trade, *AM* 108–24. Ships, *SSAW* 169–82. Thanks for safe crossing: In comedies of the time, when a returning merchant comes on stage, his first words are often fervent thanks to the gods for a safe arrival. 'Father Neptune!' says Theoproprides in *The Haunted House* (431–7), re-written by Plautus from a comedy of the late fourth century B.C., 'Many thanks for letting me off and sending me home still alive. But believe me, if you ever hear of my getting within a foot of the water hereafter, you can go right ahead and finish what you started to do this last trip. Just keep away from me, far away, from now on. I've trusted in you all I'm ever going to.'

67–8   Going by foot, Xenophon, *Mem.* 3: 13: 5 (Socrates, discussing with some one obviously well-to-do the difficulties of travelling from Athens to Olympia, a five- to six-day walk, talks only of the right attitude to take toward such a walk, never of using an animal or cart). Accompanying servant, Xenophon, *Mem.* 3: 13: 6 (Socrates reminds a traveller who complained of arriving tired that he carried only a cloak whereas his slave was burdened with the bedding and other gear). Pack-animals, *DS* s.v. *asinus, clitellae, mulus, sagma.* Litters and sedan-chairs, *DS* s.v. *lectica*. Reaction to Demosthenes, Deinarchus, *Against Demosthenes* 36. Vehicles, *Enc. Arte Ant.* s.v. *carro*; H. Lorimer, 'The Country Cart of Ancient Greece', *JHS* 23 (1903) 132–51.

68–72 Greek roads, Forbes 140–4. Pausanias' comment about the road to Delphi, 10: 5: 5. 'Impossible for vehicles', Pausanias 2: 11: 3. The Ladder, 8: 6: 4. Staff-Road, Frazer iii, pages 87–8. 'For six miles', Frazer ii, page 547. Hadrian's improvements, Pausanias 1: 44: 6. Carriage road from the Peloponnese, Plutarch, *Mor.* 304e. Greek rut roads, Forbes 142–3; Singer ii, 499. The prehistoric tracks in Malta, often cited among the earliest examples of rut roads, were simply casual grooves formed by the dragging of slide cars (cars of two shafts, supported at the front end by an animal while the rear end drags on the ground); see J. Evans, *The Prehistoric Antiquities of the Maltese Islands: A Survey* (London 1971) 202–4. A splendid example of a work road with ruts is the *diolkos*, the road built in the sixth century B.C. across the Isthmus of Corinth for dragging ships from one side to the other; see N. Verdelis in *Ath. Mitt.* 71 (1956) 51–9 and plates 33–7. Projection barring the way, E. Curtius and J. Kaupert, *Karten von Attika*, Heft ii (Berlin 1883) 45. 'I walked along', *Oed. Rex* 801–13. *Hermeia, DS* s.v. *Hermae*. In Egypt, Strabo 17: 818. 'The superstitious man', Theophrastus, *Char.* 16: 5. Description of tourist route, Muller, *FHG* ii, 256–61; cf. Frazer i, pages xlii–xlvii.

72–6 Demosthenes' cases, Demosthenes, *Against Nicostratus* 6–7, *Against Callippus* 5. Plot of comedies, H. Ormerod, *Piracy in the Ancient World* (London 1924) 263–4. 'Is the sort who', Theophrastus, *Char.* 25: 2. 'Was murdered', Lucian, *Dial. Mort.* 27: 2. Senseless taking of life for the pleasure of it was not unknown to the ancient world and posed yet another hazard for the traveller. Plutarch tells (*Mor.* 304e) of a group of families making a sacred pilgrimage from the Peloponnese to Delphi who bedded down in their wagons for the night along a body of water, and some drunken toughs who happened to come by tipped the wagons into the water drowning most of the people in them. Precious bowls, Demosthenes, *Against Timotheus* 31. Money-changing, R. Bogaert, *Banques et banquiers dans les cités grecques* (Leiden 1968) 314–26. Greek clothing, M. Bieber, *Griechische Kleidung* (Berlin and Leipzig 1928); Anderson 85–7. 'As for the length', e.g. Herodotus 1: 72. The precise cut and shape of the Greek garments mentioned varied of course from age to age and place to place. The Greek terms cited are as general in their meaning as our words 'shirt' or 'coat'.

77–9 Spartan attack, Thucydides 5: 49. The Spartans argued that their attack had been launched before the 'truce-bearers' actually arrived in Sparta to make the announcement and refused to pay. The Eleans held that the truce was in force from the moment it had been proclaimed in Elis. On the Olympic games in general, see L. Drees, *Olympia* (English trans., London 1968). Wealthy making a show: The painter Zeuxis turned up at one Olympic festival wearing a cloak with his name embroidered in gold (Pliny 35: 62). Alcibiades, Plutarch, *Alcibiades* 11–12. Aqueduct, Lucian, *The Death of Peregrinus* 19; the Greek multimillionaire, Herodes Atticus, footed the bill. The events, Drees 66–86. Formal readings: There was an apocryphal story that Herodotus had recited his history at one of the Olympics and 'everybody got to know him much better than the Olympic victors themselves' (Lucian, *Herodotus* 2). By the Middle Ages the story had acquired picturesque details—Thucydides while still a boy, it was said, had heard the readings and been moved to tears; cf. How and Wells 6. Addresses on vital issues, cf. Drees 59–60. Demosthenes, for example, at the Olympics of 324 B.C. engaged in a debate on the pros and cons of rule by Alexander the Great (Plutarch, *Demosthenes* 9: 2). Displays of art, Lucian, *Herodotus* 4. Spectators bareheaded, cf. Lucian, *Anacharsis* 16. 'Don't you get scorched', Epictetus, *Diss.* 1: 6: 26; although Epictetus lived in the first century A.D., conditions at the games were no doubt very much the same as they had been five centuries earlier. Threatening a slave, Aelian, *Var. Hist.* 14: 18. Thales died of thirst and heat prostration while watching athletic games (Diogenes Laertius 1: 39).

81–2 Criticism of the government: The Athenians had a second somewhat less important festival for dramatic competitions, the Lenaea, which took place in mid-winter when sea-borne traffic was at an almost complete standstill. Aristophanes presented his next play, *The Acharnians*, at this festival and pointedly remarked (*Ach.* 502–5), 'This time Cleon can't accuse me of running down the state in the presence of strangers: it's the Lenaea; we're by ourselves.' Athens' theatre, A. Pickard-Cambridge, *The Theatre of Dionysus in Athens* (Oxford 1946) and *The Dramatic Festivals at Athens* (Oxford 1968²). Example of brazen effrontery, Theophrastus, *Char.* 9: 5.

82–5 The fundamental work on the cult of Asclepius is E. and L. Edelstein, *Asclepius* (Baltimore 1945). 'On these tablets', Pausanias 2: 27: 3. For the text of the tablets, see Edelstein i, 229–37; those cited are Nos. 17, 20, 30. For a description of the site, see Frazer iii, 236–57. Inn at Epidaurus, W. Dinsmoor, *The Architecture of Ancient Greece* (London 1950³) 251. 'A great many Greeks', Herodotus 3: 139. Solon, Aristotle, *Ath. Pol.* 11: 1. 'If you've never', Lysippus 7 (= Muller, *FHG* ii, 255). Plato's attitude toward travel was uncompromisingly totalitarian: in his *Laws* (950–1a) he limits travel by and large to people on state business, who, moreover, are to be at least forty years old and on their return are to 'teach the young that the political institutions of other states are inferior to their own'. For sightseeing at Delphi, cf. Euripides, *Ion* 184–236.

85–9 'Stand back', Aristophanes,' *Ach.* 616–17. City streets, Forbes 166–7. 'My master said', Plautus, *Pseudolus* 596–7, 658. 'You know that house', Terence, *Brothers* 581–4. See also Homo, *Urb.* 589–93. Street signs and house numbers are quite recent inventions; Paris introduced the first in 1729 and the second in 1512 but not in a thorough-going fashion until 1800 (Homo, *Urb.* 588–9). On private hospitality, cf. Diodorus' account (13: 83) of a certain Tellias, a wealthy man of Acragas toward the end of the fifth century B.C., who posted servants before his door to invite any and all strangers; once he took in 500 cavalry-men who arrived in town in a winter storm and not only fed them but sent them off with a change of clothing. Such open-handed hospitality was already looked on as old-fashioned by this time. Theophrastus characterizes as a typical boaster the man who lives in hired lodgings but tells strangers that it is his ancestral home and that he is selling it because it does not have enough room for guests (*Char.* 23: 9). Putting up all visitors from certain places: Inscriptions found at Delphi reveal that a certain Craton who lived there kept up the custom, long current in his family, of always making his guest room available to any Thebans who came to town (E. Ziebarth, 'Gasthäuser im alten Griechenland', *Eis mnemen Spyridonos Lamprou*, Athens 1935, 339–48, esp. 340). *Xenon*, Diodorus 13: 83 (Tellias had numerous *xenones*); Diogenes Laertius 5: 14 (Aristotle's will mentions a *xenon* on a garden that seems to have been a separate lodge). Invited to host's table, Vitruvius 6: 7: 4. Inns: There are numerous other terms for inn besides *pandokeion*, e.g. *katalyma, katagogion, katalysis*. Inns along major routes, cf. the 'abun-dance of inns' between Athens and Oropus mentioned earlier (72 above). 'Landladies with the fewest bedbugs', *Frogs* 114–15. Landlady of the inn in Hades, 549–78. Other examples of landladies, Plutarch *Mor* 412c; Dio Cassius 46: 6: 4. Courtyard, see A. Furtwängler in *Mélanges Nicole* (Geneva 1905) 159–64 (vase of fourth century B.C. with picture of inn-court). Sharing rooms, see Ziebarth 342 (inn at Epidaurus which seems to have had seven 7-bed rooms). Furniture, cf. Aristides, *Or.* 27: 15 = ii, 455 Keil (Aristides was ushered into a 'chamber and was furnished with a pallet and clean spread, both most welcome since I didn't have a thing with me'); although Aristides wrote in the second century A.D., things must have been much the same centuries earlier. Buying food, Plutarch, *Mor.* 234e-f, 995b-c, and cf. 211 above. Rates including board, Polybius 2: 15: 5–6, referring to Lombardy in the second century B.C. Public inn in Epirus (at Kassope near Preveza), *JHS* 73 (1953) 120–1, 74 (1954) 159, 75 (1955) Archeological Reports p. 13, 76 (1956) Archeological

Reports p. 19. For a public inn maintained for Romans at Sparta in the second century B.C., see *RhM* 64 (1909) 335–6. For *leschai* in this age, see Diogenes Laertius 9: 17; Pausanias 10: 25. 1 (the famous *lesche* in Delphi decorated with murals by Polygnotus, the greatest painter of the fifth century B.C.). Baths, *DS* s.v. *balneum*, pp. 648–51. Robbing garments, Aristophanes, *Clouds* 175–9 (a joke to the effect that Socrates, finding himself one day without the price of dinner for himself and his disciples, improvised a pair of calipers and with them solved, not a geometry problem, but the food problem by hooking somebody's *himation* from a dressing-room); Diogenes Laertius 6: 52 (Diogenes the Cynic's crack to a thief at the baths: 'Are you here for an oiling (*aleimmation*) or a cloak (*all' himation*)?' or, more freely, 'Are you here for rubbing or robbing?'). Byzantium husbands, Athenaeus 10: 442c.

90–1 Temple inns, *IG* ii², 1638 A 30 (Delos), Diodorus 11: 89: 8 (Palike, in eastern Sicily). Plataea, Thucydides 3: 68 (two-storey inn covering a circuit of 200 feet along each side, and if we assume the rooms were cubicles ten feet square, there were some 150 of them). Banquet halls, A. Frickenhaus in *JDI* 32 (1917) 114–33. Hostelry at Olympia, see W. Dinsmoor, *op. cit.* (339 above) 114 and fig. 44; an inscription records that it was erected by one Leonidas of Naxos. Renting of temple lodgings, cf. *Syl.*³ 1106 §§ 1, 12–13, inscription of 300 B.C. dealing with the setting up of a religious foundation with *xenones* for rental to provide revenue (their use is expressly denied to the foundation personnel). Well-to-do use tents: At the Olympics of 388 B.C., Dionysius I, ruler of Syracuse, housed himself and his entourage in tents of gold cloth (Diodorus 14: 109: 1). The authorities occasionally tried to cut down on such invidious extravagance; an inscription has been uncovered which deals with an important festival at the town of Andania in Messenia and, among the provisions, is one limiting the size of the tents to be used and the value of their furnishings (*Syl.*³ 736: 34–9; early first century B.C.). Temporary shelter at international games, Aelian, *Var. Hist.* 4: 9 (Plato, incognito, shared a tent with strangers at the Olympic games); Schol. to Pindar, *Ol.* 10.55b (shelters for crowds at Olympic games set up at Pisa, a third of a mile or so from Olympia). At Atargatis' sanctuary in Hieropolis in Syria, city-states appointed locally resident nationals to put up any of their citizens who came as pilgrims (Lucian, *de Syria dea* 56).

91–2 Wine shops in Corinth, O. Broneer in *Archaeology* 7 (1954) 74–81. A building at Olynthus may have been an elegant gambling casino; see W. McDonald in *Studies Presented to David Moore Robinson* i (St Louis 1951) 365–73. 'Earrings and a rug', Lucian, *Dial. Mer.* 14: 3.

92–3 Proxenos, *DS* s.v. *Proxenia*. The text of the resolution that appointed Heracleides (*Syl.*³ 304) nicely illustrates the reasons why a man was chosen *proxenos* and the perquisites that were attached to the position:

> Whereas Heracleides of Salamis has continuously shown his dedication to the interests of the People of Athens and done for them whatever benefactions lay within his power, viz.
>
>> on one occasion, during a period of scarcity of grain, he was the first of the shippers to return to the port, and he voluntarily sold the city 3,000 *medimni* [4,500 bushels] at a price of 5 drachmas per measure [the market price was probably in the neighbourhood of 16], and
>>
>> on another occasion, when voluntary contributions were being collected, he donated 3,000 drachmas [some £6000 or $15,000 in purchasing power] to the grain purchase fund, and
>>
>> in all other respects he has continually shown his goodwill and dedication to the people,
>
> be it resolved that official commendation be extended to Heracleides, son of Charicleides, of Salamis, and
>
>> that he receive a gold crown for his goodwill and dedication to the interest of the People of Athens,
>>
>> that he and his offspring be declared *Proxenos* and Benefactor of the People of Athens,
>>
>> that they have the right to own lands and buildings [foreigners were normally forbidden the ownership of real estate at Athens] subject to the limits of the law, and
>>
>> that they have the right to undertake military service and the payment of property taxes in common with Athenian citizens.
>
> Be it further resolved that the secretary currently in office have a record of this motion and others ancillary to it inscribed on a stone slab and set up on the acropolis, and that the treasurer provide for this purpose 30 drachmas from the appropriate funds.

Another passage of the resolution reveals that the crown cost 500 drachmas (c. £1,000 or $2,500 in purchasing power)—but no doubt the cash value meant little to Heracleides who would keep the gift as an heirloom.

Notes to Chapter 5

95–6 'At a place', 4: 81. 'As an eye-witness', 2: 29. 'I didn't see it', 1: 183. Artemisia, 8: 88. Herodotus' life, How and Wells 1–9.

97–103 Interest in religion: Cf. the trouble he went to for information about Heracles (102 above). 'Sea shells', 2: 12. 'Especially inaccurate', 2:

22. Interest in river craft, 1: 194 (cf. *SSAW* 6), 2: 96 (cf. *SSAW* 14, 335). Dnieper fish, 4: 53. Egyptian linen, 2: 105. Hemp cloth, 4: 74. Tamarisk syrup candy 7: 31. 'They lay out', 4: 196. Herodotus' travels, How and Wells 16–20; J. Myres, *Herodotus, Father of History* (Oxford 1953) 1–16. 'Square in shape', 1: 178–80. 'In the middle', 1: 181. 'The walls are full', 2: 148 (of the Labyrinth). 'It was large', 2: 143. 'Just about as big', 2: 124. 'There is an inscription', 2: 125. 'We saw the upper', 2: 148; on the identification of the building, see How and Wells, note ad loc. Lake Moeris, see How and Wells, note to 2: 149: 1, and, on the present size, *Guido Blou: Egypte* (Paris 1950) 675–6. 'Wanting to learn', 2: 44. Priests washing, 2: 37. Apis bull, 2: 38–9. Bulls sacrificed to Isis, 2: 40. Pigs unclean 2: 47. Foods taboo for priests, 2: 37. Festivals, cf. 31 above. Sacred animals, 2: 65. Embalming, 2: 86–8. Greek gods derived from Egyptian 2: 43, 145–6.

103–6 Croesus' gifts, 1: 50–1; cf. 241 above. Temple of Hera, 2: 182. Fetters at Tegea, 1: 66. Tomb of Alyattes, 1: 93. Battlefield, 3: 12. Grandson of Spartan hero, 3: 55. Sounding with the lead, 2: 5. Persian words 1: 192, 2: 6. Egyptian words, 2: 69, 77, 81, 96. Scythian words, 4: 23, 27. Guides, e.g. 2:125. Priests as guides, 2: 143. 'The Egyptians were the first', 2: 123; cf. J. Wilson in *Scholae Adriani de Buck Memoriae Dicatae* (Leiden 1970) 8–11. Description of hippopotamus, 2: 71. Eating out-of-doors, 2: 35. Egyptian women's one garment, 2: 36. Phoenix, 2: 73. 'I myself didn't observe', 2: 156. 'That's what they say', 1: 182. 'It was nonsense', 2: 131.

106–11 Account of Babylon, 1: 178–99. Account of the Scythians, 4: 5–82. Ethiopians, 3: 17, 20, 114. Gold-digging ants, 3: 102–5; cf. How and Wells, note ad loc. Island where gold is fished, 4: 195. Donkeys with horns, dog-headed men, headless men, 4: 191. One-eyed men, 4: 27. Goat-footed men, hibernating men, 4: 25.

Notes to Chapter 6

115–17 Alexander's goals, his successors' goals, Greek emigration, *SEHHW* 262–63, 323–32, 472–82, 1054–57. Cosmopolitan culture, *SEHHW* 1045–53.

117–9 Pytheas, Cary-Warmington 33–40; Thomson 143–51. Arab shipping and the monsoons, G. Hourani, *Arab Seafaring* (Princeton 1951) 17–28. Eudoxus, Cary-Warmington 70–1, 98–103; Thomson 175–6, 185; for an imaginative fictional reconstruction of his voyages, L. Sprague de Camp, *The Golden Wind* (New York 1969). Arabia and

Somaliland produced both frankincense and myrrh. The first was used as incense and a drug (to stop bleeding, to aid healing), the second as incense, a drug (as an ointment, e.g. for haemorrhoids), and cosmetic (mixed with neutral oil to make anointing oil); see G. van Beek, 'Frankincense and Myrrh', *The Biblical Archaeologist* 23 (1960) 70–95. Exclusion of Greeks, Warmington 10–13; Hourani 21–2; the predecessors of Ptolemy VIII as a consequence favoured the overland routes (*SEHHW* 386–8). Bombay and Patna, Thomson 173–4. Greek knowledge of India, Cary-Warmington 152–3; Thomson 130–1.

120–1 Greek knowledge of east Africa, Cary-Warmington 67–71; Thomson 136–9.

122 Roman coinage, *SEHRE* 181. Roman law, Crook 283–5.

122–6 Knowledge of northern Europe, Thomson 233–47. Denmark and Scandinavia, 246. Fairy tales, 237–8. Russia, 250–3. Overland silk route, Needham iv, 3, 17–18; Thomson 177–81, 306–12; J. Miller, *The Spice Trade of the Roman Empire* (Oxford 1969) 119–36. The sea routes, Warmington 35–51. Routes and products, Thomson 298–301. India and Malay bottoms, Warmington 65–66. China's sea trade, J. Mills, 'Notes on Early Chinese Voyages', *Journal of the Royal Asiatic Society* (1951) 3–25, esp. 6 (not before the fifth century A.D.). Settlements in India, M. Wheeler, *Rome Beyond the Imperial Frontiers* (London 1954) 133, 145–50. Voyages beyond India, Cary-Warmington 82–4. Cloves, Warmington 199–200. 'The ninth year', W. Schoff, *The Periplus of the Erythraean Sea* (New York 1912) 276. Objects of trade, Miller 193–215; Schoff 284–9. Increased geographical knowledge, Thomson, figs 54–8. Hearsay, Cary-Warmington 83. 'Honest in their transactions', Schoff 276. Knowledge of Africa, Cary-Warmington 173–8; Thomson 271–7. Source of the Blue Nile, Thomson 138. Nero's expedition, Cary-Warmington 174–6. 'Tribes without noses', Pliny 6: 187–8.

Notes to Chapter 7

128–9 'I built myself', Petronius 76. Flavius Zeuxis, *IGRR* 4: 841· Irenaeus, *Sel. Pap.* 113. Egyptian grain fleet, *SSAW* 188, 297–9. 'The whole mob', Seneca, *Ep.* 77: 1. Roman trade, *AM* 223–39. Transport by land in Roman times, C. Yeo in *TAPA* 77 (1946) 221–5. *Stationes,* L. Moretti in *Athenaeum* N.S. 36 (1958) 106–16.

130–4 'In the case of tuberculosis', Celsus 3: 22: 8. Sanctuaries of Asclepius, Edelstein ii, 242–50 (history and location), 252 (admission to

Rome), 253–5 (Epidaurus, Cos, Pergamum). Pergamene sanctuary, Behr 27–30 (facilities and sleeping arrangements), 32–4 (ritual). On the medicine practised in the sanctuaries, see Edelstein's detailed discussion, ii, 139–80. 'It was night', *P. Oxy.* 1381. Aristides' illnesses and cures, Behr 26, 37–49, 162–70. End of the sanctuaries, Edelstein ii, 256–7.

134 Silver vessels from Vicarello, Friedländer 327–8. Coins from Vicarello, *RhM* 9 (1854) 20–8. Coins found at other baths, *RA* 4 (1847) 410 (Amélie-les-Bains); *RE* s.v. *aquae* 294 (Schwalheim, Nauheim). Hot springs in Sicily, Strabo 6: 275. 'Many people', Diodorus 5: 10.

135 Trophonius, Pausanias 9: 39: 5–14. Temple of Fortune at Praeneste, Cicero, *de Div.* 2: 41: 85–6. 'It is a fine looking horse', *CIL* i² 2177 (cf. 2173–89). Oracle of Heracles, Pausanias 7: 25: 10. 'The fame of the shrine', Lucian, *Alexander* 30.

136–7 'One could hear', Dio Chrysostom, *Or.* 8: 9. Spartan boys, Cicero, *Tusc. Disp.* 2: 34; Philostratus, *Vita Ap.* 6: 20; Plutarch, *Lycurgus* 18: 1; Libanius, *Or.* 1: 23. Nero's debut, Tacitus, *Ann.* 15: 33. 'Three times I put on', *Res Gestae* 22. Racing, gladiatorial shows, and other entertainment at Rome, Balsdon 244–339.

Notes to Chapter 8

138 'I intend', *ad Att.* 2: 8: 2. *Peregrinatio*, D'Arms 45. Spring the start of the season, 48. Cicero's villas and his relations with his neighbours, 198–200. His lodges, 49. Cicero's death, Plutarch, *Cicero* 47–8. Pompey's villas were scattered up and down the Italian boot from Etruria to Tarentum in the instep; see W. Drumann and P. Groebe, *Geschichte Roms* iv (Leipzig 1908²) 542–3. On villas and vacation times, see also Balsdon 193–213.

139–41 Villas of Republican times, D'Arms 171–201. Horace's observation, *Carm.* 3: 1: 33–7. Augustus' step-father, D'Arms 189–90. Lucullus, 184–6. 'Xerxes etc.', Plutarch, *Lucullus* 39. Villas of Imperial times, D'Arms 202–32. Nero, Tacitus, *Ann.* 14: 4–8. Vedius Pollio, D'Arms 125; he apparently made his money as one of Augustus' agents. Location and style of villas, 45–6, 127–31. Fishing from the bedroom, Martial 10: 30: 16–18; cf. Pliny, *Ep.* 9: 7. Wall-painting, *Enc. Arte Ant.* s.v. *Pompeiani stili*. For a brilliant reconstruction of the decoration in a Neapolitan villa of the second to third centuries A.D., see K. Lehmann-Hartleben in *The Art Bulletin* 23 (1941) 16–44. Plantings, Martial 3: 58: 1–3. *Piscinae*, D'Arms 41–2. Pollio's use of human flesh, Pliny 9: 77.

When Augustus was once a guest, Pollio was ready to throw in a slave who had dropped a crystal goblet; the slave begged the emperor for mercy, and Augustus not only granted it but ordered all the crystal in the house smashed and filled up the fishponds with the fragments (Seneca *de Ira* 3: 40).

141–4 The social round, D'Arms 49–51. Oyster cultivation, D. and P. Brothwell, *Food in Antiquity* (London 1969) 65–6. Lucrine oysters and their possible connection with the transfer of the base, D'Arms 136–7. 'When the fashionable crowd', Ammianus 28: 4: 18. Pursuits of the ordinary vacationer, D'Arms 52, 135–8; fig. 19 (amphitheatres, park); Seneca, *Ep.* 77: 1–2 (watching ships come in; cf 129 above). Baiae, Friedländer 405–8; D'Arms 42–3, 139–40. 'With luxury palaces', Strabo 5: 246. Shady women (*adulterae*), Seneca, *Ep.* 51: 12. Bathing in the nude (*procaces natatus*), Symmachus, *Ep.* 8: 23: 3. 'Filled the lakes', Seneca, *Ep.* 51: 4. 'Unmarried girls', Varro, *Sat. Menipp.* fr. 44 = Nonius 154: 4. 'Why must I look', Seneca, *Ep.* 51: 4. 'Squabbles of nocturnal serenaders', 51: 12. 'Her debauchery', and 'amid those crowds', Cicero, *pro Caelio* 35, 49. 'The wife, even worse', Martial 1: 62. Augustus' attitude toward Baiae, D'Arms 77. Puteoli, 138–9. Naples, 36 (Greek dress), 142-6 (cultural centre), 150–1 (Greek contests). Romulus Augustulus, 108. Eruption of Vesuvius: Pliny the Elder, admiral of the fleet based at nearby Misenum, set out for Pompeii with a squadron partly in answer to a frantic call for help from the owner of a seaside villa right under the mountain, but, when he arrived, the place had already been buried; cf. D'Arms 222–3. 'I've passed a few days', Symmachus, *Ep.* 8: 23: 2–3.

144–7 Transfer to the hills, D'Arms 48–9. Villas at Tusculum, Friedländer 397. Cicero and his villa, J. Pollitt, *The Art of Rome c. 753 B.C.–337 A.D. Sources and Documents* (Prentice-Hall 1966) 76–9. Hill villas: cf. e.g. the description of Pliny's near the Tuscan-Umbrian border in *Ep.* 5: 6. Heated pool, *Ep.* 2: 17: 11. Hadrian's villa, G. Mancini, *Hadrian's Villa* (Ministero della Pubblica Instruzione, Direzione generale delle antichità e belle arti: Guide Books to the Museums and Monuments in Italy 34). 'Is he homeward', Martial 3: 47: 15. Martial's cottage, 6: 43, 9: 18. 'So, Pannychus', Martial 12: 72.

Notes to Chapter 9

149 'What greater miracle', Pliny 19: 3–4. Cotton, Warmington 210–12.

150–2 Finger's breadth of plank, *SSAW* 204. Farewell poems, Horace 1: 3 (to Virgil on his departure for Greece), 3: 27; Statius, *Silvae*

3.2. These *propemptika*, as they were called, though a standard type of poem inherited from the Greeks, reflect quite distinctly Roman nervousness about the sea. Sailing season, *SSAW* 270–73. Chief entrepôts and routes, J. Rougé *Recherches sur l'organisation du commerce maritime en Méditerranée sous l'empire romain* (Paris 1966) 85–97. War galleys at disposition of officials, Rougé in *REA* 55 (1953) 295–7. Cicero's voyage, *ad Att.* 5: 11: 4, 5: 12, 6: 8: 4, 6: 9: 1. Voyage from Rome to Alexandria and back, Casson in *TAPA* 81 (1950) 43–51. Pliny's trip, *Ep.* 10: 15–17.

152–4 Sailing rig, *SSAW* 229–43. Speed, *SSAW* 281–96. 'In Constantinople', Libanius, *Or.* 1: 31. St Paul at Caesarea and Myra, Acts 27: 1–6. On Ostia's piazza, the so-called Piazzale delle Corporazioni, see R. Meiggs, *Roman Ostia* (Oxford 1960) 283–8, esp. 287. Provisions, cf. Synesius *Ep.* 4: 165 (because of two storms that delayed arrival a number of days, Synesius ran out of food). Passengers on Venetian galleys to the Holy Land in the fourteenth and fifteenth centuries went on board with their own bedding and generally fortified with provisions, since the ship's food included in the passage price was notably scanty; see J. Sottas, *Les messageries maritimes de Venise aux XIVe et XVe siècles* (Paris 1938) 168. Officers and crews *SSAW* 314–20. Accommodations, 175–81. Exit passes, *ESAR* ii 593–94, 715 (Nos. 64, ,66 68).

155–6 Waiting at the waterfront, Augustine, *Confessions* 9: 10. Herald announcing departures, Philostratus, *Vita Ap.* 8: 14. Superstitions, Wachsmuth 299 (ill-omened days, citing Macrobius 1: 16. 18), 119–26 (sacrifice, citing, e.g. E. Wüst in *RE* s.v. *Poseidon* 505), 188 (sneezing, citing Plutarch, *Them.* 13. 3, Polyaenus 3: 10: 2), birds (197, citing, e.g. Plutarch, *Cicero* 47: 8, Horace 3: 27: 1, 11, 15–16), 182–3 (words, citing, e.g., Artemidorus 3: 38, Cicero, *Div* 2: 40: 84), 183 (wreckage, citing Seneca, *Controv.* 7: 1: 4). See also I. Hermelin, *Zu den Briefen des Bischofs Synesios* (Uppsala 1934) 31–5 (end of month ill-omened). Dreams, Artemidorus 2: 12 (goats, boars, bulls), 2: 17 (gulls), 2: 23 (anchors), 2: 27 (turbid waters), 2: 36 (face in the moon), 2: 68 (flying on your back), 3: 16 (walking on water), 3: 54 (key), 3: 65 (owls). Birds mean land, Wachsmuth 190 (citing, e.g. Velleius Paterculus 1: 4: 1, Pomponius Mela 1: 110). Hair and nails, 302–3 (citing Petronius 103: 5, 104: 5). Blasphemies, 289 (citing, e.g. Libanius, *Ep.* 178: 1). Dancing, 289 (citing *AP* 9: 82: 5). Death, 278–9 (citing Plutarch, *Cato Min.* 15: 4, Dio Cassius 47: 49: 2).

156–8 Number of passengers, *SSAW* 172. Chair on the poop, Lucian, *Jup. Trag.* 47. Codexes useful for travelling, Friedländer 342–43. Handling the ship, *SSAW* 224–8 (steering oars), 176 (bailing), 248–9 (ship's boat). St Paul's ship in storm, Acts 27: 19, 38. Ship's boat's inadequacy as lifeboat, cf. Acts 27: 30; Achilles Tatius 3: 3–4. Sacrifice,

348 TRAVEL IN THE ANCIENT WORLD

SSAW 182. Tugs, *SSAW* 336–7. Acts of ill omen, Wachsmuth 289, citing Gregory Nazianzen, *Carm.* I, II, 33: 105–7 (*PG* 37: 995).

158–60 'From Brindisi to Syria', Philo, *In Flaccum* 26. Alexandria-Rome grain ship, Lucian, *Navigium* 5. 'And we were in all', Acts 27: 37. Vespasian preferred merchantment, cf. Josephus, *BJ* 7: 21. Synesius' voyage, *Ep.* 4. 'Our shipowner, etc.', 4: 160, 162–4.

Notes to Chapter 10

163 Etruscan roads, J. Ward-Perkins in *Mélanges Grenier* (Collection Latomus 58, Brussels 1962) 1636–43.

164–5 Date of the Via Aurelia, H. Herzig in *Epigraphica* 32 (1970) 50–65; T. Wiseman in *Epigraphica* 33 (1971) 27–32 argues that it goes back to 241 B.C. The Roman road system: *DS* s.v. *via* 790–817 provides a useful survey. Each year brings new information; see the annual volumes of *Fasti Archaeologici* s.v. *topography*. Alpine passes, W. Hyde, *Roman Alpine Routes* (Memoirs of the American Philosophical Society ii, Philadelphia 1935) 137–41 (Brenner), 185 (summary of passes used).

166–7 'The roads were carried', Plutarch, *Gaius Gracchus* 7. Roman road-building, Grenier chapter x; Fustier *passim*. British roads, Forbes 155. Tools, Fustier 78–9. Wheelbarrow, Needham iv, 2, 258–74; Singer ii, 546. Cliff at Terracina, Baedeker's *Central Italy* (1930[16]) 556. Tunnel on the Via Flaminia, 149. Other tunnels, Baedeker's *Southern Italy* (1930[17]) 106. Raising of roads, Fustier 83–4. On sides of valleys, 68–9.

168–70 Surveying instruments and uneven segments, Fustier 74–8. Erroneous view: Proposed by Nicolas Bergier (1557–1632), who was in part misled by the remains of some of the roads he examined. Often multiple layers were present because the original road had been resurfaced many times after being laid, each new surface being placed over the old; Bergier and his followers jumped to the conclusion that that was how it had been built originally (Grenier 317–27; Fustier 109–10, 115, 269–71). No use of cement, Fustier 115. Choice depends on soil and terrain, Grenier 387–9; Fustier 95. Paving, Grenier 331–45. Nature of paving stones, Fustier 103. Size, Grenier 334–6, who cites examples of oblong stones measuring as much as 55 by 35$\frac{1}{2}$ by 20 inches. Joining contiguous pieces from the quarry, Fustier 103. 'Prepare the underbody', Statius, *Silvae* 4: 3: 44–6; he is describing an extension to the Via Appia built by Domitian (A.D. 81–96). Paving set right on the ground, Fustier 100 and fig. 38, 104 and fig. 43 bis. Road-bed, Grenier 327–31; Fustier

105–8, 110–15. Use of fill from elsewhere, 110. Terrace walls, 117–18. Road-bed in marshy land, Fustier 108–9. Crown, tilting, 84–5. Stone border and paths, Grenier 342–5; Fustier 85, 103. Mounting stones, Plutarch, *Gaius Gracchus* 7; Fustier 131. *Fossae*, 85.

170–2 North Africa routes, Fustier 95. Cutting in rock, 96. Artificial ruts, Grenier 368–77, who points out that the space between the ruts varies, indicating the use in different regions of vehicles with different sized wheel-base. First-quality segments followed by poor, Fustier 67. Widths, Friedländer 319–20; Grenier 365–7; Fustier 85 and fig. 32 on page 87; *DS* s.v. *via* 786. Mountain roads, Forbes 155; Friedländer 322–3. Grades, 323. Fords, Fustier 118–20. Bridge at Narni, Singer ii, 508; Baedeker's *Central Italy* (1930[16]) 109. Pont du Gard, Baedeker's *Riviera and South-Eastern France* (1931) 126–7. Access ramps, Fustier 123–5. Paving only on approaches to towns, etc., Grenier 341. Gravel and dirt roads, 345–54; Fustier 68, 83 and fig. 26, 97–9.

172–3 Administration, O. Hirschfeld, *Die kaiserlichen Verwaltungsbeamten* (Berlin 1905) 205–11; G. Walser in *Epigraphica* 31 (1969) 102–3. Repairs, Grenier 354–65. Milestones, Plutarch, *Gaius Gracchus* 7; *DS* s.v. *via* 790–2. *Miliarium aureum*, E. Nash, *Pictorial Dictionary of Ancient Rome* ii (New York 1968[2]) 64. Names from milestones, Grenier 251–4. Religious monuments, 224–34.

174–5 Chinese roads, Needham iv, 3, 1–31, esp. 7 (gravel surface, width), 14 and 21 (straightness, bridges). Needham's suggestion (7) that the Chinese anticipated the macadam road cannot be taken seriously; the essence of a macadam road is the use of cut stones of the same size, and there is no mention in Chinese records of that. Roads and bridges in the Middle Ages, Fustier 161–8. Renaissance, 178–84. Seventeenth century use of earth, 207. McAdam, 251–3.

Notes to Chapter 11

176–8 Land travel in winter: Aristides frequently travelled about Asia Minor in December and January (Behr 23, 63, 67). For Melania the Younger's trip, see 315 above. St Basil, living in remote and mountainous Cappadocia, complained of the shutdown in communications during the winter (Ramsay 377) but not always justifiably (cf. M. Fox, *The Life and Times of St Basil the Great As Revealed in his Works*, Washington 1939, 1–4). Clothing, L. Wilson, *The Clothing of the Ancient Romans* (Baltimore

1938) 72–3 (underwear), 87–95, 100–4, 112–29 (capes). The Greek east, in addition to its traditional clothing (cf. 75 above) adapted many Roman garments. Pocket sundials, *RE* s.v. *horologium* 2423–4; R. Tölle, '*Eine spätantike Reiseuhr*', *JDI*, *Archäologischer Anzeiger* 84 (1969) 309–17. 'Bring your gold jewellery', *P. Mich.* 214 (A.D. 296). Theophanes' accounts, *P. Ryl.* 627–8, 630–8. Inventory of his baggage, 627: 1–64. 'When you come', *P. Mich.* 214. Theophanes' extra supplies, *P. Ryl.* 630–8: 462–3, 465–66. Use of vehicles, cf. Pflaum 36 (carriages used on the *cursus publicus* almost from the outset), Juvenal 3: 10 (household effects carried from Rome to Cumae in a *reda*), Fig. 13. Use of pack-animals and porters, Vigneron 140–9. Dreams, Artemidorus 1: 77 (narcissi), 2: 8 (air), 2: 12 (donkeys, boars, gazelles), 2: 28 (marshes), 2: 33 (moving statues), 2: 36 (stars), 2: 37 (gods), 3: 5 (quail), 3: 65 (owls).

178–80 Transporting luggage, cf. Juvenal 3: 10–11 (the baggage of someone leaving Rome was loaded on a wagon outside the Porta Capena, where the Appian Way began). Sidewalks, see *TLL* s.v. *crepido* 2b, *margo* 1; respectable members of society were expected to use vehicles or animals and not walk (cf. Synesius, *Ep.* 109). Various types of vehicles, see *DS* s.vv.; M. Cagiano de Azevedo, *I trasporti e il traffico* (Mostra Augustea della Romanità, Civiltà Romana 4, Rome 1938) 10–14; Vigneron 151–2, 167–70. The Greek-speaking east continued to use the traditional Greek terms (68 above) and also the general term *ochema* 'vehicle'. Lubricants, cf. Cato, *de Agr.* 97 (olive dregs). Livery stables: The *cisiarii* 'carriage handlers', 'wagon handlers' and *iumentarii* 'animal handlers' are attested in many cities, usually with quarters at the town gate (Friedländer 330–1; Pflaum 52); the first presumably offered vehicles for hire, the second horses, mules, and donkeys. Ancient hired drivers shared their modern counterparts' bad habit of driving too fast: 'If a driver (*cisiarius*)', states one of Rome's legal authorities, 'while trying to overtake, turns over the carriage and crushes or kills a servant, my opinion is that he is liable, since it was his obligation to maintain a moderate speed' (*Dig.* 19: 2: 13 *pr.*). Springs: Though the great wagon that carried Alexander's body from Babylon to Alexandria seems to have had some form of springing (54 above), springs are never heard of again until the tenth century A.D.; see L. White, Jr, 'The Origins of the Coach', *Proceedings of the American Philosophical Society* 114 (1970) 423–31. In earlier four-wheeled vehicles both axles were fixed—i.e. the front wheels were unable to pivot—and it is often asserted that Roman vehicles were made the same way (Singer ii, 545; Fustier 82; cf. Vigneron 114–15, who leaves the question open). This may have been true of rough-hewn farm carts but almost certainly not of those used on the highways; cf. Cagiano de Azevedo 17. The Celts used pivoting front wheels as early as the first century B.C.; Singer ii, plate 73a. Litters, *DS* s.v. *lectica;* Balsdon 214–15. Travelling in the grand style and special carriages, Friedländer 341–3. Horace's ridicule, *Sat.* 1: 6: 107–9.

181–2 Travelling by cob or mule, Friedländer 340. Stirrups, Vigneron 86–8. Saddles: Rigid saddles were used by barbarian horsemen as early as the fifth or fourth century B.C., but not by Greeks or Romans until shortly before the beginning of the Christian era, when they were adopted by the Roman army; cf. *DS* s.v. *sella equestris*. Horseshoes, Vigneron 44–50 and pls. 10–13. Harness, Singer ii, 552–5; Vigneron pls. 42, 43, 46, 51, 53. Shafts, Vigneron pls. 54, 55; Singer ii, 544, 553–4— the date of third century A.D. given here for the earliest example is wrong, since Fig. 11 dates from the early second; see G. Becatti, *Scavi di Ostia.* iv, *Mosaici e pavimenti marmorei* (Rome 1961) 40. Shafts had long been in use in China (25 above). Chinese post, Needham iv, 3, 34–38. Ptolemaic post, Pflaum 18–21; E. Van't Dack in *Chr. d'Eg.* 37 (1962) 338–41.

183–4 Augustus' founding of the *cursus publicus,* Pflaum 22–48. Gravestone of a *speculator,* Rostovtzeff in *Röm. Mitt.* 26 (1911) 267–83; E. Ritterling in *Bonner Jahrbücher* 125 (1919) 23–5. Couriers and *diplomata,* Pflaum 122–48. Otho, Tacitus, Hist. 2: 54. The *cursus publicus* after Severus, Pflaum 91–121; Levi 103–6; and, for its complications, T. Zawadzki in *REA* 62 (1960) 89–90. *Evectio* and *tractoria, Cod. Theod.* 8: 5: 9, 8: 6. Stopping places, Pflaum 149–91. The terms *mansio, statio,* etc., were used very loosely; cf. Levi 109–10. The Chinese post-stations that were placed every eleven miles offered change of horses and couriers, food and lodging, and the added refinement of cells for prisoners being moved under guard, Needham iv, 3, 35–6.

185–8 From Aquileia over the Alps, Pflaum 180–84. *Praetoria,* Levi 110. Services available, De Ruggiero s.v. *Cursus Publicus* 1413–14. Costs of the *cursus publicus,* Pflaum 62, 92–93, 119–21. Abuses, cf. T. Zawadzki in *REA* 62 (1960) 92–3. Rules against abuses, *Cod. Theod.* 8: 5: 1, 3, 6–7, 10, 14, 16, 18, 24–5, 50, 53. Regulations, *Cod. Theod.* 8: 5: 27, 35, 40 (number of animals); 8: 5: 17, 30 (size of wagons); 8: 5: 8, 17, 28 (maximum loads); 8: 5: 34 (number of drivers); 8: 5: 47 (weight of saddles); 8: 5: 2 (whips); 8: 5: 31 (tips). Connection of the *itineraria* and the *Tabula Peutingeriana* with the *cursus publicus,* Levi 97–124. esp. 119–24. Meaning of the symbols, Levi 66–93, 110–11. Speed of the couriers, Pflaum 192–200; C. Eliot in *Phoenix* 9 (1955) 76–80; A. Ramsay in *JRS* 15 (1925) 63–5.

188–9 'My lord', Pliny *Ep.* 10: 120. 'The man I had hopes', Libanius, *Or.* 1: 14. 'I found the government post', Sidonius, *Ep.* 1: 5: 2. Misuse: The future emperor Pertinax, when a newly fledged army officer, in going to join his unit used the public post without authorization and was caught; he was punished by being made to do the whole journey on foot

(*SHA Pertinax* 1: 6). Regulations against unauthorized use, *Cod. Theod.*
8: 5: 4, 8, 12, 41 (death for sale or purchase of post warrants or for giving
or taking bribes), 54. On the use of the public post by ecclesiastics, see
302 above. Superiority of the inns of the *cursus publicus*: A plaque found
at Ombos, a tiny Egyptian village twenty-five miles north of Aswan, is
eloquent on this point. Inscribed in the sixth or seventh A.D. and affixed to
a local hostel, it announced to the prospective guests that there had been
'carried out a complete cleaning of the public building [i.e. the hostel]
and of the vast amount of dung accumulated over so long a time ... The
whole place was renewed and rebuilt from the ground up for the shelter-
ing of strangers and those with no rights of requisition' (*SB* 7475, and
cf. G. Rouillard in *Mélanges Schlumberger*, Paris 1924, 85–100, esp. 88).
In the days before the cleaning, diploma-less voyagers must have done
their best to avoid spending a night at Ombos. Average speed of land
travel, Ramsay 386–8; L. Hunter in *JRS* 3 (1913) 78. Travelling hard:
Aristides at one time did 320 stades, i.e. c. $35\frac{1}{2}$ miles in a long day, at
another 400 stades, i.e. c. $44\frac{1}{2}$ miles in a day of non-stop riding that
ended at midnight (*Or.* 27: 14, 17 = ii, pp. 455–6 Keil); the messenger
who brought the news of Roscius' murder from Rome to Ameria
'travelling by *cisia* [179 above] at night dashed 56 miles in 10 hours'
(Cicero, *pro Roscio Amer.* 7: 19). Chinese couriers seem to have averaged
120 miles in 24 hours (Needham iv, 3, 36). Stops between Toulouse and
Carcassonne and over the Alps, Grenier 203–4.

190–1 Theophanes' party *P. Ryl.* iv, p. 106. Speed outward, p. 107.
Expenses and itinerary from 19 July to 6 August, *P. Ryl.* 630–8: 203–506.

193–4 Aristides' journey, *Or.* 27: 1–8 = ii, pp. 452–4 Keil, and
cf. W. Ramsay in *JHS* 2 (1881) 44–54. Horace's journey, *Sat.* 1: 5.

Notes to Chapter 12

197–200 'God willing, expect us', *Sel. Pap.* 140. Owning lodges at
intervals: Cicero had a lodge (*deversorium*) at Anagnia to use when going
to his property at Arpinum, and lodges at Lanuvium and Sinuessa for
the trip to his villas on the shore (D'Arms 49). Guests quarters, Vitruvius
6: 7: 4, describing Greek mansions of the third to second centuries B.C.
Quarters answering to his description have been found in the more
elegant homes at Pompeii, such as the Casa del Fauno, Casa del Labirinto;
A. Maiuri in *Accademia Nazionale dei Lincei*, ser. 8, *Memorie* 5 (1954)
461–7. Herod's palace in Jerusalem had chambers for a hundred guests;
Josephus, *BJ* 5.178. Elegant camping out, Friedländer 343. Cato the

Younger, Plutarch, *Cato Min.* 12. 'Lucius Memmius', *Sel. Pap.* 416. 'In accordance with your letter', 414. Visit of governor to Hermopolis, *W. Chrest.* 415. Performing dolphin at Bizerta, Pliny, *Ep.* 9: 33. Letters of recommendation, cf. Liebeschuetz 17–18.

200–3 Inn at Bovillae, Kleberg 67. Place-names derived from inn-names, 63–5; Grenier 284. Inn at Styria, *Jahres.* 27 (1932) Beiblatt 194–222. Inn on Little St Bernard, *Not. Sc.* (1924) 385–92. Inn on road from Aquileia, *Jahres.* 27 (1932) Beiblatt 206–7. A very similar inn has recently been uncovered at one of the stations (Vindolanda, the modern Chester-holm) just behind Hadrian's wall in northern England. It boasted two heated public rooms, six bedrooms, lavatories, and even its own bath complex, all set out around a central court (*The Sunday Times*, 28 November 1971). On the Greek terminology for inns, see 340 above. In Graeco-Roman Egypt, the common term *pandokeion* for some reason is never used, the rather unusual word *apanteterion* being preferred, at least in later centuries (*PSI* 175:5; *P. Iand.* 17: 3–4; *SB* 7475. 22–3); it occurs in inscriptions as well (L. Robert in *Hellenica* 11–12, 1960, 16). Khan at Umm el-Walid, R. Brünnow and A. Domaszewski, *Die Provincia Arabia* ii (Strasbourg 1905) 87 and figs 668–70; khan of about the same size at Kurnub, *IEJ* 16 (1966) 147; khan near Haifa, *IEJ* 19 (1969) 248. Inns at Olympia, *Olympiabericht* vi (Berlin 1958) 30–8, 55–67, and plates 6–7.

204–8 Hotels between Alexandria and Canopus, Strabo 17: 800–1; Ammianus 22: 16: 14. St Paul in Rome, Acts 28: 30. 'If you're clean', *ILS* 6039; the plaque was found at Tarragona in Spain. *Hospitium, deversorium, caupona,* Kleberg 5–7, 14, 27–8. Legislation concerning *caupones,* Crook 226–8. 'He did not', 227. Inns at city gates, cf. Plautus, *Pseud.* 658–9; Kleberg 49. *Stabulum,* 18, 28. Burning lamps, Spano 29–32. Inn signs, Friedländer 347; Kleberg 65–6; *Archaeology* 20 (1967) 36 (reproduction in colour). Decoration of façades, Kleberg 116–17. 'Here Mercury', *ILS* 6037; Kleberg 115. 'Traveller, listen', *CIL* xii 5732; Kleberg 119. 'The Walls of Thebes', Kaibel 1049. Lady innkeeper hawking, Virgil, *Copa.* 'Innkeeper, let's reckon', *ILS* 7478; Kleberg 118–19 and fig. 7. Stabulum at Pompeii, Kleberg 34–5. Inns in town, 32–3. House near Rome's forum, G. Lugli, *Monumenti minori del Foro Romano* (Rome 1947) 139–64, especially 139–41, 157–8. Terminology, Kleberg 87–9, 113. The word for 'bartender' may have been *deversitor;* see G. Bagnani in *AJPh* 79 (1958) 441–2. 'Summertime creatures', Pliny 9: 154. 'I say unto you', *Acta Ioannis* 60–1 in M. James, *The Apocryphal New Testament* (Oxford 1924) 242.

209–11 'Vibius Restitutus', *CIL* iv, 2146; Kleberg 33. 'Innkeeper', *CIL* iv, 4957; Kleberg 113. Goodbye to Puteoli, *CIL* iv, 2152; Kleberg 33. Names on wall, *CIL* iv, 2147, 2149, 2154–5. *lixa,* Kleberg 14–16, 44. Inns near baths, 51–2. Seneca's lodgings, *Ep.* 56: 1–2. Noise at night,

M

Martial 4: 64; Juvenal 3: 235–8; cf. 359 below. New brothels, Tertullian, *Apologeticus* 35: 4. Inns as brothels, Kleberg 89–91. Country inn: cf. Horace's experience in one (196 above). Using one's own food, Kleberg 98–100. Room service: One of Petronius' characters, staying at an inn, has the women in charge of rooms send up a dinner presumably from the inn's kitchen; *Satyricon* 90: 7, 92: 1, 95: 1 and cf. H. Rowell in *Classical Philology* 52 (1957) 217–27, esp. 221–3.

211–4 Location of bars and restaurants, Kleberg 49–53. Main street (Via dell'Abbondanza) with twenty eating establishments, 52. *Taberna*, 37–8. *Popina*, 36–7. Typical *popina*, A. Mau, *Pompeii: Its Life and Art*, trans. F. Kelsey (New York 1902²) 402. *Popina* with grape arbour, *Archaeology* 20 (1967) 36–44. Chairs and couches, Kleberg 114; cf. Martial's scornful reference (5: 70: 3) to *sellariolae popinae* 'eating joints with seats'. 'Cup of Setian', *CIL* iv, 1292; Kleberg 108. Hedone, *CIL* iv, 1679; Kleberg 107. Imported wines, 108–9. Beer, 110. Toddies and sale of hot water, 104–5. Mixed drinks, 109–10. Cups with inscriptions, *CIL* xiii, 10018: 59, 103, 105, 131, 135, 152; the word translated 'bartender' is *caupo* (204 above), who usually was busier issuing drinks than rooms. The cups come from Gaul and Germany and are dated fourth century A.D. (*CIL* xiii, 10018 praef.).

214–8 Watering wine, Kleberg 111–13. 'May you soon', *CIL* iv, 3948; Kleberg 112. 'Your wine is watered', Isaiah 1: 22. 'The rains this year', Martial 1: 56. 'Ravenna barman,' Martial 3: 57; the following epigram dealt directly with the scarcity of drinkable water at Ravenna:

> At Ravenna I'd sooner invest
> in cisterns than the vine,
> Since a man makes more money up there
> Selling water than wine.

'Knows of many', Galen, *de simpl. medic.* 10: 2: 2 (Kühn, vol. 12, p. 254). Meats served, Kleberg 100–1. Hours of business, Kleberg 120–1. Prostitutes, 89–90. Erotic decorations, 90. Intercourse with the proprietress, *CIL* iv, 8442; Kleberg 90. 'Serve him wine', *Copa* 37. 'This way', M. della Corte, *Case ed abitanti di Pompei* (Rome 1965³) 81–3 and Kleberg, figs. 18–20. Clientele, Kleberg 92–4. 'You will find him', Juvenal 8: 173–6. *Popina* at Catania, G. Manganaro in *Helikon* 2 (1962) 485–93, esp. 490–3. The text runs: *xvii k(alendas) Septem(bres), feridius Cereris Dominae. Hic sibi suabiter fecerun(t) tres adulescentes quorum nomina lege: Onesimus et L. Valerius Ersianus et Filumenus. Unus cum mulier(e), extremus.* Legislation restricting restaurants, Kleberg 101–2. Popina of the Seven Sages, G. Calza in *Die Antike* 15 (1939) 99–115. Church regulations, Kleberg 94–5. Brothels, see H. Herter in *Jahrbuch für Antike und Christentum* 3 (1960) 85–8.

Notes to Chapter 13

219–20   Day-runners and herald-runners, *hemerodromi, dromokerykes*. The best known *hemerodromos* is Pheidippides, who covered the distance from Athens to Sparta, some 150 miles, in two days to ask for Sparta's help against the Persians at Marathon (Herodotus 6: 105–6). *Tabellarii*, see, e.g. Cicero, *ad Att.* 6: 2: 1, 8: 14: 1. 'For many days', Cicero, *ad Quint. fr.* 3: 1: 7: 23. 'You have preposterous couriers', Cicero, *ad Fam.* 15: 17: 1. 'Finding someone going', *P. Mich.* viii, 490. 'I was delighted', *Sel. Pap.* 151. 'I sent you', 107. Synesius used to take his letters to the harbour and give them to the oarsmen aboard the merchant galleys (*Ep.* 129). 'Have Acastus', Cicero *ad. Fam.* 16: 5: 2; cf. *ad Quint. fr.* 2: 12: 3 (use of a Roman gentlemen), *ad Att.* 5: 15: 3 (a friend), Plautus, *Miles Glor.* 129–32 (use of a passing merchant to carry a letter from Ephesus to Naupactus). In Cicero's day, the only organized postal service was the one maintained by the Roman financiers who bought from the government the right to collect taxes in the provinces; even provincial governors found it at times the best way to get letters delivered (see J. Ooteghem in *Les études classiques* 27 (1959) 192–3.

221   On the making and use of papyri, see E. Turner, *Greek Papyri: An Introduction* (Oxford 1968), chapter 1, esp. pp. 2–5, and *Greek Manuscripts of the Ancient World* (Oxford 1971) plate 1. Papyrus paper was made by taking the triangular lower stem of the papyrus reed and peeling off strips from the pith, then laying the strips side by side with each slightly overlapping its neighbour, then placing a second layer of strips over the first at right angles (thus the strips on one face ran horizontally, on the other vertically). After a few blows from a wide-surfaced mallet, and without any adhesive, they stuck together to form a solid sheet. The sheet was left to dry and then rubbed smooth with pumice. The ordinary papyrus letter was usually rolled into a cylinder. A convenient way to seal it was to rip loose a strand of papyrus from one of the strips, wrap it about the cylinder, and fix it with a blob of clay, which was then impressed with a seal. Papyrus, though in general the cheapest and most convenient writing material for letters, was not the only one. The Romans also used wax tablets or sheets of parchment or of leather; see *RE* s.v. *pugillares* (xxiii. 2, cols. 2515–16). 'To Apollinarius', *Sel. Pap.* 113.

221–2   On the speed of Cicero's correspondence from nearby places, see W. Riepl., *Das Nachrichtenwesen des Altertums* (Berlin 1913) 141–2. Letters sent in the morning from Rome to the villa at Tusculum, some 17 miles away, got an answer that night; letters between Rome and Anzio, some 35 miles away, arrived the same day; letters from Rome could reach Arpinum, some 70 miles away, in two days; letters between Rome and the Naples area took four to six days (one arrived in three— *sane celeriter* 'mighty fast', as Cicero remarks, *ad Att.* 14: 18: 1). Letters from Rome to Athens, *ad Fam.* 16: 21: 1 (46 days), 14: 5: 1 (21 days). From Patras to Brindisi, *ad Fam.* 16: 9: 2. From Africa, *ad Fam.* 12: 25: 1. Syria to Rome, *ad Fam.* 12: 10: 2 (50 days), *ad Att.* 14: 9: 3 (sent 31 December and arrived sometime around 17 Apr., 44 B.C.).

222–5 'Having arrived on Italian soil', *P. Oxy.* 2191. 'Dear Mother', *Sel. Pap.* 111. 'Grateful thanks to the god', 112, second century A.D. 'Just as we were', P. Strass. 233 and *Chr. d'Eg.* 39 (1964) 150–6. 'Dear Mother, first and foremost', *P. Oxy.* 1773 in G. Ghedini, *Lettere Cristiane* (Milan 1923) no. 8. 'Dear Mother, I am writing', *P. Lips.* 110. 'Dear Zenon', *Sel. Pap.* 93. 'Send for me', 115, second century A.D. 'I'm disgusted', 97, 168 B.C. 'A fine thing', *P. Oxy.* 119.

Notes to Chapter 14

229–31 Paulus' journey, Livy 45: 27–8. 'Phidias has sculpted', Plutarch, *Paulus* 28: 2.

231–2 Cool to nature, Friedländer 459–65. Seven wonders, 444.

233–4 Mythological sights, Friedländer 418, 450–3, 463; Pfister 63–4, 93, 107, 156, 219, 221, 280–1, 286, 336, 347–50, 362–4, 368, 454; Pausanias 4: 36: 2 (Nestor's cave).

234–5 Historical sights, Friedländer 450, 454–6; Pfister 233, 237, 352, 456; Pausanias 9: 23: 2 (Pindar's tomb); Strabo 17: 794 (Alexander's tomb); Virgil, *Vita Donatiana* 36 (Virgil's tomb); Plutarch, *Demosthenes* 7: 3 (underground chamber), *Alexander* 69: 4 (Indian's tomb), 7: 3 (Aristotle's school).

236 Battlefields, Friedländer 408–9, 454–5; Pausanias 9: 40: 10 and Frazer's note (Chaeronea).

236–7 Art, Friedländer 457–9; *Anth. Pal.* 9: 715, 721, 730, 734 (Myron's cow); Cicero, *Verr.* 2: 4: 135 and cf. J. Pollitt, *The Art of Greece 1400–31 B.C. Sources and Documents* (Prentice-Hall 1965) 59, 128, 133, 166–7, 177.

Notes to Chapter 15

238–9 Shutruk-Nahhunte, E. Unger, *Assyrische und babylonische Kunst* (Breslau 1927) 62–3; *CAH* ii³, chapter 31, section 1 and chapter 32, section 1. Assyrians, Unger 63. Nebuchadnezzar's museum, 63–6; Unger, *Babylon, die heilige Stadt* (Berlin and Leipzig 1931) 224–8.

240–2 Treasury of the Corinthians, Herodotus 1: 14, 50–1; Frazer v 295–6. Temple of Hera, Pausanias 5: 17–20: 1 and Frazer iii 593-620. Herondas' sketch, *Mim.* 4: 20–95; for a translation of the skit, see above, 268–70. Figures at entrance to Delphi, Pausanias 10: 9: 5–7, 10: 10: 1. Colonnade, Pausanias 10: 11: 6. Erechtheum, 1: 27: 1. Pindar's chair, 10: 24: 5. Artaxerxes and Amasis, C. Blinkenberg, *Lindos, Fouilles de l'acropole,* ii: *Inscriptions* (Copenhagen 1941) no. 2, C xxix and xxxv. Each thread of the linen corselet was reputedly made up of 360 or 365 strands, and so many doubting Thomases had to feel it to make sure that, by the first century A.D., it was almost all worn away (Pliny 19: 12). Alexander's gear, Pausanias 8: 28: 1.

243–4 Mythological mementoes, Friedländer 450–1; Pfister 322, 331–4. Lindos inventory, Blinkenberg, *op. cit.* (see previous note) no. 2 B iii-xiv. Lindos fire, no. 2, D 39–42. The fire left only dedications made after about 330 B.C., and these were far less varied or interesting, being chiefly armour and weapons deposited by Hellenistic kings, and oxheads or ox horns from their sacrificial offerings (no. 2, C xxxvii-xlii). Helen's stool, Plutarch, *Solon* 4. Her cup, Pliny 33: 81. Same relics in different places, Friedländer 451; Pfister 341–5.

244–6 Physical remains, Pfister 208, 321, 410, 424. Giants' bones, Pfister 426–7; Frazer iv, 314–15. Miscellaneous oddments, Friedländer 447–8; Pfister 324–5. Indian ants, Pliny 11: 111. Marvels, Friedländer 449; Polybius 16: 12 (statues of Artemis); Pliny 2: 228 (torch-lighting fountain), 2: 231 and 31: 16 (wine fountain). The altar of the shrine of Venus at Paphos on Cyprus was also weatherproof (Tacitus, *Hist.* 2: 3).

246–7 Attalids' collection, *JDI* 6 (1891) 49–60.

247–9 Roman looters, Pollitt, *op. cit.* (346 above) 32, 44–8. Verres, 66–74. Cicero as collector, 76–9. Picture galleries in villas, *DS* s.v. *pictura,* p. 471; K. Lehmann-Hartleben in *The Art Bulletin* 23 (1941) 16–44. 'Banished as exiles', Pliny 35: 26. Masterpieces in Rome, Homo 21 46, 177–208. Polyclitus, Pliny 34: 55–6. Myron, Strabo 14: 637; Pliny 34: 57–8. Phidias, 34: 54. Praxiteles, 36: 20–3. Scopas, 36: 25–6, 28. Lysippus, 34: 40, 61–5; Velleius Paterculus 1: 11: 3–4. Apelles, Pliny 35: 27, 93–4. Zeuxis, 35: 66. Windows in the Temple of Concord, *Memoirs of the American Academy in Rome* 5 (1925) 73. Baths of Caracalla, Homo 199.

249–50 Oddments in Roman temples, Friedländer 447–9. Museum in the temple of the Deified Augustus, K. Lehmann, 'A Roman Poet Visits a Museum', *Hesperia* 14 (1945) 259–69.

251–2 Churches as museums, J. von Schlosser, *Die Kunst- und Wunderkammern der Spätrenaissance* (Leipzig 1908) 12–16; P. Salmon, *De la collection au musée* (Brussels 1958) 27–9. Sixtus IV, W. Heckscher, *Sixtus IIII Aeneas insignes statuas romano populo restituendas censuit*

(The Hague 1955) 46–7; E. Muntz in *RA* 43 (1882) 24–36. Earliest scholarly collections, D. Murray, *Museums, Their History and Their Use* i (Glasgow 1904) 24–9.

Notes to Chapter 16

253–4 'We travel long roads', Pliny, *Ep.* 8: 20: 1–2. Pausanias never in Babylon, Pausanias 4: 31: 5. Provincials visit Rome, Friedländer 395. Monuments of Rome, E. Nash, *Pictorial Dictionary of Ancient Rome* (New York 1968²); Homo, *Urb.* 305–24. Found a city of brick, Suetonius, *Aug.* 28: 3.

255–6 Sights of Sicily, Friedländer 408–9, 458. Sights of Corinth, 412–13; Cicero was among the number who went to see the ruins at Corinth (*Tusc. Disp.* 3: 53). The *diolkos*, 338 above. Sights of Epidaurus, Friedländer 413. Desolation in Greece, 410; Dio Chrysostom 7: 39. At Thebes, Pausanias 9: 7: 6. At Pisa, 6: 22: 1. Sights of the islands, Friedländer 414–16. Samothrace, K. Lehmann, *Samothrace*. Vol. 2, Part 1: *The Inscriptions on Stone* (New York 1960) 16–17.

256–7 Homer country and Asia Minor, Friedländer 417–20. Paris' lyre, Plutarch, *Alexander* 15. Armour, *Arrian, Anab.* 1: 11: 7. Cnidus, Lucian, *Amores* 11–15.

257–61 On the usual itinerary in Egypt, see J. Milne in *JEA* 3 (1916) 76–80; Behr 16–18 (Aristides' itinerary); and the papyrus cited 360 below. Apollonius, Philostratus, *Vita Ap.* 5: 43. View of the lighthouse, Josephus, *BJ* 4: 613. Alexandria, Friedländer 429–38. The Museum, E. Parsons, *The Alexandrian Library* (London 1952) 166–74. 'They worship', Friedländer 433, note 5. Alexandrians' musical ear, Athenaeus 4. 176e. Heliopolis, Strabo 17: 805–6. Memphis, 17: 807. 'Upon receipt of', *SB* 7263. Philae, Strabo 17: 818. The indomitable Aristides got as far as Pselchis, about sixty miles beyond Aswan (Behr 18). Only troops or exploring parties went further (126 above).

Notes to Chapter 17

262–3 Investigatory walk: cf. Lucian, *Amores* 8–9, where the narrator in the sketch reports that, when he arrived at Rhodes, 'after checking into a room right across from the temple of Dionysus, I took a leisurely stroll'. In the course of it, he 'met up with the greatest profit one gets out of being abroad—some old friends'. Street lights at Pompeii, Spano 22–3. Public lights at intersections, 99–104. Illuminated masks, 102–5 and, for an illustration, R. Calza and E. Nash, *Ostia* (Florence 1959) fig. 84. Spano argues (99–106) that such lighting goes back to Hellenistic times. Ammianus (14: 1: 9), describing the events of A.D. 353 at Antioch, mentions 'the brightness of the lights that shine all night', which certainly sounds like street lights. Constantinople had them without question in the sixth century A.D.; Procopius (*Anecd.* 26: 7) refers to Justinian's refusal to light them. Rome seems to have had a system of lighting along main streets by the early third century A.D. (Homo, *Urb.* 583–4). Until the use of street lights, after the shops were closed or on side streets walkers were helpless without torches; Petronius (*Sat.* 79) tells how his heroes would never have found the way back to their inn at night had not one of them foresightedly marked the posts and columns along the route with white chalk. Traffic dangers: Caesar's regulations for Rome, passed in 45 B.C., included one (*ILS* 6085. 56–67) which banned all wheeled traffic during the first ten hours of the day, with certain under-standable exceptions, such as carts carrying in construction materials for temples or hauling off rubble from public demolitions, garbage wagons, carts needed for the games on the days these took place, carriages used by the Vestal Virgins and other high clergy on holidays, etc. Claudius issued an edict banning passenger vehicles from all the cities of Italy at all times (Suetonius, *Claud.* 25: 2); travellers were limited to 'feet, sedan chair, or litter'. Various similar regulations continued to be laid down during the ensuing three centuries (cf. *SHA, Marcus Antoninus* 23: 8). 'There are shysters', Muller, *FHG* ii, 255.

264 Tourist portraits: Miniaturists were available, e.g. around naval bases to do portraits of the sailors to send to the folks back home (*AM* 212). It is only a guess, but a reasonable one, that they were available at tourist sites.

264–7 Guides, Frazer i, lxxvi-vii; Friedländer 451–2. 'I was going around', Lucian, *Amores* 8. 'Guides showed us', *Ver. Hist.* 2: 31. 'Zeus, protect me', Varro, *Men.* 34 in Nonius 419:4. 'The guides went through', Plutarch, *Mor.* 395a. Dinning again, 396c. Barbecue spits, *Mor.* 400f. Stolen art at Syracuse, Cicero, *Verr.* 4: 59: 132. 'Your guide amid', Aristides, *Or.* 25: 2 (ii, 72 Keil). Aristides at the pyramids, *Or.* 36: 122 (ii, 301 Keil). Temple of Ephesus, Pliny 36: 32. Geryon's remains, Pausanias 1: 35: 7–8. Argive guides, 2: 23: 5–6; at least four different places in Italy claimed to have the Palladium (244 above). 'Abolish foolish tales', Lucian, *Philops.* 4. Mucianus, H. Peter, *Historicorum romanorum reliquiae* (Leipzig 1906) 101–7; Pliny 7: 159 (Mt Tmolus), 8: 6 (learned elephant), 13: 88 (letter).

267–71 Herondas' sketch, *Mim.* 4: 20–90. Hanging of shields, Pausanias 10: 19: 4 (on the architrave), 5: 10: 4 (in the gable), 5: 10: 5 (along the frieze). Placing of statues, M. Jacob-Felsch, *Die Entwicklung griechischer Statuenbasen und die Aufstellung der Statuen* (Waldsassen, Bayern 1969) 19–21, 43–5, 58–9, 69–75, 84–7, 101–3. Back door at Cnidus, Lucian, *Amores* 14. Temple-robbing, Homo 204–6; cf. Lucian, *Jup. Trag.* 10.

271–2 Shinnying up the pyramids, Pliny 36: 76. Cleaning crocodiles' teeth, Plutarch, *Mor.* 976b. Feeding the Suchus crocodile, Strabo 17: 811–12; cf. the letter cited 198 above. Shooting the rapids, Strabo 17: 817–18; Aristides, *Or.* 36: 48–50 (ii, 279 Keil).

272–8 On Memnon in general, Friedländer 439–41. Strabo's account, 17: 816. Pausanias' 1: 42: 3. Explanation of the sound (rather unlikely) in Friedländer 441; Hohlwein in *Chr. d 'Eg.* 29 (1940) 274–5; Frazer ii 530–1. Henu, Breasted, *ARE* i nos. 427–33. Graffiti at Abu Simbel, *REG* 70 (1957) 5 ('When Pharaoh Psammetichus'), 16 ('Telephos'), 29 ('Krateros'), 42 (De Lessups). 'Soldiers of the elephant hunt', P. Perdrizet and G. Lefebvre, *Les Graffites grecs du Memnonion d'Abydos* (Paris 1919) no. 91. The Memnon graffiti, A. and E. Bernand, *Les inscriptions grecques et latines du colosse de Memnon* (Cairo 1960) 25–30; A. Bataille, *Les Memnonia* (Institut français d'archéologie orientale. Recherches d'archéologie, de philologie et d'histoire, tome xxiii, Cairo 1952) 153–68. Carefully carved, Bataille 163. A piece of papyrus found in Egypt contains what appears to be the wording for an inscription which some traveller drew up presumably to give to a stonecutter; see *P. Lond.* iii, 854, re-edited by W. Crönert in *Raccolta di scritti in onore di Giacomo Lumbroso* (Milan 1925) 481–97, esp. 486–7, 492, 495–6. It reads:

> Since many [these days go on voyages] and even set forth upon the sea to Egypt to visit the artistic creations of man, I made a voyage.
>
> Embarking upon the journey upstream, I came to Syene, from whence (the part of the river called) the Nile flows, and to Libya, where Ammon oracles to all men, and I visited The Cuttings, and for my friends, by name, I there engraved in the holy places an eternal record of their homage.

The date is first or second century A.D. The writer went upriver to Syene, the modern Aswan. From there he must have gone back downstream to Memphis or the vicinity, whence he took off for the oracle of Ammon at the Siwah Oasis in the Libyan desert, a place so renowned that even Alexander the Great made a flying visit to it. Thence he returned to Egypt and went to see 'The Cuttings', a puzzling term (cf. Crönert 486) which may possibly refer to the rock-cut tombs in the Valley of the Kings. On various temple walls he scratched messages on behalf of his friends such as the ones we find at Philae and elsewhere (285 above). Sabina, Bernand no, 32. Memnon's bad taste, no. 30 (he eventually did perform for Hadrian; see no. 28). Latest dated graffito, no. 60. Funisulanus, no. 18. Petronius Secundus, no. 13. 'Poet and procurator', no. 62. Falernus, no. 61. Mettius, no. 11. Statistics of verse vs. prose, Bernand, p. 15. Artemidorus, no. 34.

278–83 On the graffiti in the Valley of the Kings, J. Baillet, *Inscriptions grecques et latines des tombeaux des rois ou Syringes à Thèbes* (Mémoires de l'institut français d'archéologie orientale, tome 42, Cairo 1920–6); Bataille, cited in the previous note, 168–79. Forty tombs known, Strabo 17: 816. Ten with graffiti, Baillet viii. Dates of graffiti, xx–xxiv. The term *syringes*, Bataille 168. Travelling in groups, Baillet xii–xix. Tatianus, Baillet nos. 1118, 1380, 1512. His staff, nos. 1693 and 1826 (secretaries), 1680 and 1844 (assistants), 1520 (friend). Geographical origin of tourists, Baillet xxviii–xxx; Tod in *JEA* 11 (1925) 258. Officials and army officers, Baillet xxxiii–xxxix and xliv–xlvii. Intellectuals, xlviii–lxiv. Neoplatonists, lvi–lvii; Bataille 182. Bourichios, Baillet no. 1279. Merchants, Baillet lxv; Bataille 171. Tourist season, Baillet xxvii. Artemidorus, no. 1535. Distribution of graffiti in tombs, ix. Jasios, xi and nos. 13, 777. Graffiti near entrances and around pictures, ix–x. Statistics of those in ink, lxxxvi and p. 597. Palladius, no. 1814. Alexander, no. 1733. Antonius, no. 1249. 'Unique', no. 602. Januarius, nos 468, 1504, 1585, 1620. Volturius, nos 283, 588, 2003–4. Amsouphis, xi. Anagrams, nos 424, 1386; Bataille 175. Bourichios' lament, Baillet no. 1405. Hermogenes, no. 1283. Heraclius, no. 1732. 'Does your mother', nos. 1222, 1986 and cf. Tod in *JEA* 11 (1925) 256. Epiphanius, no. 1613. Dioscurammon, no. 1550. Christians, lxxii–lxxviii. Graffiti with a cross, nos 820, 2017; with abbreviations of Christ, nos 206, 706.

284–5 Roman lady, F. Buecheler, *Carmina latina epigraphica* i (Leipzig 1895) no. 270. 'This sphinx', Harpocration, Hermias, *CIG* iii add. 4700b, e, f. Graffiti on Philae, A. and E. Bernand, *Les inscriptions grecques de Philae* (Paris 1969). The visitors, i 53–4; ii 22–6. Heliodorus, no. 170. Intrepid traveller, see papyrus cited 360 above. Senators and Sudanese envoys, Bernand nos. 147, 180–1. Catilius, nos 142–4. Ammonius, no. 150. Demetrius, no. 130. Hatshepsut's temple, A. Bataille, *Les inscriptions grecques du temple de Hatshepsout à Deir-el-Bahari* (Cairo 1951) xxvii. Abydos, Perdrizet and Lefebvre, *op. cit.* (360 above) xiv. Plutarch's blast, *Mor.* 520e. Visitors' signatures were by no means the only graffiti the ancient world knew. Then as now, scribbling on the walls ran the gamut from philosophical utterrance through jokes to mere doodling. One wag signed himself on a wall of Hatshepsut's temple 'Amun, son of Nile, crocodile' (*SB* 151). A certain Plenis scratched on a mountainside between Deir-el-Bahari and the Valley of the Kings

M*

'Love that reasons is not love' and, not far away, he desultorily wrote out the Greek alphabet, once from alpha to omega—with two mistakes—a second time from both ends at once (AZBYCX, etc., as it were), and three other times the right way but never getting past the seventh letter; see *Bulletin de l'Institut français d'archéologie orientale* 38 (1939) 133, 150. Scribbling the alphabet seems to have been a common way of making time pass. Dozens of examples have been found on walls of houses in Pompeii and Herculaneum (*CIL* iv 2514-48, suppl. 10707-17). For graffiti at Clitumnus, see Pliny, *Ep.* 8.8.

286-9 Nile water, Juvenal 6.526-9. Miniature replicas: Examples are on display in many museums. For replicas of, for example, the famed Athena Parthenos, see Frazer ii, 313-15 and *Enc. Arte Ant.* s.v. *Fidia* (iii, 656); for replicas of the Tyche of Antioch, see below. Hadrian's villa: The sites reproduced, besides those mentioned, included the Lyceum, Academy, Prytanaeum and Painted Porch at Athens (*SHA, Hadrian* 26). On the art in the villa, see H. Winnefeld, *Die Villa des Hadrian bei Tivoli* (Berlin 1895) 142-68. Glass vessel from Afghanistan, J. Hackin, *Recherches archéologiques à Begram* (Mémoires de la délégation archéologique française en Afghanistan ix, Paris 1939) 43 and figs 38, 39. 'Queen vases' of Alexandria, E. Breccia, *Iscrizioni greche e latine* (Catalogue général des antiquités égyptiennes du Musée d'Alexandrie, lvii, Cairo 1911) iii-vii; B. Brown, *Ptolemaic Paintings and Mosaics* (Cambridge, Mass. 1957) 47-8. Glass flasks from Puteoli, C. Dubois, *Pouzzoles antique* (Paris 1907) 190-212; G. Picard in *Latomus* 18 (1959) 23-51. Tyche of Antioch, T. Dohrn, *Die Tyche von Antiochia* (Berlin 1960) 13-26. The statue was copied not only in glass but in marble, alabaster, clay, bronze, and silver. Those in metal were about 3-5 in. high, the smallest being 2 in. high; the marbles varied from 12½ in. to three times that size. The quack, Lucian, *Alexander* 18. Obscene pottery, Lucian, *Amores* 11. Demetrius of Ephesus, Acts 19: 24-7. Miniature temples as offerings, W. Ramsay, *The Church in the Roman Empire* (London 1900[6]) 121-9. Shopping in Rome, Martial 9: 59 (objects of Corinthian bronze, an alloy of gold and silver and copper, were collectors' items; Polyclitus was a renowned Greek sculptor of the fifth century B.C.; Mentor, fifth or fourth century B.C., was the Cellini of the ancient world). 'Artists . . . who contrive', Phaedrus 5, praef. 4-7 (Mys was a famous smith of the fifth century B.C., Zeuxis a famous painter of the fourth century B.C.).

289 Products for sale at Alexandria, etc., *ESAR* v 282-7, 293-4. Sarcophagi, J. Ward-Perkins, 'Il commercio dei sarcofagi in marmo fra Grecia e Italia settentrionale', *Atti del I Congresso Internazionale di Archaeologia dell' Italia Settentrionale* (Turin 1963) 119-24. 'If my health', *Sel. Pap.* 170 (259-7 B.C.).

290-1 Roman customs, S. de Laet, *Portorium* (Bruges 1949) 305-10 and 450–1 (rates of duty), 425–30 (what was exempt and what dutiable), 438 (*professio*), 431–5 (classes of people exempt; those who crossed a frontier to attend a festival were exempt—if they were carrying religious symbols to prove that that, indeed, was their destination). Apollonius' story, Philostratus, *Vita Ap.* 1.20. 'We get irritated', Plutarch, *Mor.* 518e. Argument over the pearls, Quintilian, *Declam.* 359. Confiscation and cost of recovery, de Laet 438–42. 'Send a bathing costume', *Sel. Pap.* 88.

Notes to Chapter 18

292–3 Pausanias' politics and religion, Frazer i, pp. xlix–lx. Hydra, 2: 37: 4, Mt Lycaeus 8: 2: 3–6, Actaeon 9: 2: 3–4. Pausanias' artistic tastes, Frazer i, pp. lx–lxvi. Similarly, the older editions of Baedeker's guides give short shrift to baroque art and architecture. Pausanias' birthplace and travels, Frazer i, pp. xix–xxii. Babylon, 253 above.

294–5 Pausanias' predecessors, Frazer i, pp. lxxxii–lxxxiv. Titles of Polemo's works, L. Preller, *Polemonis periegetae fragmenta* (Leipzig 1838) 18–19. Book 1 published separately and dates of composition, Frazer i, pp. xvi–xix.

295–6 'There is but one', 1: 22: 4–5. Pausanias' aim and bias, Frazer i, pp. xxii–xxxii. Description of Acro-Corinth, 2: 4: 6–7. Pausanias on natural features, Frazer i, pp. xxx–xxxi.

297 Pausanias' method, Frazer i, pp. xxiii–xxiv. Olympia, Frazer i, pp. 244–316; Athens, pp. 2–44; Delphi, pp. 507–47.

298–9 Interest a wider circle of readers, Frazer i, pp. xxiv–xxv. History of the Gauls, 1: 3: 5–4: 6. Survey of Hellenistic history, 1: 5: 5–13: 9. Pausanias' sources, Frazer i, pp. lxxii–lxxvii. Monuments and places described from autopsy, Frazer i, pp. lxxvii–xcvi.

299 Guidebooks were not the only form of travel literature being turned out. Some, following in Herodotus' footsteps, wrote travelogues. Though no examples are extant in their entirety, extensive fragments of a travel book on Greece written by an anonymous author probably in the second century B.C., have survived. Here is a brief sample of its nature, part of the description of Boeotia:

From there [i.e. Plataea] to Thebes is eighty stades [c. 9 miles]. The road is through a flat the whole way. The city stands in the middle of Boeotia. Its circumference is 70 stades [c. 8 miles], its shape circular. The soil is dark. In spite of its antiquity the streets are new, because as the histories tell us, the city has been thrice razed to the ground on account of the morose and overbearing character of the inhabitants. It is excellent for the breeding of horses; it is well-watered and green, and has more gardens than any other city in Greece. . . . So much for the city. The inhabitants are high-spirited and wonderfully sanguine, but rash, insolent, and overbearing, ready to come to blows with any man. . . . As for justice, they set their face against it. Business disputes are settled not by reason but by fisticuffs, and the methods of the prize-ring are transferred to courts of justice. Hence lawsuits here last thirty years at the very least. . . . Murders are perpetrated on the most trifling pretexts. . . . The women are the tallest, prettiest, and most graceful in all Greece. Their faces are so muffled up that only the eyes are seen. All of them dress in white and wear low purple shoes laced so as to show the bare feet. Their yellow hair is tied up in a knot on the top of the head. . . . They have pleasing voices, while the voices of the men are harsh and deep (trans. by Frazer i, p. xlv; for another selection from the same writer, see 72 above).

Obviously travel writers had discovered new paths to follow since Herodotus' day. His charming and easy-paced narrative is here replaced by a breathless flood of statements spiced with crotchety pronunciamentos.

Notes to Chapter 19

300–2   Junketing bishops, Gorce 35–40. Council of Sophia's restrictions, 36–7. Attendance at Councils, 28. Use of public post, 41–57. Constantine, 41–2. Saddle horses and *redae*, 52–3. Provisions, 54. Melania's troubles, Gorce, *Mélanie* 226–9. Gregory of Nyssa's travelling chapel, Gorce 48. 'The *cursus publicus* has been etc.', *Cod. Theod.* 8: 5: 12. Basil and Hilarion, Gorce 45–6.

302–3   The intelligentsia, Gorce 14–20. Government pouch closed, 205–6. Use of lectors and subdeacons, 210. Use of deacons, priests, and monks, 211–16. Casual letter-carriers, 222–4. Flashily dressed letter-carriers, 238–9, quoting Paulinus of Nola, *Ep.* 22: 2. Grumbling, and lingering, 232–3. Being in a hurry, 226–8. 'The bearer of this', Paulinus of Nola, *Ep.* 50: 1. Read confidential mail, Gorce 234–6. 'Write your letters with milk', Ausonius, *Ep.* 28: 21–2; presumably dried milk would have a certain stickiness, and shaking very fine ash over the paper would cause some to adhere and make the writing stand out in grey. Cf. Ovid, *Ars amat.* 3: 627–30, Pliny 26: 62.

304–7 'Everywhere in the world', *Ep.* 46: 8. Christian scholars, 46: 9. 'It is part of the faith', 47: 2. 'Less religion', 46: 9. Second- and third-century visitors, Fliche-Martin 364. The Anastasis and Martyrium, L. Vincent, *Il Santo Sepolcro di Gerusalemme* (Bergamo 1949) 38–41; Wilkinson 39–46. Constantine's building programme and early fourth-century travellers, Cabrol-Leclerq s.v. *Pèlerinages aux lieux saints* 75–76; Wilkinson 10–13. Paula, Tobler 29–40. Melania, Gorce, *Melanie* 166–9, 190–203. Etheria, Cabrol-Leclerq s.v. *Etheria*; Wilkinson 91–122.

307–10 Bordeaux pilgrim, Geyer 3–33; Cabrol-Leclerq s.v. *Itinéraires* 1855–8, *Pèlerinages aux lieux saints* 76–8; Pfister 370–3. Pierced stone, Hastings' *Dictionary of the Bible* s.v. *Jerusalem* 589. Memorable houses and caves, Pfister 355–6, 375. Starry-eyed report, Antoninus of Piacenza, in Geyer 159–218, esp. 161 (Nazareth), 169–70 (Sodom and Gomorrah), 71–7 (Jerusalem). Joseph's silo's, Pfister 351, citing *PG* 38: 534, 546.

310–3 Early solitaries, Fliche-Martin 302–3. Anthony, 329–30. Wadi Natrun, Macarius, and Ammonas, 322–6. Regime and temptations of the anchorites, 330–6. Simeon, *RE* s.v. *Simeon* 140–1. Pachomius, Fliche-Martin 338–41. Dangers of a visit to the Thebaid, 311. Visitors to Egypt, 366–7. 'If he doesn't get', 318. Palladius, 315–17. John Cassianus, 317. Rufinus, 324. Melania the Elder, *PL* 21: 86C. Menas, Cabrol-Leclerq s.v. *Menas* 345–73. 'Take the all-beneficial', 364.

314 Though the Holy Land was far and away the most important pilgrim goal during the early centuries of Christianity, it was by no means the only one. Runner-up was Rome, especially on the birthdays of Peter and Paul or Lawrence or Hippolytus; then the town was thronged with visitors, mostly from Italy but with sizable representations from Gaul, Spain and North Africa (Gorce 4–5). The key sight was the catacombs, which, under Pope Damasus (A.D. 366–84) in particular, had been fixed up to receive parties of tourists: openings had been punctured to let in light, stairways had been built, inscriptions provided, and some of the tombs given an elegant setting glistening with silver and marble (Gorce 6). There were other attractions as well, such as the numerous hallowed houses—the one in which Paul had lived for two years; Pudens', where Paul and Peter had been received; Aquila and Prisca's, where Paul held his first assembly; the palace where Helena had lived, and so on.

314–6 Jerome's route and Melania the Elder's, Cabrol-Leclerq s.v. *Pèlerinages aux lieux saints* 82–5. Paula's route, Tobler 30–1. Melania the Younger, Gorce, *Melanie* 166–9, 190–3. Antoninus, Geyer 159. Bordeaux pilgrim's route and distances, Geyer 3–9, 25–33. Melania's voyage and speed, Gorce 76; Gorce, *Melanie* 238–41, 274. Land travel between Constantinople and Syria, Liebeschuetz 75. Trouble in the West, cf. Sidonius Apollinaris, *Ep.* 3: 4: 1. Recrudesence of piracy, C. Starr, *The Roman Imperial Navy* (Cambridge 1960²) 192–8. Libanius, Liebeschuetz

121–2. Chrysostom's escort, Gorce 55. Isaurian and Arab maurauders, Gorce 88–9. Malchus, *PL* 23: 57B–58A.

317–9 Monasteries at Sinai, Cabrol-Leclerq s.v. *Sinai* 1472–8. Besides Etheria, Antoninus Martyr has left a report of a trip to Sinai (Geyer 182–5); cf. Cabrol-Leclerq *Pèlerinages aux lieux saints* 144–5. Nessana's garrison, C. J. Kraemer, *Excavations at Nessana*. Vol. iii, *Non-literary Papyri* (*P. Colt*) (Princeton 1958) 16–23. 'Paid to the Arab, etc.', *P. Colt* 89: 22–5. 'Reimbursement, etc.', 89: 35; see Kraemer's introduction to the document and his notes to the lines in question. 'In the name etc.', *P. Colt* 73. Abu 'l-Mughira, *P. Colt* 72.

319–21 Putting up in private houses, Gorce 137–41. *Tabernae* at Nola, 144–5. *Apostolic Constitutions* 54 (cf. Gorce 145). Council of Laodicaea, Gorce 145. Basil, 146–7. The word *xenodocheion* significantly derives from the Greek term for a private host, not an innkeeper, who in Greek was called a *pandokeus* 'one who receives *all* guests'; cf. *RE* s.v. *Xenodocheion* 1489–90. *Xenodocheia* and their spread, Gorce 146–55. Three thousand beds in Jerusalem according to Antoninus of Piacenza, (Geyer 175). Privately endowed hostels at Der Siman, Cabrol-Leclerq s.v. *Hôpitaux etc.* 2757; L. de Beylié, *L'habitation Byzantine* (Paris 1902) 45–6. Imperial foundations, Gorce 153; *RE* s.v. *Xenodocheion* 1499. Oxyrhynchus, Gorce 154 (the story comes from Palladius; see *PG* 65.447). *Xenodocheia* for Christians only, 172. This was the fourth-century attitude; by the sixth we find, for example, a hostel for pilgrims visiting St Eulalia at Merida in Spain expressly welcoming non-Christians (*RE* s.v. *Xenodocheion* 1502).

321–4 Letters of recommendation, Gorce 172–4. Paul, 2 Corinthians 3: 1. Reception and meals, Gorce 175–7. Turmanin, Cabrol-Leclerq s.v. *Hôpitaux*, *etc.* 2751–6. Der Siman, H. Butler, *Early Churches of Syria* (Princeton 1929) 105–7; one of the dormitories here measures 16½ by 29½ feet. A few inns for transient merchants have also survived in northern Syria. They are rectangular buildings with a portico in front, and are two storeys high, the ground floor being given over to stables, the upper to bedrooms; see G. Tchalenko, *Villages antiques de la Syrie du Nord; Le massif du Bélus à l'epoque romaine* (Beirut 1953–8) i, 21–5. At Qal'at Siman similar buildings were used for pilgrims to the sanctuary of Simeon Stylites, in this case both floors being given over to bedrooms; Tchalenko 250. Services, Gorce 178–84. No charges, 184. Contributions, 185–6. Sources of income, *RE* s.v. *Xenodocheion* 1493–4. 'The poor' as legatee, *Cod. Iust.* 1: 3: 48: 3. The provision has in mind chiefly hospitals, but in many places the same building served as both hospital and hospice. If there was more than one establishment in the town involved, the money was to go to the neediest. Hospitality a time-consuming affair, Gorce 187–9. Jerome's aside, *Ep.* 52: 3. Simeon's visiting hours, Gorce 188.

Location of monasteries, 156–61. On the quarters available at the Anastasis, see Gorce, *Mélanie* 192–3. Hospice staff, Gorce 164–8.

324–8 'We came to Cana', Geyer 161. Graffiti in Palestine, Cabrol-Leclerq s.v. *graffites* 1495–8; see 1459–77 for the mass of pilgrim graffiti in Rome's catacombs. Holy Land souvenirs, Cabrol-Leclerq s.v. *Ampoules* 1722; A. Grabar, *Ampoules de Terre Sainte* (Paris 1958) 64. Sanctuary of the Ascension, B. Bagatti in *Orientalia Christiana Periodica* 15 (1949) 138. Splinter of cross, Wilkinson 137. Farfa, I. Schuster in *Nuovo Bullettino di Archeologia Cristiana* 7 (1901) 259–68; Cabrol-Leclerq s.v. *Ampoules* 1735–7. Oil as souvenir, Cabrol-Leclerq s.v. *Ampoules* 1722. Silver flasks, Grabar *passim*. Glass flasks, D. Baraq in *Journal of Glass Studies* 12 (1970) 35–63, 13 (1971) 45–63. Alexandria and Smyrna as centres of production of terra cotta flasks, Cabrol-Leclerq s.v. *Ampoules* 1733–34. Jerusalem, Cabrol-Leclerq s.v. *Pèlerinages aux lieux saints* 127. Nazareth, *IEJ* 16 (1966) 73–74. Menas flasks, Cabrol-Leclerq s.v. *Ménas* 381–85 and s.v. *Ampoules* 1725–6; C. M. Kaufmann, *Die Ausgrabung der Menas-Heiligtümer in der Mareotiswüste* (Cairo 1906–1908), 1. Periode 92–102. Amulets, Grabar 63–7; Bagatti 143, 165–6; L. Rahmani in *IEJ* 20 (1970) 105–8. Menas flasks with picture of boat, A. Köster, *Das antike Seewesen* (Berlin 1923) pl. 9; *Sefunim* (Bulletin of the Maritime Museum, Haifa) 2 (1967–8) pl. iv. 3–4; Cabrol-Leclerq s.v. *Ménas* 387. Passover visitors, Josephus, *BJ* 2: 10, 6: 421–8. Guest quarters in synagogues, *RE* s.v. *Xenodocheion* 1489–90; *The Excavations at Dura-Europos. Final Report* VIII, Part I (New Haven 1956) 7–11.

328 'Do not imagine', Jerome, *Ep.* 58: 4 (*PL* 22.582).

INDEX